(continued from front page)

" I just wanted to thank you for helping me get a great score
on the AP U.S. History exam... Thank you for making great test preps! "

Student, Los Angeles, CA

" Your *Fundamentals of Engineering Exam* book was the absolute best
preparation I could have had for the exam, and it is one of the major
reasons I did so well and passed the FE on my first try. "

Student, Sweetwater, TN

" I used your book to prepare for the test and found that the advice and the
sample tests were highly relevant... Without using any other material, I earned
very high scores and will be going to the graduate school of my choice. "

Student, New Orleans, LA

" What I found in your book was a wealth of information sufficient to shore up
my basic skills in math and verbal... The section on analytical ability was
excellent. The practice tests were challenging and the answer explanations most
helpful. It certainly is the *Best Test Prep for the GRE*! "

Student, Pullman, WA

" I really appreciate the help from your excellent book. Please keep up
the great work. "

Student, Albuquerque, NM

" I am writing to thank you for your test preparation... your book helped me
immeasurably and I have nothing but praise for your *GRE* preparation."

Student, Benton Harbor, MI

(more on back page)

The Best Test Preparation For The

SAT Subject Test
Biology E/M

2nd **EDITION**

Linda Gregory, Ph.D.
Scientific Consultant and Tutor
Cobble Hill, British Columbia

Thomas Sandusky, Ph.D.
Environmental Science Teacher
Watchung Hills Regional High School
Warren, NJ

Rashmi Diana Sharma
Freelance Science Consultant
Piscataway, NJ

Judith A. Stone, Ph.D.
Adjunct Professor of Biology
Suffolk County Community College
Selden, NY

Cindy Coe Taylor, Ph.D.
Freelance Science Consultant
Indianapolis, IN

J.M. Templin, Ed.D.
Assistant Professor of Biology
Montgomery County Community College
Pottstown, PA

Clarence C. Wolfe, Ph.D.
Professor & Assistant Division
Chairperson of Biology
North Virginia Community College
Annandale, Virginia

William Uhland
Research Scientist

Research & Education Association
Visit our website at
www.rea.com

Research & Education Association
61 Ethel Road West
Piscataway, New Jersey 08854
E-mail: info@rea.com

The Best Test Preparation for the
SAT SUBJECT TEST IN BIOLOGY E/M

Printed in the United States of America

Library of Congress Control Number 2005931262

International Standard Book Number 0-7386-0143-8

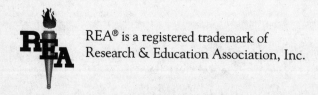

REA® is a registered trademark of
Research & Education Association, Inc.

CONTENTS

ABOUT RESEARCH & EDUCATION ASSOCIATION

Founded in 1959, Research & Education Association is dedicated to publishing the finest and most effective educational materials—including software, study guides, and test preps—for students in middle school, high school, college, graduate school, and beyond.

REA's Test Preparation series includes books and software for all academic levels in almost all disciplines. Research & Education Association publishes test preps for students who have not yet entered high school, as well as high school students preparing to enter college. Students from countries around the world seeking to attend college in the United States will find the assistance they need in REA's publications. For college students seeking advanced degrees, REA publishes test preps for many major graduate school admission examinations in a wide variety of disciplines, including engineering, law, and medicine. Students at every level, in every field, with every ambition can find what they are looking for among REA's publications.

REA's practice tests are always based upon the most recently administered exams, and include every type of question that can be expected on the actual exams.

REA's publications and educational materials are highly regarded and continually receive an unprecedented amount of praise from professionals, instructors, librarians, parents, and students. Our authors are as diverse as the fields represented in the books we publish. They are well-known in their respective disciplines and serve on the faculties of prestigious high schools, colleges, and universities throughout the United States and Canada.

We invite you to visit us at *www.rea.com* to find out how "REA is making the world smarter."

ACKNOWLEDGMENTS

In addition to our authors, we would like to thank Larry B. Kling, Vice President, Editorial, for his overall guidance; Pam Weston, Vice President, Publishing, for setting the quality standards for production integrity and managing the publication to completion; Diane Goldschmidt, Associate Editor, for post-production quality assurance; and Christine Saul, Senior Graphic Designer, for cover design.

We would also like to thank Fran Decibus, Joyce, Kirchin, and Pamela Phillips for technically editing the Ecology manuscript; James Min, Ph.D., Cindy Coe Taylor, Ph.D., and J.M. Templin, Ed.D., for technically editing the General Biology manuscript; Ellen Gong, Connie Neumann, and Adrienne Rebello for proofreading the book in its early stages of production; Dominique Won for copyediting the manuscript; Jeanne Gruver for inputting the review and practice test material for the General Biology manuscript; and Wende Solano for typesetting.

THE SAT SUBJECT TEST IN
Biology E/M

INTRODUCTION

INTRODUCTION

PREPARING FOR THE SAT BIOLOGY E/M SUBJECT TEST

ABOUT THE SAT BIOLOGY E/M SUBJECT TEST

Who Takes the Test and What Is It Used For?

Students planning to attend college should take the SAT Biology E/M Subject Test if:

(1) Any of the colleges they apply to require the test for admission;

OR

(2) The student wishes to demonstrate proficiency in Biology.

The SAT Biology E/M exam is designed for students who have taken one year of college preparatory biology (either a general survey course or one with emphasis on Ecology or Molecular Biology), a one-year course in algebra, and have laboratory experience. However, due to the variation in high school biology courses, most students will encounter questions that test material with which they are not familiar.

Who Administers The Test?

The SAT Biology E/M Subject Test is developed by the College Board and administered by Educational Testing Service (ETS). The test development process involves the assistance of educators throughout the country, and is designed and implemented to ensure that the content and difficulty level of the test are appropriate.

When Should the SAT Biology E/M be Taken?

If you are applying to a college that requires Subject Test scores as part of the admissions process, you should take the SAT Biology E/M Subject Test toward the end of your junior year or at the beginning of your senior year. If your scores are being used only for placement purposes, you may be able to take the test in the spring of your senior year. For more information, be sure to contact the colleges to which you are applying.

When and Where Is the Test Given?

The SAT Biology E/M Subject Test is administered six times a year at many locations throughout the United States; most test centers are at high schools. For more information on specific testing dates and locations, consult the registration bulletin or your high school guidance counselor.

To receive information on upcoming administrations of the exam, consult the publication *Taking the SAT II: Subject Tests,* which may be obtained from your guidance counselor or by contacting:

College Board SAT Program
P.O. Box 6200
Princeton, NJ 08541–6200
Phone: (609) 771-7600
E-mail: sat@info.collegeboard.com
Website: *www.collegeboard.com*

Is There a Registration Fee?

Yes. There is a registration fee to take the SAT Biology E/M. Consult the College Board website for information on the fee structure. Financial assistance may be granted in certain situations. To find out if you qualify and to register for assistance, contact your academic advisor.

Can I Use a Calculator?

Calculators are *not* permitted on the SAT Biology E/M. The metric system of units is used, so review of metric units may be helpful.

FORMAT OF THE SAT BIOLOGY E/M

The Biology E/M is a one-hour exam consisting of 80 multiple-choice questions. Each question has five possible answer choices, lettered (A) through (E). The common core, which appears on both the Biology-E and the Biology-M Tests, consists of 60 questions. It covers Cellular and Molecular Biology, Ecology, Classical Genetics, Organismal Biology, and Evolution and Diversity. Its emphasis is on Organismal Biology.

In addition to the common core, you will be required to take a specialty section comprised of 20 questions, making 80 the total number of questions you will be answering on any form, or in any administration, of the SAT Biology E/M. One of these specialty sections is the Biology-E Test, which covers principles and applications of Ecology. The other specialty section is the Biology-M Test which covers concepts and principles of Molecular Biology. Remember, these specialty sections are taken in addition to the common core. However, you will not be able to take both the Biology-E *and* the Biology-M Tests in the same administration.

The following chart summarizes the distribution of topics covered on the SAT Biology E/M exam:

Topics Covered in Common Core	Approximate Percentage of E Test	Approximate Percentage of M Test
Cellular/Molecular Biology	15	27
Ecology	23	13
Classical Genetics	15	20
Organismal Biology	25	25
Evolution and Diversity	22	15

Note: Every administration of the Biology E/M Test includes 60 common core questions.

ABOUT THIS BOOK

This book will provide you with an accurate and complete representation of the SAT Biology E/M Subject Test. Inside you will find a course review designed to provide you with the information and strategies needed to do well on the exam, as well as six full-length practice tests based on the actual exam. Three of our model tests are aimed specifically at students taking the Biology-E Test, and three are geared toward those taking the Biology-M Test. REA's practice tests contain every type of question you can expect to encounter on the SAT Biology E/M Test. Following each test, you will find an answer key with detailed explanations to help you master the test material.

HOW TO USE THIS BOOK

What Do I Study First?

Remember that the SAT Biology E/M Subject Test is designed to test knowledge that has been acquired throughout your education. Therefore, the best way to prepare for the exam is to refresh yourself by thoroughly studying our review material and taking the sample tests provided in this book. They will familiarize you with the types of questions, directions, and format of the SAT Biology E/M Subject Test.

To begin your studies, read over the review and the suggestions for test-taking, take one of the practice tests (Biology-E if you are studying Ecology, or Biology-M if you are studying Molecular Biology) to determine your area(s) of weakness, and then restudy the review material, focusing on your specific problem areas. The course review includes the information you need to know when taking the exam. Be sure to take the remaining practice tests to further test yourself and become familiar with the format of the SAT Biology E/M Subject Test.

When Should I Start Studying?

It is never too early to start studying for the SAT Biology E/M test. The earlier you begin, the more time you will have to sharpen your skills. Do not procrastinate! Last-minute studying and cramming is *not* an effective way to study, since it does not allow you the time needed to learn the test material. The sooner you learn the format of the exam, the more comfortable you will be when you take the exam.

TEST-TAKING TIPS

Although you may be unfamiliar with standardized tests such as the SAT Biology E/M Subject Test, there are many ways to acquaint yourself with this type of examination and help alleviate your test-taking anxieties.

Become comfortable with the format of the exam. When you are practicing to take the SAT Biology E/M Subject Test, simulate the conditions under which you will be taking the actual test. Stay calm and pace yourself. After simulating the test only a couple of times, you will boost your chances of doing well, and you will be able to sit down for the actual exam with much more confidence.

Know the directions and format for each section of the test. Familiarizing yourself with the directions and format of the exam will not only save you time, but will also ensure that you are familiar enough with the SAT Biology E/M Subject Test to avoid nervousness (and the mistakes caused by being nervous).

Do your scratchwork in the margins of the test booklet. You will not be given scrap paper during the exam, and you may not perform scratchwork on your answer sheet. Space is provided in your test booklet to do any necessary work or draw diagrams.

If you are unsure of an answer, guess. However, if you do guess—guess *wisely*. Use the process of elimination by going through each answer to a question and ruling out as many of the answer choices as possible. By eliminating three answer choices, you give yourself a fifty-fifty chance of answering correctly since there will only be two choices left from which to make your guess.

Mark your answers in the appropriate spaces on the answer sheet. Each numbered row will contain five ovals corresponding to each answer choice for that question. Fill in darkly, completely, and neatly the circle that corresponds to your answer. You can change your answer, but remember to *completely* erase your old answer. Any stray lines or unnecessary marks may cause the machine to score your answer incorrectly. When you have finished working on a section, you may want to go back and check to make sure your answers correspond to the correct questions. Marking one answer in the wrong space will throw off the rest of your test, whether it is graded by machine or by hand. When taking the test, you may want to occasionally check your answer sheet to be sure that you are filling in the oval that corresponds to the question you are answering. This is especially important for those taking the SAT Biology E/M Test. For the Biology-M Test, you will need to fill in ovals 81-100; therefore, ovals 61-80 on your answer sheet will remain blank. Be sure to pay close attention to this when you begin the Biology-M Test.

You don't have to answer every question. You are not penalized if you do not answer every question. The only penalty results from answering a question incorrectly. Try to use the guessing strategy, but if you are truly stumped by a question, remember that you do not have to answer it.

Work quickly and steadily. You have a limited amount of time to work on each section, so you need to work quickly and steadily. Avoid focusing on one problem for too long. Taking the practice tests in this book will help you to learn how to budget your time and pace yourself.

Keep track of your scores. By doing so, you will be able to gauge your progress and discover general weaknesses in particular sections. You should carefully study the reviews that cover your areas of difficulty, as this will build your skills in those areas. To help you budget your time for studying, we have provided for you a detailed study schedule.

STUDY SCHEDULE

The following is a suggested six-week study schedule for the SAT Biology E/M Subject Test. You may want to condense or expand this schedule depending on how soon you will be taking the actual exam. Set aside time each week, and work straight through each activity *without rushing*. By following a structured schedule, you will be sure to complete an adequate amount of studying, and you will be confident and prepared on the day of the actual exam.

Week	Activity
1	Acquaint yourself with the SAT Biology E/M by reading the Introduction and the review material. Keep a sheet of paper nearby and jot down any sections that are confusing or difficult for you. Locate reference sources to use for those portions of the exam.
2	Take Practice Test 1 if you will be taking the Biology-E Test or Practice Test 4 if you will be taking the Biology-M Test. Take the test as a diagnostic test to help you determine your strengths and weaknesses. After checking the answer key and the explanations, make a note of the questions that were difficult. Reread the corresponding review material.
3	Take Practice Test 2 if you are taking the SAT Biology-E Test or Practice Test 5 if you are taking the Biology-M Test. Read through all the detailed explanations carefully, and make a note of any sections that were difficult for you, or any questions that were still unclear after reading the explanations. You may want to use your textbooks, notes, or course materials, to review those areas that need clarification.
4	Take Practice Test 3 if you are taking the SAT Biology-E Test or Practice Test 6 if you are taking the Biology-M Test. Read through all the detailed explanations carefully, and make a note of any sections that were difficult for you, or any questions that were still unclear after reading the explanations. You may want to use your textbooks, notes, or course materials, to review those areas that need clarification.
5	Compare your progress between the exams. Note any sections in which you were able to improve your score, and sections in which your score remained the same or declined. Allow yourself extra study time for those areas that require added attention.
6	You may want to reread the course review and take Practice Test 1 (Biology-E) or Practice Test 4 (Biology-M) again to ensure that you are comfortable with the testing conditions and format.

SCORING THE SAT BIOLOGY E/M

The SAT Biology E/M Test, like all other Subject Tests, is scored on a 200-800 scale.

How Do I Score My Practice Test?

Your exam is scored by crediting one point for each correct answer and deducting one-fourth of a point for each incorrect answer. There is no deduction for answers that are omitted. Use the worksheet below to calculate your raw score and to record your scores for the three practice tests you take (Biology-E or Biology-M). To determine your scaled score you will need to use the Score Conversion Chart for the SAT Biology E/M. To obtain a copy of this chart, you may wish to refer to your information bulletin or contact the College Board directly (see page xvi for information).

SCORING WORKSHEET

_____ — (_____ X 1/4) = _____

number correct   number incorrect   Raw Score
                         (do not include   (round to nearest
                         unanswered questions)   whole point)

	Raw Score	**Scaled Score**
Test 1 Biology-E	_____	_____
Test 2 Biology-E	_____	_____
Test 3 Biology-E	_____	_____
Test 4 Biology-M	_____	_____
Test 5 Biology-M	_____	_____
Test 6 Biology-M	_____	_____

THE DAY OF THE TEST

Before the Test

Make sure you know where your test center is well in advance of your test day so you do not get lost on the day of the test. On the night before the test, gather together the materials you will need the next day:

✓ Your admission ticket

✓ Two forms of identification (e.g., driver's license, student identification card, or current alien registration card)

✓ Two No. 2 pencils with erasers

✓ Directions to the test center

✓ A watch (if you wish) but not one that makes noise, as it may disturb other test-takers

On the day of the test, you should wake up early (after a good night's rest) and have breakfast. Dress comfortably, so that you are not distracted by being too hot or too cold while taking the test. Also, plan to arrive at the test center early. This will allow you to collect your thoughts and relax before the test, and will also spare you the stress of being late. If you arrive after the test begins, you will *not* be admitted to the test center and you will *not* receive a refund.

During the Test

When you arrive at the test center, try to find a seat where you feel most comfortable. Follow all the rules and instructions given by the test supervisor. If you do not, you risk being dismissed from the test and having your scores canceled.

Once all the test materials are passed out, the test instructor will give you directions for filling out your answer sheet. Fill this sheet out carefully since this information will appear on your score report.

After the Test

When you have completed the SAT Biology E/M Subject Test, you may hand in your test materials and leave. Then, go home and relax! You should receive your score report which includes your scores, percentile ranks, and interpretive information about three weeks after you take the test.

THE SAT SUBJECT TEST IN

Biology E/M

CHAPTER 1

CHAPTER 1

CHEMISTRY OF LIFE

GENERAL CHEMISTRY

Definitions

Elements – An element is a substance that cannot be decomposed into simpler substances by ordinary chemical means.

Compounds – A compound is a combination of bonded elements present in definite proportions by weight. Compounds are substances that cannot be decomposed by chemical means.

Mixtures – Mixtures contain two or more substances, each of which retains its original properties and can be separated from others by relatively simple means. They do not have a definite composition and are not bonded chemically.

Atoms – Each element consists of atoms. Atoms are the smallest particles of elements that can take part in chemical changes. Atoms consist of a number of particles known as protons, neutrons, and electrons. The dense center of an atom is known as an atomic nucleus.

All atoms contain the same number of electrons and protons and are thus neutral. Protons are positively charged and are present in the nucleus. Neutrons are electrically neutral particles of the nucleus. Electrons are negatively charged particles which orbit the nucleus.

Atoms combine to form molecules which are the smallest particles of a substance that can exist by themselves.

Ions – These are produced when atoms lose or gain electrons. The ion that *gains* an electron is said to be electronegative, and the ion that *loses* an electron is said to be electropositive.

Atomic Number – This is the total number of protons in the nucleus. The atomic number determines the properties of an element.

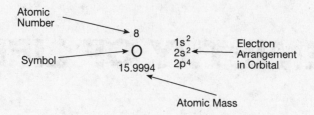

Atomic Mass – This is the total number of protons and neutrons.

Isotopes – These are atoms of the same element with the same number of protons but a different number of neutrons. Therefore, isotopes have different properties.

Chemical Bonds

Energy of bonds – Energy, in the form of heat, light, or electricity is required to form a chemical bond, and energy is released when bonds are broken.

Ionic Bonds – In these types of bonds, electrons are completely transferred from one atom to another. Ionic compounds are held together by strong electrovalent (ionic) bonds. An electrovalent bond is an electrostatic attraction between oppositely charged ions.

Ionization – When an ionic bond is broken and the compound separates into ions, a positively charged cation and a negatively charged anion are formed.

Covalent Bonds – Covalent bonds consist of shared electrons between two atoms. In a covalent bond, each atom contributes an electron to the shared pair which fills the outermost shell. The electron shells of hydrogen and helium are full when they have two electrons. For all other elements, their outer shells are full when they have eight electrons.

Polar Covalent Bonds – A polar covalent bond is a bond in which the charge is distributed asymmetrically within the bond.

Nonpolar Covalent Bonds – A nonpolar covalent bond is a bond in which the electrons are pulled equally by two atoms.

Hydrogen Bonds – A hydrogen bond is formed when a single hydrogen atom is shared between two electronegative atoms, usually nitrogen or oxygen.

Van der Waals Forces – Van der Waals forces are weak linkages that occur between electrically neutral molecules or parts of molecules which are very close to each other.

Hydrophobic Interactions – Hydrophobic interactions occur between groups that are insoluble in water. These groups, which are nonpolar, tend to clump together in the presence of water.

Lewis Electron Dot Structures

The Lewis structure simply shows the valence electrons of an atom or ion. A few examples would be

$$Na \cdot \qquad Sr : \qquad : \overset{..}{\underset{.}{S}} \cdot \qquad : \overset{..}{\underset{.}{I}} : \qquad : \overset{..}{\underset{..}{Xe}} :$$

for sodium, strontium, sulfur, iodine, and xenon, respectively. Returning to the above problem of the covalent bonding of chlorine, note from the Lewis structure,

$$: \overset{..}{\underset{.}{Cl}} :$$

that each Cl atom has one unpaired electron. If two Cl atoms were to come together and share their unpaired electron with the other, a covalent bond would be formed, and each Cl atom would have a full outer shell. This can be shown as

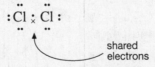

By this sharing, each Cl atom has an eighth outershell electron. Another example would be oxygen, O_2. Note the Lewis structure for O is

$$: \overset{..}{\underset{.}{O}} :$$

To form a covalent bond, two pairs of electrons will have to be shared, creating what is appropriately called a "double bond," giving the resulting structure

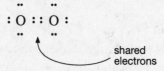

Sometimes a line is used instead of dots to represent two shared electron pairs. In this case, each line represents a pair of electrons. Such a structure for Cl_2 and O_2 would be

$Cl - Cl$ or $O = O$,

respectively. Often, unshared electron pairs are not shown.

Acids and Bases

Acids – These are substances that dissociate in water to produce hydrogen ions (H^+). A hydrogen ion is a proton. Acids are proton donors.

Bases – A base is a compound that dissociates in water and yields hydroxyl ions (OH^-). Bases are proton acceptors.

$$Cl^- \; + \; :\overset{..}{\underset{\underset{H}{\times\bullet}}{O}}{\times}H \; + \; H\overset{..}{\underset{\underset{H}{\times\bullet}}{N}}{\times}H \; \longrightarrow \; :\overset{..}{\underset{\underset{H}{\times\bullet}}{O}}{\times}H \; + \; H\overset{..}{\underset{\underset{H}{\times\bullet}}{N}}{\times}H \; + \; Cl^-$$

with H^+ above each $:O$ ... group

Reaction between hydrochloric acid (proton donor) and ammonia (proton acceptor).

pH – This is a numerical scale used to measure the relative strengths of acids and bases.

A pH of 7 is neutral.

A pH less than 7 is acidic.

A pH more than 7 is basic.

Chemical Changes

Chemical Reactions – A chemical reaction is any process in which at least one bond is either broken or formed. The outcome of a chemical reaction is a rearrangement of atoms and bonding patterns, forming a new substance.

Laws of Thermodynamics

Conservation of Energy – Energy may be exchanged between the materials and the surroundings, but the total energy of the materials and the surroundings remains constant.

First Law of Thermodynamics – Energy cannot be created or destroyed, although it can be converted from one form to another. The sum of all energy changes must be zero.

Second Law of Thermodynamics – This is used to predict whether or not a chemical reaction will take place. Entropy is a measure of disorder in a system. Any system tends toward a state of greater instability. Instability means more randomness and disorder.

Third Law of Thermodynamics – A perfect crystal which is a completely ordered system, would have perfect order at absolute zero (0 Kelvin). Therefore, its entropy would be zero. Energy released from chemical reactions opposes entropy, restoring stability.

The stability of a system depends on:

   A) Enthalpy – Total energy content of a system.

   B) Entropy – Energy distribution.

Exergonic Reactions – These types of reactions release free energy. All spontaneous reactions are exergonic.

Endergonic Reactions – These reactions require the addition of free energy from the external source.

Organic Chemistry

This branch of chemistry is devoted to the study of hydrocarbons. Carbon is a unique element. Each atom has the potential to form four covalent bonds. It can bond with itself to form long chains with branches and rings.

Hydrocarbons – The ability of carbon to form bonds to itself and hydrogen leads to the formation of stable compounds called hydrocarbons. These compounds contain only carbon and hydrogen. Hydrocarbons can exist as chains (e.g., butane) or rings (e.g., benzene).

butane   benzene

Biochemistry – This is a branch of organic chemistry that deals with compounds and reactions important to living things (plant, animal, or microbial). Today it is impossible to study biology without some knowledge of biochemistry.

Lipids – Lipids are organic compounds that dissolve poorly, if at all, in water (they are hydrophobic). All lipids (fats and oils) are composed of carbon, hydrogen, and oxygen where the ratio of hydrogen atoms to oxygen atoms in the molecule is greater than 2:1. A neutral lipid molecule is composed of one glycerol and two fatty acids (triglyceride).

Phospholipids – A phospholipid is a molecule in which a phosphate group substitutes for one fatty acid in the lipid.

Steroids – Steroids are complex molecules that contain carbon atoms arranged in four interlocking rings. Some steroids of biological importance are vitamin D, bile salts, and cholesterol.

Carbohydrates – Carbohydrates are compounds composed of carbon, hydrogen, and oxygen, with the general molecular formula CH_2O. The principal carbohydrates include a variety of sugars.

Monosaccharide – A simple sugar or a carbohydrate that cannot be broken down into a simpler sugar. Its molecular formula is $C_6H_{12}O_6$, and the most common is glucose.

Disaccharide – A double sugar with two simple sugar molecules bonded together. Sucrose is a familiar disaccharide, as are maltose and lactose.

Polysaccharide – A polysaccharide is a complex compound composed of a large number of monosaccharide units bonded together. Examples of polysaccharides are starch, cellulose, and glycogen.

Proteins – All proteins are composed of carbon, hydrogen, oxygen, nitrogen, and sometimes phosphorus and sulfur. Approximately 50% of the dry weight of living matter is protein.

> **Amino Acids** – The 20 amino acids are the building blocks of polypeptides in a protein.

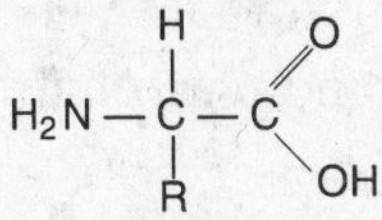

$$H_2N - \overset{\overset{\displaystyle H}{|}}{\underset{\underset{\displaystyle R}{|}}{C}} - \overset{\overset{\displaystyle O}{\parallel}}{C} \diagdown_{OH}$$

Figure 1.1 An amino acid with R representing the distinctive side chain.

> **Polypeptides** – Amino acids unite into polypeptides by peptide bonds. Two amino acids bond by a condensation reaction between the COOH (carboxyl) groups and the NH_2 (ammonia) groups.

>> **Primary Structure** – This is the number of polypeptide chains and the number, type, and sequence of amino acids in each.

>> **Secondary Structure** – The secondary structure of the polypeptide in a protein is characterized by the same bond angles repeated in successive amino acids. This gives the linear molecule a recurrent structural pattern such as an alpha helix or pleated sheet.

>> **Tertiary Structure** – This is the three-dimensional folding pattern of a polypeptide, which is superimposed on the secondary structure.

>> **Quaternary Structure** – The quaternary structure is the manner in which two or more independently folded polypeptides fit together in a protein.

Nucleic Acids – Nucleic acids are long polymers involved in heredity and in the manufacture of different kinds of proteins. The two most important nucleic acids are deoxyribonucleic acid (DNA) and ribonucleic acid (RNA).

> **Nucleotides** – These are the building blocks of nucleic acids. Nucleotides are complex molecules composed of a nitrogenous base, a 5-carbon sugar, and a phosphate group.

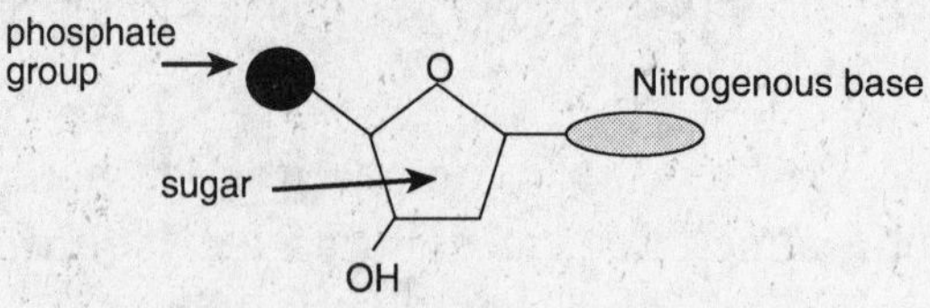

Figure 1.2 Structure of a nucleotide.

Deoxyribonucleic Acid (DNA) – Chromosomes and genes are composed mainly of DNA. It is composed of deoxyribose, nitrogenous bases, and phosphate groups.

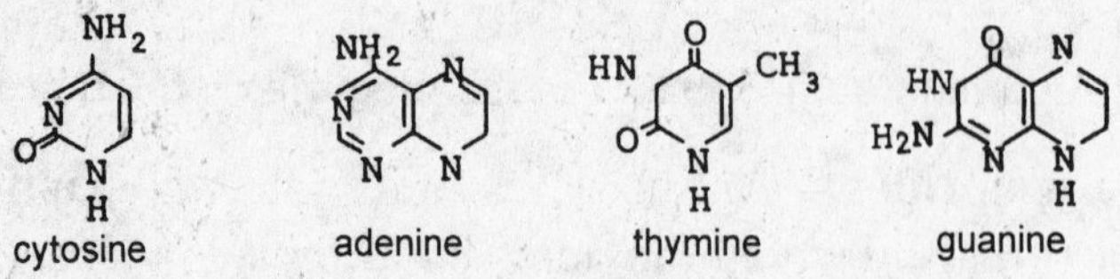

cytosine   adenine   thymine   guanine

Figure 1.3 The four nitrogenous bases of DNA.

Ribonucleic Acid (RNA) – RNA is involved in protein synthesis. Unlike DNA, it is composed of the sugar ribose and the nitrogenous base uracil instead of thymine.

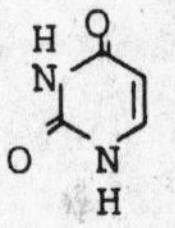

Figure 1.4 Uracil.

BIOCHEMICAL PATHWAYS

Enzymes

Enzymes are protein catalysts that increase the speed of a reaction by lowering the activation energy. Thus, equilibrium is achieved sooner. A catalyst will not cause a reaction to occur that ordinarily would not occur without the presence of a catalyst. Catalysts are not consumed during the course of a reaction, so they can be used over and over again.

Enzymes bind with a substance known as a substrate. The substrate fits into a "groove" known as the active site on the enzyme molecule. As the enzyme and substrate combine, the enzyme may change its shape to better accommodate the substrate. The enzyme and substrate are bound by weak chemical bonds, which are made and broken easily. An enzyme usually affects only one substrate.

Allosteric Enzymes – These are enzymes that exist in two different forms, one active and the other inactive.

Allosteric Inhibition – In this process an inhibitor molecule called a negative modulator combines with the inactive form of the enzyme, "locking" it into this configuration.

Coenzymes – These are also known as prosthetic groups or cofactors and consist of nonprotein organic molecules that bind briefly and loosely to some enzymes. The coenzymes are necessary for the catalytic reaction of such enzymes.

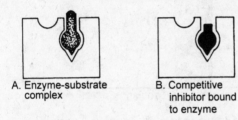 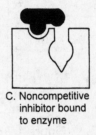

A. Enzyme-substrate complex   B. Competitive inhibitor bound to enzyme   C. Noncompetitive inhibitor bound to enzyme

Figure 1.5

Factors Influencing the Rate of Enzyme Action

1) **pH** – Every enzyme has an optimum pH at which it works best, i.e. pepsin works best at a pH of 2.0 whereas, amylase works best at a pH of 7.0.

2) **Temperature** – Proteins become denatured at high temperatures. Since enzymes are proteins, they cannot work at high temperatures. For most enzyme-catalyzed reactions, the rate doubles for each 10°C up until 40°C. The reactions finally taper off and stop at 60°C.

3) **Enzyme Concentration** – The rate of an enzyme-catalyzed reaction increases as substrate concentration increases, and as long as there is an excess concentration of enzyme present.

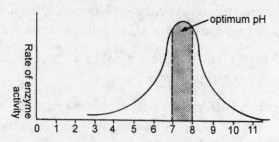

Figure 1.6 Effect of pH on rate of enzyme action.

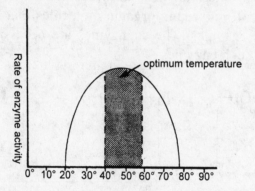

Figure 1.7 Effect of temperature on enzyme activity.

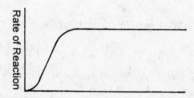

Figure 1.8 Fixed amount of enzyme and an excess of substrate molecules.

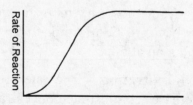

Figure 1.9 Fixed number of substrate molecules and an excess of enzyme molecules.

Photosynthesis

This is a process implemented by organisms containing chlorophyll, including green plants. These organisms convert CO_2 and H_2O

to organic compounds, namely carbohydrates. Chloroplasts utilize the sunlight energy as well as CO_2 and H_2O to produce carbohydrates of high potential chemical energy. Oxygen, a by-product of this reaction, is released to the atmosphere through the stomates (openings in leaves), stored temporarily in the air spaces, or used in cellular respiration. An overall chemical reaction of photosynthesis is the equation

$$6CO_2 + 6H_2O \xrightarrow[\text{chlorophyll}]{\text{light}} C_6H_{12}O_6 + 6O_2$$

Photosynthesis is divided into two stages:

A) A light stage which requires light but is unaffected by temperature. The light stage includes photolysis, which is the decomposition of water molecules forming hydrogen and oxygen in the presence of light. Since this stage involves chlorophyll and light, it is referred to as the light reaction.

B) A dark stage which does not require light but is affected by temperature. The dark reaction, also known as CO_2 fixation, involves hydrogen from the light reaction combining with CO_2 to form carbohydrates.

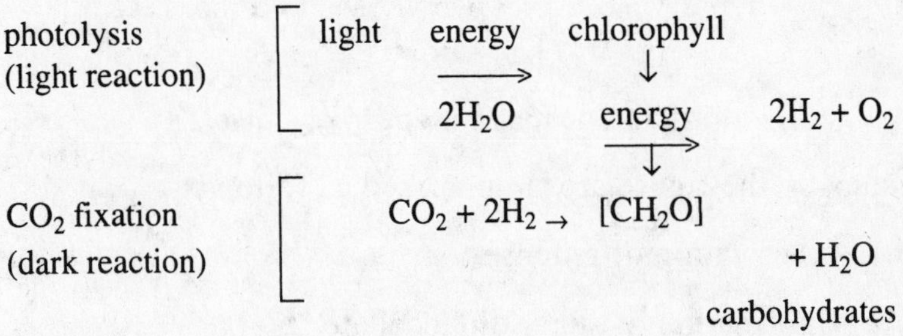

photolysis
(light reaction)

$$\text{light} \quad \text{energy} \quad \begin{array}{c}\text{chlorophyll}\\ \downarrow\end{array}$$
$$2H_2O \xrightarrow{\text{energy}} 2H_2 + O_2$$

CO_2 fixation
(dark reaction)

$$CO_2 + 2H_2 \rightarrow [CH_2O] + H_2O$$
$$\text{carbohydrates}$$

Figure 1.10 Photolysis and CO_2 fixation.

Cellular Respiration

Living organisms obtain energy from food. Once the food is consumed, it is converted to carbohydrates which are then respired.

Respiration involves the oxidation of glucose to carbon dioxide and water. Energy is released in cellular respiration.

This process occurs in living cells and causes the release of energy from glucose. It may be further subdivided into 3 steps:

1) Glycolysis

2) Krebs Cycle

3) Respiratory Chain and Hydrogen Transport System

In this process carbon dioxide is eliminated as a waste product and oxygen is utilized.

Glycolysis – This is an anaerobic process and involves the breakdown of glucose with the release of energy in the form of ATP.

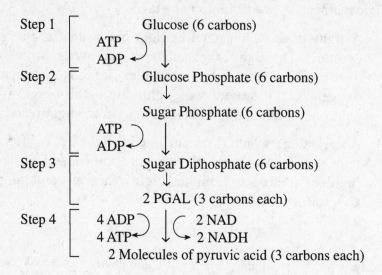

Figure 1.11 The major steps in glycolysis.

The steps in the figure are summarized as follows:

Step 1 – Activation of glucose

Step 2 – Formation of sugar diphosphate

Step 3 – Formation and oxidation of PGAL, phosphoglyceraldehyde

Step 4 – Formation of pyruvic acid ($C_3H_4O_3$), with a net gain of two ATP molecules

Krebs Cycle

If oxygen is present, the pyruvic acid formed during glycolysis is converted to acetyl coenzyme A, which is shunted into the Krebs Cycle (Citric Acid Cycle). In this process the carbon chains of amino acids, fatty acids, and carbohydrates are metabolized to produce CO_2. Pyruvic acid is converted to acetyl coenzyme A and, through a series of reactions, citric acid is formed.

The Krebs Cycle is important because

A) it supplies a rich source of hydrogen atoms that provide a large amount of energy, which is obtained by the oxidation of a glucose molecule.

B) it provides a large number of intermediate molecules that are used to produce other substances such as fatty acids, amino acids, and carotenoids.

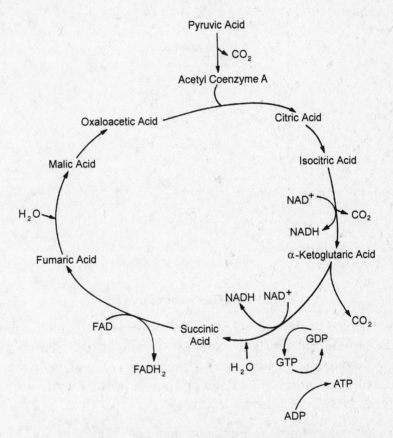

Figure 1.12 Summary of the Krebs Cycle.

ATP and NAD

ATP – This stands for adenosine triphosphate. ATP is a coenzyme essential for the breakdown of glucose. When the bonds in ATP are hydrolyzed, a large amount of energy is released.

NAD – This stands for nicotinamide adenine dinucleotide. Like

ATP, it is also a coenzyme. NAD participates in a large number of oxidation-reduction reactions in cells, including those in cellular respiration.

The Respiratory Chain (Electron Transport System)

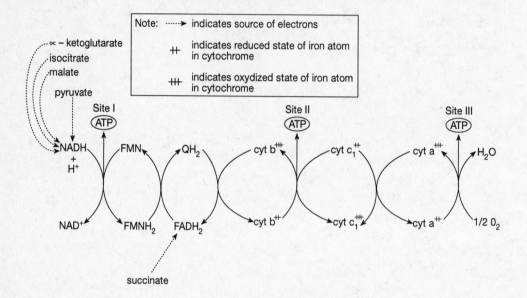

Figure 1.13 The respiratory chain.

At the end of the Krebs Cycle, derivatives of the glucose molecule have been oxidized into a new series of compounds. The bulk of the energy is contained within the hydrogen atoms of these compounds. These hydrogen atoms are passed on to a series of enzymes which are at progressively lower energy levels.

Cytochromes are the enzymes and coenzymes of the hydrogen transport chain. They are involved in the transfer of hydrogen from compounds of the Krebs Cycle. The cytochromes, together with other enzymes, split hydrogen atoms attached to compounds such as $NADH_2$ into hydrogen atoms and electrons.

The final step involves the hydrogen atoms combining with an oxygen molecule to form water. Oxygen is the final hydrogen acceptor in the chain. This step is vital since, without the presence of the oxygen molecule, the hydrogen atoms would accumulate and aerobic respiration would not occur.

Anaerobic Pathways

If no oxygen is present, the pyruvic acid does not enter the Krebs Cycle, but enters an anaerobic pathway. This is commonly known as fermentation. There are three major anaerobic pathways: acetaldehyde fermentation, alcohol fermentation, and lactic acid fermentation.

MOLECULAR GENETICS

DNA: The Basic Substance of Genes

A) **DNA** – Deoxyribonucleic acid is the genetic material of living organisms. A series of experiments proved that DNA was the hereditary material of organisms. The first such evidence resulted from the transformation experiments of Fred Griffith in 1928, involving strains of pneumococcus.

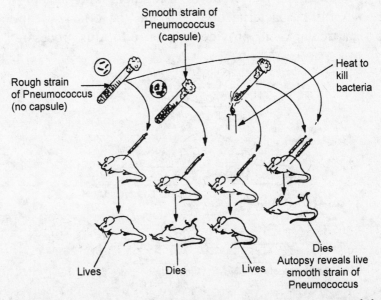

Figure 1.14 The experiments of Fred Griffith, which demonstrated the transfer of genetic information from dead, heat-killed bacteria to living bacteria of a different strain. Although neither the rough strain of pneumococcus nor the heat-killed smooth strain pneumococci would kill a mouse, a combination of the two did. Autopsy of the dead mouse showed the presence of living, smooth strain pneumococci.

Strong evidence that DNA is the genetic material came from the Hershey and Chase experiments with *E. coli* and the virus that attacks *E. coli*.

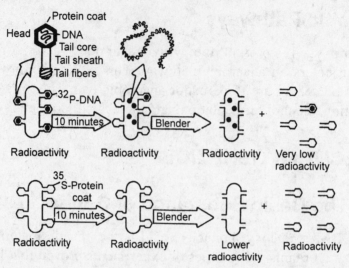

Figure 1.15 Hershey and Chase experiment demonstrating that only phage DNA enters the bacterial host cell after infection.

B) **Transduction** – A virus transfers DNA from one bacterium to another. The work of Lederberg and Zinder with two strains of bacteria, one resistant, the other susceptible to a particular virus, provided evidence for this process.

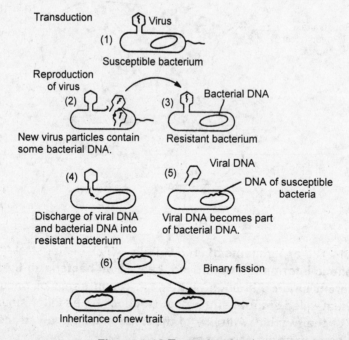

Figure 1.16 Transduction.

DNA contains instructions consisting of genetic material that is passed from one generation to the next. It encodes information that determines characteristics such as hair color and leaf size. DNA makes a messenger molecule, RNA. RNA makes proteins from amino acids. These amino acids are assembled into proteins that control metabolism.

A nucleotide of DNA consists of a nitrogen base, a five-carbon sugar, and phosphate groups. Each nucleotide contains one of four nitrogenous bases, which are the purines, adenine and guanine, and the pyrimidines, cytosine and thymine. Each nitrogenous base is attached to deoxyribose via a glycosidic linkage, and deoxyribose is attached to the phosphate group by an ester bond. This combination of an organic base attached to a pentose sugar forms a unit known as a nucleotide.

The nucleotides are joined by phosphate ester bonds into a chain. The phosphate group of one DNA nucleotide bonds to the sugar of another nucleotide. Nucleotides bond to form a long, chainlike molecule. The entire DNA molecule consists of two complimentary strands that run in opposite directions and are twisted into a double helix.

The following figures show the structural formulas of purines (adenine and guanine), pyrimidines (thymine and cytosine), and a nucleotide.

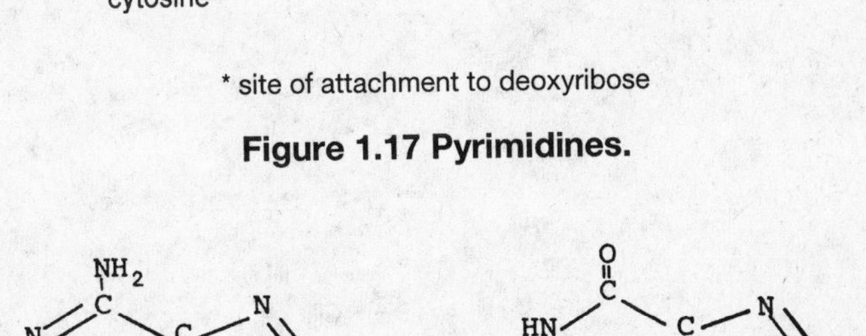

* site of attachment to deoxyribose

Figure 1.17 Pyrimidines.

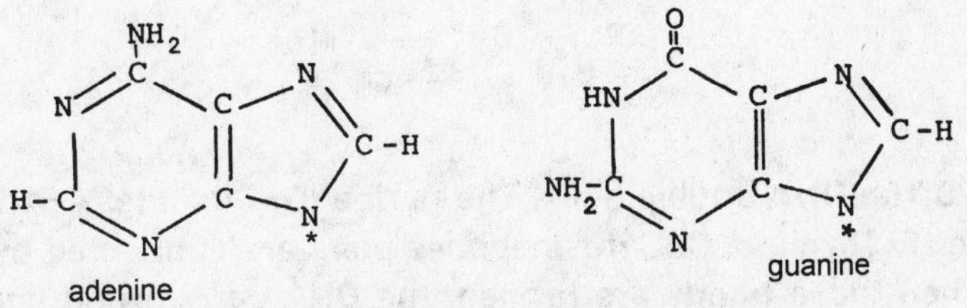

* site of attachment to deoxyribose

Figure 1.18 Purines.

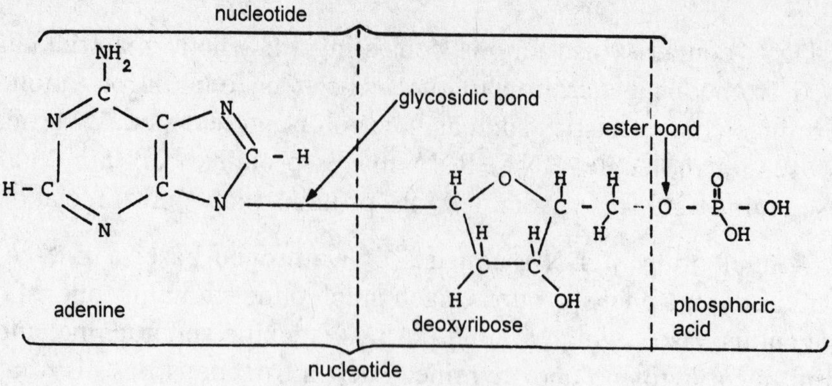

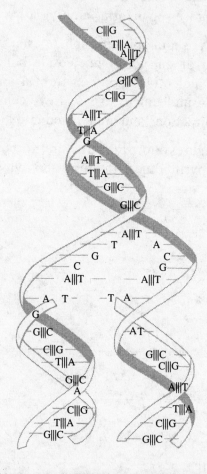

Figure 1.19 Nucleotides.

Figure 1.20 The DNA double helix. The purine (G=Guanine, A=Adenine) and pyrimidine (T=Thymine, C=Cytosine) base pairs are connected by hydrogen bonds. When these bonds are broken, the DNA can unwind and replicate (as in mitosis) or act as a template for mRNA synthesis. The deoxyribose sugar and phosphate groups act as a backbone of DNA, helping to maintain the sequential order of the nitrogenous bases. There are ten base pairs in one turn.

The Watson and Crick hypothesis was established in 1953. They proposed a model for the DNA molecule which consisted of a double helix of bonded nucleotides wherein two nucleotide chains were wound around each other, forming a double helix. Each full turn of the helix measures 34Å and contains 10 nucleotides equally spaced from each other. The radius of the helix is 10Å. These measurements were in agreement with those obtained from x-ray diffraction patterns of DNA.

The DNA double helix can be visualized as a twisted "ladder." In this structure there is a sugar phosphate backbone which is held together by bonded base pairs that form the rungs of the ladder. However, the bases are paired up in such a way that adenine always combines with thymine, and cytosine with guanine. Therefore, if we know the sequence of one strand of DNA, we can deduce the sequence of the complimentary strand.

```
A   C   T   T   A   G
|   |   |   |   |   |
T   G   A   A   T   C
```

Gene Expression

Replication of DNA occurs in the nucleus. After replication DNA remains in the nucleus. However, this DNA information needs to leave the nucleus so that it can be expressed by different cells in the body. This is achieved through the help of an intermediate substance known as RNA. RNA consists of only one chain of nucleotides which forms a single strand. It also contains the base uracil in place of thymine, while the other bases are the same as DNA.

Types of RNA

There are three different types of RNA. Each RNA consists of a single strand. RNA polymerase is an enzyme present in the nucleus which transcribes the information from a DNA template onto mRNA. This process is known as transcription.

Messenger RNA (mRNA) – The mRNA moves from the nucleus to the ribosomes in the cytoplasm where it translates the information coded in the DNA into a polypeptide chain. The two strands of the DNA separate and partially uncoil. The mRNA is copied. The strand that is transcribed is called the "sense strand." As in DNA replication, C always pairs with G, but unlike DNA replication, A pairs with U, since there is no T in RNA. After it is formed, the mRNA breaks away from the DNA template, and the DNA strands once again become double-stranded and coil up. The newly formed RNA strand leaves the nucleus and travels into the cytoplasm. The process of converting the genetic message from the DNA into RNA is called transcription.

The base pairing rules for transcription are

DNA	RNA
A	U
C	G
G	C
T	A

Proteins are made up of 20 different amino acids. Three bases code for an amino acid. These three bases, also known as a codon, can arrange themselves in 64 different ways. For example, using the following chart we can see that UUC codes for phenylalanine and CUC for leucine. An amino acid may be coded for by more than one codon. Some of the combinations are known as stop codons since they do not code for an amino acid, but instead cause the production of an amino acid to terminate.

The Genetic Code

First Position (5' end)	Second position	Third position (3' end)			
		U	C	A	G
U	U	Phe	Phe	Leu	Leu
	C	Ser	Ser	Ser	Ser
	A	Tyr	Tyr	Terminator	Terminator
	G	Cys	Cys	Terminator	Trp
C	U	Leu	Leu	Leu	Leu
	C	Pro	Pro	Pro	Pro
	A	His	His	Glu	Glu
	G	Arg	Arg	Arg	Arg
A	U	Ileu	Ileu	Ileu	Met
	C	Thr	Thr	Thr	Thr
	A	Asp	Asp	Lys	Lys
	G	Ser	Ser	Arg	Arg
G	U	Val	Val	Val	Val
	C	Ala	Ala	Ala	Ala
	A	Asp	Asp	Asp	Asp
	G	Gly	Gly	Gly	Gly

Transfer RNA (tRNA) – tRNA positions the amino acid into the correct sequence as determined by the nucleotide sequence on the mRNA. The tRNA has a sequence of nucleotides called the anticodon which pairs with the codon of the mRNA. For example, from the table we can see that valine can be coded for by the codon GUG; therefore, the anticodon will be CAC (A to U and C to G). A tRNA that carries the CAC anticodon would then also be attached to valine. Figure 1.21 is an illustration of the configuration of tRNA for alanine. It should be remembered that this is a two-dimensional representation of a three-dimensional structure.

Ribosomal RNA (rRNA) – Ribosomal RNA is the site where protein synthesis occurs.

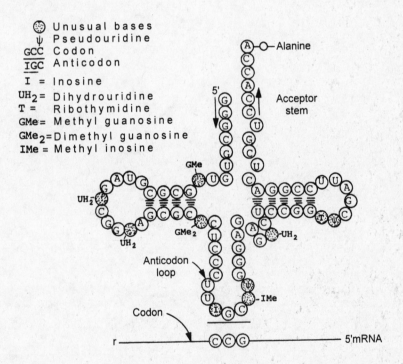

Figure 1.21 The complete nucleotide sequence of alanine tRNA showing the unusual bases and codon/anticodon position. The structure shown is two-dimensional.

THE SAT SUBJECT TEST IN
Biology E/M

CHAPTER 2

CHAPTER 2

THE CELL

CELL STRUCTURE AND FUNCTION

All living matter is composed of cells. Cells are the basic units of life. They are self-contained units and are surrounded by a cell membrane. All cells are divided into two categories; prokaryotic and eukaryotic. Prokaryotic cells are more simplified and primitive. Eukaryotic cells are more complex and advanced.

Protoplasm refers to living matter that is an organized complex of organic and inorganic substances (i.e., proteins, water, and elements). Different cell types have protoplasm of differing compositions.

Prokaryotic Cells

Prokaryotic cells are quite small and simple. It is thought that they were the first type of cell to appear on Earth. Prokaryotic cells are small in size, usually only a couple of micrometers in diameter. No structures can be seen inside prokaryotic cells using a light microscope. The liquid contents of any cell (whether prokaryotic or eukaryotic) is referred to by the generic term cytoplasm. Prokaryotic cells have such small cellular volume that their cytoplasm has nowhere to go, and hence does not move around within the cell. There is a cellular membrane that marks the barrier between the inside of the cell and its external environment. Most prokaryotic cells also have a cell wall surrounding the outside of their cellular membrane. Also present, but invisible to the light microscope, are ribosomes and a single circular chromosome made of DNA without any associated protein. It is this single molecule that regulates the cell's activities. Today, the only living prokaryotic cells are the bacteria and blue-green algae.

Eukaryotic Cells

Eukaryotic cells are much larger and more complex than prokaryotic cells. The DNA is associated with specific proteins called "histones." Together, these make linear chromosomes that can be seen easily with a light microscope during certain times in the cell's cycle. The number of chromosomes present depends upon the type of organism the cell is or comes from. In eukaryotic cells, the chromosomes are found in a special structure called the nucleus. Eukaryotic cells are so large that they usually contain many small structures, or organelles, as they are called. These cells are so large that the cytoplasm can be seen flowing from one location within the cell to another. This phenomenon is termed "cytoplasmic streaming," or cyclosis. The cytoplasm when found in the nucleus is termed "nucleoplasm." A more general term that does not reveal location is "protoplasm." The following is a list of cellular organelles that might (but not necessarily must) be found in eukaryotic cells.

Nucleus – The nucleus consists of a double unit membrane. It contains DNA stored as chromatin which becomes visible at the time of cell division as chromosomes.

Nucleolus – This is a dense region of the nucleus that is composed of protein and RNA. This is also the site where rRNA is made.

Mitochondrion – This organelle has a double-unit membrane and is the site of chemical reactions that provide the cell with energy. The mitochondria are responsible for 95 percent of all ATP produced in the cell. For this reason, the mitochondria are commonly referred to as the "powerhouse" of the cell.

Chloroplasts – These are found in plants and certain algae and are the sites of photosynthesis.

Lysosomes – These are surrounded by single-unit membranes that contain acid hydrolase, an enzyme that digests substances within the cell.

Endoplasmic Reticulum – This is a double-unit membrane which may have ribosomes present. If ribosomes are present, the rough endoplasmic reticulum synthesizes proteins. The smooth endoplasmic reticulum lacks ribosomes. The rough and smooth endoplasmic reticulum transport substances. Also, endoplasmic reticulum (present only in eukaryotic cells) accounts for about one-half the cellular membrane.

Cell Membrane – This is a double layer of lipids that surrounds the cell, thus acting as a "gatekeeper" by controlling what moves into and out of the cell. In 1972, S.J. Singer and G.L. Nicolson proposed a fluid-mosaic model that diagrammed the two phospholipid layers and the embedded proteins. Note this from the following illustration.

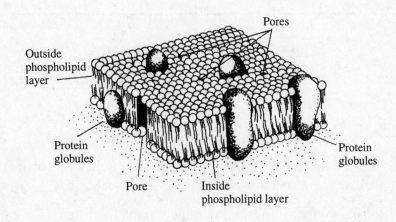

Figure 2.1 Schematic Depiction of a Typical Cell Membrane.

Ribosomes – These are small structures composed of ribosomal RNA and are the sites of protein synthesis. Messenger RNA (mRNA), which carries genetic information from the nucleus to the ribosomes, associates with the small ribosomal subunit first and then binds to the large subunit as a prelude to protein synthesis. This association of mRNA to ribosomes makes the system of protein synthesis more efficient than if the complex was dispersed freely into the cytoplasm. The mRNA then pairs with complementary molecules of transfer RNA (tRNA), each carrying a specific amino acid, which bind with each other to form a highly specific protein molecule. Thus, ribosomes are the sites where proteins are synthesized under genetic control.

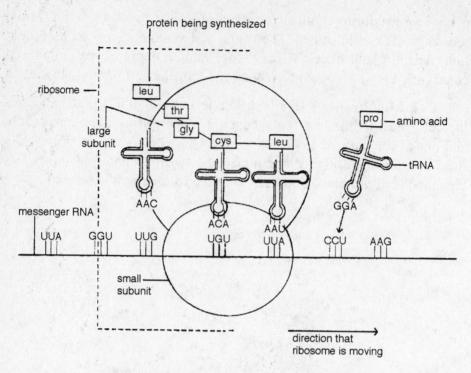

Figure 2.2 Diagram showing protein synthesis.

Golgi Apparatus – This organelle is a collection of membranes that packages and secretes proteins and polysaccharides.

Peroxisomes – These single-membraned substances contain oxidative enzymes.

Vacuoles – These are membrane-enclosed fluid-filled spaces that are involved in the storage of substances.

Cell Wall – These are present in plant cells for support and protection.

Centrioles and Centromeres – These coordinate cell division and organize locomotion.

Microtubules – These are hollow, rod-shaped structural organelles composed of tubulin protein and found in the cytoplasm, cilia, and flagella of eukaryotic cells.

Microfilaments – These are solid, rod-shaped structural organelles composed of actin protein found in the cytoplasm of most eukaryotic cells and which function in cell contraction.

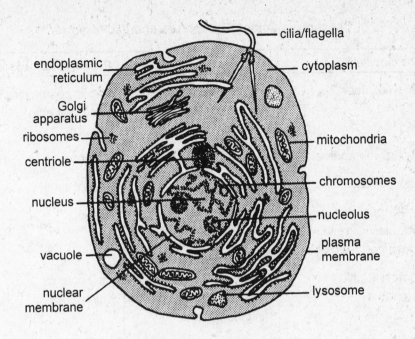

Figure 2.3 Animal Cell.

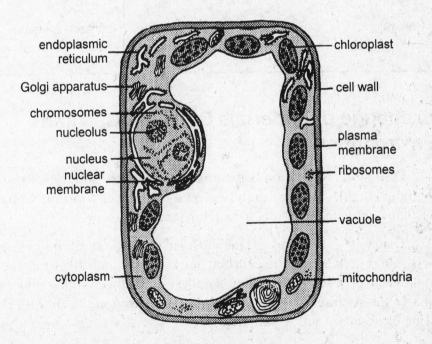

Figure 2.4 Plant Cell.

Characteristics of Eukaryotes and Prokaryotes

Characteristic	Eukaryotic cells	Prokaryotic cells
Chromosomes	multiple, composed of nucleic acids and protein	single, composed only of nucleic acid
Nuclear membrane	present	absent
Mitochondria	present	absent
Golgi apparatus, endoplasmic reticulum, lysosomes, peroxisomes	present	absent
Photosynthetic apparatus	chlorophyll, when present, is contained (in chloroplasts)	may contain chlorophyll
Microtubules	present	rarely present
Ribosomes	large	small
Flagella	have 9-2 tubular structure	lack 9-2 tubular structure
Cell wall	when present, does not contain muramic acid	contains muramic acid

Exchange of Materials Between Cell and Environment

Diffusion – Diffusion is the migration of molecules or ions from a region of higher concentration to a region of lower concentration. The particles' movement results from their random motion.

Osmosis – Osmosis is the diffusion of water through a semi-permeable membrane. At constant temperature and pressure, the net movement of water is from the solution with lower solute concentration to the solution with higher solute concentration. The solute represents osmotically active particles.

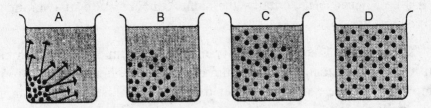

Figure 2.5 The sugar molecules, over a period of time, will be distributed evenly in the water because of diffusion.

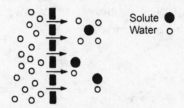

Figure 2.6 The process of osmosis.

Active Transport – The movement of ions and molecules against a concentration gradient is referred to as active transport. The particles move from lower to higher concentrations. The cell must expend energy to accomplish the transport. In passive transport, no energy is expended.

Endocytosis – Endocytosis is an active process in which the cell encloses a particle in a membrane-bound vesicle, pinched off from the cell membrane. Endocytosis of solid particles is called phagocytosis.

Figure 2.7 Endocytosis in the amoeba.

Exocytosis – Exocytosis is the reverse of endocytosis; there is a discharge of vacuole-enclosed materials from a cell by the fusion of the cell membrane with the vacuole membrane.

Pinocytosis – This is a cellular process in which an invagination forms in the cell membrane, eventually pinching both sides together to form a vesicle containing engulfed extracellular fluid and its dissolved material.

Isotonic Medium – An isotonic medium is in osmotic balance with a cell because it contains the same concentration of osmotically active particles.

Hypertonic Medium – A hypertonic medium is one in which a cell loses water because the medium contains a higher concentration of osmotically active particles. Water diffuses into this extracellular medium by osmosis.

Hypotonic Medium – A hypotonic medium is one in which a cell gains water because the medium contains a lower concentration of osmotically active particles. Water diffuses away from this extracellular medium into the cell by osmosis.

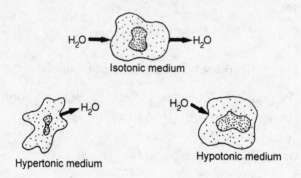

Figure 2.8 Osmotic effects of the fluids bathing cells.

Cells display the properties of life. Life activities are the basic functions of living organisms. They include the following:

Ingestion – Nutrition by heterotrophs in which food is eaten whole or in pieces.

Digestion – Food is broken down into an assimilable state by chemical and/or mechanical action.

Secretion – The production and export of a substance from cells or the body.

Absorption – The act or process of taking in or soaking up.

Respiration – Metabolic process whereby an organism releases stored energy by breaking down complex molecules.

Excretion – The process of eliminating waste matter from the cell or body.

Transport – To move from one place to another (i.e., from outside to inside a cell).

Regulation – The ability to adjust rate, amount, or flow in accordance with internal and external factors.

Synthesis – To combine elements, parts, or substances into a whole.

Assimilation – The process of taking in and incorporating substances into a body or cell.

Reproduction – The ability to generate offspring.

Irritability – Response to stimuli.

Movement – The act or process of changing positions.

Cellular Division

All cells arise from pre-existing cells. Binary fission is the process by which prokaryotes reproduce. In this method, the cell membrane invaginates. This is followed by the invagination of the cell wall, resulting in the formation of two equal halves.

Mitosis

Mitosis is the process of reproduction used by eukaryotes. It is a form of cell division in which each chromosome duplicates itself. These duplicates are separated during cell division, forming two identical daughter cells. This form of asexual reproduction is involved in growth, regeneration, and cell replacement in multicellular organisms. It is a complex division consisting of the following stages:

Interphase – During interphase, the cell undergoes a great deal of activity. The DNA replicates and forms mRNA, tRNA, and rRNA. In the cytoplasm, oxidation and synthesis reactions take place.

Prophase – The chromatids shorten and thicken and become visible as chromosomes. The nucleolus and nuclear membrane break down and disappear. The centrioles divide and move to opposite poles of the nucleus, and spindle fibers begin to form.

Metaphase – The chromosomes move to the equator of the spindle fibers (the middle). The paired chromosomes attach to the equator of the spindle at the centromeres.

Anaphase – The sister chromatids separate and move to opposite poles of the spindle fibers. Cytokinesis begins.

Telophase – Cytokinesis is complete, having formed two daughter cells. The chromosomes in each new cell uncoil, and the nucleus and the nuclear membrane reform. In plant cells, a cell plate appears dividing the parent cell into two daughter cells. In animal cells, the plasma membrane invaginates dividing the plasma membrane.

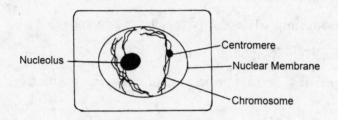

Figure 2.9 Interphase.

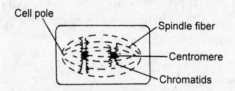

Figure 2.10 Late prophase in plant cell mitosis.

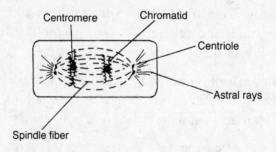

Figure 2.11 Prophase in animal cell mitosis.

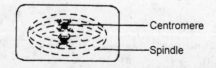

Figure 2.12 Metaphase in plant cell mitosis.

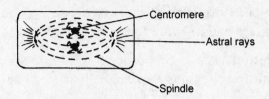

Figure 2.13 Metaphase in animal cell mitosis.

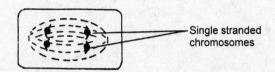

Figure 2.14 Anaphase in plant cell mitosis.

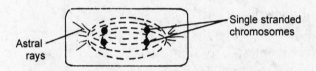

Figure 2.15 Anaphase in animal cell mitosis.

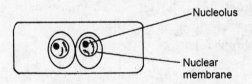

Figure 2.16 Late telophase in plant cell mitosis.

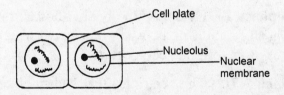

Figure 2.17 Late telophase in animal cell mitosis.

Meiosis

Meiosis – Meiosis consists of two successive cell divisions with only one duplication of chromosomes. This results in daughter cells with a haploid number of chromosomes, or one-half of the chromosome number in the original cell. This process occurs during the formation of gametes and in spore formation in plants.

Spermatogenesis – This process results in sperm cell formation with four immature sperm cells with a haploid number of chromosomes.

Oogenesis – This process results in egg cell formation with only one immature egg cell with a haploid number of chromosomes, which becomes mature and larger as yolk forms within the cell.

First Meiotic Division

A) **Interphase I** – Chromosome duplication begins to occur during this phase.

B) **Prophase I** – During this phase, the chromosomes shorten and thicken and synapsis occurs with pairing of homologous chromosomes. Crossing-over between non-sister chromatids will also occur. The centrioles will migrate to opposite poles and the nucleolus and nuclear membrane begin to dissolve.

C) **Metaphase I** – The tetrads, composed of two doubled homologous chromosomes, migrate to the equatorial plane during metaphase I.

D) **Anaphase I** – During this stage, the paired homologous chromosomes separate and move to opposite poles of the cell. Thus, the number of chromosome types in each resulting cell is reduced in the haploid number.

E) **Telophase I** – Cytoplasmic division occurs during telophase I. The formation of two new nuclei with half the chromosomes of the original cell occurs.

F) **Prophase II** – The centrioles that had migrated to each pole of the parental cell, now incorporated in each haploid daughter cell, divide, and a new spindle forms in each cell. The chromosomes move to the equator.

G) **Metaphase II** – The chromosomes are lined up at the equator of the new spindle, which is at a right angle to the old spindle.

H) **Anaphase II** – The centromeres divide and the daughter chromatids, now chromosomes, separate and move to opposite poles.

I) **Telophase II** – Cytoplasmic division occurs. The chromosomes gradually return to the dispersed form and a nuclear membrane forms.

EQUIPMENT AND TECHNIQUES

Units of Measurement

The basic scientific unit of length is the **meter** (1 m = 3.28 ft). There are 1,000 millimeters (mm) per meter.

Microbes are generally measured in micrometers (μm) or nanometers (nm).

$$1 \ \mu m = 0.000001 = 10^{-6} \ m$$

$$1 \ nm = 10^{-9} \ m$$

Microscopes

Microscopy is the process of projecting energy (visible light, ultraviolet light, or electrons) onto an object, and then using the energy that is emitted from that object to create an image on a sensing device (e.g., the lens of your eye, a screen, or a photographic film). Microscopes may differ in the kind of energy used, type of sensing device, resolution, wavelength, and magnification.

Resolution refers to the ability to distinguish adjacent objects or structures as separate and discrete entities. The **resolving power** of a microscope indicates the size of the smallest objects that can be clearly observed.

Compound light microscope – This microscope uses a two-lens system—an ocular lens and an objective lens. Total magnification (magnifying power) equals the magnification of the ocular lens *times* that of the objective lens.

Brightfield microscopy – Light is transmitted directly through the specimen. Organisms must generally be stained.

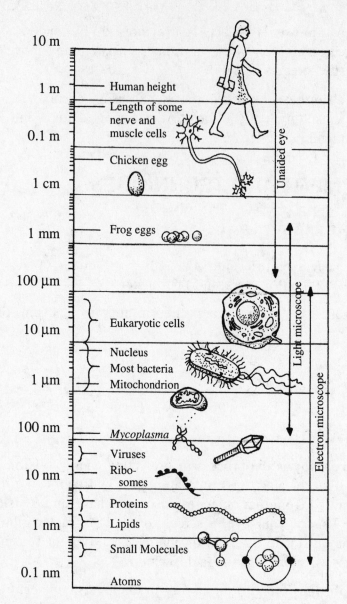

Figure 2.18 Relative sizes.

Darkfield microscope – These microscopes have a condenser that reflects light off the specimen at diverse angles and prevents most light from passing directly through the specimen. At the apex of the illuminating cone, light rays are scattered from the specimen into the objective lens, and the image is that of a light organism against a dark background. This type of microscope is good for visualizing capsules surrounding bacterial cells and in diagnosing diseases caused by spiral bacteria. Even though these organisms are near the limit of resolution, their characteristic movement is discernible in darkfield.

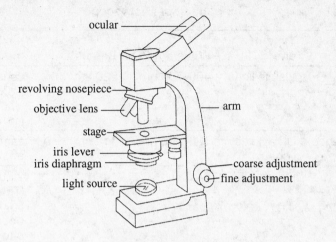

Figure 2.19 The compound microscope.

Phase-contrast microscope – This microscope is preferred for the observation of living, unstained organisms. A condenser splits the light beam, throwing the light rays slightly out of phase. Small differences in the densities and refractive indices of various structures are accentuated, and internal details of live, unstained cells can be observed.

Fluorescence microscopy – Ultraviolet light is used to excite electrons in molecules. When these electrons fall back to their original energy state, they fluoresce (emit light). Some organisms are naturally fluorescent, but most organisms observed in this way must first be treated with a fluorescent dye or *fluorochrome* (e.g., fluorescein).

Electron microscopes – These microscopes use energy in the form of a beam of electrons rather than a beam of light. This beam is focused using electromagnets rather than lenses. Viruses can be seen only by using electron microscopes. There are two types of electron microscopes: the *transmission electron microscope* and the *scanning electron microscope*.

Transmission electron microscopy (TEM) – Electrons pass through the specimen. TEM cannot be used to view whole organisms, but is very good for looking at internal structures.

Scanning electron microscopy (SEM) – Used to create three-dimensional images of surfaces, both external and internal.

Comparison of Microscopes

	Type of energy	Wavelength	Resolution	Maximum magnification
Light microscope	Visible light	400–700 nm	220 nm	usually 100×, (1,000×–2,000× with oil immersion)
Fluorescence microscope	Ultraviolet light	100–400 nm	110 nm	same as above
Electron microscope	Electrons	0.005 nm	1 nm (TEM) 20 nm (SEM)	2,000,000× (TEM) 50,000× (SEM) prior to photographic enlargement

THE SAT SUBJECT TEST IN
Biology E/M

CHAPTER 3

CHAPTER 3

GENETICS – THE SCIENCE OF HEREDITY

MENDELIAN GENETICS

In 1857, Gregor Mendel discovered the basic laws of genetics, by studying garden peas, one trait at a time.

Definitions

Genes – These are the units of inheritance. They are the part of a chromosome that codes for certain hereditary traits.

An Abstract of the Data Obtained by Mendel from His Breeding Experiments with Garden Peas

Parental Characters	First Generation	Second Generation	Ratios
Yellow seeds × green seeds	all yellow	6,022 yellow:2,001 green	3.01:1
Round seeds × wrinkled seeds	all round	5,474 round:1,850 wrinkled	2.96:1
Green pods × yellow pods	all green	428 green:152 yellow	2.82:1
Long stems × short stems	all long	787 long:277 short	2.84:1
Axial flowers × terminal flowers	all axial	651 axial:207 terminal	3.14:1
Inflated pods × constricted pods	all inflated	882 inflated:299 constricted	2.95:1
Red flowers × white flowers	all red	705 red:224 white	3.15:1

The 3:1 ratio resulting from this data enabled Mendel to recognize that the offspring of each plant had two factors instead of a single factor for any given characteristic.

Chromosomes – These are rod-like structures that contain genes in the cell nucleus.

Alleles – Alleles are forms of a gene that can be dominant (A) or recessive (a). These are alternative forms of a gene that determine a character. For example, height may be controlled by one allele for tallness and another allele for shortness.

Genotype – This is the genetic constitution of an organism.

Phenotype – This is the outward expression of the genotype in the organism.

Homologous Chromosomes – These are paired chromosomes that bear genes for the same traits. Homologous chromosomes are the same in size and shape.

Homozygote – This is an organism possessing an identical pair of alleles on homologous chromosomes for all given characters. An organism can be homozygous dominant (AA) or homozygous recessive (aa).

Heterozygote – This organism possesses different alleles on homologous chromosomes for all given characters (e.g., Aa).

Crossing Over – Paired chromosomes may break and their fragments reunite in new combinations. This occurs in prophase of meiosis I.

Translocations – The shifting of gene positions in chromosomes that may result in a change in the serial arrangement of genes. In general, it is the transfer of a chromosome fragment to a non-homologous chromosome.

Linkage – Genes that are fairly close together on the same chromosome are inherited together.

Genetic Mutation – This is a change in an allele or segment of a chromosome that causes genetic variation, a prerequisite for evolution.

Codon – This is a sequence of three nucleotides that codes for an amino acid.

Laws of Genetics

Law of Dominance – Of two contrasting characteristics, the dominant one (A) is expressed and the recessive one (a) is masked.

Law of Segregation and Recombination – Each trait is transmitted as an unchanging unit, independent of other traits, thereby giving the recessive traits a chance to recombine and show their presence in some of the offspring.

Law of Independent Assortment – Each character for a trait operates as a unit and the distribution of one pair of factors is independent of another pair of factors linked on different chromosomes. By this, two heterozygous gene pairs form four kinds of sex cells: e.g., AaBb forms AB, Ab, aB, ab.

Punnett Square – This is a method of determining the genotypes from the mating of two individuals with known genotypes.

Tt × Tt (T is dominant to t)

T = tallness
t = shortness

	T	t
T	TT	Tt
t	Tt	tt

TT = 1; Tt = 2; tt = 1
TT and Tt are the same.
TT/Tt : tt = 3 : 1

Figure 3.1

Test Cross – This method, devised by Mendel, determines the genotype of an individual to see if it is homozygous or heterozygous. It involves crossing the test individual with a homozygous recessive individual.

PP × pp

	p	p
P	Pp	Pp
P	Pp	Pp

Figure 3.2

All are purple, therefore the test plant must be homozygous for purple flowers.

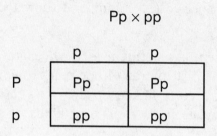

$$Pp \times pp$$

Figure 3.3

Half are purple and half are white so the test plant is heterozygous for purple.

PATTERNS OF INHERITANCE, CHROMOSOMES, GENES, AND ALLELES

In 1900, Walter Sutton compared the behavior of chromosomes with the behavior of the hereditary characters that Mendel had proposed, and formulated the Chromosome Principle of Inheritance.

The Chromosome Principle of Inheritance

A) Chromosomes and Mendelian factors exist in pairs.

B) The segregation of Mendelian factors corresponds to the separation of homologous chromosomes during the reduction division stage of meiosis I.

C) The recombination of Mendelian factors corresponds to the restoration of the diploid number of chromosomes at fertilization.

D) The factors that Mendel described as passing from parent to offspring correspond to the passing of chromosomes into gametes which then unite and develop into offspring.

E) The Mendelian idea that two sets of characters present in a parent assort independently corresponds to the random separation of the two sets of chromosomes as they enter a different gamete during meiosis.

Sutton's Chromosome Principle of Inheritance states that the hereditary characters, or factors that control heredity are located in the chromosomes. By 1910, the factors of heredity were called genes.

Genes and the Environment

An organism's particular genotype, or genetic makeup, will determine its phenotype, or physical characteristics. A gene produces a particular protein, usually an enzyme, that brings about a chemical reaction resulting in a certain characteristic. The expression of some genes is sometimes dependent upon the environmental conditions, for example, temperature or availability of light. Differences in the appearance or intelligence of identical twins that were separated at birth demonstrate the importance of environment in gene expression.

Improving the Species

Breeding for Better Plants and Animals – Humans have modified plants and animals that they find useful by selectively breeding for desirable traits (artificial selection). Artificial selection can achieve changes in the characteristics of an organism in a relatively short period of time and may result in improved yield, improved quality, increased resistance to disease, and new varieties. Other methods for artificially improving the species include hybridization, or cross-breeding, selecting for useful mutations, and genetic engineering.

SEX CHROMOSOMES

Humans have 46 chromosomes which are present as 23 pairs. The chromosomes are divided into autosomes and sex chromosomes. In humans, there are 22 pairs of autosomes and one pair of sex chromosomes.

Females contain two X chromosomes and have the genotype XX. Males contain an X and a Y chromosome and have the genotype XY. The Y chromosome is smaller than the X chromosome. During gametogenesis the X and Y chromosomes separate into different cells. During oogenesis, the X chromosomes also separate. However, all eggs contain an X chromosome, whereas the sperm cells contain either an X or a Y chromosome. Therefore, the following outcomes are possible:

1. If a sperm carrying an X chromosome fertilizes an egg the result is an individual with genotype 'XX'.

2. If a sperm carrying a Y chromosome fertilizes an egg the result is an individual with the genotype 'XY'.

Therefore, it can be concluded that the makeup of the male, and not the female, sex cell determines the sex of its offspring during fertilization.

Sex-linked Characteristics

Certain genes have been identified that are carried on the sex chromosomes and inherited along with the sex chromosomes. Examples of sex-linked traits (also called X-linked traits) include hemophilia and color blindness. They result from the expression of recessive alleles.

The inheritance of hemophilia can be represented as follows:

If X^h represents the X chromosome that carries the allele for hemophilia and X^H represents the X chromosome carrying the normal allele

	X^H	X^h
X^H	$X^H X^H$	$X^H X^h$
Y	$X^H Y$	$X^h Y$

The results of this cross are as follows:

1 normal female: $X^H X^H$

1 normal female who is a carrier: $X^H X^h$

1 normal male: $X^H Y$

1 hemophilic male: $X^h Y$

Note: If produced in another cross, a hemophilic female is: $X^h X^h$.

Inheritance of Defects

Certain inherited diseases arise due to genetic defects, such as:

Hemophilia – This is inherited as an X-linked recessive trait that mainly affects males. A hemophiliac's blood does not clot, thus the hemophiliac may bleed to death from relatively minor cuts and bruises.

Phenylketonuria (PKU) – This is an X-linked recessive trait. PKU causes elevated levels of phenylalanine, an amino acid, which results in mental retardation and brain damage.

Sickle cell anemia – This condition is brought about by a point mutation in which the amino acid glutamic acid is substituted by valine. Due to the ability of sickled cells to adhere to capillary walls, they can occlude blood vessels and prevent the flow of blood, resulting in swelling and pain. This disease may be present in a small percentage of African-Americans. Heterozygous individuals are afforded protection from malaria causing the defective gene to be selected and inherited. A homozygous recessive genotype of the sickle cell gene, $Hb^s Hb^s$ (SS), however, is lethal.

Tay-Sachs Disease – This disease is most common in those of Eastern European Jewish origin. Lipids accumulate in the various cells, especially in the brains of newborns. This results in motor and mental deterioration.

Chromosomal Aberrations – A number of chromosomal disorders occur as a result of non-disjunction during meiosis. Failure of chromosomes to divide during gametogenesis may cause monosomy or trisomy. Down Syndrome arises due to the presence of an extra chromosome at position 21. Individuals with this disease suffer from physical and mental retardation and have 47 chromosomes instead of the usual 46. Klinefelter's Syndrome, or male hypogonadism, is due to the genotype XXY. These individuals are infertile and their secondary sex characteristics do not develop.

Testing for Defects

Prenatal Testing

This is a method used to examine the chromosomes and genes of the unborn fetus for any abnormalities. Examples of these procedures include amniocentesis and chronic villi sampling.

1) *Amniocentesis*

In this procedure, a hollow needle is inserted through the uterine wall during the fourth month of pregnancy and amniotic fluid containing sloughed cells from the developing fetus are drawn. After being placed in a centrifuge and grown on a nutrient medium, these cells are examined for chromosomal defects. The chromosomes are examined for defects which may bring about abnormalities in the fetus. This method is especially important in families in which genetic defects are present. Genetic counseling is given to those women carrying a fetus with an inherited defect.

2) *Chronic Villi Sampling*

This procedure may be conducted in the 9th week of pregnancy by passing a hollow tube into the uterus and collecting cells from the chorion of the developing fetus. These cells are then examined for defects. CVS is more specific and more accurate at detecting defects in the fetus.

Karyotypes

The arrangement of chromosomes in an individual differs between different individuals and species. This arrangement of chromosomes is known as karyotype. Karyotypes can be examined for abnormalities by photographing the chromosomes and then rearranging them according to size. These abnormalities in humans are compared to a normal karyotype:

> male: 44 autosomes + XY
>
> female: 44 autosomes + XX

Eugenics

Eugenics is the study of improving the human race. Using pedigree's diagrams over several generations, it uses genetics to understand patterns of inheritance. It was discovered by Sir Francis Galton during the latter part of the 19th century.

Modern Genetics

Gene Action

Genes are composed of DNA and carry the units of inheritance. They replicate and pass on a copy of themselves in the formation of a zygote. By making RNA, genes control the synthesis of proteins and enzymes. Therefore, they control cell activity.

Mutations – Mutations are changes in the genetic information of a cell. If the mutation causes an alteration in only a few nucleotides of the genetic sequence, it is known as a point mutation. A chromosomal mutation is caused by extensive chemical change in the structure of a chromosome. Mutations that occur in cells which form gametes, known as germline cells, are passed on to successive generations. Mutagens are chemicals released into the environment that cause damage to DNA.

DNA Fingerprinting – This is a procedure that has been implemented to determine paternity cases and to solve crimes. A number of steps are used to analyze DNA from small amounts of semen, hair cells, or blood. Since the base pair's sequence for each individual is different, this method has proven effective in solving crimes.

Cloning – This is a method used by scientists to generate identical replicas of an organism without prior fertilization. The new cells produced are known as clones. Although cloning has been used by scientists to generate important medical products, the use of cloning on human cells has been banned.

Recombinant DNA – This is a method of creating a DNA molecule in the laboratory by joining different genomes together in various combinations. Restriction endonucleases are enzymes used to cut the DNA source at particular sites in order to produce the desired fragments.

Genetic Engineering – Genetic engineering is a procedure that cuts up DNA into certain sequences and then rearranges these sequences. Restriction endonucleases are the enzymes used to cleave the DNA molecule. In the 1980s geneticists conducted an experiment in which they introduced the protein interferon into a bacterial cell. Interferon is a protein which protects against viral infection. The interferon proceeded to replicate in large amounts in the bacterial cell.

Another area in which genetic engineering has been implemented is in manipulating genes of certain crop plants. Genes have been isolated which may produce resistance to frost, diseases, and improve nutritional content.

Genetic engineering has also been used to produce various vaccines. Techniques have been used to produce vaccines against the herpes and hepatitis viruses.

Human Genome Project – The total number of genes in a haploid chromosome is known as the genome. Humans have 50,000 to 100,000 genes distributed over their 23 chromosome pairs. In 1988, the Human Genome Project that would determine the correct sequence of genes on a chromosome of a cell was established. The purpose of the project was to grasp a better understanding of defective genes that lead to the formation of various inherited diseases.

How Living Things are Classified

In this chapter we've reviewed important concepts in the study of genetics. We've seen that biologists rely on genetics to understand why species are different and how traits are passed on from one generation to the next. Variations in genetic codes over millions of years have led to an innumerable amount of species. With this great number of species, scientists needed a conventional way of naming all organisms so that the entire scientific community could share a common language. The naming system had to meet two requirements: 1) the language chosen for this naming system could not be preferential to any one country/nationality, and 2) the naming system needed to be highly organized.

In 1735, Carolus Linneaus created a system that met these requirements by developing what he termed taxonomy. He chose Latin as the language since it is a "dead" language; that is, people do not speak Latin anymore. In this system, each individual organism has two Latin names, a genus name and a species name, and this is known as binomial nomenclature. Organisms are classified according to their similarities in structure, development, and evolutionary history. This is called systematics. Classification groups from most different to most similar are as follows: kingdom, phylum, subphylum, class, order, family, genus, species, variety. Conventionally, there are five kingdoms of living organisms: Monera, Protista, Fungi, Plantae, and Animalia.

THE SAT SUBJECT TEST IN
Biology E/M

CHAPTER 4

A SURVEY OF BACTERIA, PROTISTS, AND FUNGI

DIVERSITY AND CHARACTERISTICS OF THE MONERA KINGDOM

The two main branches of the Monera Kingdom are Eubacteria and Archaebacteria. Most bacteria are considered Eubacteria. The other branch, Archaebacteria, live in extreme conditions in which no other forms of life are able to exist, (i.e., near thermal vents).

Archaebacteria

This branch of the Monera kingdom contains the prokaryotes that are ancient bacteria. The archaebacteria (ancient bacteria) are distinct from the more familiar eubacteria (true bacteria) by differences in their cell wall, cell membrane, and ribosome structure. The 3 main groups of the ancient bacteria are the methanogens (methane generators), halophiles (salt lovers) and thermophiles (heat lovers).

Eubacteria

The true bacteria and blue-green algae are included in this branch of the Monera kingdom. These cells, having no nuclear membrane and only a single chromosome, are termed prokaryotes. Both blue-green algae and bacteria lack membrane-bound subcellular organelles such as mitochondria and chloroplasts.

Study of Bacteria

Early History

Microbiology is the study of microbes (microorganisms), i.e., organisms too small to be observed by the naked eye, and dates back to the 17th century, when Hans and Zaccharias Janssen (ca. 1600) invented the first compound microscope.

Robert Hooke (1665) made early observations using a compound microscope. From his observations with cork, he coined the word "cell" to describe the "little boxes" he saw as the smallest structures of life, setting the foundation for "cell theory." The cell theory states that all living things are composed of cells.

Francesco Redi (1660s) was first to present experimental evidence to refute spontaneous generation. Redi used cloth-covered jars to show that maggots do not arise spontaneously in meat but that the meat must be open to contact with flies in order for maggots to appear. However, his results were not accepted by many (the experiment that finally put the theory of spontaneous generation to rest did not occur for another 200 years).

Carolus Linnaeus (1735) developed a general system of classification and *binomial nomenclature* (genus name + specific epithet or species name).

On the medical front, Edward Jenner (1798) developed and tested the first vaccine. Jenner noticed that milkmaids exposed to cowpox rarely developed the more serious smallpox. He then used cowpox to successfully inoculate patients against smallpox.

Ignaz Philipp Semmelweis (1840s) noticed a connection between doctors doing autopsies and patients developing puerperal (childbirth) fever. He is generally credited with being the first scientist to suggest that doctors should wash their hands between procedures.

The Golden Age of Microbiology

The Golden Age of Microbiology (1850-1890) was a period during which major historical figures established microbiology as a viable scientific discipline.

Louis Pasteur was the scientist responsible for the disproof of spontaneous generation/proof of biogenesis (1861). Pasteur devised a special kind of flask in order to disprove spontaneous generation. He used swan-neck flasks that were not sealed off; rather, the necks of the flasks were open, long, and curved. Such flasks were open to air and to any "vital force." However, microorganisms from the outer air became trapped in the curved neck of the flask and were prevented from contaminating the medium. Infusions or nutrient broths that had been sterilized by boiling were not contaminated in such a flask unless the neck became broken. Thus, Pasteur disproved spontaneous generation while demonstrating that the inoculating (contaminating) organisms are present in the air.

Pasteur was first to show that microorganisms are *everywhere*, including the air. This discovery provided impetus for the development of aseptic techniques in the laboratory and medical situations to prevent contamination.

Pasteur was also instrumental in work on the role of yeast and other microorganisms in fermentation, or the conversion of sugars to alcohol. He developed a heating process used to kill bacteria in some alcoholic beverages and milk, i.e., *pasteurization*.

In addition, Pasteur was a pioneer in the area of immunology. He developed "vaccines" (he coined the term) for chicken cholera and rabies (1884). In his search for a rabies vaccine, Pasteur used the brain tissue of rabid animals to inoculate rabbits. He then used the dried spinal cords of those rabbits to inoculate experimental animals.

In 1865, he used this treatment to successfully vaccinate a young boy who had been bitten by a rabid dog and, showing signs of the disease, was expected to die. The vaccine worked and the boy lived (modern vaccines are generally live, avirulent microorganisms, or killed pathogens or components isolated from pathogens, especially by use of recombinant DNA techniques).

It was one of Pasteur's publications (1857) that laid the foundation for the germ theory of disease by suggesting that microorganisms are the *cause* of disease rather than the *result* of it. This theory states that microorganisms can invade other organisms and are responsible for the transmission of infectious diseases.

Joseph Lister (1860s) introduced the use of disinfectants to clean surgical dressings and instruments.

Robert Koch's work (1870s) provided further support for the germ theory of disease. His work with the sheep disease anthrax was instrumental in establishing the concept of "one disease—one organism," which is the foundation of medical microbiology. He was the first to establish pure culture technique, and the first to use agar in growth medium. Koch's Postulates (1876) are still used today as the appropriate method for demonstrating that a specific microorganism transmits a specific disease.

Bacteria

Bacteria are unicellular prokaryotes, ranging in diameter from about 0.20 to 2.0 μm. Bacteria reproduce by binary fission. They are identified and grouped on the basis of a number of characteristics, including: morphology (size, shape, arrangement), staining characteristics (gram-positive, gram-negative, acid-fast), nutritional requirements, growth characteristics, physical requirements (e.g., temperature and pH optima).

Bacteriophages

Bacteriophages are viruses that attack bacterial cells and contain either RNA or DNA. Some have a tail-like structure through which they inject their nucleic acid into the bacterial host cell.

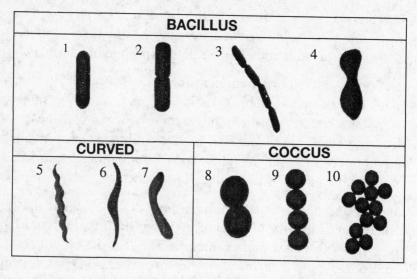

1	Single	5	Spirochete	8	Diplococcus
2	Diplobacillus (pair)	6	Spirillum	9	Streptococcus
3	Streptobacillus (chain)	7	Vibrio	10	Staphylococcus
4	Cocco-bacillus				

Figure 4.1 Primary bacterial shapes.

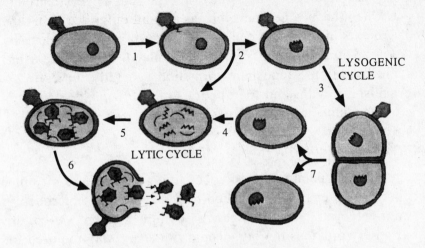

1. Phage attaches to host cell wall
2. Viral DNA is injected into cell
3. Viral DNA attaches to bacterial DNA
4. Viral DNA takes over cell and starts to reproduce
5. New protein coats are synthesized
6. Bacterium lyses and new viruses are released
7. Bacterial cell divides, producing more cells with viral DNA

Figure 4.2 Lysis and lysogeny.

Bacteriophage infection follows one of two courses—lysis or lysogeny. If the infecting virus multiplies within the host cell and destroys it, the virus is said to be lytic, or virulent. On the other hand, if the virus does not replicate but rather integrates into the bacterial chromosome, the virus is said to be temperate, or lysogenic. The phage in the lysogenic cycle can spontaneously become lytic. The presence of the integrated virus, which is called a prophage, generally renders the cell resistant to infection by similar phages. Lysogeny does not result in the destruction of the host cell.

Growth of Bacterial Populations

Growth is the orderly increase in quantity of all cellular components and structures. The growth of an individual cell leads to an increase in size and is generally followed by cell division. Thus, growth of a bacterial population is an increase in cell number.

Vegetative cell – One that is actively growing and dividing.

Cell division in bacteria usually occurs by binary fission, in which the cell divides into two new (approximately equal and identical) cells.

Cell division can also occur in some bacteria and in yeast through budding, in which the new cell develops as a small outgrowth from the surface of the existing (parent) cell. Other bacteria may reproduce by fragmentation or by endospore formation. Although it does occur under favorable conditions, endospore formation generally serves to allow the organism to withstand long periods of unfavorable conditions such as extreme temperatures or dryness.

Culturing Microorganisms

A culture is a population of microbes living in a culture medium. A liquid or solid prepared for the purpose of growing microbes is called a nutrient broth, nutrient agar, or culture medium. A culture medium generally provides the organisms with everything required for their growth.

Selective media – These encourage the growth of some organisms while discouraging the growth of others. Salts, dyes, and antibiotics are among the substances used to inhibit growth of unwanted organisms.

Differential media – These distinguish growing microbes on the basis of visible chemical changes in the medium. Reagents in the medium allow for a specific chemical reaction to take place, but only in the presence of particular microorganisms.

A medium can be both differential and selective.

Enrichment media – These contain a nutrient (or nutrients) that enhances the growth of particular microbes, e.g., addition of blood to nutrient medium enhances growth of streptococci. This technique is designed to increase the relative numbers of a particular organism; it *is* possible to obtain pure cultures with this culture method.

Selective media, differential media, and enrichment media are all diagnostic media.

Preparation of Specimens for Light Microscopy

Wet mount – A drop of medium containing the organisms is placed on a microscope slide. This technique is used to view living organisms.

Hanging drop – A drop is placed on a cover slip which is then inverted over a depression slide.

Smear – This is used to view dead organisms (the organisms are killed by the process). Microorganisms from a drop of medium are spread across the surface of a glass slide. This smear is air-dried and then heat-fixed (by passing through flame). Heat fixation accomplishes three things: (1) it kills the organisms, (2) it causes the organisms to adhere to the slide, and (3) it alters the organisms so that they more readily take up stains.

Staining

Stain (dye) – A stain is a molecule that can bind to a cellular structure and give it color, distinguishing it from the background. In addition to discerning parts of the cell, staining helps to categorize microorganisms, and is used to examine structural and chemical differences in their cell walls. Stains are used extensively in bacterial identification and classification.

Stains may be either simple or differential.

Simple stain – A single dye is used. It reveals basic cell shapes and arrangements. Examples include methylene blue, safranin, carbolfuchsin, and gentian violet.

Differential stain – Two or more dyes are used to distinguish between two kinds of organisms or between two different parts of the same organism. Examples include the Gram stain, Schaeffer-Fulton spore stain, and Ziehl-Neelsen acid-fast stain.

> **The Gram stain** (Christian Gram 1884) – This procedure reveals fundamental differences in the nature of the cell wall (probably due to differences in the amount of peptidoglycan in the cell wall—gram-positive bacteria have more peptidoglycan than do similar gram-negative ones). Often used in bacterial taxonomy, the Gram stain is used on air-dried, heat-fixed (therefore, killed) specimens.

Biogeochemical Cycles

Microbes are essential to the recycling of chemical elements such as carbon, nitrogen, phosphorus, sulfur, and oxygen. They also solubilize minerals, such as sulfur, potassium, iron, and others, making them available for plant metabolism.

In the carbon cycle, photoautotrophs fix CO_2, providing nutrients for chemoheterotrophs. Chemoheterotrophs release CO_2, which can then be used by the photoautotrophs.

In the nitrogen cycle, bacteria are involved in the decomposition of proteins from dead cells, ammonification of the amino acids, and reduction of nitrites to nitrates to molecular nitrogen (N_2). Nitrogen-fixing bacteria are responsible for converting molecular nitrogen back into ammonium and nitrate, which can then be used by other bacteria and plants in the synthesis of amino acids.

Applied Microbiology

Microbes and the Recycling of Nutrients

Microbes, especially bacteria and fungi, play an important role in the decomposition of organic matter and the recycling of chemical elements.

Bioconversion – The microbial conversion of organic waste materials into alternative fuels.

Bioremediation – The use of bacteria to clean up toxic wastes.

Microbes in the Food Industry

Alcoholic beverages and vinegar – Fermentation by yeasts is responsible for the production of ethanol; *Acetobacter* and *Gluconobacter* oxidize the alcohol in wine to acetic acid (vinegar).

Dairy – Lactic acid bacteria are used to curdle cheese and to produce hard cheese; lactobacilli, streptococci, and yeasts are used in the production of buttermilk, sour cream, and yogurt.

Nondairy fermentation by various microbes is involved in making sauerkraut, pickles, olives, and soy sauce. The fermentation of yeast produces ethanol and CO_2, which makes bread dough rise.

Industrial Microbiology

Microbes are used to manufacture or help manufacture useful products or to dispose of waste. They can produce acetone, alcohols, glycerol, and organic acids. Some microbes can extract mineral ores.

Microbes and Medicine

Pharmaceutical microbiology – Microbes are used to manufacture products used in medicine.

Bacteria produce most of the amino acids used in medicine and food. Microbes can produce antibiotics, enzymes, vitamins, and hormones.

Microbes and Recombinant DNA Technology

The ability to genetically engineer cells has paved the way for the production of many new products.

Applications in Medicine

Currently, such important substances as insulin and interferon are produced from genetically engineered microorganisms.

DNA probes provide rapid identification of pathogens in food and body tissues.

Applications in Agriculture

Cells from plants with the desired characteristics can be cloned.

E. coli can be used to produce bovine growth hormone.

THE KINGDOM PROTISTA

Most protists are unicellular. Some are composed of colonies. All protists are eukaryotes. That is, they are characterized by nuclei bounded by a nuclear membrane. Examples of protists are flagellates, the protozoans, and slime molds.

The members of this kingdom occupy different phyla based on motility: the ciliates, flagellates, sarcodinians (pseudopods), and sporozoans.

Algae—photosynthetic protists—range from single-celled to complex multicellular forms. Most are aquatic, living in all of the earth's waters, and in a few instances on land. Included are the vast, floating, microscopic marine phytoplankton and the marine seaweeds and kelps.

THE KINGDOM FUNGI

Fungi are multicellular, nonmotile heterotrophs, lacking tissue organization except in their reproductive structures. Some are coenocytic (made up of a multinucleated mass of cytoplasm without subdivision into cells), while others are cellular. Most have chitinous cell walls, while a few have walls of cellulose. One example of fungi is the molds. The filaments of molds, hyphae, form a mycelium.

THE SAT SUBJECT TEST IN

Biology E/M

CHAPTER 5

CHAPTER 5

A SURVEY OF PLANTS

DIVERSITY, CLASSIFICATION, AND PHYLOGENY OF THE PLANT KINGDOM

Plants are organisms that are multicellular and photosynthetic, most with tissue, organ, and system organization (roots, stems, leaves, flowers). They develop from protected embryos, contain chlorophylls -a and -b, produce starches, and have walls of cellulose.

Plants are classified into five categories:

1) **Nonvascular Plants** – They have little or no organized tissue for conducting water and food (xylem and phloem), e.g., mosses.

2) **Seedless Vascular Plants** – They have organized vascular tissue, limited root development, many primitive traits, and chlorophylls -a and -b.

3) **Seed-Producing Vascular Plants** – They have seeds, organized vascular tissues, and extensive root, stem, and leaf development.

4) **Gymnosperms** – They have seeds without surrounding fruit.

5) **Angiosperms** – They have flowers, seeds with surrounding

fruit; e.g., magnolia, cabbage, tobacco, cotton, iris, orchids, and grains.

Adaptations to Land

To adapt to land, plants (except for the nonvascular plants) grew much larger due to the presence of vascular tissue, including the woody, hardened xylem, and tough accompanying supporting tissues. Apparently, large size provided a novel way of adapting to the terrestrial environment. Also, deep root systems allowed the plants to obtain water and allowed them to grow larger.

The Life Cycle (Life History): Alternation of Generations In Plants

The alternation of generations in plants has two phases in the life of a single individual, including a diploid spore-producing phase (sporophyte) and a haploid gamete-producing phase (gametophyte).

Plant	Alternation of Generation
Moss	Separate generations, gametophyte usually dominant, swimming sperm, egg, and zygote protected
Fern	Separate generations, dominant sporophyte, minute gametophyte, swimming sperm
Pine	Nonmotile sperm, wind-pollinated
Angiosperms (Flowering Plants)	Nonmotile sperm, both wind- and insect-pollinated

ANATOMY, MORPHOLOGY, AND PHYSIOLOGY OF VASCULAR PLANTS

A mature vascular plant possesses several distinct cell types which group together in tissues. The major plant tissues include epidermal, parenchyma, sclerenchyma, chlorenchyma, vascular, and meristematic.

Transport of Food in Vascular Plants

For transport, a plant has three major organs:

A) **Leaf** – The leaf consists of an upper epidermis, mesophyll layer, and lower epidermis. Its primary function is to change inorganic substances to organic substances by the process of photosynthesis. A leaf also functions in the exchange of gases between the plant and the atmosphere. Stomata are where the lower epidermis exchanges gases.

The main photosynthetic organs of most plants usually consist of a flattened blade and stalk. The upper epidermis has a waxy cuticle to prevent water loss, while the lower epidermis contains pores called stomata for gas exchange. The mesophyll between these two layers consists mostly of chloroplast-packed parenchyma cells.

The veins in the leaf, known as xylem and phloem tubes, transport fluid materials in the leaf.

1) **Xylem** – This transport tissue carries water and dissolved minerals from the stem and roots to the leaf cells.

2) **Phloem** – This transport tissue carries organic (e.g., sugars) materials from the leaf to the stem and roots.

B) **Stem** – The stem consists of an epidermis, sclerenchyma, parenchyma, and conducting tissue which are the xylem and phloem. One of the primary functions of the stem is to transport raw materials from the roots to the leaves and manufactured products to the roots and other plant organs.

This above ground part of a plant has thickened cell walls for support and protection and openings called lenticels for gas exchange.

C) **Root** – The water that is needed by the plants enters by way of the roots. Water and dissolved minerals diffuse into the root hairs and pass through the cortex cells to the cells of the xylem.

This subterranean part of the plant anchors the plant, stores food, and absorbs and conducts nutrients, minerals, and water. Root hairs occur near the root tips and increase the surface area for absorbing nutrients and water.

Plant Tissues

Covering tissue – Epidermis covers the plant surface.

Conducting tissue – Within the stems, vascular tissue is collected in bundles which conduct nutrients (phloem) and water (xylem). Xylem is composed of non-living, woody, thick-walled cells, while phloem consists of living, thin-walled sieve tube cells.

Growing tissue – Growth occurs at a region called the meristem which consists of embryonic plant tissue that continues to actively divide throughout the plant's life span.

Food-making tissue – Parenchyma cells are relatively unspecialized cells of a plant. Photosynthesis occurs within the chloroplasts of parenchyma cells located in the mesophyll. There are two distinct regions of mesophyll. The upper half is palisade mesophyll made up of columnar-shaped cells with many chloroplasts. The lower half is spongy mesophyll made up of loosely packed cells; the air spaces between function in gas exchange.

Supporting tissue – Plants have woody xylem cells and living cells with thickened cell walls to help keep them upright and rigid. In addition, plant cells may become more rigid as a result of water entering the cell (turgidity).

Storage tissue – Food may be stored in the stems within thin-walled cells called pith. Roots may also be enlarged to provide for storage of food.

Reproductive tissue – A flower is a modified leaf that is specialized for reproduction. The parts of a flower include the stamen (contains sperm nuclei, or pollen), the carpel (contains one or more ovules which house the female gametes), and sterile sepals and petals. Pollination occurs when pollen is deposited on the stigma of the carpel. Fertilization occurs with the joining of the male and the female nuclei. The fertilized ovule becomes the seed. Fruit is a ripened ovary containing the seeds that functions in protection and dispersal of the seeds.

Summary of Plant Tissues

Tissue	Location	Functions
Epidermal	Root	Protection; Increases absorption area
	Stem	Protection; Reduces H_2O loss
	Leaf	Protection; Reduces H_2O loss, Regulates gas exchange
Parenchyma	Root, stem, leaf	Storage of food and H_2O
Sclerenchyma	Stem and leaf	Support
Chlorenchyma	Leaf and young stems	Photosynthesis
Vascular a. Xylem	Root, stem, leaf	Upward transport of fluid
b. Phloem	Leaf, root stem	Downward transport of fluid
Meristematic	Root and stem	Growth; formation of xylem, phloem, and other tissues

REPRODUCTION AND GROWTH IN SEED PLANTS

Mitosis and differentiation in the primary endosperm and zygote will produce the embryo which, along with the food supply and seed coat, makes up the seed.

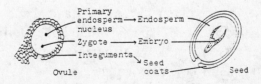

Figure 5.1 Development of an ovule into a seed.

For many seeds, germination (the emergence from dormancy) simply requires the uptake of water, suitable temperatures, and the availability of oxygen, but others require special conditions, such as exposure to freezing temperatures, fire, abrasion, or exposure to animal digestive enzymes.

Reproduction in Higher Plants

A flower is specially designed for plant reproduction. A flower has brightly colored petals that attract pollinators (i.e., birds, insects) arranged in a circle (corolla). Stamens consist of a stalk with an anther on the top containing the pollen. The pistil contains an ovary with one or more ovules. The pistil narrows at the top to form the style, the topmost, sticky region which is known as the stigma and functions in pollen collection.

Pollination occurs when pollen is transferred from the stamen to the stigma. Pollination may occur within the same flower (self-pollination) or among different flowers (cross-pollination). After pollination occurs, the pollen grains germinate and begin to grow down through the stigma, in the process forming a pollen tube. The pollen tube, carrying two sperm nuclei, enters the ovule through a pore called a micropyle. Both sperm nuclei combine with egg cells within the enlarged embryo sac, in a process known as double fertilization.

Following double fertilization, the ovule matures into a seed. The seed may have one seed leaf (monocotyledon) or two (dicotyledon). Endosperm provides nutrients for the developing embryo, which eventually ruptures from the seed coat and develops into a seedling (germination).

In many plants, after fertilization the ovary enlarges to become fruit, which provides protection and a mechanism for seed dispersal, as the fruit and seeds are eaten by animals and disposed of elsewhere. Other mechanisms of seed dispersal include scattering by wind (i.e., dandelion), expulsion (i.e., witch-hazel), attachment to fur (i.e., cocklebur), and floatation (i.e., coconut).

Photosynthesis

Chlorophyll – The green color of the leaf is due to the presence of chlorophyll, a green pigment that absorbs light and uses it to synthesize organic compounds from carbon dioxide and water. Chlorophyll is found in specialized organelles called chloroplasts.

Requirements of photosynthesis – Light (sunlight or artificial light), carbon dioxide, and water must be available for photosynthesis to occur. A by-product of photosynthesis is oxygen which is used by other organisms in respiration. The glucose formed in photosynthesis may be used as energy, stored as starch, or converted to fats and oils, proteins, or vitamins.

Light Reaction (Photolysis)

A first step in photosynthesis is the decomposition of water molecules to separate hydrogen and oxygen components by photolysis. This decomposition is associated with processes involving chlorophyll and light and is thus known as the light reaction. Oxygen gas is formed and the released hydrogen is picked up by NADP.

Dark Reaction (CO_2 Fixation)

In this second phase, the hydrogen is released from NADP. It reacts with CO_2 and carbohydrate forms. CO_2 fixation does not require light.

Plant Functions

Transport – There are three types of transport (translocation) in plants: 1) water and solutes are taken up by individual cells, 2) substances are moved short distances from cell to cell, and 3) sap is transported long distances by way of phloem and xylem.

The roots play an integral role in the absorption of water and nutrients from the soil. The structures and functions of different types of roots are as follows:

Taproot (long and strong, support), fibrous (branched, support, and increased surface area for water/nutrient absorption), fleshy (food storage), brace (large and growing down from the main stem, support), and aerial (above ground).

Soil water (water that contains nutrients) passively diffuses across the cell membranes of the roots. Minerals are actively transported into the cell. Water and minerals reach the rest of the plant via xylem vessels. Over large distances (i.e., from the roots to the highest branches of a tall tree) water moves as a result of the following forces: 1) water potential (the tendency for water to move from one place to another), 2) root pressure (upward push of water caused by the active pumping of minerals into the xylem by root cells), and 3) transpiration (the loss of water from a plant by evaporation).

Gas Exchange in Plants

A) Gas Exchange in Roots and Stems

Plants are able to exist without specialized organs for gas exchange because:

1) There is little transport of gases from one part of the plant to another;

2) Plants do not have great need for gas exchange;

3) The distance gas must diffuse is not large; and

4) Most cells have at least a portion of their outer surface in contact with air.

B) Gas Exchange in the Leaf

The exchange of gases in the leaf for photosynthesis occurs through pores in the surface of the leaf known as the stomata. Usually, the stomata open in the presence of light and close in its absence. The most direct cause of this is the change of turgor in the guard cells.

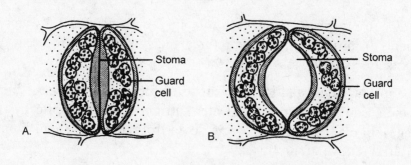

A. Stoma
Guard cell

B. Stoma
Guard cell

Figure 5.2

A. Stomata closed.

B. Stomata open when turgor builds in guard cells.

Plant nutrition – Plants require water and minerals (primarily carbon, oxygen, hydrogen, nitrogen, sulfur, and phosphorus) to form organic compounds. Micronutrients are also required in relatively small quantities. Carbon, oxygen, and hydrogen are available from carbon dioxide and water; the rest must be obtained from the soil or growing medium.

Plants obtain the nitrogen that they require from the soil after nitrogen-fixing bacteria convert it to a usable form. Some plants (i.e., legumes, alders) have nodules on their roots that contain nitrogen-fixing bacteria.

Nutritional adaptations of plants – Some plants have developed ways to obtain supplemental nutrition. Plants may be carnivorous (kill and digest insects and small animals), parasitic (obtaining nourishment by attaching to other organisms), or exist as mycorrhizae (mutualistic associations of roots and fungi).

Excretion in Plants

Plants lack specific organs of excretion and reuse most of the wastes that they produce.

A) Catabolism (breakdown) in plants is usually much lower than in animals; therefore, metabolic wastes accumulate at a slower rate.

B) Green plants use much of the waste products produced by catabolism in anabolic (build-up) processes.

Plant Hormones: Types, Functions, Effects on Plant Growth

Auxins – These plant growth regulators stimulate the elongation of specific plant cells and inhibit the growth of other plant cells.

Gibberellins – In some plants, gibberellins are involved in the stimulation of flower formation. They also increase the stem length of some plant species and the size of fruits. Gibberellins also stimulate the germination of seeds.

Cytokinins – Cytokinins increase the rate of cell division and stimulate the growth of cells in a tissue culture. They also influence the shedding of leaves and fruits, seed germination, and the pattern of branch growth.

Ethylene – This is the only gaseous plant hormone. It diffuses through the intracellular spaces within the plant and is thought to play a role in fruit ripening, aging of plant cells, and it may inhibit root growth and development of auxiliary buds in the presence of auxin.

Phytochrome – A plant pigment that detects specific wavelengths of light and plays a role in the measurement of the length of darkness in a photoperiod.

Florigen – This is a hormone that promotes flowering.

ENVIRONMENTAL INFLUENCES ON PLANTS AND PLANT RESPONSES TO STIMULI

Auxin is involved in tropisms, or growth responses. They involve positive phototropism (bending or growing toward light), negative phototropism (bending or growing away from light), geotropism (influenced by gravity), and thigmotropism (mechanical or touch).

Photoperiodism is any response to changing lengths of night or day. Flowering in plants is often photoperiodic, but so far no specific hormonal mechanism has been found.

Plant photoperiodism – The stages of plant development are regulated, at least in part, by the plant's responsiveness to the relative lengths of light and darkness. Photoperiodism is defined in terms of day length, though it usually depends on critical night length. Flowering occurs following a maximum (short-day plants) and minimum (long-day plants) number of hours of uninterrupted darkness. Day-neutral plants flower without regard to photoperiod.

THE SAT SUBJECT TEST IN
Biology E/M

CHAPTER 6

ANIMAL TAXONOMY AND TISSUES

DIVERSITY, CLASSIFICATION, AND PHYLOGENY

The phylogenetic tree representing animal evolution reveals the separate origins of metazoans and parazoans. An early major split produced the protostomes and deuterostomes, which include the higher invertebrates and the vertebrates, respectively.

SURVEY OF ACOELOMATE, PSEUDOCOELOMATE, PROTOSTOME, AND DEUTEROSTOME PHYLA

The acoelomates are animals that have no coelom (body cavity). They include the phylum Platyhelminthes (flatworms) and the phylum Nematoda. In acoelomate animals, the space between the body wall and the digestive tract is not a cavity, as in higher animals, but is filled with muscle fibers and a loose tissue of mesenchymal origin called parenchyma, both derived from the mesoderm.

The pseudocoelomates consist of the following phyla: Nematoda, Rotifera, Gastrotricha, Nematomorpha, and Acanthocephala. These animals have a body cavity that is not entirely lined with peritoneum.

A major division in animal evolution produced the protostomes and deuterostomes. Each has bilateral symmetry, a one-way gut, and a true coelom (eucoelomate). During primitive gut formation in protostome embryos, the blastopore forms the mouth of the animal, while in deuterostomes this is the anal area.

STRUCTURE AND FUNCTION OF TISSUES, ORGANS, AND SYSTEMS

The cells that make up multicellular organisms become differentiated in many ways. One or more types of differentiated cells are organized into tissues. The basic tissues of a complex animal are the epithelial, connective, nerve, muscle, and blood tissues.

Animal Tissues

Muscle Tissue

A) Kinds of Muscles

    1) **Smooth Muscle** – Smooth muscle is found in the walls of the hollow organs of the body (e.g., stomach, bladder).

    2) **Cardiac Muscle** – Cardiac muscle is the muscle that comprises the walls of the heart.

    3) **Skeletal Muscle** – Skeletal muscles are muscles attached to the skeleton. They are also known as striated muscles.

B) The Structure of Muscles and Bones

Bones move only when there is a pull on the muscles attached to the bone. A single skeletal muscle consists of:

    1) **Tendon** – A tendon is a band of strong, connective tissue that attaches muscle to bone.

    2) **Origin** – The origin is one end of the muscle that is attached to a bone that does not move when the muscle contracts.

    3) **Insertion** – The insertion is the other end of the muscle that is attached to a bone that moves when the muscle contracts.

    4) **Belly** – The belly is the thickened part of the muscle that contracts and pulls.

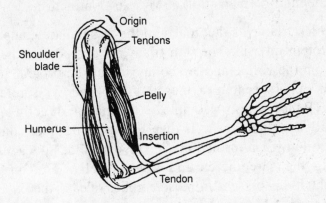

Figure 6.1 The mechanism of movement of the upper arm. When a muscle contracts, it pulls the insertion bone toward the origin bone, producing motion.

C) Skeletal Muscle Activation

The nervous system controls skeletal muscle contraction. End brushes of motor neurons come in contact with muscle fibers at the motor end plate, in a synapse-like junction. This association is called a motor unit. Muscle contraction occurs when acetylcholine is discharged on the muscle fiber surface after the impulse reaches the motor end plate.

D) Structure of a Muscle Fiber

Skeletal muscle is composed of long fibers (cells) whose cytoplasm possesses alternating light and dark bands. These bands are part of myofibrils which lie parallel to one another in the muscle cell. The dark bands are A-bands and the light bands are the I-bands. The H-band bisects the A-bands while the Z-line bisects the I-band. The contractile unit, from Z-line to Z-line, is called a sarcomere. A myofibril is a series of sarcomeres.

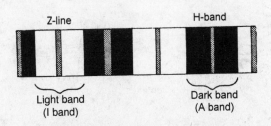

Figure 6.2 Single muscle fibril.

E) Chemical Composition of Muscle Contraction

Thick filaments that make up the A-band are composed of the protein myosin. The thin filaments extend in either direction from the Z-line and are composed of the protein actin. When an impulse enters a muscle fiber, energy is released from ATP molecules. A complex combination of actin and myosin, called actinomyosin, is then formed. The fiber contracts with actinomyosin formation. The myosin slides the actin, shortening the sarcomeres and muscle cells. The mitochondria, which are present in muscle cells, release the energy needed to form ATP.

Nerve Tissue

Neurons

The neuron is the unit of structure that conducts electrochemical impulses over a certain distance. In many neurons, the nerve impulses are generated in the dendrites. These impulses are then conducted along the axon, which is a long fiber. A myelin sheath covers the axon. The nerve impulse travels from dendrites to the axon of a neuron.

A) **Sensory neurons** – Sensory neurons conduct impulses from receptors to the central nervous system.

B) **Interneurons** – Interneurons are always found within the spinal cord and the brain. They form the intermediate link in the nervous system pathway.

C) **Motor neurons** – Motor neurons conduct impulses from the central nervous system to the effectors which are muscles and glands. They will bring about the responses to the stimulus.

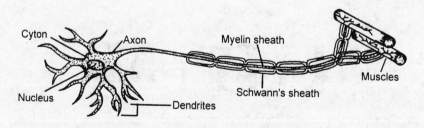

Figure 6.3 The structure of a neuron.

Blood

The Components of Blood

A) **Plasma** – Plasma is the liquid part of the blood which constitutes 55% of the total blood volume. Blood plasma is essential for homeostasis.

B) **Blood Cells** – These constitute 45% of the blood.

   1) **Red blood cells (erythrocytes)** – The erythrocytes are the most numerous of the three blood cell types. Formed in the marrow of bones, the red blood cells first possess a nucleus and not very much hemoglobin. As they mature, hemoglobin constitutes 90% of the dry cell weight. A mature erythrocyte lacks a nucleus. The chief function of erythrocytes is to carry oxygen to all parts of the body and to remove some carbon dioxide.

   2) **White blood cells (leukocytes)** – A white blood cell has a nucleus but lacks hemoglobin. White blood cells are larger than red blood cells and generally function to protect the body against disease. There are five types of white blood cells, divided into two groups. These are the granulocytes (neutrophils, monocytes, and lymphocytes), and agranulocytes (eosinophils and basophils). Some are formed in certain bones, others are formed in the lymph nodes.

   3) **Platelets** – These are cell fragments which are produced by large cells in the bone marrow. Platelets are much smaller than red or white blood cells. They play an important role in blood clotting.

Epithelial Tissue

These are layers of tightly packed cells that line organs and cavities within a body and cover body surfaces. Cells making up the epithelial tissue may be squamous (flat), cuboidal, or columnar. The arrangement of these differently shaped cells can be simple (one layer) or stratified. They may function in protection (e.g., skin), absorption (e.g., lining of the small intestine), secretion (e.g., exocrine glands), or sensation (e.g., retina).

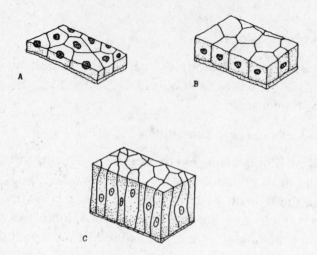

Figure 6.4 Types of Epithelial Cells
(a) simple squamous epithelium, (b) simple cuboidal epithelium,
and (c) simple columnar epithelium.

Connective (Supporting) Tissues

Connective (supporting) tissues function to bind and support other tissue. Cells of connective tissue are sparsely packed in an extracellular, non-living matrix generally consisting of a web of fibers in a liquid, jellylike, or solid ground substance.

Bone – Hard, connective tissue consisting of a porous network of fibers, cells, and calcium salts that makes up the skeletal system of most vertebrates.

White fibrous connective tissue – Dense tissue rich in collagenous fibers organized in a parallel manner to maximize tensile strength; found in tendons (attach muscles to bones) and ligaments (join bones together at joints).

Yellow elastic connective tissue – Made up of long threads of stretchable protein called elastin.

Cartilage – Found at various joints.

Areolar – Loose connective tissue found in all body regions.

Fat (adipose) tissue – Specialized type of loose connective tissue in which fat and oils are stored; functions as an insulator and in storage of fuel molecules.

Summary of Animal Tissues

Tissue	Location	Functions
Epithelial	Covering of body Lining internal organs	Protection Secretion
Muscle		
Skeletal	Attached to skeleton bones	Voluntary movement
Smooth	Walls of internal organs	Involuntary movement
Cardiac	Walls of heart	Pumping blood
Connective		
Binding white, yellow	Covering organs, in tendons and ligaments	Holding tissues and organs together
Bone	Skeleton	Support, protection, movement
Adipose	Beneath skin and around internal organs	Fat storage, insulation, cushion
Cartilage Areolar	Ends of bone, part of nose and ears	Reduction of friction, support
Nerve	Brain	Interpretation of impulses, mental activity
	Spinal cord, nerves, ganglions	Carrying impulses to and from all organs
Blood	Blood vessels, heart	Carrying materials to and from cells, carrying oxygen, fighting germs, clotting

THE SAT SUBJECT TEST IN

Biology E/M

CHAPTER 7

CHAPTER 7

DIGESTION/ NUTRITION

THE HUMAN DIGESTIVE SYSTEM

The digestive system consists of the alimentary canal and several glands. The alimentary canal consists of the oral cavity (mouth), pharynx, esophagus, stomach, small intestines, large intestines, and the rectum.

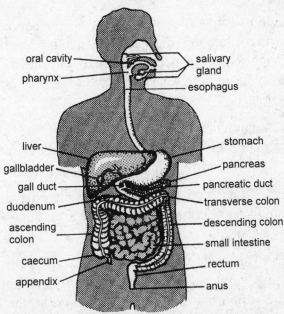

Figure 7.1 Human digestive system. (The organs are slightly displaced, and the small intestine is greatly shortened.)

The digestive system breaks down large food molecules into sub-units for use in the body.

Oral cavity – In the mouth, food is broken down into chewable and swallowable chunks by the teeth and tongue. The presence of food in the mouth causes the salivary gland to release saliva, which contains an enzyme that begins the digestion of starch. Saliva also lubricates and moistens the food and protects against bacteria.

Ingestion and Digestion

Teeth – The teeth of humans (32 adult, 20 child) are located within the oral cavity and arranged in rows on the upper and the lower dental arches. Humans have teeth of various shapes and sizes enabling the shearing (by incisors) and grinding (by premolars and molars) of many kinds of food.

    Structure of teeth – Teeth are made up primarily of dentin, which is similar to bone. On the exposed part of the tooth (crown), the dentin is covered by a thin layer of extremely hard enamel. Inside the tooth is the pulp, which consists of nerves and blood vessels. The root of the tooth extends below the gum (firm connective tissue surrounding the base of the teeth) and into the jawbone.

Salivary digestion – The digestive process begins in the mouth (oral cavity) where mucous and salivary glands release liquid secretions (mucus and saliva, respectively) that wet the food. Saliva also contains the enzyme ptyalin, an amylase that breaks down starch into smaller sugar units.

Pharynx – The food then passes from the oral cavity into the pharynx. Once in the pharynx, swallowing becomes involuntary. The medulla is the part of the brain that contains the swallowing center.

Esophagus – The food passes from the pharynx into the esophagus. The food moves down the esophagus by involuntary muscle action known as peristalsis.

Stomach – The food enters the stomach from the esophagus by passing through a valve known as the cardiac sphincter. The primary functions of the stomach involve liquefying, grinding, and storage of food. The various cells of the stomach produce hydrochloric acid and gastric juice. The hydrochloric acid is used to kill bacteria in food. The gastric juice initiates the digestion of proteins. The semi-liquid mass of partially digested food (chyme) enters the duodenum through the valve known as the pyloric sphincter.

Small Intestine – The small intestine is composed of the duodenum, jejunum, and the ileum. The presence of chyme in the duodenum causes the release of pancreatic fluid from the pancreas. The pancreas is a gland formed by the duodenum and the under surface of the stomach. Pancreatic juice is an alkaline solution of sodium bicarbonate, amylase, lipase, trypsin, chymotrypsin, carboxypeptidase, and nucleases. These various secretions further break down the food into disaccharides and peptides. Bile is also released into the duodenum. Bile is produced in the liver and stored in the gall bladder. It is involved in the emulsification of lipids and increases the surface area for the action of the various enzymes. The final digestion and absorption of the disaccharides, peptides, fatty acids and monoglycerides involves absorption across the finger-like projections known as villi. This occurs by a process known as active transport. By absorption, digested nutrients leave the tract and enter the blood.

Liver – The liver is an accessory digestive organ. It secretes bile, which aids in digestion by neutralizing the chyme from the stomach and emulsifying fats. The liver is also responsible for the chemical destruction of excess amino acids, the storage of glycogen, and the breakdown of old red blood cells.

Gall bladder – The gall bladder is an accessory organ to the liver. The gall bladder stores the bile produced by the liver. Bile contains bile salts that aid in the digestion and absorption of fats.

Large Intestine – The large intestine plays almost no role in the digestion of food but does reabsorb water and electrolytes. In addition, it stores feces until defecation of indigestible food components, such as fiber. Feces pass through the rectum and out the anus.

Summary of the Action of Enzymes

Gland	Place of Action	Enzymes	Substrates	End Products
Salivary	Mouth	Ptyalin (amylase)	Starch	
Gastric	Stomach	Pepsin	Proteins (minerals)	(Dissolved minerals)
		Rennin	Milk	Coagulated milk
		Lipase	Emulsified lipids	Fatty acids and glycerol
Liver	Small intestine	None		
Pancreas	Small intestine	Trypsin (protease)	Proteins	
		Amylopsin (amylase)	Starch	
		Steapsin (lipase)	Emulsified lipids	Fatty acids and glycerol
		Nucleases	Nucleic acids	Nucleotides
Intestinal	Small intestine	Peptidases	Polypeptides and dipeptides	Amino acids
		Maltase	Maltose	Glucose
		Sucrase	Sucrose	Glucose and fructose
		Lactase	Lactose	Glucose and galactose

Digestive System Disorders

Dental cavities and gum disease – Dental cavities (caries) are caused by the acidic by-products of bacterial metabolism within the oral cavity (plaque). If the acid makes its way through the enamel and dentin, it can be very painful and may abscess. Brushing and flossing the teeth help to remove food particles that promote bacterial growth, and fluoride hardens the enamel. Both may help to prevent cavities and gingivitis (gum disease).

Ulcer – Lesion of the digestive tract lining.

Constipation – Difficulty or inability to empty the bowels.

Diarrhea – Frequent or excessively loose bowel movements.

Appendicitis – Inflammation of the appendix, usually requiring surgical removal.

Gallstones – Small, hard deposits that form in the gall bladder or bile ducts.

HUMAN NUTRITION

Oxidation – The cells of humans and other living organisms derive energy through the oxidation of food, primarily carbohydrates and fats. Food is not used directly for energy, however, but is used to produce adenosine triphosphate (ATP). When energy is needed, the ATP molecule is cleaved and energy is released. Metabolism is the sum of all physical and chemical processes required to maintain life. The minimum amount of energy that is required by an organism to carry out life functions is known as basal metabolism and is measured by the amount of oxygen consumed and carbon dioxide released while at rest.

A *calorie* is the heat energy required to raise the temperature of 1 gram of water 1 degree Celsius. When food is completely oxidized to carbon dioxide and water, the heat energy that is released in the process represents the calorie content of that food item. A calorimeter is a device that measures the calorie content of a food item by burning it in pure oxygen and measuring the temperature increase in the surrounding water. The number of calories required by different people varies depending upon their basal metabolic rate and activity level.

The basis of good health is directly related to good nutrition. A healthy diet is composed of water, carbohydrates, fats, proteins, vitamins, and minerals.

Carbohydrates

Present in vegetables, beans, peas, fruit, bread, and milk products, carbohydrates are involved in energy production. The body receives its main source of glucose from carbohydrates. They may be simple or complex. Sucrose, lactose, and fructose are disaccharides and are known as simple carbohydrates. Fruits are the primary source of simple carbohydrates. Complex carbohydrates are found in beans, peas, vegetables, and breads. Carbohydrates provide the body with blood glucose. This is a major energy source. The glucose may be stored as glycogen in the liver to be used in the future.

Fats

Fats are present in foods like ham, cream, butter, and cheese. Fats provide twice as much energy per gram as carbohydrates and proteins. High levels of fat contribute to colon cancer, high blood pressure, obesity, and coronary heart disease.

Proteins

The building blocks of proteins are amino acids. Proteins provide the body with energy but may also function as enzymes, structural framework, antibodies, and hormones. Proteins are present in cheese, milk, egg, and fish. Protein malnutrition results in a condition known as *kwashiorkor,* which is characterized by retardation in mental and physical development.

Vitamins

Vitamins are micronutrients needed by the body in small concentrations. They are involved in the regulation of biochemical reactions. Vitamins can be divided into two categories: water soluble and fat soluble. The water soluble vitamins include vitamins B and C. Since these are excreted and cannot be stored, they need to be replenished daily. The fat soluble vitamins include A, D, E, and K. These vitamins can be stored in the body. Vitamims may be obtained naturally or from synthetic sources. Natural vitamins are obtained from the diet through the food we eat.

Vitamin A – Vitamin A protects against cancer formation, prevents eye problems like night blindness, protects against skin ailments, colds and influenza, infections of various organs, and is involved in the formation of bones and teeth.

Vitamin B complex – The role of the B vitamins includes maintenance of skin, hair, nails, nerves, and muscles, as well as proper functioning of the brain. The B vitamns are vitamin B1, vitamin B2, vitamin B3, vitamin B5, vitamin B6, and vitamin B12.

Folic Acid (folacin) – It is involved in the formation of red blood cells, protein metabolism, and in the production of energy. It is very important in pregnancy since it plays a role in fetal nerve cell formation.

Vitamin C (ascorbic acid) – Vitamin C has antioxidant properties by scavenging free radicals in the body which cause cell injury. It is also involved in the maintenance of healthy gums, growth and repair, as well as the healing of wounds and burns.

Vitamin D – Involved in the absorption of calcium and phosphorus from the intestinal tract. It is imperative for the proper growth and development of bones and teeth.

Vitamin E (tocopherol) – Has antioxidant properties and is also involved in the maintenance of nerves and muscles.

Vitamin K (phylloquinone) – It is a vital component of the blood clotting process. Deficiency of this vitamin may cause bleeding.

Minerals

Minerals (ions) are important for the proper functioning of living cells. They are involved in energy production, growth, and formation. Minerals can be divided into two groups: macrominerals and microminerals. The macrominerals like sodium, potassium, calcium, magnesium, and phosphorus are needed in larger quantities than the microminerals. Minerals are found naturally as mineral salts within rocks.

Calcium – It plays a part in preventing cardiovascular disease, lowering cholesterol levels, building bones and teeth, and nerve transmission.

Phosphorus – It is involved in the building of bones and teeth, energy production, and kidney function.

Sodium – Sodium is involved in nerve transmission, muscle function, and the maintenance of water balance and blood pH.

Potassium – This mineral is involved in conducting electrical impulses and regulating the heartbeat. It is also involved in the maintenance of water balance in the body.

Micronutrients – Micronutrients also known as trace elements are needed in only minute amounts in the body. Cobalt, chromium, and manganese are also needed by the body.

Iodine – Iodine is an element that is vital for physical and mental development. It is involved in the maintenance of a healthy thyroid gland.

Iron – Iron is involved in the production of hemoglobin and myoglobin, which are proteins found in red blood cells and muscle. It is also involved in energy production and required by enzymes.

Copper – Copper is involved in energy production and the formation of red blood cells, hemoglobin, and bone.

Fluorine – Fluorine is an element involved in the development of teeth and bones. However, large amounts may build up in the body and cause damage to the immune system.

Manganese – Manganese is involved in energy production, reproduction, bone formation, and regulation of the central nervous system.

Zinc – It is involved in the development of reproductive organs, regulation of the immune system, and protein and collagen formation.

Chromium – It is involved in glucose metabolism and energy production.

Water

The body is composed of over 70 percent water. Water is involved in various bodily functions including excretion, digestion, and absorption. Water is the medium by which nutrients are transported throughout the body and wastes are eliminated. To maintain the composition of water required by the body, it is recommended that you drink eight 8-ounce glasses of water daily.

Conserving the nutrients in food – There are numerous ways to gain the maximum nutrient value from food: 1) avoid overcooking vegetables, 2) eat fresh, unprocessed foods whenever possible, 3) when fresh foods are unavailable, those that are quick-frozen may retain more vitamins than those that are canned, and 4) use foods that are enriched (i.e., breads, milk, pastas).

The Food Guide Pyramid – The Food Guide Pyramid was introduced in 1992 by the U.S. Department of Agriculture to assist people in making daily food choices that will optimize nutrition. The Food Guide Pyramid has replaced the original "Four Food Groups." The recommendations of the food pyramid are that most of the calories come from complex carbohydrates, vegetables, and fruits; meats and milk products are used moderately; and oils and fats are used sparingly. See figure 7.2.

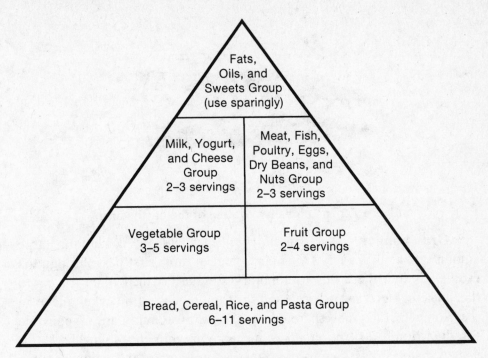

Figure 7.2 The Food Guide Pyramid.

Ingestion and Digestion in Other Organisms

Many protozoa of the Protista kingdom ingest food using a specialized feeding structure called an oral groove which leads to a mouth-like structure called the cytostome. Food is packaged and broken down within a vacuole that serves as a digestive compartment. Nutrients pass through the vacuole membrane into the cytoplasm, and waste is eliminated via exocytosis through the anal pore, a specialized region of the plasma membrane.

Hydra – The hydra possesses tentacles which have stinging cells (nematocysts) that shoot out a poison to paralyze the prey. If successful in capturing an animal, the tentacles push it into the hydra's mouth. From there, the food enters the gastric cavity. The hydra uses both intracellular and extracellular digestion.

Earthworm – As the earthworm moves through soil, the suction action of the pharynx draws material into the mouth cavity. Then from the mouth, food goes into the pharynx, the esophagus, and then the crop which is a temporary storage area. This food then passes into a muscular gizzard where it is ground and churned. The food mass finally passes into the intestine; any undigested material is eliminated through the anus.

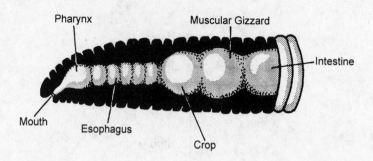

Figure 7.3 The digestive system of the earthworm.

Grasshopper – The grasshopper is capable of consuming large amounts of plant leaves. This plant material must first pass through the esophagus into the crop, a temporary storage organ. It then travels to the muscular gizzard where food is ground. Digestion takes place in the stomach. Enzymes secreted by six gastric glands are responsible for digestion. Absorption takes place mainly in the stomach. Undigested material passes into the intestine, collects in the rectum, and is eliminated through the anus.

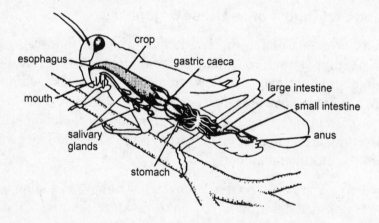

Figure 7.4 The digestive system of the grasshopper.

THE SAT SUBJECT TEST IN
Biology E/M

CHAPTER 8

CHAPTER 8

RESPIRATION AND CIRCULATION

RESPIRATION IN HUMANS

In humans, the respiratory system begins as a passageway in the nose. Inhaled air then passes through the pharynx, the larynx, the trachea, the bronchi, and the lungs.

Nose – The nose is better adapted than the mouth to inhale air. The nostrils, the two openings in the nose, lead into the nasal passages which are lined by the mucous membrane. Just beneath the mucous membrane are capillaries which warm the air before it reaches the lungs.

Pharynx – Air passes via the nasal cavities to the pharynx where the paths of the digestive and respiratory systems cross.

Larynx – The larynx is the voice box, located between the pharynx and trachea. The glottis is the opening in the larynx; the epiglottis, which is located above the glottis, prevents food from entering the glottis and obstructing the passage of air.

Trachea – The trachea, or windpipe, conducts inhaled air from the larynx to the bronchi.

Bronchi – The trachea divides into two branches called the bronchi. Each bronchus leads into a lung.

Lungs – In the lungs, the bronchi branch into smaller tubules known as the bronchioles. The finer divisions of the bronchioles eventually enter the alveoli. The cells of the alveoli are the true respiratory surface of the lung. It is here that gas exchange takes place.

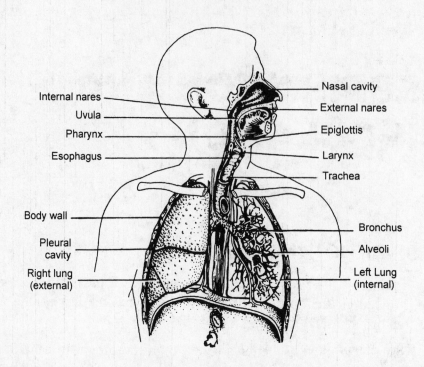

Figure 8.1 Diagram of the human respiratory system.

Mucous cells secrete mucus and trap ingested particles. These particles are finally moved out of the respiratory tract by ciliary action.

Breathing

Mechanics – The lungs are contained within the thoracic cage and come into contact with the chest wall through a thin layer of pleural fluid, which enables smooth movement during breathing. With each breathing cycle, air is pumped into (inspiration) and out of (expiration) the lungs. During inspiration, the thoracic cavity enlarges due to contraction of the diaphragm, a dome-shaped muscle at the base of the thorax. This action reduces the internal pressure within the lungs and draws air into them. Expiration during quiet breathing is usually passive, such that when the diaphragm relaxes and returns to its resting curved shape, it pushes upward on the thoracic cage. Thus, the lungs and chest wall return to their former position, and air is driven out of the lungs.

Control – Voluntary control of breathing originates in the cerebral cortex, while automatic control originates in the medulla. At rest, the breathing center of the medulla sends impulses approximately 10 to 14 times per minute, signaling the diaphragm to contract.

Inhaled and Exhaled Air – Air is composed primarily of oxygen and nitrogen. In breathing, oxygen and carbon dioxide are exchanged with the air. The air that is inhaled contains about 79 percent nitrogen, 20.9 percent oxygen, and 0.04 percent carbon dioxide, while exhaled air contains 79 percent nitrogen, 16.3 percent oxygen, and 4.5 percent carbon dioxide.

Lung Disorders

Lung cancer – A disease of the lung cells in which they exhibit unregulated growth. Lung cancer is primarily a disease of smokers.

Asthma – An often allergy-induced respiratory disease characterized by constriction of the bronchial tubes, difficulty breathing, and coughing.

Emphysema – Primarily a disease of smokers in which the alveoli of the lungs break down causing the lungs to lose their elasticity and resulting in labored breathing and susceptibility to infection.

Infectious diseases – Airborne pathogenic microorganisms, spread by coughing, sneezing, speaking, and close proximity, may be breathed into an organism and disease may ensue. Some bacteria and viruses thrive in the moist environment of the lungs, and may cause such diseases as influenza, tuberculosis, and pneumonia.

Respiration in Other Organisms

Protozoa

Amoeba – Simple diffusion of gases between the cell and water is sufficient to take care of the respiratory needs of the amoeba. Oxygen diffuses into the cell and carbon dioxide diffuses out of the cell.

Paramecium – The paramecium takes in dissolved oxygen and releases dissolved carbon dioxide directly through the plasma membrane.

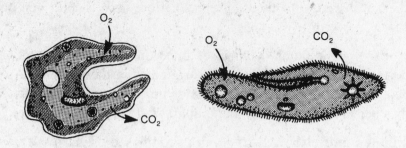

Figure 8.2
A. Respiration in the amoeba.   **B. Respiration in the paramecium.**

Hydra

Dissolved oxygen and carbon dioxide diffuse in and out of two cell layers through the plasma membrane.

Grasshopper

The grasshopper carries on respiration by means of spiracles and tracheae. Blood plays no role in transporting oxygen and carbon dioxide. Muscles of the abdomen pump air into and out of the spiracles and the tracheae.

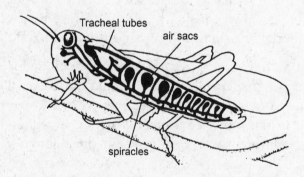

Figure 8.3 Respiration in the grasshopper.

Earthworm

The skin of the earthworm is its respiratory surface. Oxygen from the air diffuses into the capillaries of the skin and joins with hemoglobin dissolved in the blood plasma. Carbon dioxide from the tissue cells diffuses into the blood. When the blood reaches the capillaries in the skin again, the carbon dioxide diffuses through the skin into the air.

Fish

The gills are specialized organs of respiration in fish. Fish continuously pump water through the mouth and over the gills. As water passes over the gills, oxygen in the water is picked up by the capillaries within the gills and is distributed throughout the body. At the same time, carbon dioxide in the blood diffuses out of the gill capillaries and into the water.

Comparison of Various Respiratory Surfaces Among Organisms

Organism	Respiratory Surface Present
Protozoan	Plasma membrane
Hydra	Plasma membrane of each cell
Grasshopper	Tracheae network
Earthworm	Moist skin
Human	Alveoli in lungs

CIRCULATION IN HUMANS

The circulatory system consists of the heart, blood vessels, blood, and the lymphatic system. Humans have a closed circulatory system in which the blood moves entirely within the blood vessels.

The heart is a four-chambered pumping organ, covered by a protective membrane known as the pericardium. The upper chambers are the atria. The lower ones are the ventricles.

Atria – These chambers receive blood from the superior and inferior vena cava and then pump the blood to the ventricles.

Ventricles – These chambers have thicker walls compared to the thin walls of the atria. They are involved in pumping blood out of the heart to the lungs and to other distant parts of the body.

Various valves are located in the heart which prevent the backflow of blood.

Contraction of the heart is known as systole. Relaxation is known as diastole. The sinoatrial node in the wall of the right atrium is known as the pacemaker, since this is where the heartbeats originate. The sympathetic nervous system causes an increase in heart rate and contraction, and the parasympathetic system causes a decrease. The vagus nerve is a parasympathetic nerve that decreases the heart rate.

The blood vessels consist of the arteries, capillaries, and veins. The arteries carry blood away from the heart and are made of smooth muscle and elastic tissue. The capillaries are involved in the transfer of blood from the blood vessels to the tissues and consist of only endothelial cells. The veins carry blood back to the heart and have less muscle and elastic tissue than arteries.

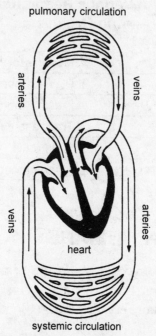

Figure 8.4 Schematic representation showing pulmonary and systemic circulation.

Blood

The composition of blood is about 55% plasma and 45% cells. The cells include red blood cells (erythrocytes), white blood cells (leukocytes), and platelets.

Red Blood Cells

The primary function of the red blood cells involves the transportation of respiratory gases. They contain the pigment hemoglobin which consists of iron. Hemoglobin removes oxygen from areas where there is a high oxygen concentration, and releases it to areas of low oxygen concentration.

There are five million red blood cells per cubic mm. of blood. They are produced in the bone marrow and eliminated in the spleen and liver. Anemia is a condition characterized by too low a number of red blood cells.

Adult hemoglobin picks up oxygen at the lungs and disassociates from oxygen at the tissue cells, supplying them with oxygen. Fetal hemoglobin has a greater affinity for oxygen. Therefore, the fetus is able to acquire oxygen through the placenta from the mother's blood.

White Blood Cells

These cells are also known as leukocytes and have a primary function which is the defense of the body. This occurs by two methods:

1. **Phagocytosis** – This is a process used by neutrophils to remove the foreign matter from the body, since neutrophils are the first white blood cells to arrive at the injured site.

2. **Antibody Production** – The presence of foreign material, known as antigens, in the body causes antibody production by lymphocytes.

Platelets

Platelets are cell fragments involved in the clotting process. Platelets swarm to a cut area of the body, rupturing and releasing platelet factors. They react to form a clot. The steps of blood clotting are:

fibrinogen → fibrin

The "threads" of fibrin form a "web" which entangle the red blood cells, and thus a clot is formed.

$$\text{platelets}$$
$$\downarrow Ca^{2+}$$
$$\text{prothrombin} \xrightarrow{\text{vitamin K}} \text{thrombin}$$
$$\downarrow$$
$$\text{fibrinogen} \to \text{fibrin}$$
$$\downarrow$$
$$\text{scab}$$

Plasma

This is the straw-colored fluid that is devoid of red blood cells. It contains hormones, waste products, and the end products of digestion.

Blood Groups

The red blood cells contain cell surface antigens of which there are two types, A or B; or both or neither. The plasma contains antibodies to A and/or B. If transfused blood is incompatible between the donor and/or the recipient, the blood will clump. There are four ABO blood groups, based on the presence or absence of two antigens on the surface of red blood cells. The four blood groups are: A, B, O, and AB. Note that the antigen names the blood group. An antibody, found in the blood plasma, is always the opposite by name. Type O is the universal donor, as it has no antigen to cause agglutination of a recipient's blood. Type AB is the universal receptor, as it lacks antibodies to react against donated blood.

Blood group	Antigen in red blood cell	Antibody present in plasma
A	A	B
B	B	A
AB	A, B	Neither
O	Neither	A, B

Rhesus Factor

Rhesus factor, or Rh, is an antigen that may be present in the blood. A person whose blood contains Rh is said to be Rh positive, since their red blood cells contain the Rh antigen. During pregnancy some fetal blood is passed into the mother's bloodstream. This may cause future complications if an Rh^- mother is carrying an Rh^+ fetus, since the mother produces Rh^+ antibodies which affect future pregnancies, but not this pregnancy. These antibodies cross over into the bloodstream of the fetus and cause the fetal red blood cells to be destroyed. This condition is known as *erythroblastosis fetalis*. To prevent this from happening, the mother is injected with Rh antibodies that prevent the build-up of antibodies to the Rh factor. This occurs immediately after the delivery of her baby.

Lymph

Tissues are bathed by a fluid which has a low protein content, water, and dissolved nutrients. This fluid leaves the capillaries and flows in the intercellular spaces. This fluid reenters the general circulation via the right lymphatic duct and the thoracic duct. The fluid is known as lymph and moves along the lymphatic vessels which contain valves.

The thoracic duct carries lymph upward across the chest and empties into a large vein near the base of the neck. Lymph travels in only one direction, from the body organs to the heart.

1) **Lymph nodes** – Lymph nodes are the thousands of pea-shaped structures lining the lymph vessels. They filter out bacteria from the lymph. The white blood cells produced by the lymph nodes destroy bacteria.

2) **Spleen** – The spleen is a sac-like mass of lymphatic tissue located near the stomach. The blood that passes into it is filtered. The spleen stores red blood cells so that when bleeding occurs, it contracts and forces the stored red blood cells into circulation.

CIRCULATION OF BLOOD

The blood circulates in three different systems: 1) the pulmonary system, which involves the heart and lungs; 2) the systemic circulation system, which involves the rest of the body; and 3) the portal circulation system, which is also part of the systemic circulation, draining digestive organs into the liver.

The superior and inferior vena cava return blood to the right atrium of the heart. The superior vena cava drains blood from the heart and upper body, and the inferior vena cava from the lower body. From the right ventricle the blood enters the lungs via the pulmonary artery. Here, carbon dioxide and water are eliminated and oxygen is absorbed. The pulmonary vein returns this oxygenated blood to the left atrium of the heart. The aorta carries oxygenated blood from the left ventricle to various parts of the body.

Arteries carry oxygenated blood to various parts of the body, and the veins return deoxygenated blood to the heart. The exception to this rule is the pulmonary artery, which contains deoxygenated blood, and the pulmonary vein, which contains oxygenated blood.

Portal Circulation

The portal vein carries blood, which consists of digested food absorbed from capillaries of the small intestine, to the liver. In the liver, any excess glucose is converted to glycogen and stored. The hepatic vein conveys this blood from the liver to the inferior vena cava.

TRANSPORT MECHANISMS IN OTHER ORGANISMS

Protozoans – Most protozoans are continually bathed by food and oxygen because they live in water or another type of fluid. With the process of cyclosis or diffusion, digested materials and oxygen are distributed within the cell, and water and carbon dioxide are removed. Proteins are transported by the endoplasmic reticulum.

Hydra – Like the protozoans, materials in the hydra are distributed to the necessary organelles by diffusion, cyclosis, and by the endoplasmic reticulum.

Earthworm – The circulatory system of the earthworm is known as a "closed" system because the blood is confined to the blood vessels at all times. A pump that forces blood to the capillaries consists of five pairs of aortic loops. Contraction of these loops forces blood into the ventral blood vessel. This ventral blood vessel transports blood toward the rear of the worm. The dorsal blood vessel forces blood back to the aortic loops at the anterior end of the worm.

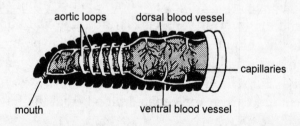

Figure 8.5 "Closed" circulatory system of the earthworm.

Grasshopper – The grasshopper possesses an "open" circulatory system in which the blood is confined to vessels during only a small portion of its circuit through the body. The blood is pumped by the contractions of a tubular heart and a short aorta with an open end. Blood from the heart flows into the aorta and then into sinuses. The blood then returns to the heart.

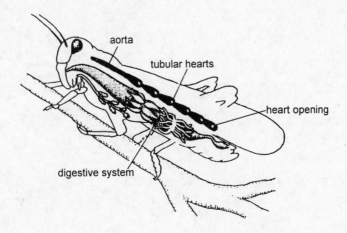

Figure 8.6 "Open" circulatory system of the grasshopper.

Fish – Fish have two-chambered hearts, with one atrium and one ventricle. Blood pumped from the ventricle travels to the gills, where oxygen from the water is taken up and carbon dioxide is removed. The oxygenated blood is carried to other parts of the body, and deoxygenated blood is returned to the atrium by veins. Thus, blood passes through two capillary beds, one in the gills and one in the other body organ.

Amphibians – Frogs and other amphibians have three-chambered hearts, with two atria and one ventricle. Blood that is pumped out of the ventricle enters either the pulmonary (to the lungs and skin) or the systemic (to all other organs except the lungs) circuit. The pulmonary circuit picks up oxygen in the lungs and the oxygenated blood returns to the heart and is pumped to the rest of the body systems. This is known as double circulation.

THE SAT SUBJECT TEST IN

Biology E/M

CHAPTER 9

CHAPTER 9

THE ENDOCRINE SYSTEM

THE HUMAN ENDOCRINE SYSTEM

The major glands of the human endocrine system include the thyroid gland, parathyroid gland, pituitary gland, pancreas, adrenal glands, pineal gland, thymus gland, sex glands, stomach, and small intestine. These glands secrete substances called hormones into the bloodstream that have an effect upon a target organ. Hormones play a major role in coordinating the body's activities through regulating the activity of organs and cells.

Hormone – a circulating chemical signal that is released from one organ and travels through body fluids to a target organ where it exerts its effects.

Cyclic AMP (cAMP) – Cyclic AMP, or adenine 3′,5′-monophosphate, generally acts as an intracellular second messenger to propagate and amplify the signal from a first messenger, such as a hormone. Many hormones interact with a cell surface receptor, which causes an increase in the activity of adenylate cyclase, thus converting ATP to cAMP. The increased amounts of cAMP within the cytoplasm alter cellular function. Calcium may also act as a second messenger.

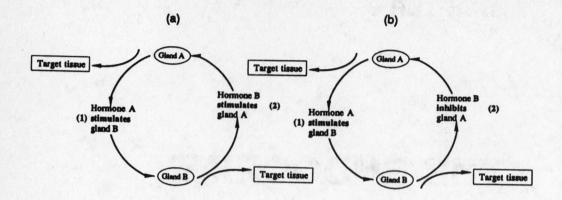

Figure 9.1 (a) Positive and (b) negative feedback regulation.

Thyroid Gland

This two-lobed structure is located in the neck in front of the respiratory tract. It secretes the hormones thyroxin and calcitonin. Thyroxine increases the rate of metabolism. Calcitonin lowers the calcium levels in the blood by causing the calcium to move into the bones.

Parathyroid Gland

This gland is located at the back of the thyroid gland. It produces parathyroid hormones which control calcium and phosphate levels. It causes calcium and phosphorous to be released from the bones and increases their concentration in the blood.

Pituitary Gland

This gland is located at the base of the brain. It is divided into three lobes: the anterior lobe; the intermediate lobe, which is only a vestige in adulthood; and the posterior lobe.

Hormones of the Anterior Lobe

Growth Hormone (GH) – Causes growth of tissues. Excess secretion of growth hormones results in a condition known as gigantism in children and acromegaly in adults. A deficiency of this hormone causes pituitary dwarfism.

Thyroid Stimulating Hormone (TSH) – Stimulates the thyroid gland to produce thyroxin.

Prolactin – Stimulates milk secretion in women after childbirth and regulates development of the mammary glands of a pregnant woman.

Adenocorticotrophic Hormone (ACTH) – Stimulates the secretion of glucocorticoids by the adrenal cortex. The glucocorticoids are involved in blood cell production and metabolism.

Follicle Stimulating Hormone – This hormone acts upon the gonads, or sex hormones.

Luteinizing Hormone (LH) – In males, LH causes the cells in the testes to secrete androgens. In females, LH causes the follicle in an ovary to change into the corpus luteum.

Hormones of the Intermediate Lobe

This lobe secretes a hormone that has no known effect in humans.

Hormones of the Posterior Lobe

Vasopressin (ADH) – This hormone causes the muscular walls of the arterioles to contract, thus increasing blood pressure. It regulates the amount of water reabsorbed by the nephrons in the kidney. Specifically, it stimulates water reabsorption.

Oxytocin – This hormone causes the muscles of the walls of the uterus to contract. It induces labor and causes milk ejection in lactation.

Pancreas

This is considered both an endocrine and an exocrine gland. Its endocrine function is exemplified by the release of insulin and glucagon by the Islets of Langerhans cells.

Insulin – It lowers the glucose levels in the bloodstream by converting glucose to glycogen. Diabetes mellitus is brought about by insulin deficiency.

Glucagon – It increases the glucose levels in the bloodstream by causing glycogen breakdown and the synthesis of glucose from amino acids in the liver.

Adrenal Glands

The two adrenal glands are located on top of each kidney. They are composed of the adrenal cortex and the adrenal medulla.

Hormones of the Adrenal Cortex

Cortisone – These hormones are steroids. ACTH stimulates the cortex to release cortisol, a glucocorticoid. This increases the glucose levels in the bloodstream and also helps to fight infections.

Aldosterone – This causes sodium reabsorption which reduces urinary output, promotes water retention, and increases extracellular fluid volume. Aldosterone exerts its effect on the tubules of the kidney. It also causes potassium to be secreted.

Sex hormones – They are called androgens, and are similar in chemical composition to hormones secreted by the sex glands.

Hormones of the Adrenal Medulla

Epinephrine – This hormone is a sympathetic stimulant that causes the release of glucose from the liver. It also relaxes the smooth muscles of the bronchioles, dilates the pupils of the eye, reduces the clotting time of blood, and increases heart rate, blood pressure, and respiration rate.

Norepinephrine – This hormone signals the same responses as epinephrine.

Pineal Gland

The pineal gland is attached to the brain above the cerebellum. It is responsible for the production of melatonin.

Thymus Gland

The thymus gland is located under the breastbone. It contributes to T-cell development as the immune system develops.

Sex Glands

The sex glands include the testes of the male and the ovaries of the female.

Testes – A luteinizing hormone stimulates specific cells of the testes to secrete androgens. Testosterone, which controls the development of male secondary sex characteristics, is the principal androgen.

Ovaries – Estrogen is secreted from the cells that line the ovarian follicle. This hormone is responsible for the development of female secondary sex characteristics.

Hormones of the Alimentary Canal

Secretin – Released by cells of the small intestine due to the presence of acid in the duodenum; it stimulates the secretion of bicarbonate ions from the pancreas. The bicarbonate ion buffers the acidity of the chyme entering the small intestine from the stomach.

Cholecystokinin – Originates in the duodenum of the small intestine; it causes the gallbladder to contract and release bile into the duodenum and stimulates the production and release of pancreatic enzymes.

Gastrin – Released by the stomach wall upon stimulation caused by certain substances in food; stimulates the stomach to secrete gastric juice and stimulates the stomach's muscular wall to increase mobility.

Gastric Inhibitory Peptide (GIP) – Originates from the duodenum of the small intestine; it inhibits the stomach glands and muscles, decreasing their secretion and motility, and thus protecting the duodenum against excessive acid and regulating the rate of gastric emptying. This hormone is also known as enterogastrone.

Atrial Natiuretic Factor – A peptide hormone that helps to regulate salt and water balance and thus also regulating renal and cardiovascular homeostasis. It opposes the action of aldosterone.

Human Endocrine Glands and Their Functions

Gland	Hormone	Function
Pituitary		
Anterior lobe	Growth hormone	Stimulates growth of skeleton
	FSH	Stimulates follicle formation in ovaries and sperm formation in testes
	LH	Stimulates formation of corpus luteum in ovaries and secretion of testosterone in testes
	TSH	Stimulates secretion of thyroxine from thyroid gland
	ACTH	Stimulates secretion of cortisone and cortin from adrenal cortex
	Prolactin	Stimulates secretion of milk in mammary glands
Posterior lobe	Vasopressin (ADH)	Controls narrowing of arteries and rate of water absorption in kidney tubules
	Oxytocin	Stimulates contraction of smooth muscle of uterus
Thyroid	Thyroxin	Controls rate of metabolism and physical and mental development
	Calcitonin	Controls calcium metabolism
Parathyroids	Parathormone	Regulates calcium and phosphate level of blood
Islets of Langerhans		
Beta cells	Insulin	Promotes storage and oxidation of glucose
Alpha cells	Glucagon	Releases glucose into bloodstream
Thymus	Thymus hormone	Contributes to T-cell development as immune system develops
Adrenal Cortex	Cortisones	Promote glucose formation from amino acids and fatty acids
	Cortins	Control water and salt balance
	Sex hormones	Influence sexual development
Medulla	Epinephrine (adrenalin) or norepinephrine (noradrenalin)	Releases glucose into bloodstream, increases rate of heartbeat, increases rate of respiration, relaxes bronchial smooth muscle in air passages
Gonads, Ovaries, follicle cells	Estrogen	Controls female secondary sex characteristics
Corpus luteum cells	Progesterone	Helps maintain attachment of embryo to mother
Testes	Testosterone	Controls male secondary sex characteristics

Disorders of the Endocrine System

Hyperthyroidism and Hypothyroidism – Some diseases are results of hormone imbalances. Excessive secretion of thyroxin may occur if the body produces antibodies against the TSH receptors, thus stimulating the thyroid cells. Grave's disease may serve as one example of hyperthyroidism. Hyperthyroidism is characterized by a high basal metabolic rate (BMR), weight loss, irritability, nervousness, and increased cardiovascular and respiratory activities. A deficiency of thyroxin in children results in cretinism, which is characterized by retarded mental and physical growth. Severe hypothyroidism in adults results in myxedema. Regular hypothyroidism is characterized by low BMR, thick skin, puffy face, husky voice, and coarse hair.

Thyroxin is also thought to play a role in the metamorphosis of a tadpole into an adult frog.

THE ENDOCRINE SYSTEM IN OTHER ORGANISMS

Insect Hormones

Ecdysone – A steroid hormone secreted by a pair of thoracic glands just behind the head; triggers the molt and the development of adult characteristics.

Brain hormone – A peptide from the brain that promotes development by stimulating the prothoracic glands to create ecdysone.

Juvenile hormone – Secreted by a pair of small glands just behind the brain; balances ecdysone and brain hormone by preventing the action of ecdysone and actively promoting the retention of larval characteristics.

THE SAT SUBJECT TEST IN

Biology E/M

CHAPTER 10

CHAPTER 10

THE NERVOUS SYSTEM

THE NERVOUS SYSTEM

The nervous system is a system of conduction that transmits information to appropriate structures for action.

Neurons

Neurons conduct electrical impulses over large distances. Neurons consist of a cell body, short projections called dendrites, and a larger projection called an axon. Impulses may travel in either direction; however, impulses are usually conveyed from dendrites to cell body to axon. Axons are covered by a myelin sheath which helps speed up the transmission of the impulse.

Sensory (Afferent) Neurons – Sensory neurons conduct impulses from receptors to the central nervous system.

Interneurons – Interneurons are always found within the spinal cord and the brain. They form the intermediate link in the nervous system pathway.

Motor (Efferent) Neurons – Motor neurons conduct impulses from the central nervous system to the effectors, which are muscles and glands. They bring about the responses to the stimulus.

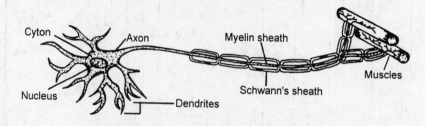

Figure 10.1 The structure of a neuron.

Nerve Impulse

The nerve impulse is the signal that is transmitted from one neuron to another. When a neuron is not stimulated, the outside of the neuron is positively charged and the inside is negatively charged. However, when there is neuron stimulation, the inside of the neuron is temporarily positively charged and the outside is temporarily negatively charged. This marks the beginning of the generation and flow of the nerve impulse.

Synapse

The synapse is the junction between the axon of one neuron and the dendrite of the next neuron. An impulse is transmitted across the synaptic gap by a specific chemical transmitter called acetylcholine. When a nerve impulse reaches the end brush of the first axon, the end brush secretes acetylcholine into the synaptic gap. It is here that the acetylcholine changes the permeability of the dendrite's membrane of the second neuron.

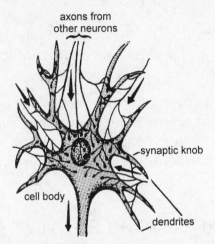

Figure 10.2 Nerve impulse across a synapse.

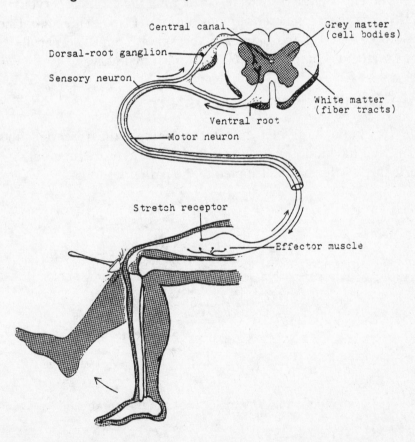

Figure 10.3 A simple reflex arc that elicits a knee-jerk response.

Reflex Arc

The unit of function of the nervous system. It is formed by a sequence of sensory neurons, interneurons, and motor neurons which conduct the nerve impulses for the given reflex.

Impulses are transferred from different sense organs to the sensory neurons. From here they pass to the interneurons and then to the motor neurons. The motor neurons connect to the various muscles and glands, also known as the effector organs. The effector is the organ making a reflex response.

THE HUMAN NERVOUS SYSTEM

The nervous system is divided into the central nervous system (CNS) and the peripheral nervous system (PNS). The central nervous system consists of the brain and the spinal cord. The peripheral nervous system is comprised of cranial and spinal nerves.

The Central Nervous System

The brain is divided into three regions: the forebrain, the midbrain, and the hindbrain. Most of these divisions are bilateral, and each has a specific function attributed to the particular lobe.

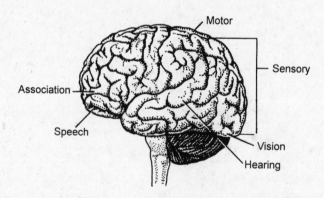

Figure 10.4 The major areas of the cerebrum.

Brain

Forebrain – The most prominent portions of the forebrain are the cerebral hemispheres that compose the higher forebrain. All sensory and motor activity is interpreted here. It is also involved in memory, emotions, speech, and learning. The surface of the cerebrum is known as the cerebral cortex. The thalamus, hypothalamus, and pineal gland are also part of the lower forebrain. The hypothalamus regulates the internal environment of the body. It works closely with the pituitary gland and controls the release of the various hormones produced by this gland. It is also involved in the regulation of thirst, hunger, water balance, behavior, and temperature.

Cerebrum – The axons and dendrites of CNS neurons are organized into bundles (tracts) that are white in appearance because of the presence of the myelin sheath. This tissue is known as white matter. The bodies of these cells are localized in the outer region known as gray matter. The cerebrum contains both sensory and motor areas and is highly convoluted in most mammals. The size of the cerebrum from smallest to largest is as follows: fish, amphibians, reptiles, birds, and mammals, with the primates having the largest cerebrum of all mammals.

Midbrain – The midbrain is one of the smallest regions of the brain. It acts as a relay station, transferring nerve impulses between the two other parts of the brain.

Hindbrain – The two main regions of the hindbrain are the medulla oblongata and the cerebellum.

1) **Medulla oblongata** – Its functions are respiratory and circulatory regulation, cough reflex, swallowing, sneezing, and the vomiting reflex.

2) **Cerebellum** – It is involved in the coordination of muscle activity, locomotion, and maintenance of balance. It is initiated by impulses originating in the forebrain.

Lateralization refers to the fact that each side of the brain controls different functions. For most people, the right brain controls artistic concepts and spatial perception, while the left brain is the speech, language, and calculation center. The corpus callosum is a thick band of fibers that connects the two halves of the brain.

Endorphins are peptide hormones produced in the brain and anterior pituitary that inhibit pain reception through binding to the same neuroreceptors as morphine.

The Spinal Cord

The spinal cord runs from the medulla oblongata down through the backbone. It is comprised of an interior of gray matter and an exterior of white matter. The gray matter consists of neuron cell bodies and the white matter consists of myelinated axons. The white matter also contains descending and ascending tracts that run from the spinal cord to the brain. Throughout its length, it is enclosed by three meninges and by the spinal cord vertebrae. Running vertically in the spinal cord center is a narrow canal filled with cerebrospinal fluid.

The spinal cord controls the centers for reflex acts occurring below the neck, and it provides the major pathway for impulses between the peripheral nervous system and the brain. It is also a connecting center between sensory and motor neurons.

The Peripheral Nervous System

The peripheral nervous system consists of the autonomic and somatic nervous systems. It contains nerve fibers that connect the brain and the spinal cord to the sense organs, glands, and muscles.

Somatic Nervous System

The somatic nervous system consists of nerves that transmit impulses from receptors to the central nervous system and from the central nervous system to the skeletal muscles of the body.

Autonomic Nervous System

This system is further divided into the sympathetic and parasympathetic systems. The ANS controls the motor responses of the internal organs.

Sympathetic Nervous System – This system consists of motor neurons arising from the spinal cord. This system is involved in the "fight or flight" response, which is a condition that moves the body away from homeostasis. This system causes acceleration of heart rate, relaxes the bladder but tightens the sphincter, slows digestion, constricts most arteries, increases blood flow to the heart and muscles, slows peristalsis, and causes dilation of breathing passages and pupils.

Parasympathetic System – This system consists of fibers arising from the brain. It maintains homeostasis (maintenance of a constant internal environment). The system tends to oppose the effects of the sympathetic system. It dilates arteries, slows heartbeat, and increases the digestive process.

Some Problems of the Human Nervous System

Cerebral palsy – Impaired muscle control due to brain damage by infection or injury before or after birth.

Meningitis – Inflammation of the membranes (meninges) that surround the brain and spinal cord; may be caused by infection with a bacterium or virus.

Stroke – Caused by a blood clot in the brain or a decreased amount of blood flowing to the brain; causes the portion of brain tissue supplied by the artery to die.

Poliomyelitis – A viral disease that attacks nerve cells and can result in paralysis. This disease is not seen very often due to the vaccine.

RELATIONSHIP BETWEEN THE NERVOUS SYSTEM AND THE ENDOCRINE SYSTEM

The nervous and endocrine systems generally act as a functional unit. The two systems are structurally related in that many endocrine glands are made up of (i.e., hypothalamus) or were originally evolved from (i.e., adrenal medulla) nervous tissue. Additionally, they are chemically related, as both systems use some of the same hormones for signaling (i.e., epinephrine). Finally, they are functionally related such that the systems may act in a series to elicit a specific response, or one system may affect the output of the other. They differ, in that the nervous system can conduct a signal much more rapidly than the endocrine system; the nervous system response is generally transient while that of the endocrine may be more sustained, and hormones of the endocrine system generally have to travel long distances through the bloodstream to reach their target tissue.

Actions of the Autonomic Nervous System

Organ Innervated	Sympathetic Action	Parasympathetic Action
Heart	Accelerates heartbeat	Slows heartbeat
Arteries	Constricts most arteries	Dilates most arteries
Lungs	Dilates bronchial passages	Constricts bronchial passage
Digestive Tract	Slows peristalsis rate	Increases peristalsis rate
Eyes	Dilates pupils	Constricts pupils
Urinary Bladder	Relaxes bladder	Constricts bladder
Sphincter	Constricts	Relaxes

THE NERVOUS SYSTEMS IN OTHER ORGANISMS

Protozoans – Protozoans have no nervous system; however, their protoplasm does receive and respond to certain stimuli.

Hydra – The hydra possesses a simple nervous system known as a nerve net. The hydra lacks centralization of a nervous system. A stimulus applied to a specific part of the body will generate an impulse which will travel to all body parts.

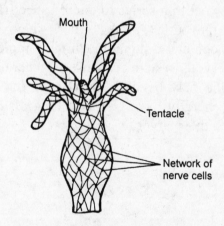

Mouth

Tentacle

Network of nerve cells

Figure 10.5 Nerve net of the hydra.

Earthworm – The earthworm possesses a central nervous system that includes a brain, a nerve cord (which is a chain of ganglions), sense organs, nerve fibers, muscles, and glands.

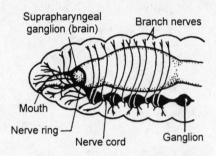

Figure 10.6 Nervous system of the earthworm.

Grasshopper – The grasshopper's nervous system consists of ganglia bundled together to form the peripheral nervous system. The ganglia of the grasshopper are better developed than that of the earthworm.

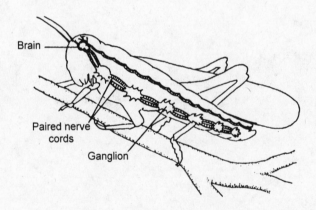

Figure 10.7 Nervous system of a grasshopper.

Fish – The brains of fish are composed of a pair of olfactory lobes (smell), a cerebrum with two hemispheres, two optic lobes (sight), a cerebellum, and a medulla. Additionally, the lateral lines that run the length of both sides of a fish contain mechanoreceptors that are sensitive to movement, particularly to the water–current pressure.

Frogs – The brains of frogs are similar to those of fish in that they also are composed of olfactory and optic lobes, a cerebrum, a cerebellum, and a medulla, though the cerebrum of a frog is larger than that of a fish.

Birds – The optic lobes and cerebellum of birds are relatively large to accommodate for their well-developed sense of sight and to enable the functions of coordination and balance in flight, respectively.

THE SAT SUBJECT TEST IN
Biology E/M

CHAPTER 11

CHAPTER 11

SENSING THE ENVIRONMENT

COMPONENTS OF NERVOUS COORDINATION

Three components are needed to develop a sense.

Receptor – This is a structure that must have the ability to detect a change in the environment and initiate a signal in the nerve cell.

Conductors – These send signals through the body. The nervous system is the conduction system.

Effectors – These are the structures that respond to the stimuli. For example, skeletal muscles are effectors. They respond by contracting when signaled by the nervous system.

Photoreceptors

The photoreceptive system includes the sense of sight. The eye is a delicate receptor which is sensitive to light.

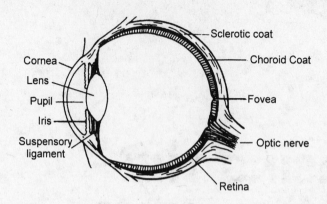

Figure 11.1 The human eye.

Sclera – This is the outer layer of the eyeball. It is white and changes into the cornea in the front of the eye. The cornea is transparent and admits light into the eye interior.

Choroid – The choroid is the middle layer of the eye. Its purpose is to stop the reflection of scattered light within the eye. The choroid coat forms the iris of the eye which has a center opening known as the pupil. The pupil, which is in front of the lens, permits light to enter the eye. The choroid also changes into the ciliary muscle and suspensory ligaments in front of the eye. This muscle-ligament system changes the shape of the lens for focusing (accomodation).

Retina – The retina is the innermost layer of the eye. It contains two types of receptor nerve cells, known as the rods and cones, which are the actual visual receptors.

1) **Rods** – These are sensitive to light and are basically used for vision in dim light.

2) **Cones** – These function as bright-light color receptors. Both rods and cones are connected to a network of nerve cells which forms the optic nerve. The optic nerve is connected to the brain.

Vision Defects

Nearsightedness (Myopia) – In most cases of nearsightedness, the eyeball is too long so the retina is too far from the lens. The light rays converge in front of the retina and diverge when they reach it.

This results in seeing distant objects as blurred images. Eyeglasses with concave lenses correct this defect.

Farsightedness (Hypermetropia) – In most cases of farsightedness, the eyeball is too short so the retina is too close to the lens. Light rays will strike the retina before they converge which results in seeing nearby objects as blurred images. Eyeglasses with convex lenses correct farsightedness.

Astigmatism – In astigmatism, there is an irregularity in the curvature of the cornea or the lens. This causes a blurred image. Astigmatism can be corrected with lenses designed specifically to correct the irregular curvature of the cornea or the lens.

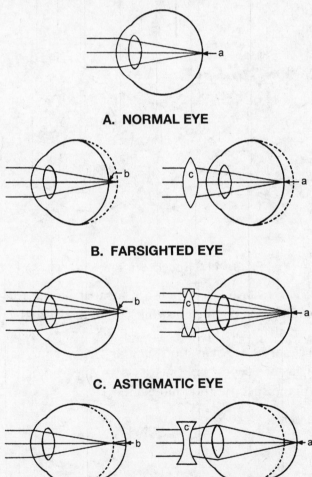

A. NORMAL EYE

B. FARSIGHTED EYE

C. ASTIGMATIC EYE

D. NEARSIGHTED EYE

a. Sharp image b. Blurred image c. Correction

Figure 11.2 Illustrations of normal eye and common eye defects with corrective lenses.

Chemoreceptors

The senses of taste and smell comprise the chemoreceptive system. These are the receptors of chemicals in the external environment.

Smell – The nose is the organ in humans that detects odors by means of receptor cells in two olfactory epithelia. An individual receptor consists of a cell with tiny hairs at one end and a nerve cell fiber at the other end. Present theories suggest that active sites on the receptor cells join with specific odor molecules. This combination forms a complex that generates a signal in the receptor cell. The signal then passes through a nerve fiber, which is part of the olfactory nerve, to the brain for interpretation.

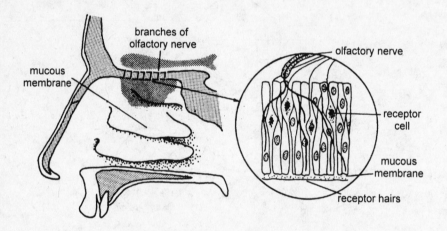

Figure 11.3 Receptors in the nose.

Taste – The taste buds, which are located on the tongue, are the principal receptors of chemical stimuli in the external environment. There are four different types of taste buds which, when stimulated, initiate one primary taste sensation such as sweet, sour, salty, or bitter. Each type of taste receptor cell has its own specific active site which combines with the specific food molecule.

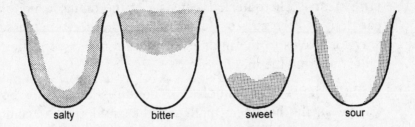

salty   bitter   sweet   sour

**Figure 11.4 Distribution of the taste buds sensitive
to salty, bitter, sweet, and sour tastes.**

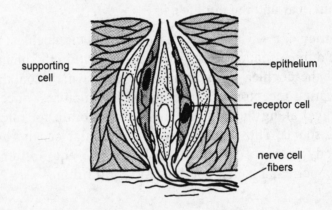

supporting
cell

epithelium

receptor cell

nerve cell
fibers

Figure 11.5 A diagram of a taste bud cell.

Mechanoreceptors

The senses involving touch and hearing comprise the category of mechanoreceptors. These receptors are sensitive to mechanical stimuli such as pressure or compression.

Touch – In humans, touch is detected by receptors near the surface of the skin next to a hair follicle. The Pacinian corpuscle is a receptor found in the skin and in some internal organs. Each Pacinian corpuscle is connected to a sensory neuron. It is a pressure receptor; therefore, any application of pressure will deform the corpuscle.

Proprioceptors are sense receptors distributed throughout skeletal muscle and tendons. Any muscle contraction or stretching will trigger the receptors to initiate nerve impulses.

Hearing – The organs of hearing and equilibrium are found in the ear. The ear is especially sensitive to sounds of varying frequencies and intensities. The human ear consists of an outer ear, a middle ear, and an inner ear.

1) **Outer ear** – The outer ear consists of the pinna, which is an ear flap, and the auditory canal, which provides the passageway for waves to the middle ear. The eardrum separates the outer ear from the middle ear.

2) **Middle ear** – The middle ear contains three tiny bones known as the hammer (malleus), the anvil (incus), and the stirrup (stapes). These bones transmit sound waves across the middle ear cavity. The Eustachian tube connects the middle ear to the pharynx and equalizes the pressure between the outer ear and the middle ear.

3) **Inner ear** – The inner ear consists of the cochlea, vestibule, and three semicircular canals. Lying within the inner chamber of the cochlea is the organ of Corti, which contains the vibrating receptors for hearing. Nerve impulses, once initiated, travel along the auditory canal to the brain for interpretation as sound. The vestibule and semicircular canals function for body balance: the vestibule for static equilibrium, and the semicircular canals for dynamic equilibrium.

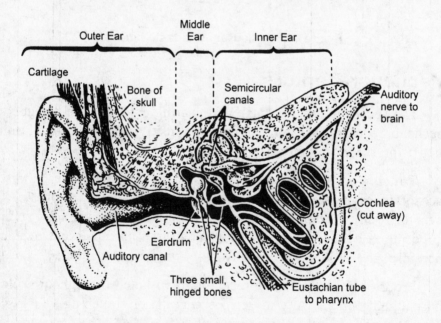

Figure 11.6 The structure of the ear.

Receptors in Other Organisms

Protozoans – The plasma membrane in these organisms is the receptor for external stimuli.

Hydra – The hydra possesses nerve endings in the ectoderm and endoderm layers that are sensitive to light, touch, and chemicals.

Grasshopper – The grasshopper possesses many sense organs which are sensitive to external stimuli. The compound and single eyes are sensitive to bright light and dim light, respectively. Hairs that are found in various areas on the body are sensitive to touch. The tympanic membranes, located on the grasshopper's abdomen, transmit sound vibrations to receptor cells.

Earthworm – The nerve endings in the skin of the earthworm possess receptors for touch, chemicals, and temperature changes. Light receptors are mainly found in the head and tail areas.

THE SAT SUBJECT TEST IN

Biology E/M

CHAPTER 12

CHAPTER 12

THE EXCRETORY SYSTEM

EXCRETION IN HUMANS

The organs of excretion which remove metabolic wastes from a cell or organ in humans include the skin, lungs, liver, kidneys, and large intestine.

Skin

The skin functions as an organ of excretion as well as protection against injury and regulation of body fluids. The sweat glands of the skin remove water, mineral salts, and urea from the blood.

Skin Structure

The skin is variably thick, sensitized, and vascular, and functions in protection, body temperature regulation, excretion, sensation, and the production of vitamin D. The skin of mammals contains fat and hair, which aids in insulation. Skin consists of two layers of tissue: the thin epidermis (stratified epithelium) and the thick, fibrous dermis. Components of the skin, such as sweat glands, blood vessels, oil glands, and nerves, are found within the dermis. The release of water from sweat glands in the skin and subsequent evaporation helps to cool the skin and regulate body temperature.

Effects of Sun Exposure

Prolonged exposure of the skin to the sun's ultraviolet rays (UVA and UVB) may have damaging effects on the skin, such as producing leathery, wrinkled skin and inducing skin cancer. The use of sunblock is a good way to minimize the damaging effects of sun exposure.

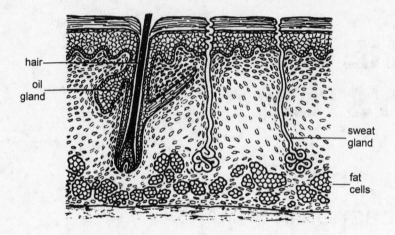

Figure 12.1 Section of the human skin.

Lungs

The lungs excrete water and carbon dioxide.

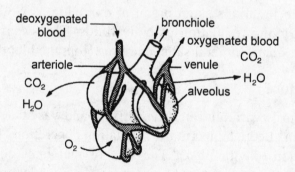

Figure 12.2 Representation of alveoli where carbon dioxide and water are eliminated.

Liver

The liver is the gland that synthesizes bile for the emulsification of fats. It is considered an organ of excretion because it removes the following:

1) old red blood cells from the bloodstream;

2) excess amino acids that are deaminated by the liver;

3) all monosaccharides, except glucose.

Urinary System

The urinary system of humans consists of a pair of kidneys, a pair of ureters, the urinary bladder, and the urethra.

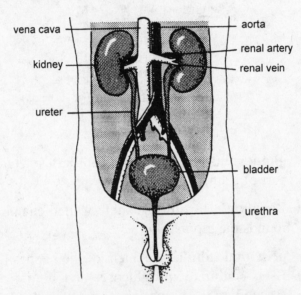

Figure 12.3 The human excretory system.

1) **Kidneys** – The kidneys are located against the dorsal body wall just above the waistline. They are composed of three distinct regions: the cortex, medulla, and pelvis. The capillaries and tubules in the kidneys form nephrons which remove metabolic wastes from the blood. Blood reaches the kidneys via a right and left renal artery and leaves via right and left renal veins. In the nephron, the blood composition is controlled by three processes: filtration, reabsorption, and secretion.

   a) **nephron** – structural and functional unit of the kidney which manufactures urine

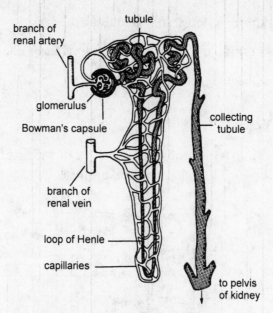

Figure 12.4 A single nephron.

b) **glomerulus** – network of capillaries which constitutes part of a single nephron

c) **Bowman's capsule** – double-walled chamber which surrounds the glomerulus

d) **proximal tubule** – segment of the nephron tubule where H_2O, sodium ions, glucose, and amino acids are absorbed into the blood

e) **loop of Henle** – The proximal tubule leads into the loop of Henle where sodium ions are actively transported out of the segment.

f) **distal tubule** – Additional sodium can be reabsorbed out by the distal tubule. Water is also reabsorbed here.

g) **collecting tubule** – receives urine from smaller tubules. Peritubular capillaries surround the tubule part of the nephron.

2) **Ureters** – Urine flows down from the kidney to the bladder by means of the ureter.

3) **Bladder** – The bladder is a hollow, muscular organ which is capable of expanding when urine flows into it.

4) **Urethra** – Urine flows to the outside from the bladder by way of the urethra.

Excretory System Problems

Kidney disease – Normal kidney function may be compromised by infections, heavy-metal poisoning (lead, mercury), and very high-protein diets. Extreme dysfunction of the kidneys may result in the need for kidney dialysis to remove wastes from the blood.

Gout – Gout is caused by the inadequate removal by the kidneys of uric acid from the blood or the overproduction of uric acid in the blood. This results in the development of uric acid crystals, which usually concentrate in the big toe or joints, causing pain.

EXCRETION IN OTHER ORGANISMS

Protozoans – Elimination of metabolic wastes occurs by diffusion through the plasma membrane. The major waste products include ammonia, carbon dioxide, mineral salts, and water. Some have contractile vacuoles for elimination.

Hydra – The metabolic wastes of the hydra are excreted by simple diffusion. The major wastes of the hydra include ammonia, water, carbon dioxide, and salts.

Grasshopper – The excretory system of the grasshopper is made up of Malpighian tubules. Wastes such as water, salts, and dissolved nitrogenous compounds diffuse into the blood in the body cavity. The Malpighian tubules absorb these wastes. Water present in the Malpighian tubules is reabsorbed into the blood. Any remaining waste passes into the intestine where it is eliminated. Salts, uric acid, and small quantities of water are the major metabolic wastes.

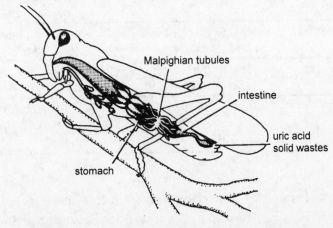

Figure 12.5 Excretory organs of a grasshopper.

Earthworm – The nephridia are the major excretory structures of the earthworm. They are needed for the elimination of water, urea, ammonia, and mineral salts. Each nephridium consist of a nephrostome which lies within the body cavity. This body cavity is filled with fluid which enters the nephrostome and passes down a long tubule. As it travels down this tubule, useful materials are reclaimed by cells which line the tubule. Useless materials leave the earthworm by the nephridiopores, which are openings to the outside.

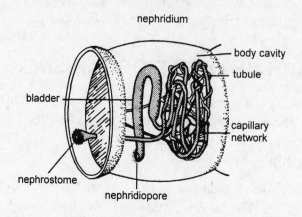

Figure 12.6 Excretory system of the earthworm.

Summary of Excretion

Organism	Major Organs for Excretion	Major Waste Products
Protozoans	Plasma membrane	water, ammonia, carbon dioxide, salts
Hydra	Plasma membrane	water, ammonia, carbon dioxide, salts
Grasshopper	Malpighian tubules and intestine	uric acid, salts, very little water
Earthworm	Nephridia and intestine	urea, water, salts, ammonia
Human	Lungs, kidneys, skin, liver, large intestine	urea, water, bile salts, carbon dioxide

Fish – Instead of conserving water like most terrestrial animals, freshwater fish need to release excess water because of their aqueous surroundings. To do this, the nephrons of fish kidneys use cilia to sweep large amounts of dilute urine from the body. Bony fishes that live in saltwater have the opposite problem and must excrete large amounts of ions, such as Ca^{2+} and Mg^{2+}, and very concentrated urine.

Frogs – In frogs, urine is produced by the kidneys and travels through the ureters to the cloaca, a common duct opening for the digestive, urinary, and reproductive tracts. Urine leaves the body, along with solid wastes, through the anus.

THE SAT SUBJECT TEST IN
Biology E/M

CHAPTER 13

CHAPTER 13

THE SKELETAL SYSTEM

THE SKELETAL SYSTEM

Functions

The skeletal system consists of 206 bones that are large enough to be counted. It provides at least five functions for the human body.

Protection – Many organs are contained within spaces formed by the bones. The cranium, which is the superior portion of the skull, houses the brain. The vertebral column surrounds the spinal cord. Twelve pairs of ribs and the sternum, composing the thoracic cage, protect many organs in the central body cavity. Examples include the heart, lungs, stomach, and liver.

Support – The vertebral column has four different curvatures along its length. These curvatures give the backbone a great ability to support body weight. The arch formed by the bones of the foot also support body weight. Other bones, such as the long bones in the legs and arms, contribute great mechanical strength.

Movement – Skeletal muscles attach to the bones. As the muscles contract, they pull on the bones and produce movement. For example, the forearm bones (radius and ulna) are pulled toward the upper arm bone (humerus) as the biceps brachii muscle contracts. The forearm bones and humerus are connected by a hinge joint. This joint permits the bending (flexion) of the forearm when the biceps muscle in the upper arm contracts.

Mineral Storage – Calcium and phosphorus are stored in the bones. If the concentration of these minerals is too high in the blood, the excess amount is stored in the bones. If more of these minerals is needed in the blood, they are released from the bones.

Blood Cell Formation (Hemopoiesis) – Bones are not solid structures. Cavities in the cranial bones, vertebrae, ribs, sternum, and ends of long bones contain red marrow. This blood-forming tissue produces erythrocytes (red blood cells), leukocytes (white blood cells), and thrombocytes (platelets). From these sites of production, these cells are released into the circulation.

Growth and Development

Based on shape, there are five kinds of bones that develop in the body.

Long bones – Found in the arms (i.e., humerus, the upper arm bone) and legs (i.e., femur, the thighbone).

Short bones – Include the carpals (wrist) and tarsals (ankle).

Flat bones – Such as the sternum (breast bone).

Irregular bones – Such as the mandible (jawbone) and vertebrae.

Sesamoid bones – Are seed-shaped, found in joints (i.e., patella, the kneecap bone).

Long bones increase in diameter through the activity of cells. Cells called osteoblasts on the surface of the bone produce layers of new bone cells, called osteocytes. These bone cells mature and produce a matrix, surrounding inorganic material, to increase the amount of compact (dense) bone tissue. As this process progresses, the long bone increases in diameter.

The activity of osteoblasts and osteocytes also produces compact bone tissue in the other kinds of bones (short, flat, irregular, and sesamoid).

Axial Skeleton

The axial skeleton is one branch of the skeletal system. It forms the midline of the skeleton. This branch consists of the skull, hyoid bone, vertebral column, and thoracic cage. Eighty of the 206 bones of the skeleton are axial.

Skull – Twenty-eight bones are found in the skull. Eight bones make up the cranium or superior portion of the skull.

Hyoid Bone – This is a horseshoe-shaped bone suspended by muscles from the floor of the oral cavity.

Vertebral Column – The backbone consists of four curvatures: cervical (neck), thoracic (chest), lumbar (lower back), and pelvic. Each consists of a serial arrangement of vertebrae. These vertebrae form a continuous tube, housing the spinal cord.

Thoracic Cage – The thoracic cage consists of the sternum (breastbone) and 12 pairs of ribs.

Appendicular Skeleton

The appendicular skeleton is the other branch of the skeletal system. It contains 126 bones. This branch consists of the pectoral (chest) girdle and arm bones as well as the pelvic (hip) girdle and leg bones.

Pectoral Girdle – Each half of the pectoral girdle consists of the clavicle (collarbone) and scapula (shoulder blade). The medial end of the clavicle articulates to the manubrium of the sternum. Laterally it attaches to the acromion of the scapula.

Arm Bones – The arm bones consist of the humerus and the ulna and radius. The wrist consists of the carpal bones. The metacarpals are the bones in the palm of the hand and the phalanges are the bones of the fingers.

Pelvic Girdle – The pelvic girdle consists of the two hip bones. They connect by a slightly movable joint. Combined with the sacrum and coccyx of the axial skeleton, they form the pelvis.

Leg Bones – The leg bones consist of the femur, tibia, fibula, and patella (kneecap bone). The ankle consists of the tarsal bones, and the metatarsals compose the arch of the foot. The phalanges are the bones of the toes.

Articulations (Joints)

Articulations (joints) are the structures where bones connect. There are three main classes of articulations based on the amount of motion they allow:

Synarthroses – Immovable joints.

Amphiarthroses – Joints permitting slight mobility.

Diarthroses – Joints allowing free mobility (synovial joints). Types of these joints include:

Ball and Socket – The head of one bone fits into a shallow depression. Motion occurs here in three different planes.

Hinge – Examples include the knee joint and the elbow joint.

Pivot – The ring of one bone rotates around the process of another. The atlas pivots on the axis.

Gliding – Bones can slide over each other (i.e., carpal and tarsal bones).

Saddle – The bones have a saddle shape (i.e., carpals and metacarpals).

THE SKELETAL MUSCLES

Functions

Skeletal muscles carry out several important body functions.

Movement – Skeletal muscles attach to the bones. As a muscle contracts, it pulls on a bone (or bones) to produce movement. For example, the hamstring muscles are found in the posterior thigh. As each contracts, it pulls the calf toward the thigh, producing flexion (bending) of the calf. As it contracts, a muscle pulls an *insertion bone* (movable end) toward an *origin bone* (fixed end). In this example, the tibia represents the insertion bone and the femur represents the origin bone.

Heat Production – Numerous chemical reactions in muscle cells liberate heat. This heat contributes to the maintenance of body temperature.

Posture – Some skeletal muscles pull on the vertebral column and other parts of the skeleton, helping to maintain an upright stance and posture of the body.

Structure of a Skeletal Muscle

There are more than 600 skeletal muscles in the human body. Each one has the same basic structure at several levels of organization: organ (the muscle), tissue (striated, skeletal), cell (fiber), organelles (e.g., mitochondria and myofibrils), and molecules (e.g., water, actin, myosin).

As an organ, a skeletal muscle consists of several tissue types. Skeletal muscle fibers are long, thread-like cells that compose skeletal (striated) tissue. These cells have the ability to shorten their length or contract.

The interior of a muscle also contains the axons of motor neurons. Each axon signals a group of muscle fibers. This association (one neuron, group of muscle fibers) is called a motor unit.

Muscles also contain an abundant supply of blood vessels. The blood delivers glucose and other nutrients, along with oxygen, that are needed for cell metabolism. There are also fat deposits in muscles that store energy.

Muscle cells contain many organelles common to most cells (i.e., mitochondria). Myofibrils are organelles that establish the contractile ability of muscle cells. Each myofibril is a linear succession of box-like units called sarcomeres. Each sarcomere contains the contractile proteins (myofilaments) actin and myosin. The myosin is the thicker central protein. The actin is the thinner protein at each end of the sarcomere.

Actin and myosin are organized in each sarcomere in the following regions:

A Band – actin and myosin

H Zone – myosin only, within the A band

I Band – actin only

Z Line – boundary of the sarcomere where actin molecules are attached at each end

Mechanism of a Muscle Contraction

A skeletal muscle contracts by the following series of steps:

1. A motor nerve signals the muscle. Some of the neurons in the

nerve develop electrical impulses that signal some fibers in the muscle. Each axon secretes a neurotransmitter (chemical signal) called acetylcholine at the synapse (motor end plate) between the neuron and some muscle fibers. This signal excites each signaled muscle cell.

2. An electrical signal spreads out along the sarcolemma (cell membrane) of each muscle cell that is signaled.

3. This signal continues transversely into the sarcoplasm (cytoplasm) of each muscle cell along the membranes of the T (transverse) tubules.

4. The T tubules join the SR (sarcoplasmic reticulum) in the sarcoplasm (cytoplasm). The signal spreads from the T tubules to this tubular SR, releasing Ca ions.

5. The release of Ca^{+2} from the SR blocks the action of troponin, a protein in the myofibrils. Troponin normally inhibits the interaction of actin and myosin, contractile proteins in the sarcomeres of the myofibrils.

6. With troponin inhibited, actin and myosin can interact. Crossbridges on the myosin slide the actin molecules toward the center of the sarcomere. As the actin molecules are attached to the Z lines, boundaries of the sarcomeres, this shortens the sarcomeres according to the sliding filament theory. The actin molecules slide between the central myosin molecules.

7. Hydrolysis of ATP in the cells, into ADP and phosphate, releases energy to drive the sliding of the filaments (actin and myosin). ATP is rebuilt from an energy-storage compound, creatine phosphate.

8. If enough sarcomeres shorten, myofibrils shorten. If enough myofibrils shorten, the fibers (cells) shorten. If enough fibers shorten, the muscle shortens or contracts.

Each muscle responds by an all-or-none law. If stimulated sufficiently, it contracts fully. The force of contraction from an entire muscle depends on the percentage of cells that are active, each cell responding by all-or-none.

THE SAT SUBJECT TEST IN
Biology E/M

CHAPTER 14

CHAPTER 14

HUMAN PATHOLOGY

DISEASES OF HUMANS

How Pathogens Cause Disease

Bacterial pathogens must first adhere to a host. Adhesions are projections on the surface of the bacterium that adhere to complementary receptors on host cells. Adherence is followed by colonization of the tissues (in complex multicellular organisms), and may also involve invasion of cells.

Disease-causing bacteria may produce toxins. Bacterial toxins include endotoxins and exotoxins. An endotoxin is a lipid component of some bacteria's cell walls. It is released when the bacterium divides or dies. Inactivated toxins that retain their antigenic properties are called toxoids. These can be used to vaccinate humans against such diseases as tetanus infection. An exotoxin is a poisonous substance released from the bacterium into the surrounding medium. They include neurotoxins, which affect the nervous system, and enterotoxins, which affect the gastrointestinal system. Antitoxins are antibodies that are produced against toxins.

Pathogenic viruses, fungi, protozoans, and helminths also damage host cells and tissues. Cytopathic effects (CPEs) are the signs of cell damage due to viral infection. Viruses release digestive enzymes and alter host DNA. Fungal pathogens digest cells; some produce toxins or allergic reactions. Protozoans and helminths produce symptoms through direct damage to host tissues, release of toxic waste products, or by causing allergic reactions.

Pathogens

Pathogen – A parasitic microorganism that causes disease.

Pathogenicity – The ability of a microbe to produce disease.

Virulence – The power of an organism to cause disease.

Infection – Pathogen invasion of the body.

Disease – Disturbed health due to a pathogen or other factor.

Pathogens gain access to a host via a portal of entry and leave via a portal of exit. Portals of entry include the mucous membranes (including those lining the respiratory, gastrointestinal, and genitourinary tracts) and parenteral entry (direct inoculation through the skin via bites, injections, or other wounds). The most frequently used portal of entry is the respiratory tract. But many pathogens cannot cause infection unless they enter through a specific (preferred) portal of entry. Portals of exit include the respiratory tract (coughing, sneezing), the gastrointestinal tract (saliva, feces), and secretions from the genitourinary tract. Microbes may also leave the body via blood into syringes or biting arthropods.

Host Defense Mechanisms

Resistance is the ability to ward off disease. It is the result of genetically predetermined (innate) resistance and other factors such as the individual's age, sex, and nutritional status. Susceptibility is lack of resistance.

Predisposing factors, such as age, fatigue, stress, and poor nutrition, can make a host more susceptible to infection and disease.

Nonspecific defenses (e.g., fever, inflammation) are used to protect the body from all kinds of pathogenic organisms. They generally serve as a first line of defense.

Specific defenses include innate resistance and acquired resistance to specific pathogens.

Nonspecific Host Defense Mechanisms

Nonspecific defenses include mechanical barriers such as skin, saliva, the lacrimal apparatus, and mucous membranes, as well as the outward flow of urine, vaginal secretions, and blood (from wounds).

There are three categories of white blood cells (leukocytes): the granulocytes (neutrophils, basophils, eosinophils), which predominate early in infection; agranulocytes: (the monocytes, which predominate late in infection); and the lymphocytes.

Phagocytosis is the cellular ingestion of a foreign substance (including microorganisms). Certain types of white blood cells are phagocytes. Phagocytes locate microorganisms through chemotaxis. They then adhere to the microbial cell. Pseudopods then encircle and engulf the microbe. The phagocytized microbe, enclosed in a vacuole called a phagosome, is usually killed by lysosomal enzymes and oxidizing agents.

Fever is abnormally high body temperature produced in response to infection. It serves to augment the immune system, inhibit microbial growth, increase the rate of chemical reactions, raise the temperature above the organism's optimum growth temperature, and decrease patient activity.

Inflammation is a response to cell damage. Initiation of inflammation is caused by the release of histamine (a vasodilator), kinins, and prostaglandins. Redness, heat, swelling, pain, and sometimes loss of function are characteristic of inflammation.

Tissue injury also stimulates blood clotting, which may help to prevent dissemination of the infection.

The complement system refers to a group of blood serum proteins that activate a cascade series of reactions to destroy invading pathogens. It causes cell lysis, inflammation, and opsonization (in which the microbial cell is coated by plasma proteins). Complement deficiencies result in reduced resistance to infection.

Specific Host Defense Mechanisms—Types of Immunity

Immunity – The ability of the body to recognize and defend itself against an infectious agent.

Specific immunity – Characterized by specificity, recognition of self vs. nonself, heterogeneity, and memory.

Heterogeneity – The ability to respond specifically to a variety of substances.

Memory (anamnestic response) – The ability to recognize and respond to a substance previously encountered.

Innate immunity/resistance – Genetically predetermined immunity or resistance that an individual is born with, including species resistance.

Acquired immunity – Specific immunity developed during an individual's lifetime.

> **Actively acquired immunity** – Involves the production of antibodies or specialized lymphocytes in response to exposure to an antigen; it is usually long-lasting. Naturally acquired active immunity is a result of an infection. Artificially acquired active immunity is a result of vaccination.

> **Passively acquired immunity** – Antibodies produced by another source are transferred to an individual to confer immunity; they are generally not long-lasting. Naturally acquired passive immunity involves transfer of antibodies from mother to fetus (via the placenta) or from mother to newborn (via the colostrum). Artificially acquired passive immunity involves acquisition of antibodies by injection.

An antigen is a chemical substance (usually foreign) that elicits a specific immune response. It may be a protein, glycoprotein, lipoprotein, nucleoprotein, or large polysaccharide.

An antibody (immunoglobulin) is a protein produced by B lymphocytes in response to an antigen. Antibodies bind to antigenic determinant sites or epitopes on the antigen. There are five different immunoglobulin (Ig) classes: IgG, IgM, IgA, IgD, and IgE.

> *IgG* antibodies provide naturally acquired passive immunity; they enhance phagocytosis, neutralize toxins and viruses, and protect both fetus and newborn.

> *IgM* antibodies are the first antibodies produced in response to an infection.

> *IgA* antibodies protect mucosal surfaces.

> *IgD* antibodies appear to be involved in initiation of the immune response.

IgE antibodies are involved in allergic reactions and possibly in responding to protozoal and parasitic infections.

There are two components of the immune system: humoral immunity and cell-mediated immunity. Lymphocytes differentiate into either B cells (which are involved in humoral immunity), or T cells (which are involved in the cell-mediated response).

Humoral immunity involves antibodies defending against toxins, bacteria, and viruses in extracellular body fluids such as plasma and lymph.

Cellular immunity (cell-mediated immunity) is involved in the body's response to multicellular parasites, transplanted tissues, cancer cells, and intracellular viruses. T cells do have receptors for antigens, but they do not make antibodies.

Vaccines and toxoids (inactivated toxins) are used to confer active immunization.

Vaccines can be made from live attenuated (weakened) organisms, parts of organisms (subunit vaccines), or dead organisms. Subunit vaccines are generally safer than either attenuated organisms or whole killed cells. Recombinant vaccines, in which the antigen genes of pathogens are inserted into the DNA of a nonpathogen, are very safe.

Diseases Caused by Microbes

Microbial Diseases of the Skin and Eyes

Bacterial diseases of the skin include staphylococcal, streptococcal, and pseudomonad infections. Most of these organisms are opportunists, generally part of the normal flora, that gain access through cuts, burns, or surgical incisions.

Viral diseases of the skin include smallpox, chickenpox, shingles, herpes, measles, rubella, and warts.

Fungal skin diseases include athlete's foot, ringworm, and candidiasis.

Microbial Diseases of the Respiratory System

Infections of the upper respiratory system can be caused by several bacteria and viruses, often in combination. These infections include pharyngitis, laryngitis, bronchitis, epiglottitis, and sinusitis.

Bacterial diseases of the upper respiratory system include strep throat, scarlet fever, diphtheria, and otitis media (middle ear infections).

The common cold is caused by about 200 different viruses; about half are rhinoviruses. Ear infections and sinus infections may occur as complications.

Bacterial diseases of the lower respiratory system include whooping cough, tuberculosis, and pneumonia.

Tuberculosis (caused by *Mycobacterium tuberculosis*) is a major, worldwide health problem, and its incidence is increasing in the U.S.

Pneumonia is often caused by members of the normal flora. Most infections are due to *Streptococcus pneumoniae*, or *Haemophilus influenzae*.

Viral infections cause influenza and pneumonia as well. The influenza virus exhibits antigenic variation.

Microbial Diseases of the Digestive System

Tooth decay (dental caries) and periodontal disease – *Streptococcus mutans* is involved in the production of plaque. Bacterial acids destroy tooth enamel, and filamentous bacteria and gram-positive rods invade the underlying dentin and pulp. Gram-negative anaerobes, streptococci, and actinomycetes can cause gingivitis and decay of the underlying cementum, leading to periodontal disease.

Gastrointestinal distress can be caused by pathogens growing in the intestine or from the ingestion of toxins (bacterial intoxication). Both infections and intoxications can cause diarrhea, dysentery, or gastroenteritis.

Microbial Diseases of the Cardiovascular System

Septicemia – growth of microorganisms in the blood—can cause inflamed lymph vessels (lymphangitis), septic shock, and decreased blood pressure. Symptoms are usually the result of endotoxins.

Peurperal sepsis – A uterine infection following childbirth or abortion; it is usually caused by *Streptococcus pyogenes*.

Bacterial endocarditis – Infection (usually streptococcal or staphylococcal) of the inner layer of the heart.

Rheumatic fever – A possible complication following streptococcal infection.

Anthrax and Lyme disease are other bacterial diseases of the cardiovascular system.

Viral diseases include infectious mononucleosis and Burkitt's lymphoma.

Microbial Diseases of the Nervous System

Bacterial meningitis can be caused by nearly 50 species of opportunistic bacteria. Leprosy, tetanus, and botulism are also caused by bacteria.

Protozoal diseases of the nervous system include African sleeping sickness.

Viral diseases of the nervous system include rabies.

Microbial Diseases of the Genitourinary System

Bacterial diseases of the urinary system include cystitis, glomerulonephritis, and pyelonephritis.

Bacterial diseases of the reproductive system include gonorrhea, nongonococcal urethritis, syphilis, vaginitis, chancroid, granuloma inguinale, and lymphogranuloma venereum.

Viral diseases of the reproductive system include cytomegalovirus, genital herpes, and genital warts.

Candidiasis, a fungal disease, and trichomoniasis, a protozoal disease, also affect the genitourinary system.

Insect and Tick Transmitted Diseases

Bubonic plague – Bubonic plague is caused by the bacillus *Yersinia pestis*. It is transmitted to humans by the bite of an infected flea, which may reside on rodents. Characteristics include blackish areas on the skin caused by subcutaneous hemorrhages, enlarged lymph nodes (buboes), and fever. The mortality rate is relatively high.

Lyme disease – Lyme disease is a tick-borne disease caused by spirochete *Borrella burgdorferi*. Deer and field mice are common hosts. The sign of the illness is an expanding, ring-shaped, localized red rash and flu-like symptoms. Neurological abnormalities, heart inflammation, and arthritis may develop weeks or months later, and symptoms resembling Alzheimer's disease and multiple sclerosis may develop years later. A vaccine has recently developed that may prevent *Borella* infection.

Malaria – The parasitic protozoan Plasmodium causes malaria and it is spread by way of the *Anopheles* mosquito. Malaria is characterized by bouts of high fever and chills that occur at regular intervals.

Rocky Mountain spotted fever – This is a disease caused by *Rickettsia rickettsii*, which is transmitted by ticks. The disease is characterized by the sudden onset of a headache, high fever, chills, and a skin rash. Antibiotic therapy is usually effective in treating the disease.

Typhus fever – Epidemic (louse-borne) typhus is caused by *Rickettsia prowazekii*, which is transmitted from person to person by the louse. The rickettsias infect the intestinal tract of the louse and appear in their feces, which may then be transmitted to the bite wound. The rickettsias cause inflammation of the blood vessels, which produces headache, fever, and muscle aches. Mortality rates are very high unless treated with an antibiotic.

Sexually Transmitted Diseases

Chlamydia – *Chlamydia trachomatis* and *C. psittaci* cause chlamydia, which may include infections of the eye, pharynx, respiratory tract, urethra, cervix, and fallopian tubes.

Genital herpes – Genital herpes is caused by the herpes simplex type II virus. It is characterized by fever, burning and sore genitals, and fluid-filled, infectious blisters.

Genital warts – These soft, pink warts are caused by the human papilloma virus. They occur on the external genitalia, in the vagina, on the cervix, or in the rectum.

Gonorrhea – Gonorrhea is a disease of the mucous membranes of the genitourinary tract, eye, rectum, and throat caused by *Neisseria gonorrhoea*. In males, the symptoms of the disease are a yellow, creamy urethral discharge and frequent, painful urination. Females may experience some vaginal discharge which may lead to a serious condition such as pelvic inflammatory disease (PID).

HIV is the virus that is thought to cause most cases of AIDS (Acquired Immunodeficiency Syndrome). This virus destroys T4 cells and eventually impairs almost all types of immune response. HIV may remain latent for many years or it can begin replicating immediately. HIV is transmitted through bodily fluids (blood, semen, vaginal secretions, and breast milk) or across the placenta. Researchers are working to develop a vaccine against HIV.

Syphilis – Syphilis is a sexually transmitted disease caused by the spirochete *Treponema pallidum*. The initial symptom is a small, painless, reddened lesion called a chancre that contains the microorganism. The secondary stage occurs within 2 to 10 weeks following the lesion and is characterized by a skin rash. The tertiary stage develops after many years, in which degenerative lesions (gummas) form in the skin, bone, and nervous system.

Diseases Caused by Worms

Hookworm – Hookworms are tiny, round worms that enter the body by boring into the feet from the soil. They travel through the bloodstream to the lungs, and later the small intestine, causing tissue damage, bleeding, anemia, and lethargy.

Tapeworm – Tapeworms are flattened, segmented worms. The larva of many species of tapeworms may be spread to humans through the ingestion of undercooked meat. The larva may develop into full-sized worms within the intestine, where they attach to the intestinal wall.

Trichinosis – Trichinosis is a disease resulting from infection with the larvae of the worm *Trichinella spiralis*. These larvae may be present in undercooked meat, especially pork. It is characterized by muscle pain, fever, and edema.

Other Diseases

Cancer

Cancer is an uncontrolled growth of cells beginning at any part of the body with a tendency to spread (metastasize). Cancer may be treated by surgery, radiation therapy, and chemotherapy. A *carcinogen* is a cancer-causing agent or substance.

Heart disease

Angina pectoris – is chest pain that is always associated with a lack of oxygen to the heart.

Coronary heart disease (atherosclerosis) – is characterized by deposits of pulpy fat-containing material on the artery walls which often causes thickening or hardening of the arteries and an increase in blood pressure.

Coronary thrombosis – is characterized by an obstructive blood clot (thrombus) a coronary artery, usually associated with atherosclerosis and often leading to myocardial infarction or sudden death.

Hypertension – is high blood pressure, which may be associated with other primary diseases of the circulatory system (atherosclerosis), stress, sedentary lifestyle, and/or diet.

Control of Microbial Growth

Disinfection and Antisepsis: General Terms

There are various ways in which microorganismal growth can be inhibited.

Sterilization – The process of killing (or removing) all microorganisms on an object or in a material (e.g., liquid media).

Disinfection – The process of reducing the numbers of or inhibiting the growth of microorganisms, especially pathogens, to the point where they no longer pose a threat of disease.

Disinfectant – A chemical agent used to destroy microorganisms on inanimate objects such as dishes, tables, floors. Disinfectants are not safe for living tissues.

Antiseptic – A chemical agent that can be administered safely to external body surfaces or mucous membranes to decrease microbial numbers. Antiseptics cannot be taken internally.

-static agents – Those which inhibit growth of microorganisms, but do not kill them. A bacteriostatic agent is one that inhibits bacterial growth.

-cidal agents – Those which kill microorganisms. A bactericide is a chemical agent that kills bacteria. A viricide is an agent that inactivates viruses. A fungicide is an agent that kills fungi. A sporicide is an agent that kills spores (bacterial or fungal).

Germicides – Broad-spectrum cidals, including both antiseptics and disinfectants.

Physical Methods of Disinfection and Antisepsis

There are physical and chemical methods of disinfection and antisepsis. Physical methods include the use of heat (pasteurization is an example of a moist heat method), filtration, and radiation. Chemical methods (also referred to as cold sterilization) utilize chemical agents such as alcohols (ethanol, isopropanol), oxidizing agents (peroxide), and surface-acting agents (i.e., soaps and detergents).

Moist heat methods include boiling, pasteurization, and autoclaving (steaming under pressure).

> **Boiling** is very inexpensive and readily available; usually 100°C for 15 minutes—many vegetative cells and viruses are killed/inactivated within 10 minutes at 100°C.

> **Pasteurization** is primarily used to decrease the number of pathogenic organisms in food without adversely affecting the flavor; usually 72°C for 15 minutes or 63°C for 30 minutes. It is often used to sterilize milk.

> **Autoclaving**, which is steam under pressure, is the most effective moist heat method; usually 121.5°C at 15 psi for 15 minutes.

Dry heat methods of sterilization include direct flaming or incineration and hot-air (160°C–170°C).

Low temperatures can be used to inhibit growth but generally do not kill microbes. Many microorganisms can survive subzero temperatures.

Desiccation through drying or freeze-drying can be used to inhibit growth (via inhibition of enzymes); organisms remain viable.

Osmotic pressure or extremely hypertonic conditions can cause plasmolysis (i.e., contraction of all the cell membrane away from the cell wall).

Filtration is a mechanical means of removing microorganisms. This method can be used for substances that are sensitive to heat.

Radiation effects are dependent on wavelength and on intensity and duration of exposure. Ionizing radiation (including x-rays), ultraviolet radiation, microwaves, and visible light are all examples.

THE SAT SUBJECT TEST IN

Biology E/M

CHAPTER 15

CHAPTER 15

REPRODUCTION AND DEVELOPMENT

REPRODUCTION

There are two types of reproduction: sexual and asexual.

Asexual reproduction – This type of reproduction usually involves only a single parent or single parent cell and no involvement of gametes.

1) **Binary fission** – In this type of asexual reproduction, a parent cell divides to form two new daughter cells the same size as the parent and with the same kind and quantity of DNA. This is common in protozoans, bacteria, and some species of algae, but is rare in animals.

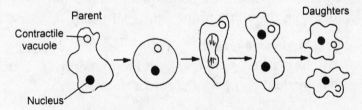

Figure 15.1 Binary fission in the amoeba.

2) **Budding** – Budding is a type of asexual reproduction in which an outgrowth on a yeast cell grows and separates from the parent cell and functions as an individual. It also occurs in the hydra and its relatives.

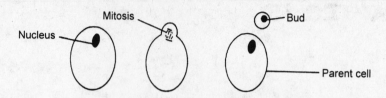

Figure 15.2 Budding in a yeast cell.

3) **Spore formation** – In this process, a cell undergoes a series of cell divisions inside its own cell wall. Each new cell produces a thick wall of its own, and the old cell wall becomes a spore case (sporangium) holding small thick-walled cells, the spores. These are liberated and they grow into new individuals.

4) **Fragmentation** – This type of asexual reproduction is characterized by regeneration of any fragmented structure of a particular plant or animal.

5) **Conjugation** – This is a sexual-like process in some organisms that allows for the exchange of genetic material through a cytoplasmic bridge joining two cells. Conjugation is carried out by spirogyra, bread mold, and paramecium.

Sexual reproduction – This is a type of reproduction in which two parents or parent cells give rise to offspring that have unique combinations of genetic material.

1) **Gonads** – The gonads are structures which produce gametes. A testis is a male gonad, an ovary is a female gonad.

2) **Sperm cells** – The sperm cells are the male gametes. They consist of a head, a middle piece, and a tail piece or flagellum. The flagellum propels the sperm cell.

> **Spermatogenesis** – This process results in sperm cell formation with four immature sperm cells that have a haploid number of chromosomes.

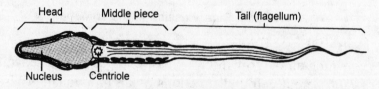

Figure 15.3 A male sperm cell.

3) **Egg cells** – The egg is the female gamete. It is larger than a sperm cell and its cytoplasm contains yolk which provides energy for the zygote divisions and the embryo's growth.

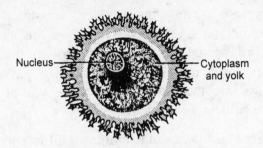

Figure 15.4 An egg cell.

4) **Zygote** – A zygote is a fertilized egg formed by the union of two gametes (sperm and egg).

Parthenogenesis – A type of reproduction in some lower organisms (i.e., aphids, Daphnia) in which females produce offspring from unfertilized eggs.

Fertilization – Sexual reproduction in which two haploid (1N) gametes combine to form one diploid (2N) zygote.

Reproduction in Humans

The male and female reproductive systems produce sex cells. In addition, the female system provides the internal environment for fertilization and for the development of the embryo and fetus.

Male Reproductive System

The male reproductive system consists of the pair of testes, ducts, glands, and external genitalia.

Testis – Each testis, an oval-shaped structure, is suspended in the sac-like scrotum.

The seminiferous tubules are the site of spermatogenesis, sperm cell production.

The interstitial cells produce and secrete the hormone testosterone. This substance promotes the development of the male reproductive organs and secondary male characteristics (e.g., pitch of voice, hair growth on the face).

Ducts – The ducts form a connected series of passageways for the migration of sperm cells when they are ejaculated. This series of ducts forms the male reproductive tract.

The epididymis is a site where sex cells are stored and where they mature. Each vas deferens, along with blood vessels and nerves, is part of a spermatic cord. From each side of the scrotum, this combination of structures passes through the inguinal canal, a passageway leading from the scrotum into the pelvic cavity. The vas deferens conducts ejaculated sperm cells into this cavity.

Glands – Several glands add seminal fluid to sperm cells migrating through the male tract. Semen is the mixture of sperm cells and seminal fluid formed by this addition.

The epididymis is a part of the tract, storing cells from the testis before they enter the vas deferens. It also adds a small percentage of the seminal fluid.

A pair of seminal vesicles add about 60% of the seminal fluid. Each gland secretes fluid into the ampulla of the vas deferens. The single, large prostate gland adds about 30% of the seminal fluid to the prostatic urethra. A pair of Cowper's (bulbourethral) glands adds a small amount of fluid to the urethra as it passes into the posterior part of the penis.

External Genitalia – The scrotum is covered with skin externally. This structure is made up of two sacs separated by a septum. Each sac houses one testis, epididymis, and the beginning of each spermatic cord.

Female Reproductive System

The female reproductive system consists of a pair of ovaries and two uterine tubes, plus the uterus and vagina. The external genitalia are also part of this system.

Ovary – The pair of ovaries stores nearly one-half million immature sex cells. During ovulation one sex cell matures and is released from the ovary into the oviduct. The ovaries also secrete changing levels of two hormones, estrogen and progesterone, during each female reproductive cycle.

Oviduct – On each side of the body, the expanded end of the oviduct (uterine tube, Fallopian tube) curves over the ovary. A sex cell released from the ovary during ovulation enters the oviduct, drawn in by the muscular contractions of this part of female reproductive tract. Normally the cell is fertilized in the oviduct, becoming an embryo of about 200 cells by the time it arrives in the cavity of the uterus.

Uterus – The uterus resembles an inverted triangle. The cervix is the most inferior region, which fits into the vagina. The endometrium is a mucous membrane that lines the cavity of this organ. It is the site where the embryo implants after arriving from the uterine tube. The uterus provides the internal environment for the prenatal development of the embryo and fetus.

Vagina – The vagina is the organ of copulation, a four- to six-inch muscular tube that accepts the penis.

DEVELOPMENT

Viviparous – This is a type of development in which the young are nourished within the body of the female, then are born alive.

Oviparous – This is a type of development in which the young hatch from eggs that are laid outside of the female's body.

Ovoviviparous – This is a type of development in which the young hatch from eggs that are retained within the female's body.

Nonplacental mammals – Some mammals, such as the duckbill platypus, lay eggs but nourish their young with milk from the mother. Marsupials, such as koalas and kangaroos, are mammals that give live birth, but their young develop inside a maternal pouch called a marsupium.

Stages of Embryonic Development

The earliest stage in embryonic development is the one-cell, diploid zygote which results from the fertilization of an ovum by a sperm.

The zygote begins to divide immediately to produce an early embryo by mitosis. The early stages of the embryo are: 2-cell, 4-cell, 8-cell, 16-cell, and 32-cell. This early division pattern is called cleavage, as the cell number increases without any increase in the cytoplasm. The 32-cell stage, for example, is the same size as the zygote.

Several days after fertilization a mulberry-shaped mass, the morula, is formed in the oviduct. The morula develops into a blastocyst, a fluid-filled hollow ball of cells. This blastocyst will enter the uterus and implant on the endometrium at about 8 to 10 days after fertilization.

The early embryo changes from a hollow ball of cells through two processes: morphogenesis and cell differentiation. Morphogenesis is the movement of cells to establish a human outline. Cell differentiation means that cells specialize into different kinds. All cells descending from the zygote have a full complement of chromosomes and genes through mitosis. Depending on which genes are expressed in a group of cells, they specialize to become nerve cells, muscle cells, etc.

Morphogenesis and cell differentiation establish three primary germ layers in the embryo, called the gastrula, by about two weeks after fertilization: the ectoderm, mesoderm, and endoderm. A continuation of these two processes in these germ layers form all future tissues and organs.

Early forms of all major structures are laid down in the gastrula period.

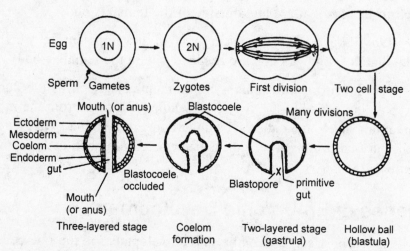

Figure 15.5 Early embryonic development in animals.

Gestation, the period of pregnancy, normally takes place over about nine months. Development before birth (prenatal development) begins with fertilization, the union of the sperm cell and female sex cell. Fertilization produces the zygote, or fertilized egg, in the oviduct. A series of events unfolds producing the embryo (first two months) and fetus (last seven months).

Table 15.6 Derivatives of the Primary Germ Layers

Primary Germ Layer	Derivatives
Endoderm	Inner lining of alimentary canal and respiratory tract; inner lining of liver; pancreas; salivary, thyroid, parathyroid, thymus glands; urinary bladder; urethra lining
Mesoderm	Skeletal system; muscular system; reproductive system; excretory system; circulatory system; dermis of skin; connective tissue
Ectoderm	Epidermis; sweat glands; hair; nails; skin; nervous system; parts of eye, ear, and skin receptors; pituitary and adrenal glands; enamel of teeth

Cleavage and Gastrulation

Cleavage and Gastrulation of a Mammalian Egg

During morula formation, the zygote subdivides into an inner cell mass (from which the embryo develops), and an enveloping layer of cells, called the trophoblast. The cells of the inner cell mass differentiate further into a thin layer of flat cells, called the hypoblast. The remaining cells of the inner cell mass become the epiblast.

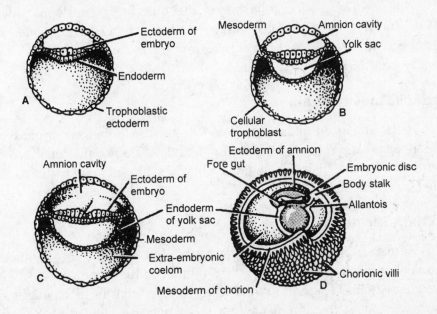

Figure 15.7 Diagrams of human embryos ten (A) to twenty (D) days old showing the formation of the amniotic and yolk sac cavities and the origin of the embryonic disc.

Development of the Embryo

Upon fertilization, the zygote, dividing rapidly, moves down the oviduct. It enters the uterus as an early embryo. Differentiation of the embryo body begins. Tissues from the embryo and the endometrium of the uterus combine to form the placenta, a disk-shaped organ that supplies the developing embryo with blood and nutrients and removes waste products through the umbilical cord that connects the embryo to the placenta. When the major organs and body structures are in place (by the end of the eighth week) the embryo is called a fetus.

Embryonic Membranes

The amnion – The amnion is filled with a lymph-like fluid, the amniotic fluid, that bathes and protects the embryo in a watery environment. It surrounds the embryo.

The yolk sac – Many blood vessels develop in the walls of the yolk sac, so that food material is transported from the yolk to the cell of the developing embryo. It grows around the yolk in the egg.

The allantois – The allantois is a sac-like structure that covers both the embryo and the yolk sac. The capillaries of the allantois exchange carbon dioxide and oxygen with the atmosphere.

The chorion – The chorion is the outermost embryonic membrane, forming a moist lining underneath the other membranes. The chorion helps in the exchange of respiratory gases between the shell and the capillaries of the allantois.

Artificial insemination

Artificial insemination, or *in vitro* fertilization, is a process by which eggs are removed from the female's body and fertilized by sperm in a petri dish. Then the embryo is placed in the uterus and allowed to implant.

Multiple births

Humans generally have single births, but multiple births do happen. Two offspring born to the same mother in the same pregnancy are known as twins. Fraternal twins (dizygotic twins) are not genetically the same; they develop from two eggs that were fertilized by two separate sperm, and are nourished by two separate placentas. Identical twins (monozygotic twins) are genetically identical because they develop from one fertilized egg that split in the early stages of development. Though genetically identical, identical twins may show slight differences in appearance or intelligence due to the influence of different environmental factors.

Reproduction and Development in Other Organisms

Cleavage and Gastrulation

Starfish – Cleavage is radial in the isolecithal starfish egg. The egg is split into two equal daughter cells. The second cleavage plane is vertical but at right angles to the first, separating the two cells into four. With further divisions, a blastula forms. It is a simple layered blastula which is later converted into a double-layered sphere, the gastrula, by the invagination of a section of a wall of the blastula.

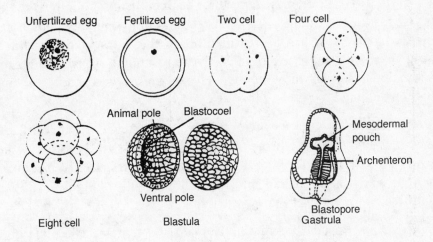

Figure 15.8 Some development stages in the sea star (starfish).

Amphibians – The cleavage pattern in amphibians is radial but because of the unequal distribution of yolk in the telolecithal egg, the blastomeres are not of equal size. At the eight-celled stage, the egg consists of four smaller animal pole blastomeres (micromeres) and four larger, yolk-laden vegetal pole blastomeres (macromeres). The egg then becomes a gastrula. To form a gastrula, a groove appears on one side of the blastula and cells at the bottom of the groove stream into the interior of the embryo. This groove extends transversely until it is ring-shaped, at which point, the yolk-filled cells remain as a yolk plug.

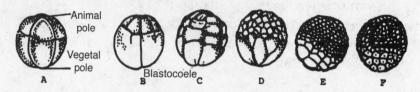

Figure 15.9 Early embryology in a frog.

Birds – Telolecithal avian eggs display meroblastic radial cleavage. Cleavage occurs in a small disc of cytoplasm in the animal pole. Horizontal cleavage separate upper blastomeres and lower blastomeres. The blastomeres at the margin of the disc, and the lower cells in contact with the yolk, lose the furrows that partially separated them and fuse into the periblast. The free blastomeres become incorporated into two layers, an upper epiblast, and a lower hypoblast. Between them is a blastocoele. The subgerminal space separates the hypoblast from the underlying yolk. Gastrula is formed by cell migration.

Hydra – Hydra may reproduce asexually by budding, but may also reproduce sexually. An ovary containing one egg and a testis containing many sperm are formed along the sides of the hydra. Because they have both sex organs, they are known as hermaphrodites. Sperm are released into the water, one unites with the egg, and a zygote is created.

Earthworm – An earthworm is a hermaphrodite, but fertilization takes place when two worms transfer sperm cells to the other's sperm receptacle. A mucous ring around each worm's body becomes a cocoon, which is deposited into the soil and within which fertilization and the development of the zygote occurs.

Insects – Insects are distinctly male and female. The male deposits sperm into the sperm receptacle of the female where the sperm are stored. When the female produces eggs, the eggs pass over the receptacle while they are being laid and are fertilized. In complete metamorphosis an insect goes through the egg, larva, pupa, and adult stages. In incomplete metamorphosis the egg becomes a nymph (larval stage) and then an adult.

Fish – Most fishes use external fertilization in which the female lays the eggs in the water and the male deposits sperm-containing fluid (milt) over the eggs, resulting in fertilization without the two parents making physical contact. Pheromones released into the water by individuals may help to ensure that the release of eggs and sperm are properly timed. After fertilization, the zygotes develop into small fish (fry) that are nourished by an attached yolk sac. By external fertilization, they develop outside the female's body. In some fish, fertilization occurs in an oviduct within the female's body and therefore develops within the female's body.

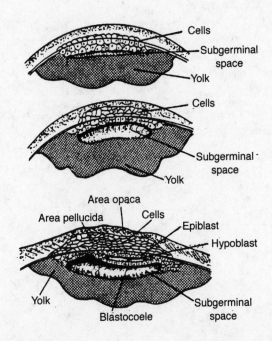

Figure 15.10 Successive stages on the cleavage of a hen's egg.

THE SAT SUBJECT TEST IN

Biology E/M

CHAPTER 16

CHAPTER 16

EVOLUTION

THE ORIGIN OF LIFE

Soon after the earth's formation, when conditions were quite different from those existing today, a period of spontaneous chemical synthesis began in the warm ancient seas. During this era, amino acids, sugars, and nucleotide bases—the structural subunits of some of life's macromolecules—formed spontaneously from the hydrogen-rich molecules of ammonia, methane, and water. Such spontaneous synthesis was only possible because there was little oxygen in the atmosphere. The energy for synthesis came in the form of lightning, ultraviolet light, and higher energy radiations. These molecules polymerized due to their high concentrations, and eventually the first primitive signs of life arose. Life as we know it is thought to have evolved from the interaction of these molecules into organized forms capable of carrying out metabolism and self-replication, and maintaining an internal environment different from their surroundings.

Evidence for Evolution

The evidence for evolution can be explained by these eight facts:

1) **Comparative Anatomy** – Similarities of organs in related organisms show the common ancestry.

2) **Vestigial Structures** – Structures of no apparent use to the organism, they may be explained by descent from forms that used these structures.

3) **Comparative Embryology** – The embryo goes through developmental stages in common with other types of species.

4) **Comparative Physiology** – Many different organisms have similar enzymes. Mammals have similar hormones.

5) **Taxonomy** – All organisms can be classified into seven taxons, from broadest to most specific: kingdom, phylum, class, order, family, genus, and species. This commonness in classification seems to indicate relationships between organisms.

6) **Biogeography** – Natural barriers, such as oceans, deserts, and mountains, which restrict the spread of species to other favorable environments. Isolation frequently produces many variations of species.

7) **Genetics** – Gene mutations, chromosome segment rearrangements, and chromosome segment doubling produce variations and new species.

8) **Paleontology** – Present individual species can be traced back to origins through skeletal fossils.

   Evidence from a "living fossil" – The coelacanth is a fish found in the Indian Ocean that is thought to be an intermediate life form between amphibians and fish.

Historical Development of the Theory of Evolution

In 1809 Jean de Lamarck proposed that from generation to generation, acquired characteristics are inherited. Lamarck believed that new organs arise in response to demands of the environment, and that the organs' size is proportional to their "use or disuse." These changes in size were believed to be inherited by succeeding generations. This theory has been rejected because of an overwhelming amount of evidence which indicates that acquired traits cannot be inherited.

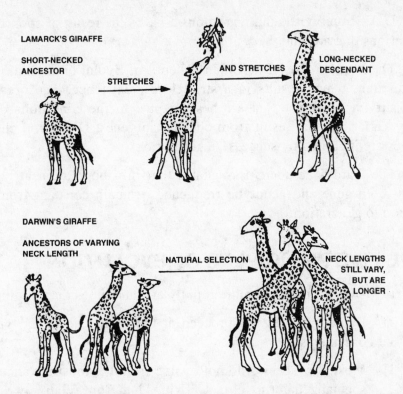

LAMARCK'S GIRAFFE

SHORT-NECKED ANCESTOR

STRETCHES

AND STRETCHES

LONG-NECKED DESCENDANT

DARWIN'S GIRAFFE

ANCESTORS OF VARYING NECK LENGTH

NATURAL SELECTION

NECK LENGTHS STILL VARY, BUT ARE LONGER

Figure 16.1 Rival explanations of evolution were advanced by Lamarck and Darwin. According to Lamarck, the long neck of the giraffe arose as a result of generations of stretching to reach food. According to Darwin, giraffes with longer necks arose as a result of natural selection.

The Darwin-Wallace theory of natural selection states that a significant part of evolution is dictated by natural forces, which select for survival those organisms that can respond best to certain conditions. Since more organisms are born than can be accommodated by the environment, a limited number are chosen to live and reproduce. Variation is characteristic of all animals and plants, and it is this variety which provides the means for this choice. Those individuals chosen for survival will be the ones with the most and best adaptive traits. These include the ability to compete successfully for food, water, shelter, and other essential elements; the ability to reproduce and perpetuate the species; and the ability to resist adverse natural forces, which are the agents of selection. Therefore, according to Darwin, organisms that are more likely to survive and reproduce direct the evolution of a population.

DeVries proposed that variations arise as the result of spontaneous mutations that are inherited.

The Modern (Neo-Darwinian) Theory of Evolution includes over-production, which results in a struggle for existence. The organisms that survive are those that are best adapted to the conditions of life. Only variations that result from changes in genes, DNA, and chromosomes are inherited by successive generations.

The Hardy-Weinberg Law states that in a population at equilibrium, both gene and genotype frequencies remain constant from generation to generation.

THE FIVE PRINCIPLES OF EVOLUTION

1) Evolution occurs more rapidly at some times than at others.

2) Evolution does not proceed at the same rate in all types of organisms.

3) Most new species do not evolve from the most advanced and specialized forms already living, but from relatively simple, unspecialized forms.

4) Evolution is not always from the simple to the complex, but may act in such a way that complex forms have given rise to simpler ones. This is termed as "regressive evolution."

5) Evolution occurs in populations (not in individuals) in a gradual process over very long periods of time.

adaptive radiation
divergent evolution

convergent evolution

Figure 16.2 Diagram illustrating the difference between divergent and convergent evolution.

Definitions:

1) **Adaptive radiation** – A single ancestral species evolves to a variety of forms that occupy somewhat different habitats.

2) **Convergent evolution** – Two or more unrelated groups of organisms become adapted to a similar environment and develop characteristics that are more or less similar.

MECHANISMS OF EVOLUTION

Evolution is the result of the interaction of four major forces. These are mutation, genetic drift, migration, and natural selection.

Mutations are random events that occur at a very low rate of approximately one out of every 1,000,000 genes. Mutation introduces variety into a population.

Genetic drift refers to the absence of natural selection. Random changes in gene frequencies occur, including the random loss of alleles. This often occurs in small populations. Random changes in the gene pool can be produced by catastrophic events in which there are few survivors. Following such events, allele frequencies in the population may become quite different through chance alone. Such events are sometimes called population bottlenecks. A bottleneck effect can be created where a few people colonize a new territory, the founder effect.

Migration occurs when individuals from one breeding population leave to join another. Migration may lead to either more variation in a population due to the introduction of new genes, or less variation due to the loss of genes through emigration.

Natural selection assures that the changes in allele frequency caused by migration, mutation, and genetic drift are adaptive. Natural selection operates through differential reproduction, which occurs when certain individuals are able, by surviving and/or reproducing at a higher rate, to preferentially propagate and transmit their respective genes over those of other individuals.

The variation that leads to evolution is now understood at the genetic level. Variation is caused by gene and chromosome mutations, as well as recombinations (reshuffling) of genes.

Mechanisms of Speciation

The following three mechanisms are fundamental in speciation:

A) Allopatric speciation is the formation of new species through the geographic isolation of groups from the parent population (as occurs through colonization or geological disruption).

B) Sympatric speciation occurs within a population and without geographical isolation. It is rare in animals, but not in plants.

C) Adaptive radiation is the formation of a new species arising from a common ancestor, resulting from their adaptation to different environments.

Evolutionary Patterns

Gradualism is the belief that evolution occurs very gradually, or in such small increments as to be nearly unobservable. In contrast, punctuated equilibrium describes evolutionary change occurring in relatively sudden spurts, following long periods of minor change or no change.

HOW LIVING THINGS HAVE CHANGED

The Record of Prehistoric Life

Paleobiologists are scientists that study the life of the past. Paleontologists study fossils, which are any preserved remnants or impressions of organisms that lived in the past. By studying fossils, scientists may reconstruct evolutionary history. Fossils are found in sedimentary rock, or rock that is formed from sand and mud that has been compressed over many years (i.e., sandstone, shale). Fossils may be formed when minerals dissolved in groundwater seep into the tissues of a dead organism and turn it to stone (petrification); when imprints are preserved in soil that is eventually changed into sedimentary rock; or when casts or molds are created by the eventual decay of an organism buried in mud, by freezing, or by an organism being trapped in tar pits or amber.

The relative dating of fossils is carried out by studying the relative position of the fossil within layers of sedimentary rock, while the absolute dating of fossils (the age is given in years, but is not errorless) is determined by radioactive dating in which the half-lives of radioactive isotopes within a fossil are used to date the specimen.

Geological Eras

The history of the earth, as determined by geologists, is divided into six geological eras. These eras, from oldest to most recent, are as follows:

1) the azoic era (no life forms; lasting for over 600 million years);

2) the archaezoic era (simple life forms; lasting for over 600 million years);

3) the proterozoic era (simple plants and bacteria; lasting about 600 million years);

4) the paleozoic era (many lifeforms including trees, fishes, amphibians, reptiles, and insects; lasting 400 million years);

5) the mesozoic era (dinosaurs, reptiles, birds, modern trees, flowering plants; lasting about 125 million years); and

6) the cenozoic era (modern plants, mammals, humans; from 60 million years ago to present).

Human Evolution

Early humans – Evidence of the first hominid (human-like primate) was found in the fossils of *Australopithecus africanus* (Southern Man of Africa). *Australopithecus* lived approximately three million years ago, walked fully upright, and had human-like hands and teeth, though its brain was only about one-third of the size of a modern human's. *Homo habilis* lived approximately two million years ago, had an enlarged brain compared to *Australopithecus*, and had the ability to use simple tools. This species led to the evolution of *Homo erectus*, which was the first hominid to leave the tropics and inhabit colder climates. It likely displayed intelligence and social cooperation and was the ancestor to *Homo sapiens sapiens*, our species.

Characteristics of *Homo sapiens* include full upright posture and ability to walk erect, an opposable thumb, the capacity for speech and communication, and a well-developed brain. Neanderthals (*Homo sapiens neanderthalensis*) were thought to be the earliest *Homo sapiens*, but DNA testing has demonstrated that they were a different species from modern humans. They lived approximately 150,000 years ago to about 25,000 years ago and had heavier brow ridges and less pronounced chins than modern humans.

Cro-Magnon man lived about 50,000 years ago and was probably the hominid ancestor of modern man, with a high forehead and a well-developed chin. Cro-Magnon was also somewhat taller than modern man and had a slightly larger brain capacity (1,500 cubic centimeters). Most scientists agree that humans are not direct descendants of apes, but because of their similarities they are likely derived from the same common ancestor that is thought to have lived approximately 10 million years ago.

THE SAT SUBJECT TEST IN
Biology E/M

CHAPTER 17

CHAPTER 17

BEHAVIOR

BEHAVIOR OF ANIMALS

Learned Behavior

Conditioning, habits, and imprinting are all specific types of behavior that are learned and acquired as the result of individual experiences.

Conditioning – Conditioned behavior is a response caused by a stimulus, different from that which originally triggered the response. Experiments conducted by Pavlov on dogs demonstrate the conditioning of behavior.

ringing of bell (stimulus 1) → barking (response 1)

food + ringing of bell (stimulus 2) → saliva flow (response 2)

ringing of bell (stimulus 1) → saliva flow (response 2)

Conditional behavior of Pavlov's dogs.

Habits – Habit behavior is learned behavior that becomes automatic and involuntary as a consequence of repetition. The behavior soon becomes automatic.

In addition to repetition, a habit is formed because there is a desire to learn the habit and satisfaction resulting from the habit. In order to break a habit it is necessary to have the desire to break it, and to concentrate on not performing the habit.

Imprinting – Imprinting involves the establishment of a fixed pathway in the nervous system by the stimulus of the very first object that is seen, heard, or smelled by the particular organism. The research of Konrad Lorenz using newly hatched geese demonstrated this type of learning.

Innate Behavior

Taxis, reflexes, and instincts are all specific types of behavior that are inborn and involuntary.

Taxis – Taxis is the response to a stimulus by automatically moving either toward or away from the stimulus.

1) **Phototaxis** – Photosynthetic microorganisms move toward light of moderate intensity. This is known as a positive phototaxis. Moving away from the light is a negative phototaxis.

2) **Chemotaxis** – Organisms move in response to some chemical.

Figure 17.1 *E. coli* **bacteria congregate near a specific chemical.**

Reflex – A reflex is an automatic response to a stimulus in which only a part of the body is involved; it is the simplest inborn response.

The knee jerk is a stretch reflex that is a response to a tap on the tendon below the knee cap which stretches the attached muscle. This tapping activates stretch receptors. Stretching a spindle fiber triggers nerve impulses.

Instinct – An instinct is a complex behavior pattern which is unlearned and automatic and is often beneficial in adapting the individual to its environment.

1) Instinct of self-preservation – This is characterized by the "fight or flight" behavior of animals.

2) Instinct of species-preservation – This is characterized by the instinctive behavior of the animal not to escape or fight, but to find a safer area for habitation.

3) Releasers – The releasers are signals which possess the ability to trigger instinctive acts.

The nest-making of birds and web-spinning by spiders are examples of instinctive behavior.

Circadian Rhythm and the Biological Clock – Numerous organisms exhibit circadian rhythms in which certain physiological functions cycle approximately every 24 hours. A biological clock controls the cycle of a circadian rhythm by matching it with an exogenous, environmental cue, thus enabling the behavior to be properly timed with the real world. Light is probably the most common exogenous cue.

Voluntary Behavior

Voluntary behavior includes activities under direct control of the will, such as learning and memory.

Learning – Intelligence measures the ability to learn and properly establish new patterns of behavior. Humans demonstrate the highest degree of intelligence among all animals. This is due, in part, to the highly developed cerebrum which contains a great quantity of nerve pathways and neurons.

Human Intelligence – Intelligence is the capacity to learn and solve problems. Tests of human intelligence have been developed by psychologists, such as those used to determine the intelligence quotient of a person (obtained by dividing the score on the mental age tests by the score on the chronological age tests and multiplying by 100). These tests measure verbal, mathematical, spatial, and reasoning ability, and memory and speed of recognition. However, these tests do not measure other forms of intelligence, such as artistic, musical, and athletic abilities.

Trial-and-Error Learning – Many animals do not have the ability to size up a problem in order to solve it correctly the first time it is encountered (lack of insight). Thus, they must try different ways of solving the problem and will generally come to learn the correct way from their successes and failures (trial-and-error learning).

Memory – All learning is dependent upon one's memory. Memory is essential for all previous learning to be retained and used.

Memory is the ability to store past experiences and recall them at will. Short-term memory occurs before the image is stored within the brain and corresponds with immediate perception. Long-term memory allows objects or ideas to be recalled some time later.

PLANT BEHAVIOR

Hydrotropism – The growth of a plant's roots toward water.

Other plant responses – Some plants have the ability to respond to touch stimuli. This is especially true of the carnivorous plants, such as the Venus flytrap, sundew, and bladderwort, which have specialized movements to trap insects upon appropriate stimulus.

Plants also exhibit phototaxic behavior.

BEHAVIOR OF PROTOZOA

Amoeba – The structurally simple amoeba may respond to such stimuli as light, chemicals, and food. It shows irritability and moves away from irritants such as bright light or chemicals and moves toward food.

Paramecium – Paramecia exhibit taxis, in which they move in response to a stimulus.

Euglena – The light-sensitive eyespot of the euglena allows it to move toward light, where it can use the light source for photosynthesis.

BEHAVIOR OF OTHER ORGANISMS

Touch and light are common stimuli that produce an automatic behavior in many organisms. These organisms may be either simple or complex.

Taxis – The usually automatic movement of an organism to or away from a stimulus.

Rheotaxis – The movement of fish to automatically align themselves in an upstream direction.

Kinesis – The change in activity rate in response to a stimulus.

DRUGS AND HUMAN BEHAVIOR

External factors can affect behavior. One such factor is drugs. Today, young adults between the ages of 18-25 years are more likely than those of any other age group to use illegal drugs. The following are common drugs of abuse:

Alcohol – Alcohol is a depressant of the central nervous system. There is a greater loss of body heat due to an increased flow of blood through the blood vessels. As a consequence of this, the person appears flushed. If pregnant women drink alcohol they may bear children with *fetal alcohol syndrome,* or FAS. These children have reduced height and weight, mental retardation, and facial abnormalities.

> **Alcoholism** – Studies have found that men abuse alcohol more than women abuse it. Due to gender differences attributed to alcohol metabolism, women incur more serious health effects than men at lower alcohol consumptions. The adverse effects associated with alcohol use include liver dysfunction, Korsakoff's and Wernike's syndrome, and hallucinations.

Tobacco – Tobacco smoke contains carbon dioxide, nicotine, tars, and other substances that irritate the lungs. The primary cause of death related to cigarette smoking is heart attack. Cigarette smoking also causes lung cancer, as well as cancer of the lip, oral cavity, larynx, and esophagus. Passive smoking (or second-hand smoking) has been documented as having a lasting effect on one's health.

Barbiturates – Barbiturates are synthetic chemicals that depress the respiratory system. They are used as sedatives, tranquilizers, anesthetics, and sleeping pills.

Amphetamines – These are known as stimulant drugs because they cause euphoria, increase performance, reduce fatigue, and elevate the pain threshold. They may be prescribed to treat mild depression, attention deficit disorder, and narcolepsy.

Cocaine – Cocaine is a drug that blocks the reuptake of certain neurotransmitters at the synapse. It causes an intense euphoria for about an hour or so which is followed by severe depression.

Marijuana – Marijuana causes sleepiness, euphoria and relaxation, alteration of time perception, increasing appetite, and impairment of memory. At high doses an individual may experience hallucination, paranoia, anxiety, and delusions. Adverse effects include a decrease in motivation.

Heroin – Heroin is an opioid that causes euphoria and sedation, and depresses the respiratory system.

Morphine – Morphine is a major analgesic drug, which means it relieves pain without the individual losing consciousness. Morphine enhances the threshold of pain; thus the individual is aware of the presence of pain but the pain sensation in not unpleasant. It also suppresses the cough reflex.

Codeine – Codeine is a much less potent analgesic drug than morphine. The pain-relieving effects of codeine are similar to those of aspirin.

Hallucinogenic drugs – These include LSD and PCP. The name is attributed to the fact that these drugs alter perception and emotional states.

THE SAT SUBJECT TEST IN

Biology E/M

CHAPTER 18

CHAPTER 18

PATTERNS OF ECOLOGY

ECOLOGY

Ecology is the study of organisms and their relationships to each other and to their environment.

There is a diverse array of ecological topics and methodologies; thus there are numerous approaches to summarizing ecological subjects. For instance, some ecologists are interested in particular organisms or habitats and spend hours in the field observing and analyzing them. Others may work only in labs testing different hypotheses. Still others may work almost exclusively developing and testing mathematical models. One common approach is to divide ecology into a hierarchical set of subjects: populations, communities, and ecosystems.

POPULATIONS

A population is all of the individuals of a particular species within a defined area. It is always only one species, but the area may be large or small. For instance, population may be the fleas on a dog, the Poison Arrow frogs in Costa Rica, or the humans in North America.

Population ecologists attempt to explain the distribution of species, why the numbers of individuals of the species fluctuate over time and space, and what factors control the numbers. In doing so, population ecologists study three main characteristics of populations: life histories, population structure, and population dynamics.

Life History Characteristics

The life history characteristics of a species are the life events of the individuals from birth to death.

Reproduction

The first life history trait is reproduction which is an obvious requirement for population growth. The contribution of an organism to future generations is referred to as the fitness of the organism. The fitness depends on the age at sexual maturity (maturity), the number of offspring produced each mating (parity), and the number of reproductive events (fecundity). Trade-offs, whereby a species produces either a large number of eggs, usually with low survivorship, or a smaller number of eggs with a higher probability of survival is observed in many species.

Growth and Associated Development

Growth is the increase in size of the individual. Development includes both the changes in form and the attainment of sexual maturity. Growth and development is an important life history characteristic of all organisms, and information on growth and the life forms of a species is critical in studying the population of that species. The life stages vary among species, as do the requirements for each stage. Many insects have egg and larval stages but the adults do not eat, surviving only long enough to lay eggs. Finding a suitable location for the eggs is thus critical for the adult. Some sharks do not reach sexual maturity until 10 to 15 years and produce few but well-developed young. Growth and development require significant food input and are long processes. Death of one female can thus have a significant long-term effect on the population.

Dispersal

Dispersal is the movement away from the breeding site. Dispersal reduces inbreeding. All species disperse to a greater or lesser extent. Some species depend only on the movement of air or water for dispersal. Others, such as the seeds of maple trees, have wings to enhance movement.

Population Structure

Many countries conduct a census on a regular basis. On the day of the census, every household must complete a form giving the address, number, sex, and age of all residents of the household. This information is used to determine and provide information on the density, the spacing and age distribution, and the characteristics that define the structure of a population.

Density

Density is determined by counting the inhabitants in a given area. However, counting the number of individuals in a population is not always possible. For instance, it is impossible to count the number of oak trees in a forest or the number of sunfish in a lake. In these cases the density is estimated using one of two main procedures.

The number of sunfish in the lake can be estimated by mark-recapture studies. In its simplest form, the procedure is to collect, mark, and release a sample of the species, and after a short period of time to obtain a second sample. The ratio of the number of marked species in the second sample to the total number of marked species is an *estimate* of the ratio of the number of species in the sample to the number of species in the population. The second general approach to estimating the population density is to divide a sample area into some form of sub-samples, and the information from the sub-sample is extrapolated to the whole population.

Sometimes the density is given as a relative measure. For example, the Christmas Bird count is an example of a relative measure. Each year, on a day close to Christmas, bird watchers record the number of each species of bird they see. Because the number of observers, the locations, and even the weather vary, this is not a precise method but it may suggest long-term increases or decreases.

Spacing

Spacing is determined by factors such as dispersal distance, competition for resources, and ability to defend an area. For example, people in Canada live primarily in large metropolitan areas; these areas are most abundant along waterways and are concentrated in the southern part of the country. Initially, travel was by water and towns built up along watercourses. Also, largely due to climate, the south is more heavily populated than the north. Thus, the spacing of the human population in Canada is clumped. Other types of spacing are random and even. The extreme of even spacing is a pine plantation or an apple orchard.

Age Distribution

Plots of age distribution can show the potential for growth of future populations and the effect of past events on certain age groups. The age distribution of the population of British Columbia, Canada, in 1989 is given in figure 18.1. Three points warrant mention. First, the large number of people that were 25 to 45 years old in 1989 are the baby boomers, the babies born in the prosperous years after the Second World War. A bulge representing the baby boomers is typical of the North American population. Second, the relatively high number of people over 65 years of age is due, in large part, to movement of people to this province to retire. Third, this is a stable or aging population. In a rapidly growing population the age distribution would decrease with age and there would be a very high number of young people.

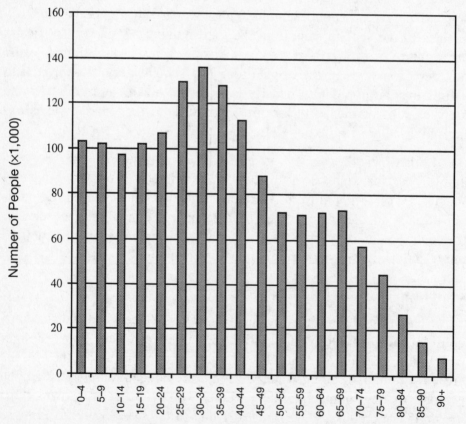

Figure 18.1 Age distribution of the people in British Columbia, Canada, in 1989. From: Province of British Columbia, 1990.

Population Dynamics

Population dynamics is the study of how and why the numbers of individuals in a population change. The size of the change depends on the initial size and the number of births, deaths, immigrants, and emigrants. Births and immigrations increase the population, and deaths and emigrations decrease the population. If the number of births and the number of immigrants is less than the number of deaths and the number of emigrants, then the population decreases.

There are two types of factors that affect the change in the size of populations. These are called density-dependent and density-independent factors. Density-dependent factors are those whose effect increases as the density increases. They include resources such as food, shelter, water, space, and events such as diseases. Density-independent factors are those whose effect is not dependent on the density of the population. Some density-independent factors are fires, hurricanes, droughts, floods, and severe cold. However, density-dependent and density-independent factors are not always mutually exclusive. For instance, severe weather (a density-independent factor) can affect available food or space (density-dependent factors).

A continual decrease in a population can result in the extinction of a population. This may result from either a decrease in the birthrate or an increase in the death rate. Both the birth and the death rates are affected by natural and imposed (e.g., decreased space, harvesting) conditions.

COMMUNITIES

Components of Communities

In general, communities are defined and studied in two different ways: by their components and by their interactions. The former is explicit; the community is named after the dominant organisms, frequently a plant (e.g., prairie grassland community, red cedar forest community), and is described with respect to the number of different species present, called the biological diversity (biodiversity). Information on biodiversity is usually calculated as the species diversity index. This index, once calculated, is a measure of both the species' richness (number of species) and the species' evenness (relative abundance of each species).

In the past few years, biodiversity has been frequently mentioned in the news, usually with respect to its decrease in populated areas, the anticipated and realized extinction of species, the loss of species that may have been valuable in medicine, and its importance to the maintenance of a healthy environment. Although biodiversity is a measure of the components of a community, an understanding of the long-term consequences of a change in the components is crucial to the survival of the world in general.

Biodiversity depends on factors such as climate and latitude, and the size and complexity of the community. In addition, in a given area it is modified by disturbances. The change in biodiversity of a community after a disturbance is called ecological succession.

Traditionally, succession is referred to as primary or secondary. Primary succession is the change in a community following a disturbance that virtually eliminates the existing life (e.g., on the volcanic ash of Mount St. Helens). Secondary succession refers to changes following less dramatic disturbances (e.g., fires, floods, and hurricanes) that leave the soil intact. In both primary and secondary succession, there is a gradual re-colonization of the area. The first species present, the pioneer species, are different from the dominant ones present before the disturbance. The species that colonize the area depend on the composition of the surrounding communities, the ability of a species to invade a disturbed area, and the response of the species to change during succession. The ultimate association of species is called the climax community.

Interactions within Communities

The second approach to studying communities is based on the definition of a community as the assemblage of populations that live and interact, directly or indirectly, in a given area. When two species interact, there are three possible outcomes for each species: it may benefit (positive effect), be harmed (negative effect), or be unaffected (zero or neutral effect). Interactions may be between two animals, between two plants, or between animals and plants.

Competition

Competition harms both species. When it occurs between individuals of different species it is called interspecific competition and when it occurs between individuals of the same species it is called intraspecific competition. Intraspecific competition is an important consequence of the effects of density-dependent factors on population growth; it acts to reduce the rate of population growth. Interspecific competition can have two different outcomes: the eventual elimination of one species, called competitive exclusion, or the sharing of the resources by the two species, called resource partitioning.

Predator-Prey vs. Parasite-Host Relationships

Predators feed on prey and the predator/prey interaction benefits the predator but harms the prey. Parasites are predators that feed on their hosts; the parasite benefits and the host is harmed. Parasites do not usually kill their hosts. However, parasitoids are a specific kind of parasite that do kill their hosts. For instance, larvae of some wasps and flies consume the eggs, larvae, and pupae of other insects. Predators include herbivores, carnivores, omnivores, and filter feeders. Filter feeders consume plankton or small (microscopic) plants and animals in water. A predator can also be prey.

Commensalism

Commensalism is an interaction in which one species benefits but no harm comes to the second species. An example of commensalism is the sitting of egrets on the backs of grazing cattle. The cattle's movement flushes insects from the vegetation and the egret, with its vantage point on the cattle's back, readily obtains the food. There is no effect on the cattle, but the cattle helps the egret obtain the food.

Amensalism

Amensalism is an interaction that is not consistently included in the summary of the interactions between species in a community. Although one species is harmed, there is no direct benefit (from the harm) to the first species. In a forest, dead branches on a tree fall to the forest floor and damage small plants or animals there. The tree that loses the branch may benefit from the loss because it no longer has to support the branch and because other living branches are exposed to more sunlight. However, the tree does not benefit from the damage to the small plant or animal.

Mutualism

The interaction in which both species benefit is called mutualism. Mutualism occurs between many different kinds of organisms. Many flowering plants produce excess nectar, a sugar solution within the flower. Bees, moths, butterflies, birds, bats, and even some small rodents eat the nectar. The nectar is within the flower, and thus they must touch the stamens containing the pollen to obtain the nectar. These organisms, referred to as *pollinators,* then move to other flowers while carrying the pollen. The flowers benefit because the pollen is passed among the flowers, resulting in cross-pollination or mixing of the genetic material; the pollinators benefit because they obtain the high-energy sugar solution.

Lichens consist of two organisms, a modified fungi and an algae. The algae lives on the fungi hyphae and receives water and nutrients from the fungi. The algae provides sugars, produced by photosynthesis, to the fungi. This close and usually obligatory mutualistic relationship is called symbiosis.

Consequences of Interactions

There are four main types of consequences resulting from the interactions within a community. They are 1) the realized (actual) vs. the fundamental niche, 2) coevolution of species, 3) adaptation and thus evolutionary change in one of the species, and 4) community structure and the role of keystone species.

Realized (Actual) Niche vs. the Fundamental Niche

The niche is the sum of all resources used by an organism in the environment. The *fundamental niche* is a species interaction with these resources under ideal conditions. Often, not all of these resources are utilized. The *realized niche* is the interactions that actually occur.

Coevolution of Species

Organisms interact, and a new genetically determined trait that improves an organism's situation in the interaction is an adaptation. Because two species are involved in the interaction, an adaptation in one will act as a new selective pressure on the second. The result is like a see-saw, with each adaptation in one effecting a change in the second. This reciprocal selection and the resulting adaptations is called coevolution. Coevolution can occur in predator-prey, parasite-host, and mutualistic interactions. General coevolution results when several species interact with several other species and the adaptations within each of the groups are similar. For example, in a mutualistic interaction, flowers that attract bees are brightly colored, usually blue and yellow but not red because bees cannot see red. In addition, the flowers are fragrant to attract the bees, have a landing platform positioned so that the stamen and pistil contact the bee's body, and have a narrow floral tube. The mouth parts of the bee are fused into a long tube that contains a tongue, an adapter for sucking the nectar. This tube fits into the flower's floral tube. Insects cannot fit into the floral tube. Several different flowers attract bees. In general, these flowers mature at different times of the year. Therefore, the bees have a continuous food supply, and there is reduced opportunity for bees to deliver pollen from one species to another.

Adaptation and Evolutionary Change

Both plant and animal prey evolve in response to their predators. One form of adaptation is mimicry, in which a prey resembles an unpalatable or poisonous organism that may also be a prey item. Some nonpoisonous snakes mimic the poisonous coral snake. Plants are prey to herbivores and some plants have developed spines or tough surfaces as physical defenses. Plants also have chemical defenses which may be unpalatable or even toxic.

Community Structure and Keystone Species

The community structure is the sum result of all of the interactions. However, some species have a greater effect on the community structure than is expected on the basis of their numbers and the general types of interactions in which they are involved. One of these is a keystone predator. A keystone predator consumes several different kinds of prey and keeps the population numbers of each of the prey populations at levels that reduce competition. This reduces the chance of competitive exclusion. The net result is that a keystone predator helps to maintain the diversity of a community. Keystone species do not all act as keystone predators. Woodpeckers, such as the red-naped sapsucker, drill holes in trees to obtain sap and insects and to nest. Once the holes are drilled, other species can eat the sap and insects and use the holes for nesting. The red-naped sapsucker thus provides food and habitat that would otherwise not be available for other species; it enhances the diversity of the community more than is immediately apparent from its numbers or lifestyle.

ECOSYSTEMS

Definitions

Ecosystems are defined as the biotic (living) and abiotic (non-living) components of an area or habitat that interact in the exchange of energy and nutrients. The biotic components are the different populations that comprise the community. The abiotic components are the physical habitats of the organisms and the conditions (i.e., pH and temperature) of the habitats (soil, water, and the atmosphere). The habitats include the soil, water, and the atmosphere; their conditions are parameters such as pH, temperature, and nutrient content.

These interactions have a profound influence on the interchanges of energy and nutrients in a specific environment. However, the first objective in studying ecosystems is to show the general pathways of the movement of energy and nutrients in ecosystems. This movement is related but different. It is related because the movement is through the same components, but different because energy flows, whereas nutrients are cycled.

Energy Flow Through Ecosystems

The sun's energy is the initial energy source in ecosystems. This energy is used by plants to fix atmospheric carbon, contained in carbon dioxide, into sugars in a process called photosynthesis. Chemically, the sun's energy is contained in the organic sugar molecules and can be released and used by the plant for growth and maintenance. When the plants are eaten by animals, energy is passed to the animals. Similarly, consumption of the animal by another animal passes energy to the second animal. This results in the flow of energy.

Different groups of organisms obtain their energy in different ways. Plants produce their own food using the sun's energy. They are called autotrophs because they make sugars by photosynthesis. Animals do not make their own food and are called heterotrophs; they obtain food from plants or animals and are called consumers. Primary consumers eat plants (herbivores), and secondary consumers eat animals (carnivores). Omnivores are consumers that eat plants and animals and function as both herbivores and carnivores. When the plant or animal dies, the energy contained in the dead organism is used by decomposers. Because consumers use the food contained in producers to grow, they are sometimes referred to as secondary producers.

The groups of animals that obtain their energy in similar ways are combined in trophic levels. There are three main trophic levels: producers, consumers, and decomposers.

A linear series of organisms that transfer the energy is called a food chain. An example of a food chain is the consumption of plants by mice that are in turn consumed by hawks. However, the transfer of energy among the organisms is usually more complex than a food chain because one organism may consume several organisms or several organisms may consume the same one organism. The result is a food web. The relationship between a food chain and a food web is shown in the following figure.

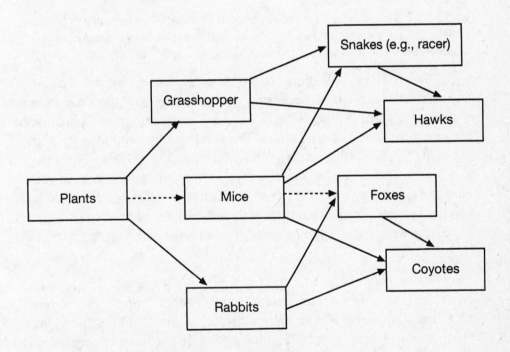

Figure 18.2 An example of a food chain (- - -►) within a food web (───►).

The transfer of energy from one individual to another is not 100 percent efficient, because each individual uses energy to maintain itself. This energy is dissipated as respiratory heat and wastes, and is not all used for growth. Therefore, not all of the energy in the primary producers is passed to the primary consumers or herbivores. Similarly, not all of the energy in the primary consumers is passed to the secondary consumers. Normally, about 10% of the energy is useful to the next step of the food chain. This decrease in energy through a food chain is represented in an energy flow pyramid. The typical energy pyramid does not include decomposers. However, energy contained in the feces and dead organisms from all levels of the pyramid is passed to the decomposers.

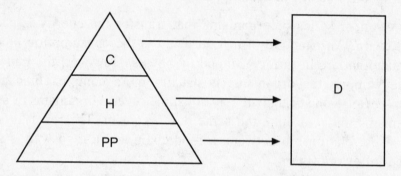

Figure 18.3 The energy flow (kcal/m²/year) through the primary producers (PP), primary consumers or herbivores (H), secondary consumers or carnivores (C), and to the decomposers, in a generalized ecosystem.

The efficiency of energy transfer at each step varies. To determine the efficiency, it is necessary to determine how the total energy produced in photosynthesis, or ingested by consumers, is partitioned between growth and maintenance. The total energy produced by photosynthesis is called the gross primary production (GPP). The energy used for maintenance in both plants and animals is the respiratory energy. The energy put to growth in animals is net production (NP) or growth. The net production or growth is the ingested energy (E_I) minus the respired energy (E_R). In plants it is called net primary production (NPP).

The total available energy from primary producer to final consumer decreases, but decomposers obtain energy from both producers and consumers and thus can have a greater amount of energy available for ingestion. Production efficiencies, which are independent of total energy ingested, vary due to metabolic rate and time of digestion.

BIOGEOCHEMICAL CYCLES

Biogeochemical cycles define the movement of elements between the physical environment and the organisms. The elements most commonly examined are the nutrients carbon (C), nitrogen (N), and phosphorus (P) that are required in large quantities by the organisms. In addition, water, which is an important medium for and transporter of the nutrients, moves in a global cycle. The physical environment includes land, air, and water. Within each of these environments, the nutrients may be available, or unavailable, for immediate uptake by the organisms. Unavailable nutrients include organic material buried, such as coal and other fossil fuels, and inorganic material such as phosphorus contained in minerals in rocks or carbon contained in limestone. The living organisms are the producers, consumers, and decomposers. Recall that one important similarity between the flow of energy and the cycling of nutrients is that both occur through the same organisms.

A general biogeochemical cycle and the general types of movement among the components are summarized in Figure 18.4.

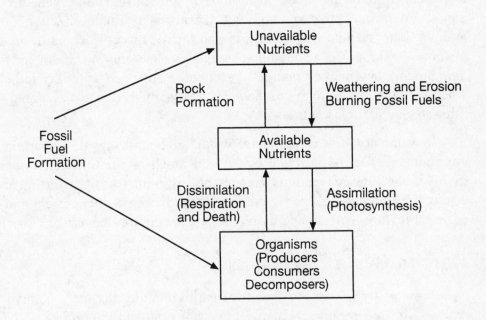

Figure 18.4 An outline of a general biogeochemical cycle.

Hydrological Cycle

The global hydrological cycle is the movement of water between the land and the oceans. On the oceans and land there is both precipitation and evaporation. Over the oceans, evaporation exceeds precipitation. The excess moisture condenses in clouds and moves toward the land. On the land, precipitation exceeds evaporation. The excess water moves into the ground (groundwater), through the soil (subsurface flow) and over the land (surface flow) to the oceans. Therefore, the overall cycle is evaporation from the oceans, movement via clouds to the land, precipitation on the land, and runoff to the oceans.

Nitrogen Cycle

In living organisms, nitrogen is a main component of proteins. As an inorganic nutrient, nitrogen exists in several forms. Interconversions among these forms are a major part of the nitrogen cycle.

The atmosphere is an important part of the cycle because it is the initial source of nitrogen. Some nitrogen is also returned to the atmosphere during denitrification and volatilization. Mineralization and nitrification occur in water and in the soil. They are the processes that are responsible for the decomposition of organic nitrogen in organisms. Uptake of nitrate or ammonium by organisms is immobilization or assimilation, and like mineralization and nitrification, it occurs in water or soil. Some organisms are selective and use only nitrate or only ammonium, but many organisms use both. Nitrogen is unavailable when it is lost as nitrate to groundwater or adsorbed (tied up) as ammonium to clay particles in the soil.

In summary, the atmosphere, water, and land are all important environments for the nitrogen cycle; and much of the nitrogen cycle involves the interconversions among the different forms of nitrogen. The rate of the many steps are controlled by the organisms present and physical features (pH, temperature, etc.) of the environment.

Carbon Cycle

A summary of the movement of carbon among the main components of the general biogeochemical cycle are shown in Figure 18.5.

The carbon cycle is closely allied with energy flow, and it is important to understand both the similarities and the differences. In energy flow, the first step is the fixation of carbon using energy from the sun in the process of photosynthesis. Similarly, a major part of the carbon cycle is the uptake of carbon by the organisms during photosynthesis (4a and 4b). The carbon is from carbon dioxide in the air or bicarbonate ions (HCO_3^-) in water. Carbon is present as bicarbonate in the water because carbon dioxide and water combine to form carbonic acid and, in water, the acid dissociates, forming bicarbonate and some-times carbonate (CO_3^-). Whether it is carbonate or bicarbonate depends primarily on the pH of the water. In energy flow, the energy moves through the trophic levels. However, as a nutrient, the carbon moves through the organisms and is returned to the atmosphere or water dur-ing respiration and when the organisms die (5a and 5b). The land (soil) is not given as a source of available carbon because available carbon is present in the air and water in the soil. Overall, the exchange of carbon between the organisms and the available nutrient source is by photo-synthesis, respiration, death, and decomposition of the organisms.

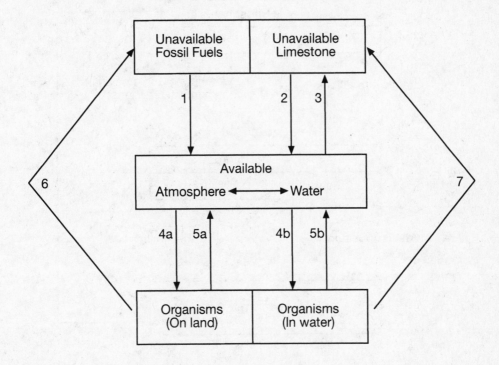

Figure 18.5 Summary of the carbon cycle.

Some of the organisms may be buried, or at least were buried in geological time (6). These buried organisms are the present source of fossil fuels. In addition, the shells of marine organisms contain calcium carbonate. Death and accumulation of these shells is the source of limestone deposits (7). However, limestone takes millions of years to form from the shells. Before limestone is produced, the carbon in shells is made unavailable (3) simply as shells on the bottom of water bodies. Burning of fossil fuels (1) and removal of limestone from the ground for use as dimension stone in construction, or release of carbon from limestone in the water body (2), releases the unavailable carbon.

Phosphorus Cycle

The chemistry of phosphorus is extremely complex and thus a chemical explanation of the phosphorus cycle is not realistic. A summary of the movement of phosphorus among the three parts of the biogeochemical cycle is summarized in the following figure.

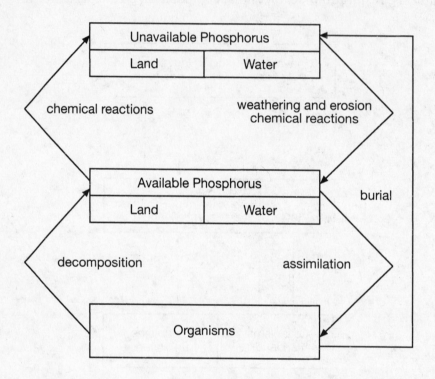

Figure 18.6 A summary of the movement of phosphorus among the three parts of the biogeochemical cycle.

In organisms, phosphorus is contained primarily in high-energy molecules of adenosine triphosphate (ATP) and in deoxyribonucleic acid (DNA). In the soil, phosphorus is present in numerous compounds that are not available to the organisms, and as the ion phosphate which is available and used by organisms. Unavailable phosphorus is also found as an element in the minerals of numerous rocks. Unavailable phosphorus is released and made available by the weathering and erosion of rocks, and by chemical reactions in the soil and in the sediments of water bodies. In addition to its presence in the soil, available phosphorus is present in marine and fresh water. In marine water, phosphate is part of the salt that makes the ocean "salty." There is a rare phosphorus gas, but in reality there is not an atmospheric component of the phosphorus cycle. Therefore, the movement of phosphorus from land to water is by runoff from the soil to the water. Movement from the water (oceans) to land requires animals such as birds to obtain phosphorus from marine sources and then die or leave feces on the land. As with all of the cycles, death and decomposition of the organisms returns the phosphorus to the available pool of nutrients, or to the unavailable pool if the organisms are buried or the chemical form of the phosphorus cannot be used by the organisms.

In fresh water, but not in the soil, phosphorus is the limiting nutrient to primary production. This means that the addition of available phosphorus, usually as phosphate, will result in increased primary production. This is because all of the other nutrients are present in larger quantities than are being used.

Types of Ecosystems

Recall that the definition for ecosystems is the biotic (living) and abiotic (non-living) components of an area or habitat that interact in the exchange of energy and nutrients. The abiotic components are the physical habitats of the organisms and the conditions of the habitats. The habitats include the soil, water, and atmosphere. The atmosphere is not generally considered a separate habitat, thus there are two main categories of ecosystems: terrestrial (land-based) and aquatic (water-based).

Terrestrial Ecosystems

The interaction of climate, topography, and soil parent-material dictates the abiotic conditions in terrestrial ecosystems. The resulting abiotic factors are temperature, wind, moisture, sunlight (solar radiation), and soil-type. These factors affect the physiology of the organisms and are important selective agents in evolution. In addition, they are critical to the flow of energy and the cycling of nutrients.

On a global scale, the commonality of the abiotic factors, particularly temperature and precipitation, results in similar global climates that contain similar types of plants. Although the plant communities are similar in their abiotic requirements, they do not necessarily have the same species. These terrestrial ecosystems (the community types and associated abiotic factors) are called biomes.

Decreasing Temperature →

Tropical	Temperate	Arctic

Forests
    Deciduous
    Evergreen
	Forests
	    Deciduous
	    Boreal (Evergreen)
		Tundra

Grassland Savanna	Grassland Chaparral	
Alpine Deserts	Alpine Deserts	

Decreasing Precipitation ↓

Figure 18.7

Types of Biomes

Tundra Biome – A tundra is a band of treeless, wet, arctic grassland stretching between the Arctic Ocean and polar ice caps and the forests to the south. The main characteristics of the tundra are low temperatures and a short growing season.

The Forest Biomes

1) The northern coniferous forest stretches across North America and Eurasia just south of the tundra. The forest is characterized by spruce, fir, and pine trees and by such animals as the wolf, the lynx, and the snowshoe hare.

2) The moist coniferous forest biome stretches along the west coast of North America from Alaska south to central California. It is characterized by great humidity, high temperatures, high rainfall, and small seasonal ranges.

3) The temperate deciduous forest biome was found originally in eastern North America, Europe, parts of Japan and Australia, and the southern part of South America. It is characterized by moderate temperatures with distinct summers and

winters and abundant, evenly distributed rainfall. Most of this forest region has now been replaced by cultivated fields and cities.

4) The tropical rainforests stretch around low lying areas near the equator. Dense vegetation, annual rainfall of 200 cm. or more, and a tremendous variety of animals characterize this area.

The Grassland Biome – The grassland biome usually occupies the interiors of continents, the prairies of the western United States, and those of Argentina, Australia, southern Russia, and Siberia. Grasslands are characterized by rainfalls of about 25 to 75 cm. per year, and they provide natural pastures for grazing animals.

The Chaparral Biome – The chaparral biome is found in California, Mexico, the Mediterranean, and Australia's south coast. It is characterized by mild temperatures, relatively abundant rain in winter, very dry summers, and trees with hard, thick evergreen leaves.

The Desert Biome – The desert is characterized by rainfall of less than 25 cm. per year, and sparse vegetation that consists of greasewood, sagebrush, and cactus. Such animals as the kangaroo rat and the pocket mouse are able to live there.

The Marine Biome – Although the saltiness of the open ocean is relatively uniform, the concentration of phosphates, nitrates, and other nutrients varies widely in different parts of the sea and at different times of the year. All animals and plants are represented except amphibians, centipedes, millipedes, and insects. Life may have originated in the intertidal area of the marine biome, which is the area between the high and low tides. The marine biome is made up of four zones.

Freshwater Zones – Freshwater zones are divided into standing water—lakes, ponds and swamps, and running water—rivers, creeks, and springs. Freshwater zones are characterized by an assortment of animals and plants. Aquatic life is most prolific in the littoral zones of lakes. Freshwater zones change much more rapidly than other biomes.

Aquatic Ecosystems

The marine biome as listed above is a habitat found in aquatic ecosystems. Aquatic ecosystems are defined more on the basis of their physical conditions than on the dominant organisms present. There are two general types of aquatic ecosystems: freshwater and marine.

Freshwater ecosystems include rivers, lakes, and marshes. Rivers vary from the headwaters to the mouth. In the headwaters, the flow is rapid, the water is usually cooler, and there are few primary producers; the energy source is primarily detritus (dead organic material) from the adjacent land, although there is usually some attached algae (periphyton) on the rocks. Immature stages of invertebrates, such as mayflies and caddisflies, are the consumers and decomposers. Fish represent the secondary consumers. Near the mouth, rivers are larger and slower moving than at the headwaters. They may also carry sediment eroded from upstream areas and thus appear quite muddy. The primary producers are plants that grow in the shallow shoreline areas and algae that live in the open water. Consumers include invertebrates and fish. Much of the dead material is carried downstream to the mouth or estuary where decomposers use the energy and recycle the nutrients.

Lakes are similar to large, slow-moving rivers, and in many cases they are the result of the widening of rivers. The primary producers in lakes are the phytoplankton. Phytoplankton require sunlight and can only live up to depths that sunlight penetrates. These primary producers also require nutrients and thus the nutrient content of the lake water is important. The nutrients enter lakes from the surrounding land and rivers and nutrients can be regenerated within the lake by decomposition of dead organisms. As organisms die, they settle to the bottom of the lake where decomposition occurs, releasing the nutrients. To return these nutrients to the water column, the lake water must be mixed. In many temperate area lakes, the most significant lake mixing, called lake turnover, occurs in the fall. As the surface waters cool, this dense water falls to the bottom, initiating mixing of the water by convection. Additional mixing occurs due to wind and some mixing may be mediated by the movement of organisms. In very deep lakes and many tropical lakes, this turnover of lake water and the resulting recycling of the nutrients does not occur. The nutrients are "trapped" in the sediments, and the lakes are nutrient poor (oligotrophic). The numbers and kinds of consumers and decomposers present in the lake depend on its size, location, and water chemistry.

Marshes are shallow bodies of standing water with extensive emergent vegetation. In addition, they contain diverse communities of animals.

HUMAN INFLUENCES ON ECOSYSTEMS

Humans are one of the earth's species that have a tremendous influence on the world's ecosystems. The first and most obvious influence is the physical space used by people and thus the loss of habitat for other organisms. The consequences to the displaced populations depend on all of the factors that affect the growth and structure of populations. Other influences can be categorized as use of non-renewable resources, use of renewable resources, and the use of synthetic chemicals.

Use of Non-renewable Resources

Non-renewable resources are materials that exist in a set quantity. As a result, these materials have the potential to be used up. Two important examples of non-renewable resources are fossil fuels and metals.

Fossil Fuels

The exploration for fossil fuels and their extraction from the ground or ocean floor is an obvious disruption of the habitat. The burning of fossil fuels releases carbon dioxide into the atmosphere. Carbon dioxide does not affect the amount of energy received on the earth from the sun, but it absorbs the heat energy that is released from the earth and keeps this heat energy in the atmosphere. This is why carbon dioxide is called a greenhouse gas. If this heat energy was not maintained in the atmosphere, the temperature of the atmosphere would be significantly colder and be able to support less life forms. However, an increase in carbon dioxide increases the temperature in the atmosphere. This is what is referred to as global warming. The consequences of global warming may be complex but the explanation is simple.

Burning of fossil fuels releases not only carbon dioxide, but also oxides of nitrogen and sulfur. These combine with water in the atmosphere; thus producing nitrous (or nitric) and sulfuric acid, respectively. These acidic compounds make up acid rain. Nitrogen is contained in fossil fuels because fossil fuels are produced from buried organisms. The sulfur content depends on the conditions under which the organisms were buried. These conditions vary and thus the sulfur content of fossil fuels, particularly coal, is quite variable.

Mining

During various geological events minerals contained in rocks are oxidized, or dissolved and moved in solution, and precipitated in various locations. These are slowly leached from the rocks and enter the available component of biogeochemical cycles. The mineral ores are first extracted from the ground, and then from the rock (the refining process). They are used for many purposes (e.g., copper wire, zinc plating, steel girders, stainless steel cookingware). Extraction from the rock frequently involves acids, and the resulting pollution must be contained in holding ponds or chemically treated to avoid contamination of adjacent areas.

Use of Renewable Resources

Renewable resources are those that can be regenerated or renewed within a reasonably short period of time, generally within a person's lifetime. Important renewable resources are fisheries, forestry, agriculture, and water.

Fisheries

The effect of the overharvesting of many species of fish is being realized in both the Atlantic and Pacific oceans. Fish are a critical component of food chains and webs, and altered fish populations affect the structure and size of the populations of their prey and predators.

Forestry

Forestry products (wood, paper, etc.) are used in large volumes. The trees are logged from natural forests and from forest plantations. The trees are primary producers and are an important component of the food web in the forest. They are consumers of carbon dioxide and thus important as potential mediators of the effects of increasing carbon dioxide levels in the atmosphere. In addition, trees are an important part of all of the nutrient cycles. If trees are removed, the nutrients contained in the trees are removed, and nutrients remaining in the soil can readily be leached from the soil and passed to surface waters or groundwater. The consequences are similar to loss of nutrients from agricultural land. Loss of the nutrients means that the area must be fertilized extensively. Since trees also hold the soil, the loss of trees can lead to erosion.

Agriculture

Agriculture uses land for production of non-native plants or animals because the large population of humans requires food. Thus, one consequence of agriculture is loss of habitat for other organisms. However, agriculture can also have negative impacts that affect people. First, there are non-point discharges (pollutants that can not be traced to any single site of discharge) from agricultural land to groundwater and adjacent surface water. These discharges can contain nutrients from fertilizers (e.g., phosphates and nitrates) and pesticides. The excess nutrients, if added to lakes, can increase the primary production of the lake. The visible result is algal blooms and the change in the lake is called *eutrophication*. The change in the numbers (and kinds) of primary producers affects the numbers and kinds of consumers. Furthermore, decomposition which requires oxygen, increases. The decreased oxygen content further alters the species composition of the water. The consequence to people is a decrease in the water quality of the lake for drinking water and recreational activities.

Second is the use of water to fertilize agricultural land. The water is taken from surface waters or groundwater which alters the local water cycle. Water taken from rivers and added to adjacent agricultural land leaches back into the river as part of a natural cycle, but the new water may contain significant levels of nutrients and pesticides.

Third, the irrigation of agricultural land leaches not only nutrients and pesticides but also small soil particles. Accumulation of these small particles in the soil results in the development of a pan (impermeable) layer. Once this layer is formed, additional water cannot infiltrate to lower depths. The water may move up in the soil and evaporate or move laterally through the soil to low lying areas. In addition, nutrients and pesticides accumulate in the soil.

Water

Most of the world's water is in the oceans. Only about three percent is freshwater, and most of this is contained in glaciers and groundwater. All organisms require water, and contamination or overuse of water is a serious potential problem. Water, like fish and forests, is a renewable resource but overexploitation can have dire consequences. The regeneration time for rivers is much faster than that for groundwater or glaciers.

Water flows in rivers from the land to the ocean. Dams are

constructed to generate electric power or to control the flow of rivers. Dams are usually constructed where the river gradient is steep and erosion exceeds deposition within the river. The presence of the dam reduces the flow and deposition occurs. Therefore, dams have a finite life span. In addition, the material deposited in the reservoir behind the dam is the material that was previously transported downstream and deposited in the estuary, or mouth of the river. The presence of dams alters the flow and the physical conditions of the river's ecosystem. Therefore, dams affect the kinds of organisms that can live in the new habitat. Second, dams restrict the movement of organisms such as migratory fish. Third, dams reduce the amount of material deposited in the estuaries and mouths of rivers. As this material contains much of the dead organic matter from the river, it is the basis of good soil and explains why river mouths and estuaries are areas of good agricultural land.

When precipitation reaches the ground, it infiltrates into the ground (ultimately to groundwater), or passes over the ground surface (runoff) to nearby surface waters. Precipitation is therefore an important source of fresh water in surface and groundwater. Anything that limits the movement of water to groundwater or surface waters will affect the water cycle and the quantity of water in the surface waters and groundwater. In cities and towns, the roads and houses prevent the input of water to the ground. Water is collected in drains and sent directly to the rivers or ocean. In this case not only is the water cycle altered, the water that is passed directly to the rivers contains potentially toxic chemicals.

Use of Synthetic Chemicals

Synthetic chemicals are used widely in North America. The chemicals include household cleaners, pesticides, preservatives, and refrigerants. In general, these pose problems to the ecosystems because they are not part of natural cycles and are not readily broken down. The result is that the potential contaminants are passed through the food web unaltered, and accumulate in consumers (bioaccumulation) or accumulate as an inorganic component of the biogeochemical cycle. In addition, many are toxic. Chlorofluorocarbons (CFCs) are an example of a synthetic substance that accumulates in the stratosphere of the atmosphere. CFCs used in refrigerators and air conditioners are referred to as ozone-depleting substances. The ozone layer filters out most of the sun's harmful ultraviolet rays, particularly ultraviolet-B

(UV-B) rays, and thus a decrease in the ozone layer increases the ultraviolet radiation reaching the surface of the earth. Excessive exposure to UV-B rays is a serious health risk to humans. However, high UV-B radiation may also inhibit plant growth and contribute to the decline of amphibian populations.

SUGGESTED READINGS

Kormondy, E. J. 1984. *Concepts of Ecology*, 3rd ed. Prentice-Hall, Inc., Englewoods Cliffs, New Jersey. 298 pp.

Mackenzie, Aulay, Andy S. Baul and Sonia R. Virdee. 1998. *Instant Notes in Ecology*. BIOS Scientific Publishers, Oxford UK.

Pielou, E. C. 1998. *Fresh Water*. The University of Chicago Press, London. 275 pp.

Purves, W. K, G. H Orians, and H. C. Heller. 1995. *Life: The Science of Biology*, 4th ed. Volume II, Evolution, Diversity, and Ecology.

Ricklefs, R. E. 1996. *The Economy of Nature*, 4th ed. W. H. Freedman and Co., New York, New York. 678 pp.

Smith, R. L. 1992. *Elements of Ecology*, 3rd ed., HarperCollins Publishers Inc. New York, New York. 617 pp.

Smith, R. L. 1996. *Ecology and Field Biology*. 5th ed. HarperCollins College Publishers. New York, New York. 740 pp.

THE SAT SUBJECT TEST IN
Biology E/M

PRACTICE TESTS

If you are preparing for the Biology-E Test, take Practice Tests 1-3. If you are preparing for the Biology-M Test, take Practice Tests 4-6.

SAT Biology E/M
Practice Test 1

(Answer sheets appear in the back of this book.)

TIME: 1 Hour
            80 Questions

BIOLOGY CORE SECTION

DIRECTIONS: The lettered or numbered choices below refer to the questions or statements that immediately follow them. Pick the best answer choice and fill in the correct oval on your answer sheet. An answer choice may be used more than once or not at all.

Questions 1–2 refer to the following.

    (A) parasitism

    (B) mutualism

    (C) predation

    (D) commensalism

    (E) competition

1.   A deer tick biting a deer is an example of

2.   Two species of frogs colonize the same lake. One increases in number, while the other decreases in number.

ABO Blood Group
Agglutination Results

Individual	Antiserum	
	Anti-A	Anti-B
1	+	+
2	–	+
3	–	–
4	+	–
5	–	+

I^A = antigen A
I^B = antigen B
i = neither

Questions 3–4 refer to the results of a blood typing test done on five individuals.

3. From the results shown above, which individual has blood type AB?

   (A) 1   (D) 4

   (B) 2   (E) 5

   (C) 3

4. Which individual above has the genotype ii?

   (A) 1   (D) 4

   (B) 2   (E) 5

   (C) 3

DIRECTIONS: The questions or incomplete statements below are followed by five possible answers or completions. Pick the answer choice that best answers or completes the question or incomplete statement and then fill in the correct oval on your answer sheet.

5. Light energy is captured in the plant by

   (A) NADP.   (D) glucose.

   (B) ATP.   (E) carbon dioxide.

   (C) chlorophyll.

6. Bacteria have

   (A) a cell wall.   (D) mitochondria.

   (B) a nuclear membrane.   (E) rod-like chromosomes.

   (C) chloroplasts.

7. Intense physical activity can result in all of the following EXCEPT

   (A) large amounts of glucose being converted to glycogen.

   (B) the breakdown of glucose.

   (C) an oxygen debt.

   (D) ATP production.

   (E) muscle fatigue.

Questions 8 refers to the following graph showing the effect of pH on enzyme activity.

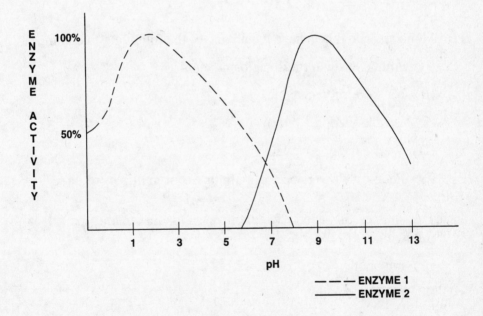

8. Judging from the graph, which one of the following is correct?

   (A) An enzyme has some activity at all pH values.

   (B) One enzyme may have more than one optimum pH.

(C) The activity curve for an enzyme found in the stomach would be similar to enzyme 1.

(D) Both enzymes have an optimum activity at about pH 7.

(E) Enzyme 2 works best at high acidity.

9. When an animal learns to make a strong association with another organism during a brief period early in development, this is called

(A) conditioning.

(D) habituation.

(B) imprinting.

(E) trial-and-error learning.

(C) reinforcement.

10. The most abundant plants living in temperate, terrestrial habitats are

(A) conifers.

(D) flowering plants.

(B) ferns.

(E) horsetails.

(C) club mosses.

11. Monocots and dicots have which one of the following in common?

(A) Annual growth rings enclosing a pith

(B) Network of veins in leaves

(C) One cotyledon

(D) Well-developed xylem

(E) Petals of flowers occurring in threes or multiples of three

12. The sources of genetic variation in a population include all of the following EXCEPT

(A) mutation.

(B) natural selection.

(C) fertilization of egg by sperm.

(D) crossing over.

(E) meiosis.

13. The nineteenth-century monk Gregor Mendel discovered that

    I.   heredity factors blend together in new individuals.

    II. heredity factors act as particles when transferred to the next generation.

    III. some heredity factors mask the effect of other heredity factors.

(A) I only.   (D) II and III.

(B) II only.   (E) I, II, and III.

(C) III only.

14. The term *primary productivity* refers to which part of the food chain?

(A) Herbivores   (D) Plants

(B) Carnivores   (E) Decomposers

(C) Omnivores

15. Nutrient absorption occurs primarily in the

(A) esophagus.   (D) large intestine.

(B) stomach.   (E) rectum.

(C) small intestine.

Question 16 refers to the following.

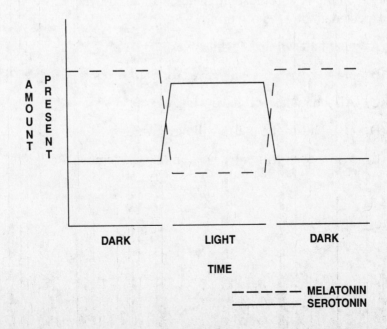

245

16. The graph shows the production of serotonin (a precursor of melatonin) and melatonin (a hormone made by the pineal gland) during a 24-hour period. From this graph, which one of the following is true?

    (A) Light increases melatonin production and increases serotonin production.

    (B) Light increases melatonin production and inhibits serotonin production.

    (C) Light inhibits melatonin production and inhibits serotonin production.

    (D) Light inhibits melatonin production and increases serotonin production.

    (E) Serotonin inhibits melatonin production.

17. Which one of the following groups is most closely related?

    (A) ciliates - sponges

    (B) flatworms - roundworms

    (C) sea anemones - flagellates

    (D) segmented worms - insects

    (E) clams - squid

18. If a red-eyed female fruit fly who carries a recessive gene for white eyes on the X chromosome mates with a red-eyed male, what will be expected among the offspring?

    (A) One-half will have white eyes.

    (B) 3/4 red eyes, 1/4 white eyes for both sexes

    (C) All the males will have white eyes.

    (D) One-half of the males will have white eyes.

    (E) White eyes will only show among the females.

19. Bone-to-muscle connections are made by

    (A) tendons.   (D) cartilage.

    (B) ligaments.   (E) striated muscle.

    (C) bone.

20. Natural selection depends upon all the following EXCEPT

    (A) more individuals are born in each generation than will survive and reproduce.

    (B) there is genetic variation among individuals.

    (C) some individuals have a better chance of survival than others.

    (D) some individuals are reproductively more successful.

    (E) certain acquired traits can be passed on to the next generation of organisms with the phenotypes.

21. In the cross tall smooth × tall smooth, the offspring were

    9/16 tall smooth

    3/16 tall wrinkled

    3/16 short smooth

    1/16 short wrinkled

    From this we can conclude

    (A) the genes for tall and smooth are linked.

    (B) the genes for tall and wrinkled are dominant.

    (C) at least one of the parents was homozygous for smooth.

    (D) at least one of the parents was homozygous for tall.

    (E) at least one of the parents was heterozygous for tall.

22. Which one of the following situations is most likely to result in an evolutionary change?

    (A) Athletic ability by extensive training

    (B) Maintenance of health by correct diet

    (C) Prompt medical attention when exposed to disease

(D) Increased resistance to a disease because of a mutation

(E) Vitamin supplements

23. The liver does all of the following EXCEPT

(A) make bile.

(B) store glucose.

(C) make urea.

(D) convert glucose into fat.

(E) make white blood cells.

24. Which one of the following does NOT match?

(A) ribosomes - RNA production

(B) mitochondria - ATP formation

(C) Golgi apparatus - packaging of secretory products

(D) lysosomes - storage of digestive enzymes

(E) centrioles - formation of spindle fibers

25. The life cycles of moss and fern are similar in all of the following EXCEPT

(A) they both have alternation of generation.

(B) the gametophyte generation of both is the most conspicuous.

(C) they both produce spores.

(D) in both, the gametophyte generation produces sperm and eggs.

(E) in both, the cells of gametophytes have one-half the normal number of chromosomes.

26. The life cycles of moss and fern are both dependent on a moist habitat because

I. in both, sperm swim to the egg.

II. both lack true roots.

III. the embryo is not protected.

(A) I only.

(B) II only.

(C) III only.

(D) I and III.

(E) I, II, and III.

248

27. Which of the following is expected to have the largest mass of living material (biomass)?

    (A) Producers

    (B) Herbivores

    (C) Decomposers

    (D) Carnivores

    (E) Predators

28. Evidence for evolution includes all of the following EXCEPT

    (A) fossil record.

    (B) similarities of proteins in different organisms.

    (C) homologous limb structures.

    (D) similarities in chromosome banding patterns.

    (E) differences in physical appearance of individuals within a species.

29. In the spring, the ice on a lake melts. The cooler surface water settles to the bottom, displacing the warmer bottom water. All of the following will happen EXCEPT

    (A) nutrients will be brought to the surface.

    (B) phosphorus will be made available to living organisms.

    (C) algae will increase in growth.

    (D) upwellings of bottom water will occur.

    (E) extremes in water temperature will form from top to bottom.

30. DNA replication occurs immediately before

    I.   mitosis
    II. meiosis 1
    III. meiosis 2

    (A) I only.

    (B) II only.

    (C) III only.

    (D) I and II.

    (E) I, II and III.

31. Assuming the environmental factors remain constant, which one of the following successional stages represents the most stable community?

(A) Lake

(B) Freshwater marsh

(C) Meadow

(D) Low shrubs

(E) Forest

32. Which is NOT a correct match?

(A) ectoderm - nervous system

(B) mesoderm - muscle

(C) ectoderm - lens of the eye

(D) endoderm - skin

(E) mesoderm - bone

33. When distinguishing between DNA and RNA, DNA uniquely contains

(A) guanine.

(B) ribose.

(C) phosphorus (phosphates).

(D) one strand.

(E) thymine.

34. The functions of meiosis might include any of the following EXCEPT

(A) reduction of the chromosome number by half.

(B) production of many sperm.

(C) providing the egg with a large volume of cytoplasm.

(D) allowance for crossing over.

(E) providing for identical offspring.

Questions 35–36 refer to the following.

Two species of flour beetles were grown together. In one case, they were grown in pure flour. In the second case, they were grown under the same conditions, including the same amount of flour, except that glass tubing was added.

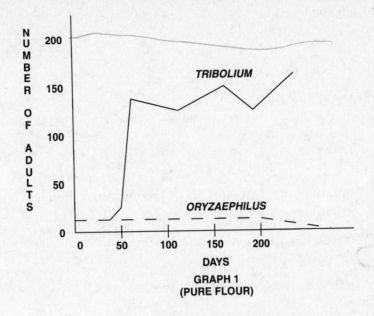

GRAPH 1
(PURE FLOUR)

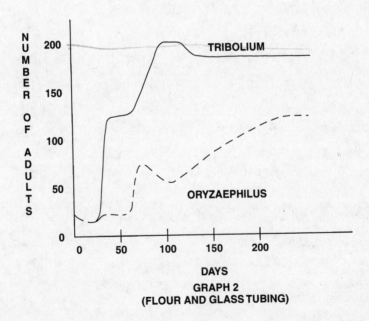

GRAPH 2
(FLOUR AND GLASS TUBING)

35. When grown in pure flour, the number of *Tribolium* adults increases at the greatest rate between

(A) day 0 and 25 days.

(B) 25 and 50 days.

(C) 50 and 100 days.

(D) 100 and 150 days.

(E) 150 and 200 days.

36. The presence of glass tubing

(A) inhibits growth in both species.

(B) improves the growth of *Oryzaephilus*, but does not affect *Tribolium*.

(C) improves the growth of *Tribolium*, but does not affect *Oryzaephilus*.

(D) improves the growth of both species.

(E) causes the extinction of *Oryzaephilus*.

Questions 37–40 refer to the following.

	Total cross-sectional area	Velocity	Blood pressure
aorta	4 cm^2	40 cm/sec	100 mmHg
arteries	20	10	80
capillaries	4,000	0.05	20
veins	50	4	10
vena cava	12	10	8

37. In what part of the circulatory system does blood flow the slowest?

(A) Aorta

(B) Arteries

(C) Capillaries

(D) Veins

(E) Vena cava

38. Which part of the circulatory system allows for exchanges of nutrients, gases, and waste products between the blood and tissues?

(A) Pulmonary arteries

(B) Systemic arteries

(C) Capillaries

(D) Systemic veins

(E) Pulmonary veins

39. Which one of the following statements is true?

    (A) Blood pressure increases as cross-sectional area decreases.

    (B) Blood pressure decreases as cross-sectional area decreases.

    (C) As cross-sectional area increases, velocity increases.

    (D) As cross-sectional area increases, velocity decreases.

    (E) As velocity increases, blood pressure increases.

40. Blood that enters the aorta flows from the

    (A) pulmonary arteries.   (D) right ventricle.

    (B) right atrium.   (E) left ventricle.

    (C) left atrium.

Questions 41–42 refer to the following.

A particular strain of bacteria does not have the ability to make the amino acid histidine because of a defective gene. If histidine is supplied in the medium, the bacteria will grow normally, as shown on plate I. When grown on minimal medium, few, if any, colonies grow (plate II). This strain was grown on two petri plates containing minimal medium. Chemical A was added to plate III and chemical B was added to plate IV. All the plates were grown at 37°C with colony counts made at the end of 48 hours.

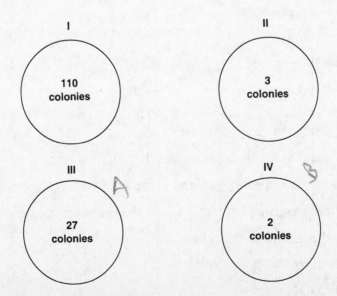

41. Which one of the following statements about the experiment above is correct?

    (A) Petri dishes I and III are the experimental sets.

    (B) Dish I is the control for dish III.

    (C) Exposure to the chemicals is the independent variable.

    (D) The colony count is the independent variable.

    (E) Temperature is the independent variable.

42. The results of this experiment indicate that

    (A) chemical A has no effect upon survival of cells.

    (B) some bacteria have become sensitive to complete medium.

    (C) bacteria are always killed by minimal medium.

    (D) chemical A has caused mutations of the defective histidine gene.

    (E) chemical B has caused mutations of the defective histidine gene.

Questions 43–44 refer to the following.

The diameter of sea urchin eggs was measured before they were placed in different concentrations of saltwater. After five minutes their diameters were again measured.

Concentration of saltwater	Percent change in diameter of eggs
0.0%	+20%
0.5	+10
2.5	+ 5
3.5	0
5.5	−20

43. The change in size is because of

    (A) the movement of salt across the cell membranes.

    (B) the movement of salt and water across the cell membranes.

    (C) the movement of water across the cell membranes.

    (D) the growth of the cells.

    (E) the loss of cell proteins.

44. If plant cells were placed in the same salt concentrations, what would happen?

  (A) The cells in the highest salt concentration would enlarge the most.

  (B) The cells in salt-free water would burst.

  (C) All the cells would change uniformly.

  (D) No water would cross the cell membrane in the cells in 0.5% salt concentration.

  (E) The cells in salt-free water would be most firm.

Questions 45–46 refer to the following situation:

While traveling various islands in the Pacific, you observed that tortoises are common. To your surprise, one of the islands had a different habitat and the tortoises had longer necks.

45. The habitat of this island was

  (A) open grassland with few trees or shrubs.

  (B) tropical forest with little growth on the forest floor.

  (C) thick shrubs shading out growth on the floor.

  (D) rocky with little vegetation.

  (E) an active volcanic island with little land around the volcano.

46. Finding long neck tortoises on one island and not on the other islands is an example of

  I. natural selection.

  II. survival of the fittest.

  III. acquired characteristics.

  (A) I only.   (D) I and II.

  (B) II only.   (E) I, II, and III.

  (C) III only.

47. The smallest type of cell in humans is a(n)

  (A) nerve cell.   (D) red blood cell.

  (B) ovum.   (E) white blood cell.

  (C) skeletal muscle fiber.

48. In the genetic cross AaBb × aabb, assume that each lettered gene pair independently controls a separate trait of phenotype. Assuming independent assortment, the probability of an offspring appearing dominant for each trait is

    (A) 0%.

    (B) 25%.

    (C) 50%.

    (D) 75%.

    (E) 100%.

    $\frac{1}{2} \times \frac{1}{2} = \frac{1}{4}$

49. A parent cell with 64 chromosomes engages in meiosis. At the end of the second division process, each daughter cell has a chromosome number equaling

    (A) 8.

    (B) 16.

    (C) 32.

    (D) 64.

    (E) 128.

50. Another name for throat is

    (A) esophagus.

    (B) larynx.

    (C) nasal cavity.

    (D) pharynx.

    (E) trachea.

51. After storage in the epididymis, migrating sperm cells next encounter the

    (A) penis.

    (B) prostate.

    (C) testis.

    (D) urethra.

    (E) vas deferens.

52. Which one of the following pairings of plant structures/functions does NOT match?

    (A) roots - nutrient storage

    (B) xylem - movement of water

    (C) phloem - movement of sap

    (D) leaves - nitrogen uptake

    (E) stem tip - growth

53. When a young bird learns to follow the first large, moving object it sees and hears, this is an example of

   (A) trial-and-error learning.   (D) taxis.

   (B) imprinting.   (E) kinesis.

   (C) habituation.

54. Heterotrophic bacteria and fungi are similar in that both

   (A) possess food vacuoles.

   (B) have gastrovascular cavities.

   (C) undergo extracellular digestion.

   (D) have cilia for filter feeding.

   (E) undergo intracellular digestion.

55. Because whales are classified as mammals, you would expect them to have all of the following characteristics EXCEPT

   (A) a vertebral column.

   (B) a dorsal hollow nerve cord.

   (C) scales.

   (D) warm-bloodedness.

   (E) the ability to nurse their young.

56. Natural selection can occur because

   (A) fossils have been found.

   (B) the limbs of amphibians, reptiles, birds, and mammals are similar in structure.

   (C) all living things contain DNA.

   (D) more organisms are produced than can survive.

   (E) extinction decreases genetic variability.

57. One important reason for classifying fungi in a separate kingdom from plants is that fungi

   (A) may be multicellular.   (D) produce spores.

   (B) are eukaryotic.   (E) have cell walls.

   (C) are nonphotosynthetic.

Questions 58–60 refer to the growth of algae in a lake. The graph below shows the number of algae present throughout the year, as well as changes in nutrients, light, and temperature.

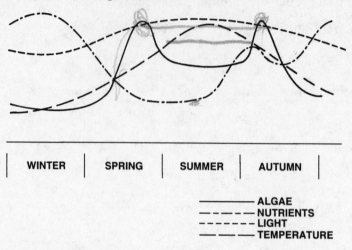

| WINTER | SPRING | SUMMER | AUTUMN |

——————— ALGAE
— — — — NUTRIENTS
- - - - - - LIGHT
— — — TEMPERATURE

58. The rate of growth of algae is greatest in the

   (A) winter.

   (B) spring and summer.

   (C) spring and autumn.

   (D) winter and summer.

   (E) summer and autumn.

59. During the summer, growth of algae is limited by

   (A) light.

   (B) temperature.

   (C) light and temperature.

   (D) nutrients.

   (E) light, temperature, and nutrients.

60. Peaks in growth of algae depend upon

   (A) light alone.

   (B) temperature alone.

   (C) nutrients alone.

   (D) light and temperature together.

   (E) light, temperature, and nutrients.

If you are taking the Biology-E test, continue with questions 61–80.

BIOLOGY-E SECTION

DIRECTIONS: The questions or incomplete statements below are followed by five possible answers or completions. Pick the answer choice that best answers or completes the question or incomplete statement and then fill in the correct oval on your answer sheet.

61. Which one of the following represents a population?

    (A) The plants in the everglades

    (B) The salamander and frogs in a marsh

    (C) The decomposers in a marsh

    (D) The red-winged blackbirds in a marsh

    (E) The red worms and sediment in a marsh

62. In a simple ecosystem there exists a field of clover (with 10,000 calories available). Mice eat the clover and skunks eat the mice. The skunks are in turn eaten by wolves. According to the 10 percent rule of ecological efficiency, how much energy would a wolf receive from the original clover plants?

    (A) 10   (D) 10,000

    (B) 100   (E) 100,000

    (C) 1,000

63. Which one of the following types of organisms occupies the trophic level of the least biomass?

    (A) Herbivores   (D) Secondary consumers

    (B) Plants   (E) Tertiary consumers

    (C) Primary consumers

64. The abiotic source of nitrogen in the nitrogen cycle is in the

    (A) atmosphere.   (D) minerals.

    (B) biomass.   (E) water.

    (C) ground.

65. The effect of _____ on population growth increases as the population size increases.

(A) density-dependent factors

(B) density-independent factors

(C) dispersal

(D) fitness

(E) spacing

66. Epiphytic plants grow on the limbs of trees, using the tree only for support. This relationship is known as

(A) predation.

(B) commensalism.

(C) mutualism.

(D) competition.

(E) amensalism.

67. Two individuals, A and B, live in marshes. If only A is present, it is found throughout the marsh, similarly for B. However, when A and B are both present, A lives in the water and B lives in the emergent vegetation. The words that describe the new position of B are

(A) fundamental niche.

(B) producer component.

(C) consumer component.

(D) realized niche.

(E) selected habitat.

68. Plant A and plant B flower at the same time but plant A attracts bees and plant B attracts insects. The bees have a mouth in the shape of a tube that fits into the floral tube of the flower. Insects cannot enter the floral tube. These adaptations of the flower and the bee are called

(A) coevolution.

(B) competitive exclusion.

(C) fertilization.

(D) keystone positioning.

(E) parasitism.

69. If there is a third plant that flowers at the same time as plants A and B in question 68, it would most likely be pollinated by

(A) bees.

(D) birds and bees.

(B) bees and insects.

(E) insects.

(C) birds.

70. Decomposers, also called detritivores, have a high production efficiency because

(A) they are the major secondary producers (consumers).

(B) they receive partially digested food.

(C) they live in all kinds of habitats.

(D) they are a diverse group of organisms.

(E) they have a high metabolic rate.

Questions 71–72 refer to the following.

Huge areas in both the temperate and tropical regions of the world are covered by these biomes. They are typically areas with relatively low total annual rainfall or uneven seasonal occurrences of rainfall. This type of climate is unfavorable for forests but suitable for growth of grasses. The temperate and tropical versions of this biome are remarkably similar in appearance, although the particular species they contain may be very different. In both cases, there are usually vast numbers of large herbivores, which often include the ungulates (hoofed animals). Burrowing rodents or rodent-like animals are also common.

71. This describes which biome?

(A) Taiga

(D) Grasslands

(B) Tundra

(E) Desert

(C) Chapparal

72. The biome characterized by location around the equator, large trees, high humidity, and a large variety of species is the

(A) taiga.

(D) deciduous forest.

(B) grasslands.

(E) None of the above.

(C) marine biomes.

Question 73 refers to the following.

It is known that phosphorus combines with iron under aerobic (with oxygen) conditions and that nitrate is lost (denitrification) under anaerobic (no oxygen) conditions. An experiment was conducted in which a lake was treated in several ways. The results are summarized in the following table.

Treatment	Observation
1. Aerate the lake	Decreased productivity
2. Add nitrate	No change
3. Add phosphate	Increased productivity
4. Add nitrate and phosphate	Increased productivity
5. Add bicarbonate	No change

73. Which treatment(s) suggest(s) that phosphorus is a limiting nutrient?

(A) Treatment 1   (D) Treatments 3 and 4

(B) Treatment 3   (E) Treatments 1, 2, 3, and 4

(C) Treatment 2

Questions 74–75 refer to the following.

E_R = respiration energy

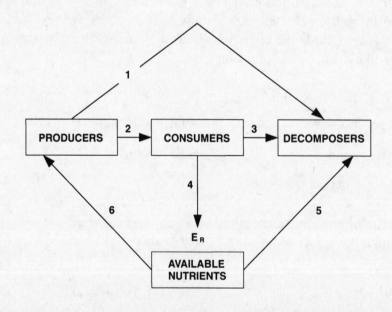

74. Which arrow(s) represent(s) only nutrient movement?

    (A) 1   (D) 4

    (B) 1 and 4   (E) 5 and 6

    (C) 2 and 3

75. Which one of the arrows represents only energy movement?

    (A) 1   (D) 4

    (B) 2   (E) 5

    (C) 3

76. Under which conditions would you expect an increase in acid rain?

    (A) Denitrification   (D) Nitrogen adsorption

    (B) Mineralization   (E) Volatilization

    (C) Nitrification

77. A town is located near the coast on the west slope of a mountain, 13°
    north of the equator. The prevailing winds are from the west. Which
    biome would be present?

    (A) Temperate chaparral   (D) Tropical grassland

    (B) Tropical alpine   (E) Tropical forest

    (C) Temperate forest

78. Which one of the following is TRUE about all temperate grassland
    areas?

    (A) The species composition is the same in similar biomes.

    (B) The abiotic requirements of the species are similar.

    (C) The pioneer species are the same.

    (D) The altitude is similar.

    (E) The amount of fresh water present is the same.

79. A river runs for 100 km from town A to town B, through agricultural land. Water from the river has been used to irrigate the fields for 50 years. Recently, the farms around town B found that the crops being produced were of a lower quality. The same was not apparent at town A. One probable explanation for the change at town B is

   (A) the ground water level at town B was decreasing and roots could not get to the water.

   (B) the pests were increasing their resistance to the pesticides.

   (C) leachates containing pesticides were passing through the soil between town A and town B and back to the river.

   (D) the development of a pan layer at site A and retention of the nutrients in the soil.

   (E) the decrease in the ozone layer was allowing more UV-B to get to the crops.

80. The burning of fossil fuel is a major source of

   (A) chlorofluorocarbons.   (D) ammonia.

   (B) carbon dioxide.   (E) dioxins.

   (C) gaseous phosphorous.

STOP
If you finish before time is called, you may check your work on the entire Biology-E test only. Do not turn to any other test in this book.

SAT Biology E/M
Practice Test 1

ANSWER KEY

BIOLOGY CORE SECTION

1.	(A)	16.	(D)	31.	(E)	46.	(D)
2.	(E)	17.	(E)	32.	(D)	47.	(D)
3.	(A)	18.	(D)	33.	(E)	48.	(B)
4.	(C)	19.	(A)	34.	(E)	49.	(C)
5.	(C)	20.	(E)	35.	(B)	50.	(D)
6.	(A)	21.	(E)	36.	(D)	51.	(E)
7.	(A)	22.	(D)	37.	(C)	52.	(D)
8.	(C)	23.	(E)	38.	(C)	53.	(B)
9.	(B)	24.	(A)	39.	(D)	54.	(C)
10.	(D)	25.	(B)	40.	(E)	55.	(C)
11.	(D)	26.	(D)	41.	(C)	56.	(D)
12.	(B)	27.	(A)	42.	(D)	57.	(C)
13.	(D)	28.	(E)	43.	(C)	58.	(C)
14.	(D)	29.	(E)	44.	(E)	59.	(D)
15.	(C)	30.	(D)	45.	(C)	60.	(E)

BIOLOGY-E SECTION

61.	(D)	66.	(B)	71.	(D)	76.	(A)
62.	(A)	67.	(D)	72.	(E)	77.	(E)
63.	(E)	68.	(A)	73.	(E)	78.	(B)
64.	(A)	69.	(C)	74.	(E)	79.	(C)
65.	(A)	70.	(B)	75.	(D)	80.	(B)

DETAILED EXPLANATIONS OF ANSWERS

PRACTICE TEST 1

BIOLOGY CORE SECTION

Questions 1–2

This set of questions asks you to analyze and categorize particular organism interactions.

1.　**(A)**

A deer tick inhabits as well as feeds off the deer by sucking the deer's blood. This is an example of parasitism. The tick is the parasite. The deer is the host.

2.　**(E)**

Two species of frogs are, in this case, related enough to share the same ecological needs. This might be food sources, avoidance of predators, etc. Therefore, they are competing for a particular place in the ecosystem. One frog gains from this relationship, the other does not.

3.　**(A)**

Antiserums Anti-A and Anti-B contain antibodies that react with antigens A and B, respectively, causing agglutination (clumping of red blood cells). Anti-A causes clumping of cells containing antigen A. Likewise, Anti-B causes clumping of cells containing antigen B. Since an individual with type AB has cells with both antigens, agglutination occurs in the presence of both Anti-A and Anti-B.

4.　**(C)**

The simplest explanation of ABO blood group inheritance is based on three alleles: I^A, I^B, and i. I^A codes for antigen A. I^B codes for antigen B. Neither antigen A nor antigen B is coded for by i. I^A and I^B are codominant alleles, and both of them are dominant to alleles, therefore, both of them are dominant to allele i. Postulated genotypes for each blood group are:

Blood Group	Genotype(s)
A	I^AI^A or I^Ai
B	I^BI^B or I^Bi
AB	I^AI^B
O	ii

An individual with genotype ii has blood type O and produces neither antigen A nor B.

5.   **(C)**
Chlorophyll is the pigment that absorbs light energy, raising electrons to a higher energy level. These excited electrons transfer their energy to chemical bond energy. NADP has the ability to pick up hydrogen atoms from water. ATP stores chemical bond energy. Carbon dioxide is the source of carbon for making glucose, the end product of photosynthesis.

6.   **(A)**
Because bacteria are prokaryotes lacking membrane-bound cell structures, they do not have a distinct nucleus separated by a nuclear membrane. In addition, their chromosome is circular. They have neither chloroplasts nor mitochondria. However, they have a cell wall, which is a complex of proteins and carbohydrates.

7.   **(A)**
This question tests your understanding of intermediary metabolism. Glycogen is converted to glucose to supply the large amounts of energy required by intense physical activity. The reverse reaction does not occur to supply energy. Because glycolysis can take place more rapidly than oxidative phosphorylation, its products (pyruvic acid and NADH) are produced faster than they can be used by the mitochondria. Instead of accumulating, they react to produce lactic acid in animals. This allows NAD, which is in limited supply, to recycle and glycolysis can continue. As lactic acid builds up, the acidity of the muscle increases until the muscle can no longer function. At that point, muscle fatigue occurs. To process the lactic acid buildup, the oxygen debt must be paid.

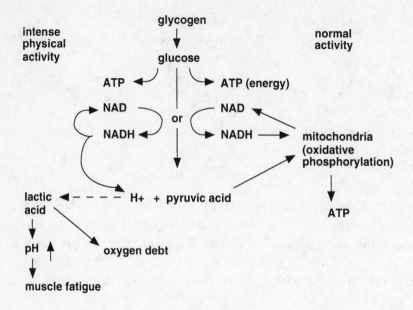

8. **(C)**

The enzymes shown have specific ranges of activity and do not function at all pH values. Each enzyme has only one optimum pH as shown by the peak for each curve. The optimum for enzyme 1 is pH 2 and the optimum for enzyme 2 is pH 9. Enzyme 2 works best at low acidity, which is represented by a high pH value. Enzyme 1 works best at high acidity as indicated by a low pH. The enzyme activity curve for pepsin, which is found in the acidic stomach, has an optimum pH of about 2, thus being most like enzyme 1.

9. **(B)**

Conditioning is a type of learning that involves an association of a novel stimulus with a stimulus that is readily recognized. When the conditioning includes reward and punishment as part of the learning, it is called trial-and-error learning, or reinforcement. Habituation is a gradual decline in response to sensation. Imprinting, on the other hand, involves the learning of a strong association that occurs during a brief period in development and is retained indefinitely.

10. **(D)**

Ferns, club mosses, and horsetails are land plants that are dependent upon a moist environment, because the sperm must swim to the egg for fertilization. Therefore, their abundances are limited. Conifers are the most abundant larger plants in the colder latitudes, while flowering plants dominate temperate (middle latitude) regions.

11. **(D)**

Monocots have one cotyledon and flower petals that occur in threes or multiples of three. Dicots have vascular bundles arranged as annual growth rings and leaves with net venation. As an adaptation to land, both types of flowering plants have a well-developed xylem for transporting water. Both are vascular plants.

12. **(B)**

This question tests your understanding of evolution and, in particular, knowing what will increase genetic variation. Mutations may involve changes in particular genes that result in new forms of the gene being produced. Meiosis is a process that involves producing gametes with one of each chromosome of a homologous pair. The chromosomes for each egg or sperm are selected at random and, thus, result in each gamete having its own combination of chromosomes. During meiosis, crossing over may occur between homologous chromosomes. This allows new combinations of genes to be located near each other and inherited as a unit on the new chromosome. The process of fertilization also increases genetic variability, since each egg and sperm contains its own combination of chromosomes. Natural selection is not a source of genetic variation, but rather acts on the genetic variation that already exists. Natural selection could, in fact, lead to decreased genetic variability.

13. **(D)**

Mendel discovered that heredity factors (alleles) inherited from parents do not blend together in their offspring but act as separate particles (Law of Segregation). These particles were later called alleles, which are different forms of a gene. Also, Mendel discovered that some of the heredity factors mask the expression of other heredity factors. This is the Law of Dominance.

14. **(D)**

This question relates to energy flow in a food chain. Primary productivity is the amount of energy from the sun that is converted to chemical bond energy during photosynthesis. Plants and other organisms with chlorophyll (e.g., phytoplankton) are the only members of the ecosystem that can accomplish this conversion. Energy can then move to other organisms (herbivores, carnivores, omnivores, decomposers) through the food chain.

15. **(C)**

For this question, you must be familiar with the functions of the various parts of the digestive tract. Absorption of most digested materials and water occurs in the small intestine. Final water reabsorption occurs in the large intestine. The esophagus functions in the transport of food to the stomach. The stomach functions in the digestion of proteins. The rectum functions in the storage of fecal matter.

16. **(D)**
The graph shows the amounts of melatonin and serotonin present during a 24-hour period. During the time of light exposure, melatonin production decreases and serotonin production increases, making (D) the correct choice. Furthermore, serotonin increases melatonin production in the dark, since serotonin is a precursor of melatonin.

17. **(E)**
This is a question about systematics. Four of the pairs of organisms represent different phyla:

ciliates (Ciliata) - sponges (Porifera)
flatworms (Platyhelminthes) - roundworms (Aschelminthes)
sea anemones (Cnidaria) - flagellates (Mastigophora)
segmented worms (Annelida) - insects (Arthropoda)

Only the clams and squid are members of the same phylum (Mollusca) and, therefore, are most closely related.

18. **(D)**
For this question you must understand how sex-linked traits are inherited. The female fruit fly is heterozygous for eye color and produces eggs that carry either an X containing a gene for red eyes or an X containing a gene for white eyes. The male produces sperm containing either an X chromosome containing a gene for red eyes or a Y chromosome that does not have an eye color gene. The Punnett square that follows indicates that all the female offspring will have red eyes, because they receive the dominant red eye gene from the father. The male offspring will have either red eyes (having received the red eye gene from the mother and a Y from the father) or will have white eyes (having received the white eye gene from the mother and a Y from the father).

Key R = red eye gene
r = white eye gene
Y = Y chromosome

Cross: red eye female × red eye male
Rr   RY

Eggs: 1/2 R   1/2 r   Sperm: 1/2 R   1/2 Y

Punnett square:

	sperm	
	1/2 R	1/2 Y
1/2 R	1/4 RR	1/4 RY
1/2 r	1/4 Rr	1/4 rY

eggs

Results:

genotypes	phenotypes
RR	red-eyed females
Rr	red-eyed females
RY	red-eyed males
rY	white-eyed males

19. (A)

This question requires a sense of the anatomical relationships of the portions of the body devoted to motion. Tendons connect bone to muscle, while ligaments provide bone-to-bone connections at the joint.

20. (E)

This question deals with the assumptions upon which evolution is based. Certain individuals have a better chance of survival because of their genetic makeup. Since more individuals are born than can survive and reproduce, those individuals with the genetic advantage will have greater reproductive success. Acquired traits will not be passed on to the next generation, because there is no genetic basis for them.

21. (E)

Because short and wrinkled are traits that show up in the offspring and were not present in the parents, they must be caused by recessive genes. Therefore, the traits, tall and smooth, must be determined by dominant genes. In addition, both parents must have been heterozygous for both tall and smooth. Finally, the genes for height and texture assort independently as indicated by the 9:3:3:1 ratio and they must, therefore, be on separate chromosomes.

Key: T = tall
      t = short
      S = smooth
      s = wrinkled

Cross: TtSs × TtSs

Gametes: 1/4 TS 1/4 Ts 1/4 tS 1/4 ts (same for both parents)

Punnett square: Results:

	TS	Ts	tS	ts
TS	TTSS	TTSs	TtSS	TtSs
Ts	TTSs	TTss	TtSs	Ttss
tS	TtSS	TtSs	ttSS	ttSs
ts	TtSs	Ttss	ttSs	ttss

9/16 T_S_ – tall smooth

3/16 T_ss – tall wrinkled

3/16 ttS_ – short smooth

1/16 ttss – short wrinkled

22. (D)

This question focuses on one of the basic requirements for evolutionary change to occur. If change is to occur, there must be genetic variation for natural selection to act upon. Athletic training, correct diet, medical care, and vitamin supplements may all improve the physical well-being of the individual, but the improvements would not be passed on to the next generation. They are environmental changes. Mutation provides the raw material for evolution.

23. (E)

The liver makes bile, which is then stored in the gallbladder. It is also responsible for a variety of metabolic conversions. These include conversions of glucose and glycogen to storage of glycogen; conversion of nitrogenous wastes to urea; and conversion of excess glucose to fat. White blood cells are manufactured in bone marrow or lymphoid tissue, not the liver.

24. (A)

For this question you must know the functions of the organelles. The ribosomes are the site of protein synthesis. They contain RNA, but RNA production occurs in the nucleus under the direction of DNA. RNA is then stored in the nucleolus of the nucleus.

25. (B)   26. (D)

Both the life cycles of moss and fern have alternation of generation. In the gametophyte generation, sperm and eggs are produced. The cells of the gametophyte generation have one-half the normal number of chromosomes (1N). The small green moss plants you see are the gametophytes. The gametophyte of the fern is a small structure (quarter-size) usually under the leaf litter; therefore, it is not as conspicuous in the fern. The sporophyte grows from the fertilized egg. The fern frond you see is the sporophyte generation. The sporophyte of moss is a very small brown stock with a capsule growing from the top of the female gametophyte. The cells of the sporophyte have the normal number of chromosomes (2N). The sporophytes produce spores by the process of meiosis in both moss and fern. The spores can withstand harsh environmental conditions. Both moss and sperm need a moist habitat because the sperm swims through a thin film of water to the egg. Also, the embryo is not protected inside a seed from drying out.

27. **(A)**
Biomass is limited by the energy available to manufacture organic matter in living organisms. Energy enters the food chain via the producers who convert light energy to chemical bond energy. Since each transfer of organic material involves a loss of energy, each successive level of the food chain has less energy than the preceding level. Therefore, the first level has the most energy and, thus, the largest amount of organic material or biomass.

28. **(E)**
This question requires some knowledge of the experimental data that support the concept of evolution. The more traditional evidence includes the fossil record and similarities in limb structures in different organisms. More recent evidence comes from molecular studies that include similarities in proteins and chromosome banding patterns. Differences in physical appearance within a species merely reflect individual variation with no evidence of whether these traits are acquired or inherited, or whether changes have occurred over time.

29. **(E)**
Familiarity with aquatic ecosystems is important in this question. Dead plants and animals settle to the bottom of lakes and undergo decomposition. Nutrients, such as nitrogen, phosphorus, etc., are released during this process of decay. In order to sustain life in the lake, these nutrients must be recycled. Ice floats on water and, as it melts, this cold water becomes denser and settles to the bottom of the lake. The warmer bottom water moves to the top as an upwelling, carrying the nutrients with it. These nutrients support the growth of living organisms, especially plants. This recycling of water also prevents temperature stratification of the lake during the period of upwelling.

30. **(D)**
Mitosis is the process of cell division that results in two daughter cells that are exactly the same as the original parent cell. Meiosis results in

gametes (eggs or sperm) or spores (in plants) with half the number of chromosomes (haploid) as the original cell. Meiosis is the preparation for fertilization, since fertilization returned the chromosomes to the original diploid number. DNA replication occurs in preparation for mitosis and meiosis 1. Chromosomes must duplicate before the duplicates can be separated in cell division. Meiosis 2 involves the delivery of the chromosomes to their respective cells, but does not involve another round of DNA replication.

31. **(E)**
The most stable community is the climax community. This type of community is marked by a large biomass, complex organization, and the fact that it does not change its environment. A lake tends to fill in with the accumulation of organic material. It will first become a marsh and then a meadow. A meadow provides open areas for the growth of shrubs, and trees then replace the shrubs. A forest is the end stage of succession, a climax community.

32. **(D)**
This question tests your knowledge of the development of the three germ layers. The outer layer (ectoderm) develops into the nervous system, the lens of the eye, as well as the skin. The middle layer (mesoderm) will develop into muscle and bone. The endoderm (inner layer) becomes the digestive tract.

33. **(E)**
DNA is a double-stranded nucleic acid, with a sugar (deoxyribose) and phosphate backbone. RNA is single-stranded with a sugar (ribose) and phosphate backbone. Both nucleic acids contain the bases adenine, guanine, and cytosine. In addition, DNA contains the base thymine, while RNA contains uracil.

34. **(E)**
The primary purpose is to reduce the chromosome number from the normal diploid number in order to produce eggs and sperm with half that number (haploid). Then, when fertilization occurs the diploid chromosome number is restored. A side benefit of meiosis occurs during prophase I when like chromosomes pair up. At this point, crossing over can occur, and, thus, increase genetic variability. Meioses in sperm production results in four sperm for each event, while meiosis in egg production gives only one egg. Because cell division is uneven in egg production, one of the cells receives most of the cytoplasm. The process of meiosis insures genetic variability, and, therefore, does not result in identical offspring.

Questions 35–36

This group of questions refers to experiments on competition between two species of flour beetles when grown together in flour.

35. **(B)**
You are asked to determine which portion of Graph I shows the greatest rate of increase of *Tribolium* adults. Days 0 to 25 show no increase. Days 50 to 100, 100 to 150, and 150 to 200 show minor fluctuations, but no overall increase in numbers of adults. The largest increase (from 10 to 120 adults) occurs from day 25 to day 50. Compare the various slopes of the lines in the graphs to assess growth rate.

36. **(D)**
In order to answer this question, you need to compare the difference in growth of both species when grown in pure flour (Graph I) vs. growth in the same amount of flour with glass tubing added (Graph II). Graph II shows more *Tribolium* adults and more *Oryzaephilus* adults than Graph I. Therefore, the presence of glass tubing has resulted in an increase in growth of both species. The glass tubing probably offered a habitat choice to reduce competition.

Questions 37–40

This set of questions tests your general knowledge of the circulatory system as well as your ability to interpret data about the circulatory system that is presented in graph form.

37. **(C)**
The capillaries have the slowest rate of blood flow with a velocity of 0.05 cm/sec. This is consistent with the function of the capillaries to allow for exchanges of materials. Capillary beds have the greatest overall cross-sectional area, reducing blood flow velocity.

38. **(C)**
To answer this question you must realize that the exchanges of nutrients, gases, and waste products occur across blood vessels that are especially adapted for this purpose. These adaptations are found in the capillaries. They are both thin-walled and contain blood flowing at a slow rate.

39. **(D)**
The ability to interpret the data presented in the table will yield the answer to this question. We cannot make a direct correlation of blood

pressure with cross-sectional area. This is because blood pressure decreases as the distance from the heart increases, while cross-sectional area increases, then decreases. A velocity first decreases, then increases, while blood pressure continues to decrease. A comparison of cross-sectional area and velocity indicates that as the cross-sectional area increases, the velocity decreases.

40. **(E)**

An understanding of the anatomy of the circulatory system will lead to the answer to this question. The blood that leaves the heart, leaves via the left ventricle and enters the aorta. This is why the blood pressure is the highest in the aorta. The heart, as a pump, is the source of the pressure.

Questions 41–42

For this set of questions you must be familiar with experimental design and you must know that it is possible to induce mutations.

41. **(C)**

Petri plate I shows normal growth of the bacteria. Plate II containing minimal medium alone is the control for the experimental plates (plate III containing chemical A and plate IV containing chemical B). Thus, chemicals A and B are the independent variables in this experiment. Temperature is one of the conditions held constant during the experiment, and the colony counts are the results. These counts are the dependent variables.

42. **(D)**

Since more colonies appear on plate III which was treated with chemical A, mutations must have occurred in the defective histidine gene. This gene now has the ability to produce histidine and can survive without histidine in the medium. Since plate IV containing chemical B has the same growth as the control (plate II), we must conclude that chemical B does not cause mutations of the defective histidine gene.

43. **(C)**

The membranes of living cells carefully control the internal salt concentration, but water moves according to its relative concentration. Because the inside of the cell has a particular salinity, water will move across the membrane from its area of higher concentration to its area of lower concentration, causing a change in cell diameter. Water, by osmosis, moves into a hypertonic environment.

44. **(E)**

To answer this question you must know something about the structure of plants and the osmotic relationship of plants to their environment. Plants have a cell wall which prevents them from bursting no matter how hypotonic their environment. Plant cells in a hypertonic environment will lose water to the environment. If the environment is isotonic, there will be an equal exchange of water with the environment. When plant cells are in a hypotonic environment, they take in water and become firm. This is what is found naturally, and accounts for the turgor pressure characteristic of plant cells. A salt-free environment is hypotonic.

45. **(C)**   46. **(D)**

The long neck variation had an advantage on the island with thick shrubs shading out growth on the floor. The tortoises could browse the shrubs with their long necks. The tropical forest, rocky, and active volcanic islands did not support low vegetation or the terrain was not suitable for tortoises. Tortoises did not need long necks to survive on the open grassland island. This is an example of Darwin's theory of natural selection, the theory that explains why evolution occurs. The theory has four principles. Because each species produces more offspring than can survive (overpopulation), there is competition (struggle for existence). In every population, organisms have different traits (variations), and these traits can be inherited. The individuals with favorable variations in a particular environment will most likely live longer and produce more offspring (survival of the fittest). The long-neck tortoise is an example of natural selection and is a culmination of all the principles which include survival of the fittest. Acquired characteristics is the theory of Lamarck in which he proposed that organisms could change through "use or disuse" of body parts and pass these changes on to their offspring. Now we know that change comes through genetic mutation or genetic recombination.

47 **(D)**

Red blood cells are the smallest body cells, seven to eight micrometers in diameter. White blood cells are slightly larger. Nerve and skeletal muscle cells are larger; the human ovum is large enough to be visible without using a microscope, approximately 1.5 mm in diameter.

48. **(B)**

Consider the following Punnett square that summarizes this genetic cross. On the far left block of the genetic grid, there is a genotype AaBb. This is the only genotype endowing the organism with at least one dominant allele in each gene pair for development of the dominant pheno-type of each trait. The other three genotypes, Aabb, aaBb, and aabb, do not.

	AB	Ab	aB	ab
ab	AaBb	Aabb	aaBb	aabb

49. (C)

Meiosis halves the chromosome number. If sex cells fertilize, sex cells with the halved chromosome number recombine to form a zygote with the full chromosome complement.

50. (D)

The pharynx is a region in which the respiratory and digestive tracts cross over. Air moves through the nasal cavity (more anterior) into the pharynx and on to the larynx (ventral). The oral cavity (more posterior) passes food into the pharynx end of the esophagus (dorsal).

51. (E)

Sperm travel through the following structures in the following order: testis, epididymis, vas deferens, ejaculatory duct, prostatic urethra, and penile urethra.

52. (D)

This question deals with the structure and function of plant parts. Roots, among other functions, are responsible for the storage of nutrients made by the plant. Movement of water occurs via xylem, while movement of sap occurs via phloem. Meristematic tissue is where cell division occurs, and one location for this tissue is the tip of the stem.

While the nitrogen content of air is about 78%, gaseous nitrogen cannot be used by plants. Therefore, nitrogen uptake does not occur through the leaves. Nitrate and ammonia ions are formed by microorganisms in the soil from gaseous nitrogen during the process of nitrogen fixation. Nitrate and ammonium ions may also be supplied by decomposers. These ions are then taken up by the plant roots.

53. (B)

For this question you must be familiar with animal behavior, and, in particular, different types of learning. A taxis is an oriented movement in response to an environmental stimulus, while a kinesis is a random response. Neither of these are learned behaviors.

Trial-and-error, habituation, and imprinting are all considered types of learning. Trial-and-error learning involves improvement in a response based upon previous experience. Habituation, on the other hand, is a decreased response to a stimulus after continued exposure to the stimulus. The behavior of the young bird is an example of imprinting. This type of learning occurs during a sensitive period in the development of the organism and usually is irreversible.

54. (C)

This question asks you to look at a variety of ways that organisms obtain nutrients, and determine what bacteria and fungi have in common. Food vacuoles form by phagocytosis and are a means of engulfing food material for later digestion within the vacuole. This type of food procurement is characteristic of amoeba. Food may also be digested in a cavity called the gastrovascular cavity. Planaria and coelenterates have gastrovascular cavities. Clams trap food in mucus that flows along its gills. The trapped food is moved by cilia to the mouth for entry into the internal digestive system, a process called filter feeding. Food vacuole formation is a form of intracellular digestion, while the gastrovascular cavity and filter feeding provide for extracellular digestion.

Fungi and bacteria do not have internal digestive systems. They, therefore, rely upon excretion of digestive enzymes onto living or dead organic material, and absorption of the digestive end-products. Thus, digestion in fungi and bacteria is extracellular.

55. (C)

To answer this question you must apply your knowledge of the classification of mammals to a specific situation—you must predict the characteristics that you would expect whales to have. Vertebrates, in general, have a vertebral column and dorsal hollow nerve cord. Since mammals are vertebrates, they would also have these characteristics. Birds and mammals are warm-blooded, and mammals nurse their young. Scales are a characteristic of fish and reptiles, and would not be expected on whales.

56. (D)

This question asks you to determine the conditions under which natural selection occurs rather than the experimental evidence for natural selection. The fossil record and similarities in limb structure among organisms is evidence for the existence of natural selection. However, natural selection can only occur when more organisms are produced than can survive, allowing the best-adapted to survive and reproduce. The fact that all living things contain DNA is another piece of evidence that organisms may have a common heritage, but is not a precondition for evolution. Natural selection may lead to extinction, but extinction does not cause natural selection.

57. **(C)**

This question asks you to distinguish between fungi and plants. Both fungi and plants are eukaryotes, may be multicellular, produce spores during parts of their life cycles, and have cell walls. Plants carry out photosynthesis, while fungi obtain energy and raw materials for growth by decomposing living or dead organic material. They are heterotrophs, not autotrophs.

Questions 58–60

To answer this set of questions you must read and analyze results presented in graphical form showing changes in a population of algae and changes in environmental variables.

58. **(C)**

This question asks you to interpret the data shown on the graph. You must look at the unbroken line showing the number of algae present and find the steepest portions slanting upward. There are marked increases in growth in both the spring and autumn.

59. **(D)**

To answer this question you must compare the levels of nutrients, light, and temperature during the summer, yet algal peaks do not occur then. On the other hand, nutrient levels are low and must, therefore, be the limiting factors.

60. **(E)**

To answer this question you must compare the changes in environmental factors with peaks in algal growth. In the winter, nutrient levels are high, but light and temperature are at their lowest. Therefore, light and temperature must be limiting factors. Maximum growth in the spring corresponds to high nutrient levels with increasing amounts of light and temperature. As the algae grow they use up nutrients in the environment, which limits their continued growth. In the fall, nutrient levels begin to increase again. Growth increases and is sustained while temperature and light levels are still high.

BIOLOGY – E SECTION

61. (D)

A population is all of the individuals of a particular species in a particular area. The red-winged blackbirds in a marsh fit the definition of a population. The plants (A) are a large taxonomic group that includes many species. The salamanders and frogs (B) are two different species in the marsh. The decomposers (C) are one group in a trophic level that includes many species. The red worms and sediment (E) include only one species but also include an abiotic factor, the sediment.

62. (A)

The average ecological efficiency per trophic level is 10 percent. Therefore, we expect that for every 10,000 calories available from clover plants, 1,000 calories will be obtained for use by a mouse. When a skunk eats this mouse, only 100 of the 1,000 calories will be available to the skunk. In the last trophic level of this food chain, the wolf will obtain 10 percent of the 100 calories transferred to the skunk. Thus, a mere 10 calories of the original 10,000 calories can be used for the metabolic processes of the wolf.

A top trophic level carnivore that is receiving only one-thousandths of the original calories of the plants must be sparsely distributed and far ranging in its activities because of its high food consumption requirements. Wolves must travel as much as 20 miles a day to acquire enough food. The territories of individual tigers and other great cats often cover hundreds of square miles.

63. (E)

Energy flows from plants (producers) to herbivores (primary consumers) to additional levels of consumers in the food chain. As you can tell from question 62, each succeeding link has less remaining available energy. Loss of energy can be attributed to the respiration of organisms and the consequent dissipation of heat, due to the inability of most animals to digest the cellulose of plants.

64. (A)

This gas constitutes 79% of the atmosphere. Soil-dwelling bacteria create a chemical form for plant use—nitrogen fixation.

65. **(A)**

Two additional answers affect the growth of populations but only density-dependent factors always affect the growth as the size increases. Density-independent factors (B) have an effect on both small and large populations. Dispersal (C) affects the genetic diversity and the distribution but not specifically the growth. Fitness (D) contributes to the growth of populations, but it is independent of the size of the population. Spacing (E) affects the distribution of the populations.

66. **(B)**

The tree provides only support and thus is not affected, whereas the epiphytic plant benefits from the support. No other interaction results in a benefit to one species with no effect on the second. Predation (A) and mutualism (C) result in a benefit to one species, but there is either a harm or a benefit to the second species. Competition (D) results in a negative effect to both species. Amensalism (E) results in harm to one species with no effect on the second species.

67. **(D)**

The ecological position, or niche, of species B is changed because of competition. The new niche is the realized niche. The niche in absence of any interactions is the fundamental niche (A). Species B lives in the emergent vegetation which is the producer component (B) but living in a vegetation does not make the individual a producer; the type of individual is not given. Similarly, because the type of individual is not known it cannot be assumed to be a consumer (C). Because species B lived in the whole pond, the new habitat is not selected (E).

68. **(A)**

The bee obtains nectar from a flower of plant A and at the same time picks up pollen. The bee carries this pollen to other flowers of plant A, thereby acting as a pollinator. Adaptations of the flower to attract only bees means that the pollen goes only to flowers of the same species. Adaptations of the bee that enhance access to the pollen increase the bee's chance of obtaining the pollen. This is coevolution. There is competitive exclusion (B) of the insect by the bee but not between the bee and the flower. Both the bee and plant A benefit, and thus there is no parasitism (E). The cross fertilization increases the genetic diversity of plant A but it does not increase species diversity as do keystone positioning (D) of the bee and plant A. The bee carries the pollen that fertilizes other individuals of plant A but the bee does not fertilize (C) plant A.

69. **(C)**

Plant C flowers at the same time as plants A and B. Therefore, pollination by a species different than the ones that pollinate plants A and B would prevent mixing of pollen from the three plants. In each of the other cases, pollen from at least two plants would be mixed. The pollen from plant A and plant C would be mixed if bees (A) pollinated plant C. The pollen from plant A and plant B would be mixed with the pollen from plant C if bees and insects (B) pollinated plant C. The pollen from plant A and plant C would be mixed if birds and bees (D) pollinated plant C. The pollen from plant B and plant C would be mixed if insects (E) pollinated plant C.

70. **(B)**

Because much of the food that detritivores ingest is already partially digested, they put less energy into digestion. They ingest large quantities of food but are not classified as consumers (A), and quantity is not related to efficiency. Also, they do live in all kinds of habitats (C) and they are a diverse group (D), but this contributes to their major role as consumers, not to efficiency. Their metabolic rate may be high (E) at high temperatures, but this would reduce efficiency.

71. **(D)**

The biome described has relatively low rainfall, is suitable for growth of grasses but not trees, and is inhabited by many large herbivores. The taiga (A) is characterized by largely evergreen forest vegetation which eliminates this choice as the biome described cannot support trees. The tundra (B) has low temperatures unsuitable for trees or grasses, thereby eliminating this choice. The chapparal (C) is an incorrect choice because it has abundant rain in the winter and its land is favorable for the growth of evergreen trees. The desert (E) does receive little rainfall but vegetation is sparse, making it difficult for large numbers of herbivores to live in this biome. The grassland (D) is the correct answer. The grassland biome is characterized by a low amount of rainfall (25–75 cm/year) and it provides natural pastures for grazing animals and vegetation to support the large number of herbivores that exist there.

72. **(E)**

You know from the answer to question 71 that the biome described in question 72 cannot be taiga (A) or grasslands (B). Although the marine biome (C) supports a large variety of organisms, it does not have to be near the equator. (C) is incorrect. The deciduous forest (D) is characterized by different types of trees but it is not necessarily near the equator, nor does it necessarily have high humidity. The answer is none of the above (E). The biome described in the question indicates that the answer should be tropical rainforest, which was not an answer choice.

73. **(E)**

If an increase in a nutrient increases productivity and a decrease in the same nutrient reduces productivity while no change occurs with the addition of other nutrients, the first nutrient is the one that limits the productivity. Therefore, to show that phosphorus is a limiting nutrient, treatments 1, 2, 3, and 4 are required. Treatment 1 (A) suggests that a decrease in phosphorus reduces productivity. Treatment 3 (B) suggests that the addition of phosphate increases productivity. Treatment 2 (C) shows no effect due to nitrate, but without this information and because the extent of the increase is not given for treatments 3 and 4 (D), it is not clear whether the effect is due to phosphate, or to phosphate and nitrate.

74. **(E)**

The decomposers release nutrients (5) which are taken up by organisms (6). Energy and nutrients move from producers to decomposers (A) and from producers to consumers to decomposers (C). Although both energy and nutrients move from producers to consumers, only respiratory energy (B) and (D) is unavailable to organisms.

75. **(D)**

Respiratory energy is heat that is unavailable to other organisms. Both nutrients and energy move from the producer to the decomposer (A), the producer to the consumer (B), and the consumer to the decomposers (C). Only nutrients are made available by the decomposers (E).

76. **(A)**

Denitrification releases nitrogen oxides into the atmosphere. Reaction of these oxides with water forms nitric acid, one of the acids that contributes to acid rain. Mineralization (B) releases ammonium from dead organisms. Nitrification (C) converts ammonium to nitrate. Some of the ammonia is adsorbed (D) to soil particles. Volatilization (E) releases the gas ammonia, which is basic.

77. **(E)**

The town is near the coast on the windward side of a mountain in the tropics. It would be hot and receive a large amount of precipitation. It is 15° from the equator and does not have a temperate climate (A) and (C). It is near the coast on the side of the mountain, not high in the mountain and would not be in the alpine area (B). Tropical grasslands (D) have only a moderate amount of precipitation.

78. **(B)**

This question is about characteristics of biomes, not specifically about temperate grasslands. An important characteristic of biomes is the similar abiotic conditions. The types of species present, not the particular species composition (A), are similar. This is also true for pioneer species (C) in succession. The altitude (D) may or may not be similar. Altitude affects the parameters that define the abiotic conditions but by itself does not determine the biome. The amount of fresh water (E) within a terrestrial ecosystem can affect the particular characteristics of the terrestrial system, but it is not consistent among any one terrestrial ecosystem.

79. **(C)**

Town A is 100 km upstream from town B. Leaching of pesticides from the agricultural land to the river, for the 100 km between the two towns, is a reasonable explanation of the lower quality crops at town B. Remember, the river water which would receive the leachates is used to irrigate the land at town B. The development of a pan layer at town A (D) could enhance the movement of pesticides to the adjacent river, but the slope of the land is not known. In addition, the answer only says that the pan layer increased the nutrients content of the soil at town A. Decreasing groundwater level (A) is a reasonable choice but the groundwater would also be decreasing at town A, only 100 km away. Similarly, ozone depletion (E) can affect the growth of some plants and pests can increase their resistance to pesticides (B), but both should also be apparent at town A.

80. **(B)**

Carbon dioxide is the main product released from burning of fossil fuels. Chlorofluorocarbons (A) are released from refrigerants. Although fossil fuels are produced from organic matter and organic matter contains phosphorus, there is no gaseous form of phosphorus (C). Gaseous nitrogen oxides, not ammonia (D) are released from burning fossil fuels. Dioxins (E) are synthetic chemicals. They are not contained in fossil fuels.

SAT Biology E/M
Practice Test 2

(Answer sheets appear in the back of this book.)

TIME: 1 Hour
        80 Questions

BIOLOGY CORE SECTION

DIRECTIONS: The lettered or numbered choices below refer to the questions or statements that immediately follow them. Pick the best answer choice and fill in the correct oval on your answer sheet. An answer choice may be used more than once or not at all.

Questions 1–3 refer to the following.

(A) Alga   (D) Minnow

(B) Bass   (E) Sunfish

(C) Human

Assume that all of the organisms that are listed above are members of a single food chain.

1. Which organism is a primary consumer?

    D

2. The least amount of useful energy is available to which organism?

    C

3. Which organism is the producer?

    A

Questions 4–6 refer to the following blood vessels.

(A) Arteriole   (D) Vein

(B) Artery   (E) Venule

(C) Capillary

4. Which blood vessel has a higher blood pressure than any other type of vessel?

B

5. Which blood vessel returns blood directly to the heart?

∅   D

6. Which blood vessel is the site of exchange of substances with body cells?

C

DIRECTIONS: The questions or incomplete statements below are followed by five possible answers or completions. Pick the answer choice that best answers or completes the question or incomplete statement and then fill in the correct oval on your answer sheet.

---

7. A protozoan cell is immersed in pure water. Select the correct statement from the following about the cell's behavior and environment.

   (A) The cell will gain water.

   (B) The cell will lose water.

   (C) The exterior environment is hypertonic.

   (D) The cell's interior is hypotonic.

   (E) The cell is isotonic to the outside.

8. White blood cells can engulf large foreign debris in the body by

   (A) active transport.   (D) phagocytosis.

   (B) diffusion.   (E) pinocytosis.

   (C) exocytosis.

9. Cells can move particles of matter from areas of lower concentration to areas of higher concentration through the expenditure of energy. This process is termed

   (A) active transport.   (D) hydrolysis.

   (B) bulk flow.   (E) osmosis.

   (C) diffusion.

Questions 10–12 refer to the following diagram.

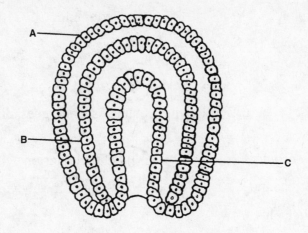

10. Embryonic layer A gives rise to

    (A) bones.

    (B) the digestive tract.

    (C) the kidney.

    (D) muscles.

    (E) the nervous system.

11. Embryonic layer B gives rise to

    (A) the digestive tract.

    (B) the kidney.

    (C) the liver.

    (D) muscles.

    (E) skin.

12. Embryonic layer C gives rise to

    (A) bones.

    (B) dermis.

    (C) the digestive tract.

    (D) epidermis.

    (E) muscles.

13. Select the light with the longest wavelength that is also absorbed during photosynthesis.

     (A) Blue

    (B) Green

    (C) Orange

    (D) Red

    (E) Yellow

14. Meiosis produces cells that are

    (A) diploid.   (D) tetraploid.

    (B) haploid.   (E) zygotes.

    (C) homologous.

15. Which one of the following organelles undergoes division during mitosis?

    (A) Ribosome   (D) Mitochondrion

    (B) Lysosome   (E) None of the above.

    (C) Nucleolus

16. A genetic counselor informs two prospective parents that they have a 100% chance of having a child who will develop diabetes mellitus. The genotype of the two parents is

    (A) both heterozygous.

    (B) both homozygous dominant.

    (C) both homozygous recessive.

    (D) one homozygous dominant, one heterozygous.

    (E) one homozygous recessive, one heterozygous.

17. A DNA strand has a base sequence of CGTAGT. The messenger RNA transcribed from it has a base sequence of

    (A) ACUACG.   (D) GACUAC.

    (B) CGTAGT.   (E) UACGUA.

    (C) GCAUCA.

18. The protein binding and blocking the operator gene in the operon model of gene control is the

    (A) inactivator.   (D) regulator.

    (B) operation.   (E) repressor.

    (C) promoter.

19. Which one of the following organisms is ciliated?

    (A) *Amoeba*

    (B) *Clostridium*

    (C) *Euglena*

    (D) *Paramecium*

    (E) *Trypanosoma*

Question 20 refers to the following diagram.

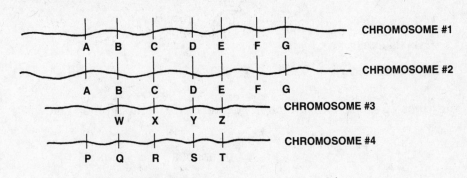

LETTERS DENOTE GENE SITES

20. A deletion could yield chromosome

    (A) ABCDEFGH.

    (B) ABCDEFGEFG.

    (C) PQRST.

    (D) WXY.

    (E) WXYZPQ.

21. Which plant tissue matures to become wood in an aging tree?

    (A) Epidermis

    (B) Collenchyma

    (C) Cortex

    (D) Phloem

    (E) Xylem

22. Impulses normally traverse the regions of a neuron in which of the following orders?

    (A) Axon, cell body, dendrite

    (B) Axon, dendrite, cell body

    (C) Cell body, dendrite, axon

    (D) Dendrite, axon, cell body

    (E) Dendrite, cell body, axon

23. The portion of the brain continuous with the spinal cord is the

   (A) cerebellum.   (D) pons.

   (B) cerebrum.   (E) thalamus.

   (C) medulla.

24. Which endocrine gland secretes human growth hormones?

   (A) Adrenal   (D) Pituitary

   (B) Pancreas   (E) Thyroid

   (C) Parathyroid

Questions 25–26 refer to the phylogenetic tree of animal phyla below.

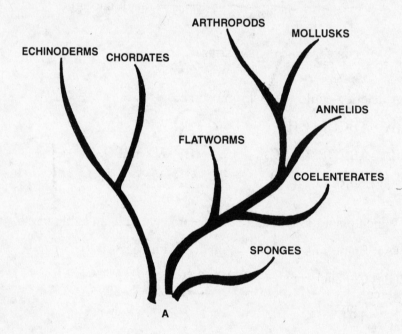

25. **A** was

   (A) a plant.   (D) a one-celled organism.

   (B) an alga.   (E) a vertebrate.

   (C) an arthropod.

26. Which two phyla are the most distantly related?

   (A) Annelids and arthropods

   (B) Arthropods and mollusks

(C) Coelenterates and flatworms

(D) Echinoderms and chordates

(E) Echinoderms and mollusks

27. Storage of fecal matter mainly occurs in what portion of the gastrointestinal tract?

(A) Large intestine

(B) Small intestine

(C) Pharynx

(D) Rectum

(E) Stomach

28. A correct summary of the normal human male chromosome complement is

(A) 42 autosomes, 2 X chromosomes, 2 Y chromosomes.

(B) 44 autosomes, 2 X chromosomes.

(C) 44 autosomes, 1 X chromosome, 1 Y chromosome.

(D) 46 autosomes, 2 X chromosomes.

(E) 46 autosomes, 1 X chromosome, 1 Y chromosome.

29. A source of genetic change in a population is

(A) catastrophism.

(B) fossils.

(C) gene flow.

(D) mutations.

(E) natural selection.

30. A female carrier of hemophilia marries a male hemophiliac. What percent of their daughters can they expect to develop hemophilia?

(A) 0

(B) 25

(C) 50

(D) 75

(E) 100

31. A community of organisms interacting with abiotic environmental factors composes a(n)

(A) biogeochemical cycle.

(B) food chain.

(C) ecosystem.

(D) niche.

(E) population.

32. Which naturalist independently came to a conclusion similar to Darwin's natural selection principle?

(A) Cuvier

(D) Malthus

(B) Lamarck

(E) Wallace

(C) Lyell

33. For a given trait, a randomly-mating population has established a dominant gene frequency of 70% in its gene pool. The frequency of homozygous recessive individuals in the population is

(A) 0.03.

(D) 0.3.

(B) 0.09.

(E) 0.7.

(C) 0.27.

34. The vertebrate class Chondrichthyes contains the member

(A) bullfrog.

(D) shark.

(B) rattlesnake.

(E) trout.

(C) robin.

Questions 35–36 refer to the cross section of a leaf viewed through a microscope.

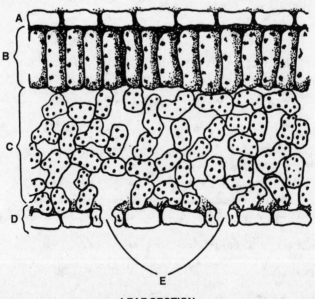

LEAF SECTION

35. The epidermal layer without stomata is labeled

    (A) A.   (D) D.

    (B) B.   (E) E.

    (C) C.

36. An accurate statement about the layer of cells that is labeled B is

    (A) 100% humidity exists between cells here.

    (B) photosynthesis can occur rapidly here.

    (C) stomata work actively here.

    (D) this is the spongy mesophyll.

    (E) this layer contains the leaf cuticle.

Questions 37–38 refer to the experimental findings required to grow a crop of corn. Results are summarized in the table below.

Nutrient	Pounds required to grow 100 bushels of corn per acre
N	160
K	80
P	40
Zn	3
Mg	.5
Mn	.2
Cu	.1
Mb	.05

37. The element to be incorporated into plant protein structure is

    (A) K.   (D) N.

    (B) Mg.   (E) Zn.

    (C) Mn.

38. Which one of the following elements is a macronutrient?

    (A) Copper

    (B) Magnesium

    (C) Manganese

    (D) Potassium

    (E) Zinc

Questions 39–41 refer to the table below. Solve in each case for the unsolved air volume from three human subjects tested in the lab.

Respiratory Rate	Tidal Volume (ml)	Respiratory Minute Volume (ml)	Expiratory Reserve Volume (ml)	Inspiratory Reserve Volume (ml)	Vital Capacity (ml)
12	500	6,000	(A)	2,500	5,000
10	400	4,000	1,500	2,400	(B)
15	(C)	9,000	2,000	3,000	5,000

These values were recorded from three separate subject readings during an experiment concerning spirometry—the measurement of air-breathing volumes.

39. Unrecorded volume A is

    (A) 1,000.

    (B) 2,000.

    (C) 3,000.

    (D) 4,000.

    (E) 5,000.

40. Unrecorded volume B is

    (A) 3,900.

    (B) 4,300.

    (C) 4,400.

    (D) 5,500.

    (E) 8,300.

41. Unrecorded volume C is

    (A) 100.

    (B) 200.

    (C) 300.

    (D) 600.

    (E) 1,000.

Questions 42–43 refer to the graph below.

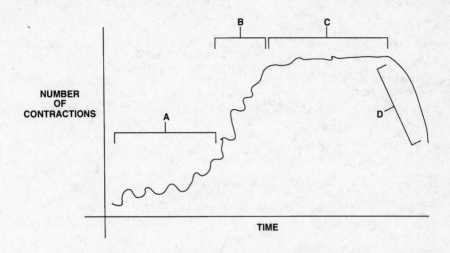

42. The graph depicts all patterns of muscle contraction EXCEPT

(A) fatigue.

(D) simple twitch.

(B) tetanus.

(E) summation.

(C) tonus.

43. The muscle response in region D is due to

(A) accumulation of lactic acid.

(B) excess glucose.

(C) lack of stimulation.

(D) presence of ATP.

(E) wasting of muscle proteins.

Questions 44–45 refer to the following drawings.

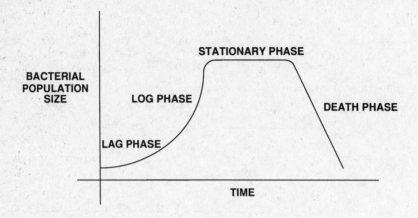

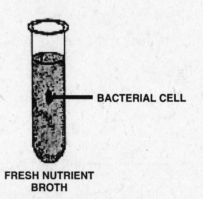

FRESH NUTRIENT
BROTH

44. One bacterial cell is placed into a nutrient broth in a test tube at noon. Its generation time is 20 minutes. By 2:00 p.m., the size of the population of bacteria in the test tube is

(A) 2.   (D) 64.

(B) 16.   (E) 128.

(C) 32.

45. A correct statement about the population's stationary phase is

(A) cells are not dying.

(B) cells are not reproducing.

(C) cell birthrate equals cell death rate

(D) cell death rate exceeds cell birthrate.

(E) cells reproduce too rapidly.

46. Which one of the following do reptiles and amphibians have in common?

    (A) Egg-laying in moist or wet environments

    (B) A four-chambered heart

    (C) Lungs in the adult form

    (D) External fertilization

    (E) Dry, scaly skin

47. Which one of the following extinct forms most closely resembles present day *Homo sapiens*?

    (A) *Australopithecus*   (D) *Cro-Magnon*

    (B) *Homo erectus*   (E) *Zinjanthropus*

    (C) *Homo habilis*

48. Poison ivy using an oak tree to reach more light is an example of

    (A) commensalism.   (D) parasitism.

    (B) mutualism.   (E) adaptive behavior.

    (C) competition.

Questions 49–51

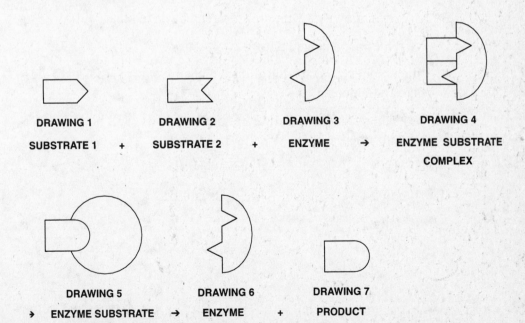

DRAWING 1   DRAWING 2   DRAWING 3   DRAWING 4

SUBSTRATE 1 +   SUBSTRATE 2 +   ENZYME   →   ENZYME SUBSTRATE
                                                   COMPLEX

DRAWING 5   DRAWING 6   DRAWING 7

→ ENZYME SUBSTRATE → ENZYME   +   PRODUCT
   COMPLEX

49. Looking at drawings 1 through 7, it can be stated that

    I.   substrates and enzymes are made of proteins.

    II.   there are specific sites on enzymes that substrates can bind or connect.

    III. enzymes speed up chemical reactions.

    (A) I only.   (D) I and III.

    (B) II only.   (E) I, II, and III.

    (C) III only.

50. By looking at drawings 1 through 7, it can be stated that

    I.   enzymes bond substrate molecules together.

    II.   substrates and enzymes are bonded together to make a new molecule before product formation.

    III. enzymes change their shape when bonding substrate molecules together.

    (A) I only.   (D) I and III.

    (B) II only.   (E) II and III.

    (C) III only.

51. By looking at drawings 1 through 7, it can be stated that

    I.   enzymes are changed during the reaction.

    II.   the product molecule has different chemical properties than the substrate molecules.

    III. if a cell produces 100 different products there will be 100 different enzymes.

    (A) I only.   (D) I and II.

    (B) II only.   (E) II and III.

    (C) III only.

Questions 52–54

Plots 1, 2, and 3 of a transect have the following distribution of juvenile and mature trees.

	Plot 1 Juvenile/Mature		Plot 2 Juvenile/Mature		Plot 3 Juvenile/Mature	
Red Oak	0	0	2	0	0	3
Sugar Maple	0	0	2	0	0	3
White Oak	0	0	3	0	0	4
White Pine	1	0	8	2	0	0
Predominant Ground Cover	Perennial Weeds and Grasses		Moss, Ferns		Wild Flowers	

52. An ecotone community is represented by

 I.   plot 1.

 II. plot 2.

 III. plot 3.

 (A) I only.   (D) I and II.

 (B) II only.   (E) II and III.

 (C) III only.

53. A climax community is represented by

 I.   plot 1.

 II. plot 2.

 III. plot 3.

 (A) I only.   (D) I, II, and III.

 (B) II only.   (E) II and III.

 (C) III only.

54. The data for plots 1, 2, and 3 indicate that a pioneer species is

 I.   red oak.

II. white oak.

III. white pine.

(A) I only.   (D) II and III.

(B) II only.   (E) I and II.

(C) III only.

55. The physical appearance that is produced by a gene is called

(A) allele.   (D) trait.

(B) phenotype.   (E) hybrid.

(C) genotype.

For **Questions 56–57**, use the following genetic crosses. You crossed black rabbits with white rabbits and all of the offspring were gray. This was a surprise because you expected all the rabbits to be black. You then crossed the gray rabbits with each other.

56. If 200 offspring were produced in the second cross, how many are expected to be black?

(A) 150   (D) 100

(B) 50   (E) 0

(C) 200

57. If 160 offspring were produced in the second cross, how many are expected to be gray?

(A) 100   (D) 80

(B) 120   (E) 160

(C) 40

58. As a seedling germinates, the young shoot bends upwards because

I. auxins cause cells to elongate on the upper side of the shoot.

II. abscisic acid prevents cell elongations on the lower side of the shoot.

III. auxins cause cells to elongate on the lower side of the shoot.

(A) I only.   (D) I and II.

(B) II only.   (E) II and III.

(C) III only.

Questions 59–60 refer to the following.

Brown field mice and white mice were allowed to breed in the laboratory. The first generation is then allowed to interbreed. 1,000 individuals of the second generation are released into a field. 723 mice are brown and 277 mice are white. The brown allele is dominant and the white allele is recessive. Red tail hawks were observed in the field having dark vegetation, where the mice were released.

59. Over time, you would expect the white allele to

    I.   become more frequent in the population.

    II. become less frequent in the population.

    III. have an equal frequency to the brown allele.

    IV. disappear.

    (A) I only.   (D) IV only.

    (B) II only.   (E) I or III.

    (C) III only.

60. Over time, you would expect

    I.   to find very few, if any, white mice.

    II. natural section to occur.

    III. a change in the frequencies of both alleles.

    (A) I only.   (D) II and III.

    (B) II only.   (E) I, II, and III.

    (C) III only.

If you are taking the Biology-E test, continue with questions 61–80.

BIOLOGY-E SECTION

61. Wolves in the Mojave desert were observed by two scientists to display peculiar behavior. When hunting a hare which can outrun wolves, one wolf would chase the hare in a large circular pattern for approximately ten minutes. It would then stop to rest and another wolf would continue the chase. These two wolves would alternate chasing the hare in this fashion until the hare was exhausted. The wolves would then catch the hare and share the meat. The type of behavior displayed by the wolves is typical of

   (A) communication.   (D) cooperation.

   (B) mimicry.   (E) None of the above.

   (C) altruism.

Question 62 refers to the following diagram. The Y-axis is either the death rate of the prey (DR) or the birthrate of the prey (BR). The X-axis is the numbers of prey, or prey density.

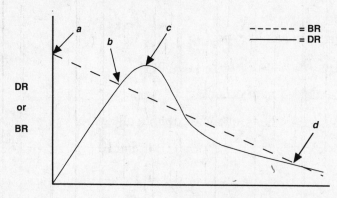

62. In the diagram, at what point(s) will the size of the prey population be stable?

   (A) **a** and **c**   (D) **a, b,** and **d**

   (B) **b** and **d**   (E) **c**

   (C) **b, c,** and **d**

63. The age distribution of a population is

    (A) always a summary of the proportional representation of the various age classes.

    (B) always a good indicator of population growth rate.

    (C) always dominated by younger age categories.

    (D) always a good indicator of population growth rate.

    (E) always all of the above.

64. Density-dependent factors are those that

    (A) cause the population size to decrease to zero.

    (B) allow birthrates to increase as population size decreases.

    (C) cause birthrates to increase as population size increases.

    (D) allow death rates to increase as population size decreases.

    (E) are always due to predation.

65. The growth of a population depends on the initial population size and which of the following parameters?

    (A) Births, deaths, immigrations, and emigrations

    (B) Maturity, parity, and fecundity

    (C) Fertility, deaths, immigrations, and dispersal

    (D) Fitness, deaths, immigrations, and spacing

    (E) Fecundity, deaths, immigrations, and dispersal

66. After a Douglas fir forest is logged, beekeepers frequently keep their beehives on the logged land. The most reasonable explanation for this is

    (A) the climax community included a major competitor of bees.

    (B) the pioneer species and the bees have a mutualistic relationship.

    (C) the bees are best kept away from people.

    (D) the bees are needed to produce honey.

    (E) the cleared forest is more accessible than the forest.

Question 67 refers to the following.

a	A larval wasp that eats its insect host.
b	A blackfly that sucks human blood.
c	A roundworm in the gut of a carnivorous fish.
d	A mink that eats fish.
e	A bird that eats conifer seeds.

67. Which one of the above are classified trophically as secondary con-
    sumers and functionally as parasitoids?

    (A) a   (D) d

    (B) b   (E) e

    (C) c

68. If a keystone species is removed from a community, the expected
    result is

    (A) coevolution.

    (B) decrease in species diversity.

    (C) increase in pollination.

    (D) increase in production.

    (E) more insects.

Question 69 refers to the following figures.

(a)   (b)

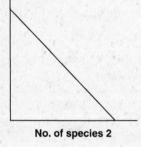

No. of
species 1

No. of species 2

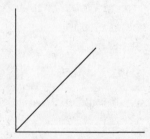

No. of
species 1

No. of species 2

(c)

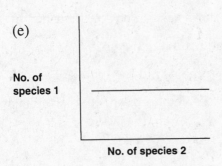

No. of species 1

No. of species 2

(d)

No. of species 1

No. of species 2

(e)

No. of species 1

No. of species 2

69. Which one of the figures shows an inverse relationship between the numbers of species 1 and species 2?

(A) (a)   (D) (d)

(B) (b)   (E) (e)

(C) (c)

70. Which one of the following terms applies to plankton?

(A) Small carnivores   (D) Small omnivores

(B) Small autotrophs   (E) Small pelagic organisms

(C) Small heterotrophs

Question 71 refers to the following.

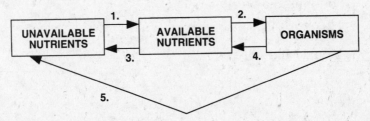

71. If the rate of decomposition of organic matter increased, which of the arrows would represent the infiltration of soluble nitrate to groundwater?

(A) 1

(D) 4

(B) 2

(E) 5

(C) 3

72. Reducing an algal growth in freshwater lakes can be accomplished by

(A) decreasing the ammonium volatilization in the lake.

(B) increasing the mineralization of organic nitrogen.

(C) increasing the conversion of available phosphorus to unavailable phosphorus.

(D) increasing the bicarbonate formation in the lake.

(E) decreasing nitrification of ammonium.

73. If the carbon dioxide increased in the atmosphere, which one of the following would you expect to occur?

(A) Increase in HCO_3^- in the ocean

(B) Decrease of biomass in the ocean

(C) Decrease in respiration by phytoplankton

(D) Increase in nitrate in the ocean

(E) No change in the ocean water

74. The two main variables used to classify terrestrial biomes are

(A) longitude and altitude.

(B) climate and topography.

(C) soil-type and precipitation.

(D) precipitation and temperature.

(E) latitude and soil-type.

75. The amount of water in the reservoir behind a dam gradually decreases over the years because

   (A) erosion below the reservoir increases.

   (B) deposition in the reservoir increases.

   (C) people use the water for drinking.

   (D) there is increased evaporation of water from the reservoir.

   (E) erosion upstream from the dam increases.

Questions 76–79

The following figure is a plot of gross primary production (GPP) vs. depth of the ocean. The energy used in respiration (E_R) is shown as the horizontal line. Note: Net primary production = GPP − E_R.

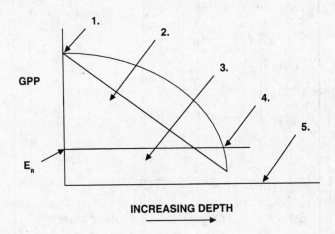

76. Which one of the following arrows shows maximum gross primary production?

   (A) 1   (D) 4

   (B) 2   (E) 5

   (C) 3

77. Which one of the arrows points to a position in the abyssal (no light) zone?

   (A) 1   (D) 4

   (B) 2   (E) 5

   (C) 3

78. Which arrow points to the area representing NPP?

    (A) 1   (D) 4

    (B) 2   (E) 5

    (C) 3

79. Which arrow shows the point where GPP = E_R?

    (A) 1   (D) 4

    (B) 2   (E) 5

    (C) 3

80. Which one of the following activities contributes to global warming?

    (A) Driving automobiles

    (B) Fertilizing a garden

    (C) Planting trees

    (D) Walking to work or school

    (E) Using refrigerants

STOP
If you finish before time is called, you may check your work on the
entire Biology-E test only. Do not turn to any other test in this book.

SAT Biology E/M
Practice Test 2

ANSWER KEY

BIOLOGY CORE SECTION

1.	(D)	16.	(C)	31.	(C)	46.	(C)
2.	(C)	17.	(C)	32.	(E)	47.	(D)
3.	(A)	18.	(E)	33.	(B)	48.	(A)
4.	(B)	19.	(D)	34.	(D)	49.	(B)
5.	(D)	20.	(D)	35.	(A)	50.	(D)
6.	(C)	21.	(E)	36.	(B)	51.	(E)
7.	(A)	22.	(E)	37.	(D)	52.	(B)
8.	(D)	23.	(C)	38.	(D)	53.	(C)
9.	(A)	24.	(D)	39.	(B)	54.	(C)
10.	(E)	25.	(D)	40.	(B)	55.	(B)
11.	(D)	26.	(E)	41.	(D)	56.	(B)
12.	(C)	27.	(D)	42.	(C)	57.	(D)
13.	(D)	28.	(C)	43.	(A)	58.	(C)
14.	(B)	29.	(D)	44.	(D)	59.	(B)
15.	(D)	30.	(C)	45.	(C)	60.	(E)

BIOLOGY-E SECTION

61.	(D)	66.	(B)	71.	(C)	76.	(A)
62.	(B)	67.	(A)	72.	(C)	77.	(E)
63.	(A)	68.	(B)	73.	(A)	78.	(B)
64.	(D)	69.	(A)	74.	(D)	79.	(D)
65.	(A)	70.	(E)	75.	(B)	80.	(A)

DETAILED EXPLANATIONS
OF ANSWERS

PRACTICE TEST 2

BIOLOGY CORE SECTION

1. **(D)**   2. **(C)**   3. **(A)**
The most likely food chain whose members are of the group of listed organisms is:

alga → minnow → sunfish → bass → human

Photosynthetic algae build organic molecules and thus are the producers. A small-sized minnow is the most likely animal to feed on the plantlike algae as a primary consumer. As energy flows through a food chain, less useful energy remains available at each successive link. Humans are the last link in the chain and are the fourth-level consumers. Therefore, in this food chain, the least amount of energy is available to the human.

4. **(B)**   5. **(D)**   6. **(C)**
Blood flows through blood vessels in the following sequence:

arteries → arterioles → capillaries → venules → veins

Blood is pumped through the arteries first; therefore the arteries have the highest blood pressure. Blood pressure slowly decreases as blood travels farther away from the heart. Veins, at the end of this route, return blood to the heart. Arterioles receive blood from arteries and supply it to the microscopic, numerous capillaries. At this level, cells are served. Nutrients and oxygen leave the blood through capillary walls to serve cells. Waste products and carbon dioxide leave body cells and enter blood for removal.

7. **(A)**
By osmosis, water will flow through the microorganism's cell membrane from the outside area of higher (100%) water concentration to inside the cell, where the concentration is lower. Choices (C) and (D) describe the reverse of the true situation. The cell's exterior is hypotonic (has a

lower solute concentration and a higher water concentration) whereas the cell's interior is hypertonic (has *higher* solute levels).

8. **(D)**
   Phagocytosis is "cellular eating," which a white blood cell performs as part of the human body's defense system. Pinocytosis is "cellular drinking." Exocytosis means the removal of substances from a cell. The other two choices are unrelated transport processes of cell molecules, atoms, or ions.

9. **(A)**
   The statement is a rote definition of active transport, which acts in opposition to diffusion and osmosis. The other choices are unrelated to energy requiring transport processes.

10. **(E)**
    The outer early embryonic layer is the ectoderm. Its cells differentiate to give rise to the epidermis and the nervous system.

11. **(D)**
    The middle layer is the mesoderm. It gives rise to bones, blood, and muscles.

12. **(C)**
    The inner layer is the endoderm. It gives rise to many internal organs such as those of the digestive tract.

13. **(D)**
    Of all the types of light that are absorbed by chlorophyll, red light has the greatest wavelength (700 nm). Blue light has the shortest wavelength (400 nm).

14. **(B)**
    Meiosis produces sex cells that have the haploid number of chromosomes. In the process, chromosome pairs are separated, so sex cells get single chromosome copies. A cell is haploid if it contains only one of each type of chromosome. Mitosis produces diploid cells with homologous chromosome pairs.

15. **(D)**
    Mitochondria, which contain their own DNA, undergo division while the cells that they are in undergo mitosis. This means that each daughter cell will have approximately as many mitochondria as the parent cell had.

Ribosomes and lysosomes do not undergo division, and nucleoli are not present during mitosis.

16. **(C)**

Diabetes mellitus is produced by a recessive gene on an autosome pair (any chromosome pair other than the sex-determining pair). Thus, a homozygous recessive genotype, aa, produces this hereditary disease. If this is to occur with a 100% chance, both parents must also be aa to ensure inheritance of the gene twice, without other possibilities. If, for example, one parent were Aa, the chance for a diabetic offspring is 50%, not 100%.

17. **(C)**

DNA-to-RNA complementarity depends on base-pairing rules, which are as follows:

DNA	RNA
A	U
C	G
G	C
T	A

The GCAUCA base-for-base readout is the only choice compatible to the given DNA. These base-pairing rules must be memorized.

18. **(E)**

The repressor is the protein made by an adjacent regulator gene, and it can bind to the operator. The adjacent promoter gene is the site at which the RNA polymerase binds to DNA. Inactivator and operation have nothing to do with the operon model of gene control.

19. **(D)**

An *Amoeba* moves using pseudopodia. The *Euglena* and *Trypanosoma* employ flagella. *Clostridium* is a bacterium that has no cilia or flagella.

20. **(D)**

A deletion is the loss of a fragment from a chromosome. Chromosome #3, WXYZ, has lost gene Z to become WXY.

21. **(E)**

New xylem is a tissue that conducts water and dissolved minerals through a plant body. With age, however, it undergoes chemical changes and hardens into wood. It then no longer functions as a conductive tissue.

Phloem conducts organic molecules, and collenchyma is a supportive tissue. Epidermis covers the plant, and the cortex is a tissue that stores materials.

22. **(E)**
This series lists the neuronal regions from end to end, over which the impulse travels. Dendrites, short and branching, carry the impulse to the cell body, which houses the neuron's nucleus and the majority of its cytoplasm. The long, single axon is the other cell process stemming from the cell's opposite end.

23. **(C)**
The medulla is at the base of the brainstem. The pons is anterior to it and the forebrain's thalamus is even more anterior in position. The cerebrum is the most anterior portion of the forebrain, whereas the cerebellum is dorsal or posterior to the hindbrain (pons and medulla) and is not continuous with the spinal cord.

24. **(D)**
This is a straightforward fact although the other listed endocrine glands also have their hormonal secretions: medulla—epinephrine; pancreas—insulin; parathyroid—parathyroid hormone; and thyroid—thyroid hormone.

25. **(D)**
A is at the base of this evolutionary tree, the suggested one-celled forerunner of all evolving multicellular animal phyla.

26. **(E)**
The echinoderms and mollusks are from separate, widely divergent evolutionary lines. The other four choices offer phylum pairs of more closely related phyla.

27. **(D)**
To answer this question you must be familiar with the functions of the various parts of the digestive tract. Absorption of most digested materials and water occurs in the small intestine. Final water reabsorption occurs in the large intestine. The esophagus functions in the transport of food to the stomach. The stomach functions in the digestion of proteins. The rectum functions in the storage of fecal matter.

28. **(C)**
An autosome is any chromosome in the complement, excepting the sex-determining pair—XX in females or XY in males. In a normal male

somatic cell complement of 46 chromosomes, there are 44 (22 pairs of) autosomes, one X chromosome, and one Y chromosome.

29. **(D)**

A population cannot change without a source of change. If only one form of a gene existed for a trait, there would not be variation. All organisms would be homozygous for that gene. Their offspring would be the same. Mutations are one way in which a population can obtain genetic variability.

30. **(C)**

Hemophilia is an X-linked recessive trait; therefore, the couple's offspring can be expected to have the following genotypes:

H dominant
h recessive

	X^H	X^h
X^h	$X^H X^h$	$X^h X^h$
Y	$X^H Y$	$X^h Y$

Thus, 50% of the couple's daughters will develop hemophilia.

31. **(C)**

An ecosystem is the interaction of biotic and abiotic components of an area or habitat. A biogeochemical cycle involves the movement of mineral ions or molecules in and out of ecosystems. A food chain is not an ecosystem though it exists in one. A niche is the sum of all resources used by an organism in the environment. A population is all of the individuals of a particular species within a defined area.

32. **(E)**

This is a fact. Wallace seldom receives the credit Darwin receives. From their independent studies, the two eventually collaborated. The people in the other choices are associated with different accomplishments: Cuvier laid the foundations of comparative anatomy and vertebrate paleontology; Lamarck put forth the theory of evolution by the inheritance of acquired characteristics; Lyell provided evidence that the earth was millions to billions of years old, not, as was believed, about six thousand years old; Malthus was an economist whose ideas influenced the formation of Darwin's theory of natural selection.

33. **(B)**

If the frequency of "A" is 0.7, the frequency of "a" is 0.3, for the two must add up to 1.0, or 100%. Therefore, the frequency of "aa" is "a" squared. 0.3 squared is 0.09.

	0.7A	0.3a
0.7A		
0.3a		0.09aa

34. **(D)**
Chondrichthyes are the cartilaginous fish, e.g., shark. Osteichthyes are the bony fish, e.g., trout. The other choices belong to other vertebrate classes: bullfrog, Amphibians; rattlesnake, Reptiles; and robin, Aves (birds).

35. **(A)**
Epidermis covers the outer surfaces of the leaf. Stomata are openings punctuating the epidermis for gas exchange. They are present throughout the lower covering but are absent in the upper layer of epidermis.

36. **(B)**
The parenchymal cells below the upper epidermal layer conduct photosynthesis. They are more densely packed, for higher photosynthetic efficiency, in the upper layer of palisade mesophyll. One hundred percent humidity exists in layer C, the spongy mesophyll. Stomata are present in the underside of a leaf, and are labeled E in the diagram. The cuticle of a leaf is an outer layer that is secreted by cells in the layer that is labeled A, and serves to protect the plant from water loss.

37. **(D)**
All plant and animal proteins contain nitrogen (N). Nitrogen is part of the amino group present in all amino acids, which are the building blocks of all proteins. Plants can synthesize most proteins from simple inorganic ingredients that include nitrogen.

38. **(D)**
K is the symbol for potassium, which is the only nutrient among the five choices listed that is needed in large amounts and is therefore a macronutrient. Copper (Cu), magnesium (Mg), manganese (Mn), and zinc (Zn) are not needed in large amounts, and are therefore, not macronutrients.

39. **(B)**
Respiratory function may be defined in terms of lung volumes and capacities. The *respiratory rate* is the number of breaths (inhalation and exhalation) per unit time. *Tidal volume* is the volume of air inspired or

expired in an unforced respiratory cycle. *Respiratory minute volume* is the total volume of air exhaled per minute. It can be the product of respiratory rate × tidal volume: e.g., $12 \times 500 = 6{,}000$ ml. *Expiratory reserve volume* is the maximum volume of air that can forcibly be exhaled immediately following tidal expiration. *Inspiratory reserve volume* is the maximum volume of air that can forcibly be inhaled immediately following tidal inspiration. *Vital capacity* is the maximum amount of air that can be expired following maximum inspiration. It is equal to the sum of the tidal volume, the expiratory reserve volume, and the inspiratory reserve volume. Thus, (A), the expiratory reserve volume, is equal to the difference of the vital capacity (5,000) and the inspiratory reserve volume and tidal volume (2,500 + 500), which is 2,000.

40. **(B)**

According to the definitions given, vital capacity is equal to the sum of the tidal volume (400), the expiratory reserve volume (1,500), and the inspiratory reserve volume (2,400), which equals 4,300.

41. **(D)**

The tidal volume multiplied by the respiratory rate is equal to the respiratory minute volume. Thus, the tidal volume is equal to the quotient of the respiratory minute volume (9,000) divided by the rate (15), which is 600.

42. **(C)**   43. **(A)**

The portion of the graph that is labeled A depicts simple twitches. A simple twitch is a muscle contraction followed by total relaxation of the contracted muscle fibers.

Portion B represents the summation of many muscle twitches. At first, various muscle fibers contract. They then begin to relax. However, in summation, another twitch occurs before the muscle fibers have had enough time to totally relax. This produces more tension and force than would normally be produced by a lone muscle twitch. This increase in contraction is repeated, until the muscle fibers can contract no further. These muscle fibers are then in a state of tetanus, represented by portion C of the graph.

Fatigue, depicted by portion D, occurs because of a buildup of lactic acid in the muscle.

Tonus, the partial contraction of various muscle fibers during a period of relaxation, is not shown by the graph.

44. **(D)**

The period from noon to 2:00 p.m. consists of six 20-minute intervals. Therefore, the size of the bacterial population will double six times by 2:00 p.m. $2^6 = 64$.

45. **(C)**

Bacterial cells would not lose their ability to reproduce in a fresh nutrient medium. If cell birth were greater, population size would increase (log phase). The opposite trend yields a population size decline (death phase). During the level stationary phase, the net growth of the size of the population is zero.

46. **(C)**

This question is looking for a feature that is shared by amphibians and reptiles. Amphibians, the first land animals, have some characteristics that tie them to a moist environment. Eggs are laid and usually fertilized in a moist environment. While the adult forms have lungs, some respiratory exchange may occur across their thin, unprotected skin. Reptiles have developed several features that improve their ability to function as land animals. Their amniotic eggs contain a water supply and have shells that are impermeable to water. The amniotic egg requires that fertilization be internal rather than external. Reptiles have dry, scaly skin that prevents water loss. Their three-chambered heart improves the efficiency of the circulatory system that must rely solely upon the lungs for gas exchange. Thus, both reptiles and adult amphibians have lungs.

47. **(D)**

Cro-Magnon people, who were essentially like present-day humans in appearance, first appeared (according to the fossil record) in Europe about 34,000 years ago, in Asia about 40,000 years ago, and in Africa perhaps 100,000 years ago. *Homo erectus, Homo habilis,* and *Australopithecus,* including *Zinjanthropus,* are much older; it is therefore thought that these species became extinct before the Cro-Magnons became dominant.

48. **(A)**

Poison ivy, using an oak tree to grow higher for more light is an example of commensalism. Commensalism is a type of symbiosis in which one organism symbiont benefits and the other organism host is not affected by the relationship. The oak tree is not affected by poison ivy growing up its trunk, but the poison ivy is benefiting by getting more light.

Questions 49–51

For this set of questions you are interpreting the role and characteristics of enzymes based on the model in drawings 1 through 7. Enzymes have the following characteristics:

- are made of proteins.
- speed up chemical reactions (organic catalysts).
- bond or break-up substrates.
- catalyzes only one reaction (enzyme specificity).
- change shape to catalyze a reaction.
- are not chemically changed by the reaction. The enzyme can be used in more than one reaction.

49. (B)
Although it is true that enzymes are made of proteins and speed-up chemical reactions, this is not evident from the drawings.

50. (D)
The drawings only show the substrates being bonded to make the product. The enzyme is not changed. The drawing 5 shows the enzyme changing its shape to bond the substrates together.

51. (E)
Since the product has a completely different shape than the substrate molecules, it can be assumed the product has different properties. The specific "fit" of the substrate molecule to the enzyme suggests this enzyme will only carry out this reaction.

52. (B)   53. (C)   54. (C)
Plot 1 represents a field community with the predominant plants being perennial weeds and grasses. There is one juvenile white pine. White pine is therefore a pioneer species that comes into an open area first. Pioneer species can tolerate a high level of light. Plot 2 is an ecotone community. An ecotone community is a transition between an open area and a climax forest community. Note the ratio of juvenile to mature plants for each species. The pioneer species (white pine) still dominates the plot but climax species (red oak, white oak, sugar maple) are starting to get established. Plot 3 is a climax community. A climax community is a stable community, which means that it does not change unless there is a distur-

bance. The transition from field to ecotone to climax is called secondary succession.

55. **(B)**
An example of phenotype, or physical appearance, is brown or blue eye color.

56. **(B)**   57. **(D)**
It was assumed that black was caused by a dominant allele and white was caused by two recessive alleles. Using this assumption, the first cross is:

	c	c	white
C	Cc	Cc	
C	Cc	Cc	

black

If black was caused by a dominant allele, then all of the offspring would have been heterozygous (Cc) and black, but they were all gray. This is an example of Incomplete Dominance. In this case, the two colors blend. The second cross is:

	C	c	gray
C	CC	Cc	
c	Cc	cc	

gray

25% of the offspring should be black (CC). 25% of 200 = 50 black
50% of the offspring should be gray (Cc). 50% of 160 = 80 gray
25% of the offspring should be white (cc).

58. **(C)**
Auxins are plant hormones that cause cell walls to soften and stretch. If the auxins accumulate on the upper side, the cells will elongate on the upper side and cause the shoot to bend down. If the auxins accumulate on the lower side, the cells will elongate on the lower side and cause the shoot to bend up. Abscisic acid is used by plants during times of stress (drought, extreme temperatures) and prevents cell division and elongation. Abscisic acid concentration drops during favorable growth conditions.

59. **(B)**   60. **(E)**
Natural selection would favor the brown mice. In a field habitat, it would be expected that all the white mice would be eliminated because of

predation pressure. The brown mice would blend into the field habitat. The white mice would be easily seen by the hawks. Over time, the brown allele frequency would increase and the white allele frequency would decrease. In a large population (1,000 individuals), the white allele should not disappear because it would be carried by heterozygous individuals.

BIOLOGY – E SECTION

61. (D)

Cooperative behavior occurs when two or more animals act toward their mutual benefit. When the animals belong to the same species, it is called intraspecific cooperation; when they belong to different species, it is known as interspecific cooperation. In the case of the two wolves (intraspecific), each wolf benefits by helping the other catch the rabbit, and each sacrifices one-half the rabbit to the other in return for help.

Communication occurs in many forms and in all kinds of behavior – friendly, hostile, aggressive. Mimicry is the adaptation of the appearance, behavior, or smell by a species of another species. Altruism differs from cooperation in that it involves an activity which benefits another organism but at the individual's own expense. A typical example of altruism is that of parents protecting their offspring.

62. (B)

The prey population will be stable when the birthrate equals the death rate. This occurs at **b** and **d**. At **a**, the birthrate is greater than the death rate, and at **c**, the death rate is greater than the birthrate. Therefore, neither (A) nor (E) is correct. Both **a** and **d** are included in (C) and (D) but **c** or **d** is present, also.

63. (A)

The age distribution of a population is a summary of the proportional representation of the various age classes. It may be an indicator of the potential for growth of future populations, but it is not a good indicator of population growth rate (B) because the data are only given for one time period. Although the age distribution may be dominated by one age category (C), this is not always the case, particularly in a distribution shown by a stable population. The distribution gives the number of individuals in each age group at a particular time but it does not indicate the number of births for each category. Therefore, it is not a good indicator of age-specific survivorship (D). The initial population size is not known and thus fecundity is unknown; therefore, the age distribution is not a measure of fecundity (E).

64. **(D)**

Density-dependent factors are those whose effect increases with population density. The effect may be to increase the death rate or decrease the birthrate as the population size increases. Of these two possible effects, only an increase in death rate was given as an option. There is an inverse relationship between birthrate and population density and thus, the birthrate would not increase as the population size increased (C) nor would the birthrate decrease as the population size decreased (A). The effect of density-dependent factors increases with increasing density but does not cause the populations to decrease to zero (B). Predation may increase as population density increases but density-dependent factors are not due to predation (E).

65. **(A)**

Many different factors affect the size, distribution, and growth of populations, but the growth depends on the initial population size and births, deaths, immigrations, and emigrations. Maturity, parity, and fecundity (B) are the factors that determine fitness or the contribution of an individual to future generations but they do not determine the growth of the population. Dispersal and spacing contribute to population distributions, and fertility is potential births. Both fertility and dispersal are included in (C) and both fitness and spacing are included in (D). Fecundity (E) could be considered as births, but dispersal is incorrect.

66. **(B)**

The forest is the climax community and once it is logged, secondary succession begins. The pioneer species are frequently species such as fireweed that are used by bees. In this question, it was not necessary to know the identity of pioneer species but to recognize that the pioneer species would not be trees, but rapidly growing small flowering plants, and that bees are pollinators that have a mutualistic relationship with flowering plants. Whether or not there was a competitor of bees in the climax forest (A) is not important because bees pollinate flowering plants, not conifers. Some people are very allergic to bee stings and like to have bees kept away from them (C), but this is not why the bees are brought to the logged land. It is true that bees are needed to make honey (D) but this is not related to why they are brought to the logged land. It is true that the cleared forest is more accessible (E), but there must be a reason to bring the bees.

67. **(A)**

The larval wasp eats the insect, an animal, and is thus a secondary consumer. In addition, it kills its host and is a parasitoid. The fly, roundworm, and mink are secondary consumers because they consume animals. However, even if the human is considered a host for the blackfly, the blackfly does not kill the human (B). Similarly, the roundworm does not necessarily kill its host (C). The mink kills the fish but the fish is not a host (D). The bird is a primary consumer and the seed is not a host (E).

68. **(B)**

A keystone species creates resources for other species and thus increases species diversity. All of the remaining choices are possible but would be the expected result only under additionally defined conditions. Coevolution (A) between members of the community is possible but it would occur after the increase in diversity. There is no particular reason that keystone species would enhance the presence of flowers or increase pollination (C). An increase in primary production (D) is possible, but it would depend on the identity of the species. The example usually given for a keystone species results in more insects (E), but this is not a general situation.

69. **(A)**

When the number of species 1 is at a maximum, the number of species 2 is zero. As the number of species 1 decreases, the number of species 2 increases. The numbers of species 1 and species 2 increase together in graph (B). In (C), the number of individuals in species 2 and species 1 fluctuates. In graph (D) there is no change in species 2 as the number of species 1 changes. In (E) there is no change in the number of species 1 as the number of species 2 changes.

70. **(E)**

Plankton, the small pelagic organisms, include both phytoplankton and zooplankton. Plankton includes carnivores (A) and omnivores (D). Phytoplankton are autotrophs (B) and zooplankton are heterotrophs (C). This is an example of the importance of understanding the exact meaning of a word.

71. **(C)**

Nitrate is an available nutrient, but if it moves to groundwater, it is no longer available. Pathway 1 (A) is the release, not the loss, of available nitrogen. The assimilation of nitrate by organisms is pathway 2 (B). The decomposition and release of nitrate is pathway 4 (D). Burial of organisms, pathway 5, (E) makes all of the nitrogen compounds in the organism unavailable.

72. **(C)**
Phosphorus is identified as the limiting nutrient for primary production in freshwater. Decreasing the phosphorus available to the algae will decrease the growth of the algae. Ammonium volatilization to gaseous ammonia (A) will reduce the nitrogen available for the algae, but nitrogen is not the limiting nutrient. Increasing the mineralization of organic nitrogen (B) will increase the available nitrogen (ammonium). Similarly, increasing bicarbonate formation will increase available carbon (D). Altering the relative amounts of available nitrogen as ammonium or nitrate (E) could affect the species composition but available nitrogen is not the limiting nutrient.

73. **(A)**
An increase in one part of the carbon cycle will result in changes in the other parts as the concentrations approach a new equilibrium. Inorganic available carbon dioxide is exchanged between the atmosphere and the water and thus, an increase in the atmospheric levels will increase the oceanic levels. In the ocean the carbon dioxide is present as bicarbonate. Inorganic available carbon dioxide can also be taken up by organisms. The result would be increased, not decreased, primary production (B), and increased, not decreased, respiration by the phytoplankton (C). If there was a decrease in primary production, the nitrate levels in the ocean could accumulate and increase (D), but a decrease in primary production is not expected. Carbon is cycled among the components of the cycle and thus an increase in one component will affect the other components, eliminating the possibility of no changes taking place in the ocean water (E).

74. **(D)**
Biomes refer primarily to terrestrial ecosystems and are defined on the basis of the main vegetation types which are dictated primarily by temperature and precipitation. Longitude and latitude (A) affect the temperature and precipitation which are products of the climate and topography (B). Soil type is also important in dictating the type of terrestrial ecosystem present but neither soil-type and precipitation (C), nor soil-type and latitude (E) combine as prime variables.

75. **(B)**

Behind a dam, the flow of the water is reduced and thus the rate of deposition increases. This decreases the volume of water that is in the reservoir. Below the dam, erosion can increase (A) but this has no effect on the amount of water in the reservoir. Water in the dam is replenished from upstream areas and the reservoir level is controlled. Water removed for drinking (C) or by evaporation (D) can be replenished.

76. **(A)**   77. **(E)**   78. **(B)**   79. **(D)**

The figure shows the decrease in gross primary production with depth. The maximum value can be read directly from the figure. The values decrease with depth due to a decrease in light penetration. The net primary production is ($GPP - E_R$) which is represented by the area shown by arrow 2 (B). The total amount of energy used in respiration is shown by arrow 3 (C). The horizontal line shows the energy used in respiration and thus at point 4 (D), where the curve showing GPP and the horizontal line indicating E_R meet, GPP equals E_R. Production ceases in the abyssal (no light) zone which is position 5 (E).

80. **(A)**

Automobiles burn fossil fuels and carbon dioxide, the most important greenhouse gas contributing to global warming is released. Carbon dioxide in the atmosphere forms two shields, trapping heat around the Earth. Fertilizing a garden (B) enhances plant growth and thus, the uptake of carbon dioxide into plants. Similarly, planting trees (C) reduces atmospheric carbon dioxide. Walking to work or school (D) consumes metabolic energy, not fossil fuels. Refrigerants (E) release chlorofluorocarbons that contribute to ozone depletion.

SAT Biology E/M
Practice Test 3

(Answer sheets appear in the back of this book.)

TIME: 1 Hour
80 Questions

BIOLOGY CORE SECTION

Questions 1–2 refer to the following.

Two different groups of people migrated into River Valley 1,000 years ago. The people migrating from the north had long straight hair and very big feet. The people migrating from the south had curly hair and normal feet. These two groups intermarried, producing 32 children. All of the children had curly hair and normal feet. The children of this group also intermarried, producing grandchildren.

(A) 135

(B) 101

(C) 45

(D) 34

(E) 11

1. One hundred eighty grandchildren are born from the above cross. If, controlling hair texture and feet size, the two genes were on two different tetrads, how many grandchildren were expected to have straight hair and normal feet?

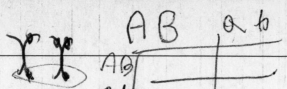

2. One hundred eighty grandchildren are born from the above cross, and if the two genes were on the same tetrad, how many grandchildren were expected to have straight hair and big feet?

Questions 3–5

(A) Cnidarians   (D) Annelids

(B) Echinoderms   (E) Arthropods

(C) Platyhelminthes

3. Have radial symmetry, but no coelom

4. Are segmented worms

5. Have a jointed exoskeleton

Questions 6–7

(A) Ligament   (D) Blood vessels

(B) Cartilage   (E) Tendon

(C) Nerves

6. Connects bone to bone

7. Provides bone with oxygen and nutrients

DIRECTIONS: The questions or incomplete statements below are followed by five possible answers or completions. Pick the answer choice that best answers or completes the question or incomplete statement and then fill in the correct oval on your answer sheet.

Question 8 refers to the following.

Laboratory Data – Enzyme Activity

Temperature (Centigrade)	Time Required (min.) to Convert 1 gram of Substance to Product
0	25
5	20
20	15
37	5
70	25

8. Select the correct statement summarizing the relationship between temperature and enzyme activity in this experiment.

    (A) As temperature decreases, enzyme activity increases.

    (B) As temperature increases, enzyme activity increases.

    (C) Enzyme activity is least at 37 degrees.

    (D) Enzyme activity peaks at 37 degrees but decreases at temperature extremes.

    (E) Enzyme activity peaks at 70 degrees.

9. Fungi have all of the following characteristics EXCEPT

    (A) the ability to undergo photosynthesis.

    (B) cell walls.

    (C) the ability to live on dead organic matter.

    (D) the ability to produce spores.

    (E) the ability to secrete digestive enzymes.

10. The gene frequencies in a population may change because of all of the following EXCEPT

    (A) mutation.   (D) nonrandom mating.

    (B) migration.   (E) a stable environment.

    (C) selection.

11. All of the following are recycled on earth EXCEPT

    (A) carbon.   (D) water.

    (B) oxygen.   (E) nitrogen.

    (C) energy.

12. Agonistic behavior may be expressed as all of the following EXCEPT

    (A) threat.   (D) kinesis.

    (B) appeasement.   (E) attack.

    (C) displacement.

13. A group of potentially interbreeding organisms that may or may not live in the same area is called a

(A) population.   (D) ecosystem.

(B) species.   (E) race.

(C) community.

Question 14 refers to the following table.

The table represents the composition of bases present in DNA extracted from different organisms.

Base Composition (percent)

Source	Adenine	Guanine	Cytosine	Thymine
human	31.0	19.6	19.3	30.1
mouse	29.0	21.1	21.2	28.7
tobacco	29.7	20.0	20.4	29.9
E. coli	24.7	25.3	25.4	24.6
sea urchin	32.7	17.7	17.3	32.3

14. From the table, which one of the following can be concluded?

(A) The nucleotide bases are bound by hydrogen bonds.

(B) The bases are attached to a sugar-phosphate backbone.

(C) The base composition of DNA is the same in all organisms.

(D) The amount of adenine equals the amount of thymine.

(E) DNA is a double helix.

15. Amino acids that must be taken in by the body in food are all of the following EXCEPT

(A) also made by the body.

(B) necessary for growth.

(C) found in the proteins that are eaten.

(D) basic components of our body proteins.

(E) as important as nonessential amino acids.

16. The ability of a plant to survive on land is not increased when that land plant

    (A) produces free-swimming sperm.

    (B) has a cuticle on the parts exposed to the air.

    (C) contains xylem.

    (D) makes seeds.

    (E) has roots.

17. Territories are areas that increase opportunities for food procurement, mating, and/or nesting sites. They are defended by the occupants against others, usually of the same species. Territories serve to

    (A) provide for equal distribution of food.

    (B) increase the time that individuals spend fighting.

    (C) regulate population size.

    (D) increase physical contact among species members.

    (E) decrease reproductive success.

18. The children of a father with type O blood and a mother with type AB blood could have the blood type

    (A) O.

    (B) AB.

    (C) O or AB.

    (D) A or B.

    (E) O, A, B, or AB.

19. The ecological role played by trees on land is the same as that played by which organisms in the ocean?

    (A) Bacteria

    (B) Algae

    (C) Fish

    (D) Shrimp

    (E) Sharks

20. All of the following are true about genes EXCEPT

    (A) they are found on chromosomes.

    (B) they contain DNA.

(C) they exist in different forms.

(D) they can undergo change.

(E) they are always beneficial.

21. A cross is made between a wild-type female fruit fly and a miniature-winged male fly. All of the offspring in the first generation are wild-type. In the second generation, one quarter of the offspring is miniature-winged and male. From this we can conclude that the gene for miniature-winged flies is

$W_X X^W$

$X^w Y$

(A) dominant and autosomal.

(B) recessive and autosomal.

(C) dominant and X-linked.

(D) recessive and X-linked.

(E) recessive and Y-linked.

Question 22 refers to the following diagram.

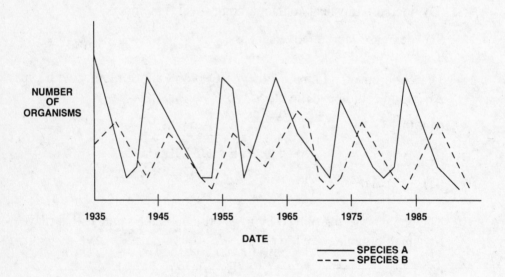

22. Species A and species B are members of the same community. From this graph we can conclude that

(A) species A eats species B.

(B) species A increases in number every five years.

(C) species B eats species A.

(D) species B can increase in number when A is low.

(E) both species are competing for the same food source.

23. Which of the following is NOT an energy-requiring process?

    (A) Operation of the sodium-potassium pump

    (B) Production of glycogen from glucose

    (C) Muscle contraction

    (D) Diffusion of water across a membrane

    (E) Uptake of calcium against a concentration gradient

24. In humans, cells with the haploid number of chromosomes occur in the

    (A) stomach.   (D) intestine.

    (B) skin.   (E) testes.

    (C) urethra.

25. Which one of the following plant modifications does NOT contribute to water retention?

    (A) Closing of stomata by guard cells in the leaves

    (B) Movement of water in xylem

    (C) Waxy cuticle on surfaces of the plant parts

    (D) Roots

    (E) Leaf shape

26. Which one of the following does NOT match?

    (A) transfer RNA - amino acid transport

    (B) nucleus - site of RNA production

    (C) ribosomes - translation

    (D) gene - protein assembly

    (E) messenger RNA - copy of gene

27. The ecosystem characterized by coniferous trees is the

   (A) temperate forest.   (D) chaparral.

   (B) tundra.   (E) tropical rain forest.

   (C) taiga.

28. Evolutionary change may occur in all of the following situations EXCEPT

   (A) some bacteria survive after exposure to antibiotics because they are antibiotic-resistant.

   (B) a small number of individuals survive a hurricane that kills most of the people on an island.

   (C) a species of birds with a variety of genetically different forms migrates to a new island.

   (D) dogs are selected for breeding because of certain behavioral characteristics that they did not acquire during training.

   (E) horses raised on a nutritionally well-balanced diet are selected for breeding.

29. Simple proteins and DNA are similar in that they both contain all of the following EXCEPT

   (A) oxygen.   (D) chlorine.

   (B) hydrogen.   (E) carbon.

   (C) nitrogen.

30. Bacteria contain

   (A) true nuclei.

   (B) chloroplasts.

   (C) mitochondria.

   (D) simple, circular DNA.

   (E) cell membranes as their outermost structures.

31. The autonomic nervous system is characterized by involuntary control of bodily functions by motor neurons. All of the following are examples of autonomic function EXCEPT

   (A) stimulation of muscles of the digestive tract.

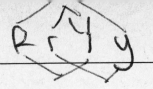

(B) increased secretion of salivary glands.

(C) contraction of skeletal muscles.

(D) release of adrenalin by the adrenal medulla.

(E) increased heart rate in response to an emergency.

32. In pea plants, the round seed allele is dominant over the wrinkled seed allele, and the yellow seed allele is dominant over the green seed allele. The genes for seed texture and those for seed color are on different chromosomes. A plant heterozygous for seed texture and seed color is crossed with a plant that is wrinkled and heterozygous for seed color. What phenotypic ratio of offspring would you expect in the next generation?

(A) 3:1

(B) 3:3:1:1

(C) 9:3:3:1

(D) 1:1

(E) 1:1:1:1

33. The greatest number of mitotic divisions occurs in

(A) meristematic tissue.

(B) xylem.

(C) phloem.

(D) guard cells.

(E) cork.

34. Where there is increased parental involvement in the raising of offspring, we would expect

(A) large numbers of offspring.

(B) a shorter time before maturation.

(C) little learning by the offspring.

(D) eating of the young.

(E) the welfare of the young placed before the welfare of the parent.

35. A single base change in the nucleotide sequence of a gene will

(A) always result in a change in the protein produced.

(B) be harmful.

(C) change the length of the gene.

(D) affect a critical portion of the protein.

(E) be inherited.

36. Protozoa

(A) are multicellular.

(B) are prokaryotic.

(C) can make their own food.

(D) have a variety of techniques for locomotion.

(E) do not have membrane-bound internal structures.

37. Which one of the following are normally diploid?

(A) Spores

(B) Eggs

(C) Drones (male bees)

(D) Zygotes

(E) Sperm

38. As one moves up an ecological pyramid, generally

(A) the biomass increases.

(B) photosynthesis increases.

(C) available energy decreases.

(D) the number of organisms increases.

(E) productivity increases.

39. If two genes are linked,

(A) they will always be inherited together.

(B) they will be inherited together unless crossing over has occurred.

(C) the frequency of chromosomal rearrangements will increase.

(D) independent assortment will occur.

(E) blending inheritance will occur.

Question 40 refers to the following graph.

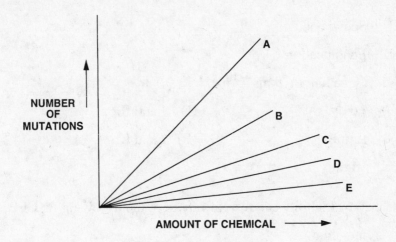

40. From the graph, we can conclude that

    (A) chemical A causes the most mutations.

    (B) all chemicals cause the same number of mutations.

    (C) as the amount of chemical increases, the number of mutations decreases.

    (D) high concentrations of a chemical always result in large numbers of mutations.

    (E) mutations are harmful.

41. How many different gametes will be produced by an organism that has the genotype AaBbCCDd for four genes that assort independently?

    (A) 2   (D) 6

    (B) 3   (E) 8

    (C) 4

42. The nutrient and energy source for the development of a plant embryo is the

    (A) seed coat.   (D) radicle.

    (B) endosperm.   (E) epicotyl.

    (C) fruit.

43. Which of the following depends upon a high degree of communications?

    I.   Social behavior

    II. Echolocation

    III. Circadian rhythms

    (A) I only.   (D) I and II.

    (B) II only.   (E) I and III.

    (C) III only.

44. Genetic variability can result from all of the following EXCEPT

    (A) mutation.

    (B) recombination.

    (C) migration.

    (D) natural selection.

    (E) chromosomal rearrangement.

45. When species A, which is not protected by an unpleasant characteristic, looks like (mimics) species B, which has an unpleasant taste, we can predict that

    (A) species A will be readily preyed upon.

    (B) species A will not be readily preyed upon.

    (C) species B will be readily preyed upon.

    (D) species A and species B will be readily preyed upon.

    (E) neither species will affect the survival of the other.

Question 46 refers to the following.

    STAGE 1   **STAGE 2**   **STAGE 3**   **STAGE 4**

46. The next stage in the process represented in the drawings is called

(A) early cleavage.

(D) blastula formation.

(B) neural tube formation.

(E) morula formation.

(C) gastrulation.

Questions 47–48 refer to the following four graphs. Graphs I, II, III, and IV show the growth of plant cells in the presence of different concentrations of the plant hormone kinetin. In addition, Graphs II, III, and IV show the growth of plant cells in the presence of three different concentrations of the plant hormone auxin.

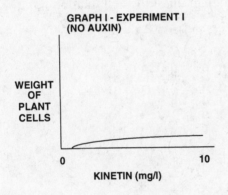

GRAPH I - EXPERIMENT I
(NO AUXIN)

WEIGHT OF PLANT CELLS

KINETIN (mg/l)

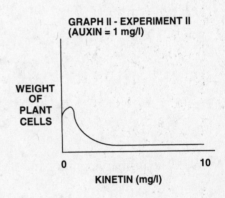

GRAPH II - EXPERIMENT II
(AUXIN = 1 mg/l)

WEIGHT OF PLANT CELLS

KINETIN (mg/l)

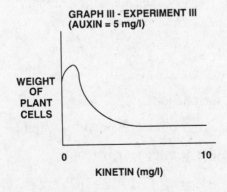

GRAPH III - EXPERIMENT III
(AUXIN = 5 mg/l)

WEIGHT OF PLANT CELLS

KINETIN (mg/l)

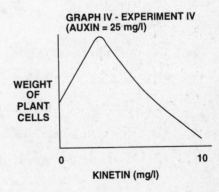

GRAPH IV - EXPERIMENT IV
(AUXIN = 25 mg/l)

WEIGHT OF PLANT CELLS

KINETIN (mg/l)

47. The optimum growth occurred when the concentration of

    (A) kinetin was 0 mg/l.   (D) auxin was 5 mg/l.

    (B) kinetin was 10 mg/l.   (E) auxin was 25 mg/l.

    (C) auxin was 1 mg/l.

48. When comparing the effects of auxin alone on growth, the control is

    (A) not present.   (D) graph III.

    (B) graph I.   (E) graph IV.

    (C) graph II.

Questions 49–50 refer to the following diagram of the cell membrane.

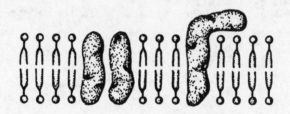

49. The primary component of this cell membrane is

    (A) carbohydrate.   (D) protein.

    (B) phospholipid.   (E) salt.

    (C) nucleic acid.

50. Which one of the following would NOT be considered true about this membrane?

    (A) It is most permeable to proteins.

    (B) Salts pass through pores in the membrane.

    (C) There is a positive charge on the outside.

    (D) Hormones and other chemicals may bind with outside receptors.

    (E) Movement of materials across the membrane may require energy.

Questions 51–52 refer to the following.

Component	Lymph	Blood	Urine	Cerebro-spinal Fluid	Inter-cellular Fluid
protein	4,000	7,000	0	20,000	0.02
glucose	100	100	0	64	100
urea	15	15	26	12	15
sodium	14.1	14.1	5-13	14.7	14.2
potassium	0.47	0.5	2-7	0.2	0.48

(amount present - relative units)

51. The fluid with the greatest variability in amounts of materials present is

    (A) lymph.

    (B) blood.

    (C) urine.

    (D) cerebrospinal fluid.

    (E) intercellular fluid.

52. From this data, we can conclude that

    (A) lymph, blood, and intercellular fluid are similar except for protein content.

    (B) glucose is normally excreted by the body.

    (C) cerebrospinal fluid is the same as blood.

    (D) the largest component in urine is protein.

    (E) the largest component in lymph is glucose.

Questions 53–54

Briggs and King and other researchers used a technique for transferring nuclei from embryonic cells into amphibian eggs whose nuclei had been removed. Nuclei were taken from blastula, gastrula, and intestinal cells and injected into the eggs. Cytoplasm by itself was also injected into some eggs. Many normal adult frogs developed from the eggs containing blastula nuclei. A few normal adult frogs developed from the eggs containing gastrula nuclei or intestinal nuclei. Eggs injected with cytoplasm alone did not develop normally.

53. In this experiment, which one was the control?

   (A) Cytoplasm alone   (D) Intestinal cell nucleus

   (B) Blastula nucleus   (E) There was no control.

   (C) Gastrula nucleus

54. This experiment shows that

   (A) the nucleus supports development.

   (B) the egg rejects the nucleus during an immune reaction.

   (C) genes are lost during development.

   (D) mutations occur in the genes in the nucleus.

   (E) the nucleus remains the same throughout development.

55. Different forms of a gene are called

   (A) alleles.   (D) traits.

   (B) phenotype.   (E) hybrid.

   (C) genotype.

Questions 56–57 refer to the following.

This information shows the amount of energy measured in kilocalories per square centimeters per year at each trophic level of a field ecosystem

Top Predators	23 Kcal
Predators	205 Kcal
Herbivores	1,980 Kcal
Producers	20,009 Kcal

56. The data of the energy pyramid best illustrates

   I. the First Law of Energy (Thermodynamics).

   II. the Second Law of Energy (Thermodynamics).

   III. the biomass distribution in an ecosystem.

   (A) I only.   (D) I and III.

   (B) II only.   (E) II and III.

   (C) III only.

57. A rule that can be established from the data is that

    I.   there are more herbivores than carnivores in a food chain.

    II. about 90% of the energy is lost as you go up the food chain.

    III. about 10% of the energy is transferred to the next highest level
         of a food chain.

    (A) I only.   (D) I and II.

    (B) II only.   (E) II and III.

    (C) III only.

58. Climate change will have the least effect on

    I.   plant germination.

    II. plant flowering.

    III. deciduous trees losing leaves in the fall.

    (A) I only.   (D) I and III.

    (B) II only.   (E) II and III.

    (C) III only.

Questions 59–60 refer to the following evolutionary inventions by vertebrates.

    I.   Lobed fins

    II. Amniote egg

    III. Internal nostrils and primitive lungs

    IV. Internal fertilization

59. What evolutionary adaptation(s) allowed vertebrates, for the first
    time, to explore land for food?

    (A) I only.   (D) I and III.

    (B) II only.   (E) II and IV.

    (C) III only.

60. What evolutionary change(s) allowed vertebrates, for the first time, to live and reproduce away from water?

   (A) II only.

   (B) III only.

   (C) II and IV.

   (D) III and IV.

   (E) II, III, and IV.

If you are taking the Biology-E test, continue with questions 61–80.

BIOLOGY-E SECTION

DIRECTIONS: The questions or incomplete statements below are followed by five possible answers or completions. Pick the answer choice that best answers or completes the question or incomplete statement and then fill in the correct oval on your answer sheet.

---

61. The movement of young salamanders from the pond where they were born to another pond is an example of

   (A) dispersal.

   (B) energy flow.

   (C) migration.

   (D) nutrient cycling.

   (E) spacing.

Questions 62–63 refer to the following table which shows the number of individuals of five different species (species 1 to 5) in five different communities (a, b, c, d, and e).

Community	Species				
	No. 1	No. 2	No. 3	No. 4	No. 5
a	18	21	22	20	19
b	150	0	0	75	5
c	47	48	0	0	46
d	100	3	5	4	5
e	6	0	6	0	0

62. Which one of the communities would have the highest species diversity index?

(A) a   (D) d

(B) b   (E) e

(C) c

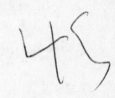

63. Which one of the communities has the lowest evenness?

(A) a   (D) d

(B) b   (E) e

(C) c

Questions 64–66 refer to the following.

The numbers of two different species in large tidal pools on the west coast of Oregon:

Observed Condition	Number of Species 1	Number of Species 2
a. Only species 1 present	60	0
b. Only species 2 present	45	0
c. Species 1 and 2 present	40	30

64. Which of the following best explains the result in condition c?

(A) Commensalism

(B) Interspecific competition

(C) Mutualism

(D) Parasitoidism

(E) Parasitism

65. If the species' numbers that were apparent after condition c were maintained, the outcome would best be described as

(A) competitive exclusion.   (D) amensalism.

(B) mutualism.   (E) resource partitioning.

(C) predation.

66. The change in the number of species 2 between conditions b and c is associated with

(A) fundamental niche of species 1.

(B) realized niche of species 2.

(C) evolutionary change in species 2.

(D) coevolution of species 1 and 2.

(E) predation of species 2 by a keystone predator.

Questions 67–68 refer to the following.

A study on a community of four species was conducted in five parts. In each part, one of the five species was removed and after six months, the number of each of the remaining species was recorded. The abiotic factors were constant. The results were as follows:

Species No.	Initial No. of Each Species	Number of Individuals after Each Treatment			
No. 1	10	removed	10	9	11	12
No. 2	30	100	removed	41	37	34
No. 3	20	1	25	removed	17	27
No. 4	30	2	40	39	removed	29
No. 5	20	3	30	33	19	removed

67. Removal of which species had the greatest effect on the community?

(A) No. 1   (D) No. 4

(B) No. 2   (E) No. 5

(C) No. 3

68. Which one of the following terms explains the results of the experiment?

    (A) Coevolution   (D) Parasitoid

    (B) Fundamental niche   (E) Intraspecific competition

    (C) Keystone predator

69. Which one of the following terms applies to phytoplankton?

    (A) Autotrophs   (D) Heterotrophs

    (B) Carnivores   (E) Omnivores

    (C) Herbivores

70. Movement of water in the hydrological cycle occurs primarily from the land to the ocean via _____ and from the ocean to the land via _____.

    (A) groundwater, clouds

    (B) groundwater, wind

    (C) low pressure systems, high pressure systems

    (D) surface water, clouds

    (E) surface water, wind

Questions 71–72 refer to the following figure.

71. If there was a net decrease in the biomass of phytoplankton, which of the following steps would decrease?

(A) 1

(D) 6

(B) 2 and 3

(E) 7

(C) 4 and 5

72. Which of the following steps contribute to greenhouse gases?

(A) 1 and 5

(D) 6 and 7

(B) 2 and 3

(E) 3 and 4

(C) 2 and 4

73. Rice paddies are anaerobic (no oxygen) and release gases. Which stage of the nitrogen cycle does this represent?

(A) Denitrification

(D) Nitrogen fixation

(B) Immobilization

(E) Volatilization

(C) Mineralization

74. In which of the following biomes is permafrost a defining characteristic?

(A) Alpine meadows

(B) Temperate deciduous forest

(C) Temperate grassland

(D) Temperate boreal forest

(E) Tundra

75. The primary initial source of energy within the headwaters of a river is

(A) caddisfly larvae.

(D) pelagic algae.

(B) dead fish.

(E) periphyton.

(C) detritus.

76. Which one of the following aquatic ecosystems would have the highest net primary production (kcal m^{-2} yr^{-1})?

(A) Abyssal zone of ocean

(D) Pelagic zone of ocean

(B) Deep tropical lake

(E) River

(C) Marsh

77. The trophic level with the greatest respiratory heat loss is the detritivores because

(A) they obtain energy from producers and consumers.

(B) they use partially decomposed material.

(C) they are small.

(D) they have a high metabolic rate.

(E) they are not selective about their diet.

Questions 78–79 refer to the following table.

The following table gives the mean monthly temperature (°C) and precipitation (mm). (Data from Environment Canada, 1990.)

Month	Mean Temperature (°C)	Mean Precipitation (mm)
January	2.5	153.8
February	4.6	114.7
March	5.8	101.0
April	8.8	59.6
May	12.2	51.6
June	15.1	45.2
July	17.3	32.0
August	17.1	41.1
September	14.2	67.1
October	10.0	114.0
November	5.9	150.1
December	3.9	182.4

78. In which month would precipitation in the form of snow be most likely?

(A) January

(B) November

(C) April

(D) October

(E) December

79. Which biome would best describe these varying conditions of temperature and precipitation?

(A) Arctic tundra

(B) Temperate forest

(C) Tropical alpine

(D) Tropical grassland

(E) Tropical forest

80. In a lake there are 3 species of fish, 14 species of invertebrates, and 19 species of algae. Which of the following represents a community?

(A) The algae

(B) The invertebrates and the fish

(C) The invertebrates and the sediment

(D) The algae, the invertebrates, and the fish

(E) The fish

STOP
If you finish before time is called, you may check your work on the entire Biology E-test only. Do not turn to any other test in this book.

SAT Biology E/M
Practice Test 3

ANSWER KEY

BIOLOGY CORE SECTION

1.	(D)	16.	(A)	31.	(C)	46.	(C)
2.	(C)	17.	(C)	32.	(B)	47.	(E)
3.	(A)	18.	(D)	33.	(A)	48.	(B)
4.	(D)	19.	(B)	34.	(E)	49.	(B)
5.	(E)	20.	(E)	35.	(E)	50.	(A)
6.	(A)	21.	(D)	36.	(D)	51.	(C)
7.	(D)	22.	(C)	37.	(D)	52.	(A)
8.	(D)	23.	(D)	38.	(C)	53.	(A)
9.	(A)	24.	(E)	39.	(B)	54.	(A)
10.	(E)	25.	(B)	40.	(A)	55.	(A)
11.	(C)	26.	(D)	41.	(E)	56.	(B)
12.	(D)	27.	(C)	42.	(B)	57.	(E)
13.	(B)	28.	(E)	43.	(A)	58.	(E)
14.	(D)	29.	(D)	44.	(D)	59.	(D)
15.	(A)	30.	(D)	45.	(B)	60.	(C)

BIOLOGY-E SECTION

61.	(A)	66.	(B)	71.	(C)	76.	(C)
62.	(A)	67.	(A)	72.	(A)	77.	(A)
63.	(B)	68.	(C)	73.	(A)	78.	(A)
64.	(B)	69.	(A)	74.	(E)	79.	(B)
65.	(E)	70.	(D)	75.	(C)	80.	(D)

DETAILED EXPLANATIONS OF ANSWERS

PRACTICE TEST 3

BIOLOGY CORE SECTION

1. **(D)**   2. **(C)**

Alleles: H = curly hair
h = straight hair
F = normal feet
f = big feet

Parent Cross: HHFF × hhff

Children's Cross (dihybrid cross): HhFf × HhFf

Question 1 assumes that the two genes are controlling these traits on two different tetrads; therefore, the Law of Independent Assortment will apply for the distribution of the gametes. When the grandchildren are produced the possible allele combinations for the grandchildren are shown in the Punnett square below:

	HF	Hf	hF	hf
HF	HHFF	HHFf	HhFF	HhFf
Hf	HHFf	HHff	HfFf	Hhff
hF	HhFF	HhFf	hhFF	hhFf
hf	HhFf	Hhff	hhFf	hhff

Results:
9/16 H_F_   9/16 × 180 = 101 curly hair, normal feet
3/16 H_ff   3/16 × 180 = 34 curly hair, big feet
3/16 hhF_   3/16 × 180 = 34 straight hair, normal feet
1/16 hhff   1/16 × 180 = 11 straight hair, big feet

Question 2 assumes that the two genes are on the same tetrad; therefore, the genes are linked on the same chromosome. The dominant genes for curly and normal hair are linked. The recessive genes are also linked. (Note that these results are rounded off to whole numbers.)

Dihybrid Cross using Linked Genes

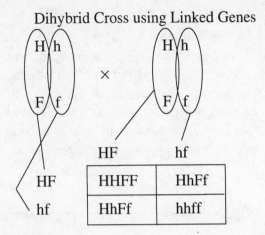

	HF	hf
HF	HHFF	HhFf
hf	HhFf	hhff

Results:

3/4 H_F_ $3/4 \times 180 = 135$ curly hair, normal feet

0/0 H_ff

0/0 hhF_

1/4 hhff $1/4 \times 180 = 45$ straight hair, big feet

Questions 3–5

This set of questions asks you to match various characteristics with their respective invertebrate phyla.

3. **(A)**

To answer this question you must know what a coelom is and which phylum has a coelom in addition to displaying radial symmetry. A coelom is a body cavity that is located completely within mesodermal tissue. It separates the body wall from the internal organs. Echinoderms have a coelom, but cnidarians do not. Cnidarians have a mesoderm that is sandwiched between an ectoderm and endoderm, with the only cavity being inside the endoderm (gastrovascular cavity). Both cnidarians and adult echinoderms have radial symmetry.

4. **(D)**

For this question you must know what is meant by segmented (metamerism) and which organisms are segmented worms. When an organism is segmented, its body is divided into roughly equal units containing repeating internal and external structures. Platyhelminthes are flatworms and do not have repeating structures. However, annelids are worms whose repeating segments contain structures such as a separate coelom, nephridia, and setae.

5. **(E)**

For this question you must be familiar with the types of skeletons found in different organisms. Cnidarians, platyhelminths, and annelids have hydrostatic skeletons. This type of skeleton depends upon alternating muscles in the body wall contracting and putting pressure on the rest of the body. Echinoderms have an endoskeleton, a skeleton made of plates embedded in the skin of the organism. An external skeleton with jointed appendages for movement is found in arthropods (arth = joint, pod = appendage).

Questions 6–7

These questions concern the functions of structures that are important in motion.

6. **(A)**

For this question you must be familiar with the way in which a joint is held together. Muscles connect to the bones of a joint and when muscles contract, they pull on bones, producing movement. Muscles are connected to bone by thick strands of dense connective tissue called tendons. The articulating surfaces of the bones are covered by cartilage. In addition, the joint is stabilized by ligaments which connect bones to each other.

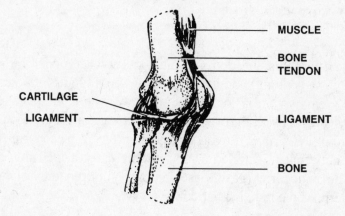

7. **(D)**

To answer this question you must realize that bones contain living cells that must receive oxygen and nutrients to survive. As with all other cells of the body, these essential materials are delivered by the circulatory system. The heart pumps blood through two series of vessels that deliver blood to structures in the body.

8. **(D)**

Since the enzyme took the least amount of time (5 minutes) to convert one gram of substrate when the temperature was 37°C, its activity was greatest at this temperature. It can be seen, therefore, that the enzyme's activity increased as the temperature increased, but peaked at a temperature of 37°C. It can also be seen that, at extremes of temperature (0°C and 70°C), enzyme activity is decreased. Choice (B) is incorrect because it does not consider the enzyme's activity at 70°C in its statement.

9. **(A)**
This question asks about the characteristics of fungi. Fungi are eukaryotes. They are multicellular and multinucleate. Structurally, they have cell walls that are composed mainly of chitin, a derivative polysaccharide containing nitrogen, and they reproduce by spore production. Lacking chlorophyll, they are not capable of undergoing photosynthesis, but instead feed on dead organic matter by secreting digestive enzymes into their environment, and breaking down food material extracellularly. The products of digestion are then absorbed through the cell wall and cell membranes by structures called haustoria.

10. **(E)**
This question relates to the Hardy-Weinberg equation, which deals with the gene frequencies of alleles in a stable population. Mutation, migration, selection, and nonrandom mating will all alter the frequency of certain genes by favoring some alleles over others. An unstable environment would also alter gene frequencies by favoring alleles that are now more beneficial in the new setting; a stable environment would not alter gene frequencies.

11. **(C)**
This question deals with biogeochemical cycles in ecology. Matter can be transferred from living material to the physical environment and back. Thus, carbon, oxygen, water, and nitrogen (matter) can be recycled. The only way that living material can obtain energy is by photosynthesis. Light energy from the sun is converted to chemical energy. As this chemical energy is transferred along the food chain, chemical bonds are broken and reformed, and heat energy is produced. Much of this heat energy is lost to the environment and cannot be recovered by living organisms. Energy flows; matter cycles.

12. **(D)**
In order to answer this question you must know what is meant by agonistic behavior and the forms it may take. Agonistic behavior is aggressive behavior. It may manifest itself in its most serious form as an attack on another organism. It may also be expressed as displays. Threat displays and appeasement displays are ways that animals have of resolving

a conflict without actual combat. The animal with the strongest threat displays (larger appearance, menacing posture) usually wins. The loser signals the end of the conflict with appeasement behavior (minimizing size, showing the most vulnerable part of the body, turning away). Displacement behavior is an irrelevant response to a situation. This may occur in response to aggressive behavior, but may also occur in other situations. A kinesis is a stable pattern of behavior that is an undirected response to a simple stimulus, and, thus, has nothing to do with agonistic behavior.

13. **(B)**

This is a straightforward question that tests your knowledge of ecological concepts. An ecosystem includes all the organisms that live in a particular area and their physical environment. Those organisms would make up a community.

Population, species, and race are terms that define a group of potentially interbreeding organisms. However, population and race refer to organisms inhabiting the same area. In fact, a race (also called a subspecies) is a type of population that is geographically more isolated and, therefore, has become genetically distinct.

A species is a group of potentially interbreeding organisms, whether or not they live in the same area. Thus, the term species is more inclusive than the terms populations and races.

14. **(D)**

For this question you must be able to interpret the data given in tabular form. While a number of true statements are offered as choices (nucleotide bases are hydrogen bonded, bases are attached to a sugar phosphate backbone, and DNA is a double helix), none of these can be concluded from the information given in the question. Looking at the percent compositions for each organism, we can see that the base composition may be different. When we compare percentages of bases, we see that the number of adenines equals the number of thymines.

15. **(A)**

In order to answer this question you must be familiar with the formation of proteins and the role of proteins in the body. Twenty different amino acids are needed by vertebrates to make proteins, important compounds necessary for growth. Humans make 12 of these amino acids, the so-called nonessential ones. However, the eight essential amino acids can only be supplied through the diet. Essential and nonessential amino acids must be present together in order for protein synthesis to occur.

16. **(A)**

To answer this question correctly you must understand that land plants must retain water in order to survive. They have, therefore, developed mechanisms to minimize water loss. All land plants have a cuticle on all parts exposed to the air to prevent water loss by evaporation. In addition, the presence of roots for water uptake, as well as vascular tissue (such as xylem) for the distribution of water and other materials, increases the ability of the plant to survive on land. Seed production among gymnosperms and angiosperms further liberates plants from a water environment. Seeds with their protective seed coats provide plants with a nonaqueous means of reproduction. With the development of seeds, free-swimming sperm have been replaced by pollen grains which contain a generative nucleus. The generative nucleus divides to produce sperm. Thus, pollen grains eliminate the need for external water for fertilization.

17. **(C)**

This question tests your ability to understand what a territory is, as defined in the question, and to apply that knowledge to understand its ecological functions. A territory is a particular area that is defended by its occupant, usually from others of the same species. Since the individual defends the borders of the territory, the territory actually decreases physical contact among species members. It, therefore, decreases the time and energy devoted to aggression.

A territory channels resources available to specific individuals, maximizing the individuals' chances of surviving and reproducing. It may insure a food supply for the individual, while limiting food available to those who have not been successful in establishing one. It also increases the reproductive success of the individual in it, by increasing the chance of mating. Therefore, it increases the reproductive success of the entire species. Equal distribution of resources among too many individuals could compromise the ability of any of them to survive. Therefore, the territory is a way of regulating population size.

18. **(D)**

In order to predict the outcome of a mating between a type O father and a type AB mother, you must know something about the forms of the genes that determine the ABO blood types. Gene I^A is a dominant gene that codes for type A antigens, proteins found on red blood cells. Gene I^B is also a dominant gene and codes for type B antigens found on red blood cells. Gene i is the recessive form that gives neither type A antigens nor type B antigens. A father with type O blood has the genotype ii, and can only produce i sperm. A mother with type AB blood has the genotype

I^AI^B, and can produce either I^A or I^B eggs. An i sperm will fertilize the I^A egg to produce a child with an I^Ai genotype, or an i sperm will fertilize the I^B egg to produce a child with an I^Bi genotype. Thus, the children of that mating can have either type A or type B blood.

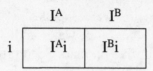

	I^A	I^B
i	I^Ai	I^Bi

19. **(B)**

For this question you must know what role trees play in the ecosystem and determine what organism plays the same role in the ocean. Trees are primary producers. They have the ability to make organic molecules from inorganic molecules using sunlight as the energy source. In other words, they are photosynthetic organisms. Algae also carry out photosynthesis and, therefore, play the same role as trees in their ecological community. Fish, shrimp, sharks, and bacteria are consumers and/or decomposers.

20. **(E)**

In order to answer this question you must be familiar with the structure and functions of genes. Genes are DNA sequences that are found on chromosomes and code for polypeptides. A particular gene may exist in more than one form, giving us alleles for the same gene. For example, two forms of the gene for a plant height would be tall vs. short. When genes undergo change, they are said to mutate. Genes may be beneficial, neutral, or harmful to the survival of the organism. It is even possible for a gene to cause the death of the organism, or in other words, to be lethal.

21. **(D)**

In order to interpret the results of this cross, we should first determine whether the gene for miniature wings is dominant or recessive. Then we can determine whether the gene is located on an autosomal, X, or Y chromosome. Because the first generation of offspring is all wild-type, the gene for miniature wings must be recessive. If the gene were on the Y chromosome, we would expect to find it passed from father to son every generation. However, it did not show up in the first generation of offspring. If the gene were on an autosomal chromosome, the 1/4 of the second-generation offspring that is miniature-winged would be expected to be both female and male. In X-linked inheritance, 1/4 of the second-generation offspring for this type of cross would be expected to show the recessive trait and, also, to be only males. Since the second generation of

358

offspring showed 1/4 miniature-winged males, the trait must be due to a recessive X-linked gene.

Key: M = wild-type gene on X chromosome
m = miniature wings gene on X chromosome
Y = Y chromosome

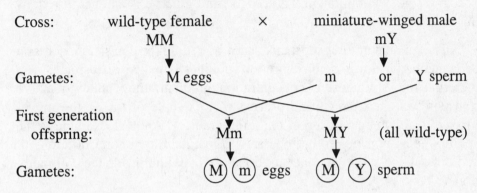

Cross: wild-type female   ×   miniature-winged male
MM   mY

Gametes: M eggs   m   or   Y sperm

First generation
offspring: Mm   MY   (all wild-type)

Gametes: (M) (m) eggs   (M) (Y) sperm

Punnett square:

	M	m
M	MM	Mm
Y	MY	mY

Second-generation offspring:

genotypes: **phenotypes:**

1/4 MM ⎫
1/4 Mm ⎭   1/2 wild-type females
1/4 MY   1/4 wild-type males
1/4 mY   1/4 miniature-winged males

22. **(C)**

This question tests your ability to interpret experimental data given in graphical form. This graph shows the changes in abundance of two species over a period of time. Species A shows a sharp increase in number every 9 to 10 years, followed by a sharp decrease. Species B increases in number following the same cycle except that the maximum abundance is about one year later than that for species A. Since species B peaks after species A, it is most likely that species B is eating species A. B is the predator, and A is the prey. When there are more species A organisms, there is more food for species B, and B increases. Larger numbers of B feed on A and cause the decline of A. As A decreases, there is less food for B, and B dies off.

23. **(D)**

In order to answer this question, you must understand what kinds of cellular activities require energy and categorize the specific choices accordingly. Energy is required for muscle contraction, for building of organic molecules, and for the movement of materials against a concentration gradient. The building of glycogen from glucose is an energy-requiring process.

The movement of a substance, such as sodium or potassium, across a cell membrane down a concentration gradient is called diffusion. When materials move against a concentration gradient, they undergo active transport, an energy-requiring process. An example of this is the movement of calcium against a concentration gradient. Another example is the sodium-potassium pump that operates to maintain high concentrations of sodium outside and high concentrations of potassium inside the cell membrane.

Osmosis is the diffusion of water across a cell membrane. Since diffusion occurs along a concentration gradient, this is not an energy requiring process. The molecules spread out by their kinetic energy.

24. **(E)**

This is a question that asks you to identify the site of meiosis. Meiosis is the process of cell division that reduces the number of chromosome sets to one. Diploid cells are converted to haploid cells, which develop into gametes with half the number of chromosomes. When haploid gametes combine at fertilization, the chromosome number doubles, and the zygote produced contains the normal diploid number of chromosomes. Therefore, the site of meiosis must be the testes in which sperm are made in preparation for fertilization.

Cell division in all other cells in the body is designed to produce daughter cells that are genetically identical to the parent cell. Therefore, cell division in the stomach, skin, urethra, and intestine is by mitosis and does not change the chromosome count.

25. **(B)**

This question deals with the problem of water loss in land plants, and asks you to figure out which mechanism would allow water loss to occur in the plant. The movement of water through the xylem occurs because the water column is "pulled" up through the plant by evaporation of water from the leaf surface, a process called transpiration.

The water loss from transpiration must be balanced by water absorption by the roots. Therefore, the roots help to retain water in the plant. In addition, the leaf shape can reduce water loss by decreasing the surface area to volume ratio (as exemplified by round pine needles). The impermeable waxy cuticle that covers plant parts exposed to the air also prevents water loss. Stomata are the gas exchange openings in leaves plus their two guard cells. Because guard cells can close when photosynthesis is not occurring and when water loss would be severe (during the heat of the day), this is an important mechanism for water retention in the plant.

26. **(D)**
For this question you need to know how protein synthesis occurs. The nucleus contains genes on chromosomes, and the genes direct the synthesis of RNA. Therefore, the nucleus is the site of the RNA production. Messenger RNA is a copy of a gene that codes for a particular protein. It travels from the nucleus to the ribosome where it attaches and directs the assembly of the protein. Thus, translation occurs at the ribosome. Transfer RNA transports the amino acids to the ribosome for protein synthesis.

27. **(C)**
This question asks you to recognize the ecosystem that is dominated by evergreen trees. This is the taiga, an area of extremely cold winters. The tundra, a region north of the taiga, has a permanently frozen subsoil (permafrost) and cannot support any large plants. The temperate forests are farther south and contain deciduous plants (plants that lose their leaves) that need more rainfall and a relatively long, warm summer. Tropical rain forests have abundant rainfall and are characterized by tremendous species diversity, with up to ten dominant trees. A chaparral is a region dominated by drought-resistant and fire-resistant small trees and shrubs because of the cool, rainy winters and hot, dry summers.

28. **(E)**
To answer this question you must know how evolution occurs, and you must figure out whether specific situations lend themselves to evolutionary change. In order for evolutionary change to occur, organisms must exist that are genetically different from each other. Acquired changes in the individual will not contribute to evolution because there is no genetic basis for these changes. Even if the acquired changes increase reproductive success, the offspring will not show an increase in the frequency of the acquired trait.

Thus, a nutritionally well-balanced diet may improve the horses that are given such a diet, but it will not change the next generation horses. On the other hand, genetically different forms of birds provide the raw materials for evolution. Those organisms that are genetically better adapted to the environment will be the most likely to survive and reproduce. For example, antibiotic-resistant bacteria will be selected for after exposure to antibiotics. Behavioral characteristics that are not acquired would be inherited and could be selected either during natural selection or selective breeding.

Another source of evolutionary change is genetic drift. Given genetic variation in a small population, it is possible that some organisms may survive based upon luck. If the individuals surviving a hurricane happen to be genetically different from the rest of the population, then evolutionary change will occur. Genetic drift does not necessarily mean that the surviving organisms are the best adapted or most fit.

29. **(D)**

To answer this question you must use your knowledge of the chemical structures of proteins and DNA to find what is different about them. Proteins are made of 20 different amino acids with the following general structure:

$$H - N - C - C - O - H$$

with R above the second C, and H, H, O below N, C, C respectively.

R is the group that is different for each amino acid. All amino acids contain carbon, hydrogen, nitrogen, and oxygen, but not chlorine.

DNA is made of nitrogen containing bases, a sugar (deoxyribose), and phosphates. The nitrogen-containing bases and sugar are organic compounds that also contain carbon, hydrogen, and oxygen. The phosphates are compounds containing phosphorus and oxygen. Therefore, DNA has all of the elements listed as choices. The fact that DNA contains phosphorus while protein does not is a way of distinguishing between the two chemically.

30. **(D)**

This is a straightforward question about the structure of bacteria. Bacteria are prokaryotes, and, therefore, have their genetic material organized as a large circular molecule of DNA. They do not have distinct nuclei, chloroplasts, or mitochondria. In addition, their cell membranes are surrounded by outer cell walls.

31. **(C)**

This question requires that you know something about the autonomic nervous system, and be able to figure out what types of activities might be autonomic in function. The autonomic nervous system is the part of the peripheral nervous system that includes the motor neurons that are not under voluntary control. These neurons control smooth muscle (found in internal organs), the heart, and glands. Thus, the autonomic nervous system controls the smooth muscle of the digestive tract, heart rate, and salivary as well as adrenal gland secretions. Contraction of skeletal muscles is under the control of the somatic nervous system.

32. **(B)**

To answer this question you must be able to solve a genetic problem. To do this you must determine the genotypes of the parents, the gametes produced, the genotypes of the offspring, and tabulate the phenotypes of the offspring. Let's begin with the gene symbols:

Key: R = round seed (dominant)
 r = wrinkled seed (recessive)

 Y = yellow (dominant)
 y = green (recessive)

Cross: RrYy × rrYy

Gametes: Because the genes are on separate chromosomes, they assort independently of each other.

 Therefore, RrYy produces RY, Ry, rY, ry gametes

 And rrYy produces rY, ry gametes

Punnett square:

	RY	Ry	rY	ry
rY	RrYY	RrYy	rrYY	rrYy
ry	RrYy	Rryy	rrYy	rryy

Phenotypes:

3/8 RrY– (round yellow seeds)   1/8 Rryy (round green seeds)
3/8 rrY– (wrinkled yellow seeds)   1/8 rryy (wrinkled green seeds)

Therefore, the phenotypic ratio is 3:3:1:1.

33. **(A)**

To answer this question you need to recognize the different types of tissues in plants. Meristematic tissue is the undifferentiated, actively dividing tissue that is responsible for growth. Therefore, the meristem would show the greatest numbers of mitotic divisions. Cork (thick, water-impermeable cells in bark) and xylem (hollow vessels that conduct water and minerals from roots to leaves) are both made of dead cells. Phloem and guard cells are highly differentiated. Phloem transports sap and guard cells regulate the size of stomata.

34. **(E)**

To answer this question you must figure out what happens when parents devote resources and energy to the rearing of the young. It might be helpful to first look at the situation in which there is no parental involvement.

Organisms that produce large amounts of offspring depend upon the sheer size of the litter for the perpetuation of their species. The young mature very quickly and are not educated, as the parents are usually involved with obtaining their own food and with reproduction. Should some of the offspring become endangered, the parents will not interfere, because it is not expected that all the young survive, which is the reason for a large litter.

Organisms that are much involved in the education of their young would place the welfare of their young above their own because such organisms usually have few offspring, as few as one per season (e.g., humans), and the death of even one of the young would seriously jeopardize the chances of any offspring surviving to maturity. In such cases, therefore, survival to maturity (of any of the young) depends upon education of the young by the parents (this means that more time is necessary in order for the parents to impart their knowledge to their young), smaller litters (it would be impossible for two parents to thoroughly educate too many offspring), and, if necessary, protection of the young (the parents have already survived to reproduce; the young have not).

35. **(E)**

To answer this question you must know what a gene is and how mutations can affect the function of the gene. A gene is a sequence of nucleotide bases that codes for the amino acid sequence of a protein. The code is a triplet code, and three bases code for each amino acid. One type of mutation that does not change the length of the gene is a change in a single base.

Let's look at what would happen to the protein if there were a single base change. Since many of the amino acids have more than one codon (base triplet), a change in the triplet code might produce an alternate code for the same amino acid. Therefore, the protein might not change at all. If the mutation does result in an amino acid change, it might not be in a critical portion of the protein. The base substitution could be beneficial, if the structure of the protein improves. It could have no effect, or it could be harmful.

36. **(D)**

This question asks you to remember the characteristics of protozoa. They are eukaryotes and, therefore, have the typical membrane-bound internal structures. They are primarily single-celled organisms that must ingest food to survive. The different groups of protozoa are characterized by the variety of techniques for locomotion: Mastigophora use flagella, Sarcodina use pseudopods, Ciliata use cilia, while adult Sporozoa lack special structures for locomotion.

37. **(D)**

It is important to know what diploid means, and you must know which cells are diploid. Diploid refers to a condition of having two sets of chromosomes. Spores, eggs, and sperm are all formed by meiosis, a process of cell division whose purpose is to reduce the amount of chromosomes to one set. Therefore, spores, eggs, and sperm are haploid. Drones develop from unfertilized eggs and, therefore, are also haploid. Zygotes are products of eggs fusing with sperm and are thus diploid.

38. **(C)**

To answer this question you must know something about ecological pyramids. Energy flow, numbers of organisms, and biomass pyramids may be constructed for a particular ecosystem. These show the primary producers (plants) at the bottom, then primary consumers (herbivores), then secondary consumers, and finally tertiary consumers at the top. Members of each level feed on the members of the level below.

Productivity (photosynthesis) is only measured at the first level, since that is where the plants are. As one moves up the pyramid, the amount of available useful energy decreases, because energy transfers between trophic levels are inefficient and result in heat loss to the environment. Since energy levels decrease, usually the biomass would also decrease and the number of organisms would also decrease (less energy supports fewer organisms). The exception to the biomass pyramid occurs when the producers have a very high rate of reproduction. The exception to the population pyramid occurs when the primary producer is very large (for example, a tree).

39. **(B)**

To answer this question you must know how chromosomes behave during meiosis. Chromosomes contain genes linked together in a linear fashion. Genes on the same chromosome are usually inherited together, unless crossing over occurs. Crossing over can occur during prophase I of meiosis, because homologous (like) chromosomes, each containing their replicated strands (chromatids), line up next to each other. During crossing over, one chromatid from each homologous chromosome breaks and reunites so that the new chromosomes contain pieces of the original chromosomes.

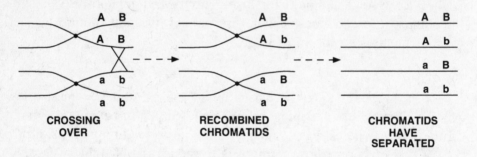

CROSSING OVER   RECOMBINED CHROMATIDS   CHROMATIDS HAVE SEPARATED

If the genes are on different chromosomes, they will assort independently of each other. The frequency of chromosomal rearrangements, such as translocations, deletions, duplication, and inversions, is not related to gene linkage. Blending inheritance occurs in some situations where the heterozygous condition shows an intermediate phenotype between an individual who is homozygous dominant and one who is homozygous recessive.

40. **(A)**

This question tests your ability to draw conclusions from experimental results shown in a graph. The graph shows the number of mutations that occur after exposure to different concentrations of a variety of chemicals. Different chemicals cause different numbers of mutations.

As the amount of chemical increases, the number of mutations also increases. In some cases (chemicals C, D, E), high concentrations of a chemical result in only a minor increase in mutations. Chemical A clearly causes the most mutations. This graph does not tell us whether the mutations are harmful, beneficial, or neutral.

41. **(E)**

To answer this question you must figure out the different kinds of gametes that can be produced.

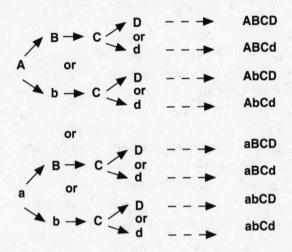

There are eight different gametes possible. An easier way of doing this is to see that there are two choices for A (A or a), two for B (B or b), one for C, and two for D (D or d). Therefore, $2 \times 2 \times 1 \times 2$ equals eight. Or you can use the formula 2^n in which the exponent n represents the number of heterozygous gene pairs; $2^3 = 8$.

42. **(B)**

This question can be answered with an understanding of the structure of the seed. The seed consists of an embryo, stored food that is endosperm or formed from endosperm, and the outer protective layers of the ovule or seed coat. As the embryo develops, one portion (the radicle) becomes the root and another portion (the epicotyl) becomes the stem. In angiosperms, the ovules are found within the ovary, which develops into the fruit. The fruit protects the seeds from water loss during development and may aid in dispersal of the seeds later.

43. **(A)**

To answer this question you need to know the functions of the three different forms of behavior. Social behavior involves the interactions of organisms within a species and includes, among others, mating behavior, caring for young, food procurement, and protection from predators. These all depend upon a high degree of communication. Echolocation is a mechanism used by bats for finding their way when they are flying. They emit sound waves that bounce off objects, and these sound waves are, in turn, perceived by the bats. Circadian rhythms are regular cycles of activity that occur about every 24 hours. Neither echolocation nor circadian rhythms depend upon interaction with other organisms, and, therefore, they do not depend upon social communication.

44. **(D)**
For this question you must recognize the different sources of genetic variability in a population. These include changes in the base sequence of a gene or in chromosomal organization which are called mutations. The chromosomal rearrangements might be translocations, duplications, deletions, or inversions. Migration of genetically different organisms into a population would also increase genetic variability. Sometimes a particular phenotype depends upon the fact that certain genes are inherited together. Either by independent assortment of different chromosomes or crossing over of homologous chromosomes, these events of genetic recombination would yield new combinations of genes that might alter the phenotype of the next generation.

Once genetic variation exists, natural selection acts to choose those individuals that are best adapted to the particular environment. Thus, natural selection is not a cause of genetic variability, but rather, a possible consequence of it.

45. **(B)**
To answer this question you must be familiar with ecological relationships among organisms, in particular predator-prey relationships and how mimicry protects the prey. If an organism has an unpleasant taste, a predator that has experienced the taste will avoid eating that organism. Another organism that looks like the first will also be protected, because it will be mistaken for the first. Therefore, mimicry of species B with the unpleasant taste will protect species A, because species A looks like species B.

46. **(C)**

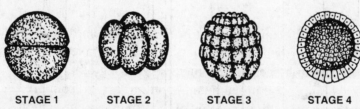

STAGE 1   STAGE 2   STAGE 3   STAGE 4

To answer this question you must recognize the stages in embryonic development and predict the next stage. The first three drawings show early cleavage leading to the formation of a ball of cells called the morula. This ball of cells hollows out to become the blastula, shown as stage 4. The next stage is gastrulation. To form a gastrula, one end of the blastula invaginates, and the cells move inward to produce a two-layered structure. Later, the dorsal surface will invaginate during formation of the neural tube, the forerunner of the spinal cord.

Questions 47–48

For this set of questions, you are asked to analyze the results of a series of experiments showing the effects of two plant hormones on growth. It is necessary to read and interpret the data as presented in graph form.

47. (E)

For this question you must be able to look at all four graphs and figure out which one shows the most plant growth. Plant cells in experiment IV show the greatest growth. This experiment involves 25 mg/l auxin and different concentrations of kinetin. The greatest growth shown for this experiment occurred when kinetin had a concentration of about 1 mg/l.

48. (B)

To answer this question you must know that a control is the experimental situation that leaves out the variable. The variable, in this case, is the amount of auxin present. Therefore, the control is experiment I, because no auxin is present in this experiment.

Questions 49–50

To answer this set of questions, you must know the chemical structure of the cell membrane and what it does.

49. (B)

For this question you must be familiar with the chemical structure of the membrane by the fluid-mosaic model. The membrane is primarily a double layer of phospholipid molecules. These phospholipids are composed of hydrophilic phosphate ends that are oriented to the surfaces of the membrane where water is present. The hydrophobic fatty acid chains point to the inside of the membrane. Interspersed between the phospholipids are proteins. Some of these proteins extend to the outside of the membrane, while others are located within the membrane. The proteins serve a variety of functions, including acting as receptors on the surface and serving as pores through which certain materials can pass into and out of the cell.

50. **(A)**

For this question, an understanding of the structure of the membrane will help you predict its behavior. Because the membrane is made primarily of lipids with uncharged fatty acid chains, charged particles, such as salts, are repelled by the lipid portion. Instead, the protein pores allow for passage of these particles. In addition, large particles, such as proteins including proteinaceous hormones, which due to their large size have difficulty passing through the membrane. However, they may have an effect on the cell by binding with protein receptors on the outside of the cell. The cell is not permeable to proteins because proteins are too large and may have charged portions.

The membrane has a positive charge on the outside because of an unequal distribution of certain ions. Positive sodium ions are found in higher concentration outside the membrane, while organic materials found inside the cell are more likely to have a negative charge. The maintenance of this concentration of sodium ions outside depends upon an expenditure of energy. This process, called active transport, also functions in moving other materials across the membrane against their concentration gradients.

Questions 51–52

For these questions, you are asked to analyze data in table form related to the different fluid compartments of the body.

51. **(C)**

This question asks you to compare the amounts of materials present in the different fluids. While urine only contains three of the five materials listed, it shows the greatest variability in the amounts of the materials present. Sodium and potassium amounts vary. Note their respective ranges of 5–13 and 2–7. This makes sense, since the function of urine is to rid the body of waste materials or materials that are present in excess. It is important for the internal body conditions to remain relatively constant, if it is to function properly. Materials, such as sodium and potassium, may vary depending upon dietary intake and metabolic needs.

52. **(A)**

For this question, you must draw a valid conclusion by analyzing the data on the table. The largest component in lymph is protein, not glucose. The largest component in urine is urea; normally no protein is found in urine. When cerebrospinal fluid and blood are compared, they have the same components, but in very different concentrations. As you can see, glucose is normally not excreted by the body, since no glucose is found in urine.

When we compare lymph, blood, and intercellular fluid, they contain the same amounts of glucose, urea, sodium, and potassium. For example, it is 100 for glucose. They do differ in the amount of protein present. The capillaries of the circulatory system are impermeable to proteins. However, slight amounts of protein leak out and are quickly picked up by the highly protein permeable lymphatic vessels.

Questions 53–54

This set of questions requires that you understand how an experiment dealing with nuclear transplants is designed and draw a valid conclusion from the experiment.

53. (A)

For this question you must know for what the experiment is testing and, from that, figure out what the appropriate control should be. These transplants are testing the effect of nuclei from various sources on the development of an egg. It is possible that some cytoplasm from the donor cell may be transferred with the nucleus, and it is also possible that the process of injection may trigger development changes. To determine the effects of cytoplasm and of the injection on the egg cell (so that if such effects occur in the experimental ova, they can be attributed to the presence of cytoplasm or the act of injection) injecting cytoplasm would serve as a control.

54. (A)

To answer this question, you must look at what the experiment is testing. It is designed to see whether the various nuclei can control development of the egg. The blastula, gastrula, and intestinal nuclei can support normal development, while cytoplasm alone cannot. However, since fewer eggs containing gastrula and intestinal nuclei develop normally, changes must have occurred in the nucleus during development. This experiment is not testing immune reactions or looking for genes that are lost or mutated.

55. (A)

Gregor Mendel discovered that there are two forms of a gene (alleles) that express a trait. Now we know that there may be more than two alleles, or more than one gene, that expresses a trait. Examples of traits are color of skin or hair, and height.

56. **(B)**   57. **(E)**

The Second Law of Energy (Thermodynamics) states that when energy is changed from one form to another, there is a loss of free energy to do work. As you go through a food chain or up the energy pyramid, there is a loss of free energy. The data shows that you lose about 90% of the energy as you go up the food chain. Another way of stating a general rule is that 10% of the energy is transferred to the next highest level of a food chain. Energy is lost to the food chain in the form of wastes and heat. The First Law of Energy (Thermodynamics) states that energy cannot be created nor destroyed, only changed in form. Food chains do transform energy. Light energy from the sun is transformed into chemical energy (carbohydrates) by producers. Chemical energy is transformed into energy (ATP) cells can use.

58. **(E)**

Both flowering plants and trees losing their leaves during the fall are controlled by the amount of light or darkness. Many plants flower when the period of darkness is longer or shorter than a certain critical time. Decreasing light causes the production of ethylene gas that stimulates the growth of a layer of cells (abscission layer) at the base of the petiole of leaves. Later, enzymes destroy the abscission layer and the leaves are easily knocked from the tree by wind or rain. The tilt of the earth and position of the earth's orbit will control flowering and leaves falling from trees.

Plant germination is dependent on favorable temperatures and sufficient moisture. Climate change can cause changes in the temperature and the amount of precipitation.

59. **(D)**

Lobed fins, internal nostrils, and primitive lungs are the invention of the Crossopterygians. These genetic mutations allowed these ancient fish to move and respire for short periods of time on land. It is thought that amphibians evolved from such lobed finned fish.

60. **(C)**

The amniote egg and internal fertilization are evolutionary inventions of the reptiles. The amniote egg, with its protective membrane and porous shell, along with internal fertilization allowed vertebrates to reproduce and have their embryos develop away from water.

61. **(A)**

Dispersal is the movement of organisms away from the breeding site. The movement of the young salamanders from the pond where they were born to a new pond is dispersal. Migration (C) involves movement but not from a specific place, the birth location. Energy flow (B) is the movement of energy. Similarly, nutrient cycling (D) is the movement of nutrients. Spacing (E) is one result of dispersal.

62. **(A)**

Species diversity is an index that measures both the number of species and the relative numbers of each species (evenness). The more evenly the species are distributed, the greater the evenness. Therefore, the community with the greatest number of species and the most even distribution of the species has the highest species diversity. Community b has the most individuals but only three species which are unevenly distributed. Community c has even distribution but only three species. Community d has five species no. 1 dominates. Community e has only two species. Community a has five species evenly distributed.

63. **(B)**

Evenness is the relative number of each of the species, regardless of the total number of species. The lowest evenness is found in the community with the most different numbers of individuals of each species. Community a has similar numbers of each of the five species. Although community c has only three species, they are present in similar numbers. Community d has a dominance of one species but the remaining four species are present in similar numbers. Community e has few individuals but the two species have the same number of individuals. Note community b with 150–0–0–75–5.

64. **(B)**

Interspecific competition is an interaction in which there is a negative effect for both species. In this example, the negative effect is the reduced numbers of each of the species. Commensalism (A) and mutualism (C) have no negative effects. Both parasitoids (D) and parasites (E) benefit and would increase in numbers. Their hosts would decrease in numbers.

65. **(E)**

Interspecific competition can have two main consequences. One of these, resource partitioning, is the one in condition c. The second, competitive exclusion (A), results in the elimination of one species. Mutualism (B) is beneficial to both species so the numbers would not decrease. Predation (C) results in a decrease in the number of only one of the species. Amensalism (D) has a negative effect on one species but no effect on the second.

66. **(B)**

The ecological position, or niche, of species 2 is changed because of the competition. The new niche is the realized niche. The niche in absence of any interactions is the fundamental niche (A). There is a negative effect on both species, and thus there is no obvious adaptation. Therefore, there is no evolutionary change in species 2 (C) or coevolution of species 1 and 2 (D). Keystone predators (E) are one consequence of the interaction of species but there is competition, not predation, in the given example.

67. **(A)**

An examination of the numbers shows that removal of species 1 resulted in a large increase in species 2. This increase was larger and more significant than any of the other changes. Read number columns 1 and 2 to see this pattern. After removal of species 2 (B), the number of individuals of species 3, 4, and 5 increased slightly but uniformly. Removal of species 3 (C) resulted in a slight increase in the numbers of species 2, 4, and 5. Both the removal of species 4 (D) and species 5 (E) resulted in slight decreases in one of the other species.

68. **(C)**

A keystone predator reduces competition among the prey items and thus reduces the opportunity for competitive exclusion. In this experiment, removal of the keystone predator increased competition among the remaining species, such that species 2 almost excluded species 3, 4, and 5. Although removal of species 2 (B), species 3 (C), species 4 (D), and species 5 (E) resulted in some changes, the same species remained in similar, relative numbers.

69. **(A)**

Phytoplankton are primary producers in water. As primary producers they use the sun's energy to fix carbon, thus making their own energy. Carnivores (B) obtain energy by eating animals. Herbivores (C) obtain energy by eating plants or plankton. Omnivores (E) obtain their energy from eating plants and animals. Carnivores, herbivores, and omnivores are heterotrophs (D) because they obtain their energy from eating other organisms.

70. **(D)**

Over the land, net precipitation exceeds net evaporation, and the excess water moves into groundwater and to the ocean via surface waters. Over the ocean, net evaporation exceeds net precipitation and the excess water in the atmosphere moves in clouds to the land. Water moves into the groundwater, but groundwater is not a major source of water from the land to the ocean (A) and (B). The wind (B) and (E) may drive the movement, but the water is contained in clouds. Similarly, air moves from high to low pressure areas (C); however, this contributes only to the driving force of moisture laden air, and movement in the atmosphere is only between the ocean and the land.

71. **(C)**
    A decrease in the amount of phytoplankton would decrease the uptake of bicarbonate (pathway 4) and reduce the decomposition of phytoplankton (pathway 5). A change in (A) would result from the burning of fossil fuels. It is shelled organisms that contribute to limestone, either as they die and accumulate on the sediments (E) or as calcium exchanged between the shells and the ocean waters (B). Phytoplankton is in water and thus, pathway (D) would not be affected.

72. **(A)**
    Two pathways are important in this question. First, burning fossil fuels (pathway 1) will increase the carbon dioxide released to the atmosphere. Second, increased loss of carbon dioxide from the organisms to the atmosphere (pathway 5), due primarily to decreased numbers of primary producers, will increase atmospheric carbon dioxide. Removal of carbon from the water column (B) and uptake of carbon by organisms (C) or both of these (D) will reduce atmospheric carbon dioxide. Conversion of organic marine shells and land organisms to unavailable carbon (E) will reduce greenhouse gases.

73. **(A)**
    Denitrification is the only stage of the nitrogen cycle that occurs under anaerobic conditions. Nitrogen oxides are released. Immobilization (B) converts inorganic nitrates and ammonium into organic matter, the organisms. Mineralization (C) releases ammonium from dead organisms. Nitrogen gas is taken from the atmosphere by bacteria on or near plants in nitrogen fixation (D). Ammonia gas is released during volatilization (E).

74. **(E)**
    The tundra is in the arctic, and permafrost is characteristic of the tundra biome. Alpine or high altitude areas (A) have permafrost only as icecaps, not where meadows occur. In addition, permafrost is not a defining characteristic of alpine biomes. Temperate areas are characteristic of warm and cold seasons. Snow and cold are continually present during the cold season of temperate deciduous forests (B), grasslands (C), and boreal forests (D), but they are not present during the warm season.

75. **(C)**

There is very low primary production in the headwaters of the stream because there is low light penetration and the water is cold and moving quickly. The initial energy source is primarily detritus (leaves, etc.) from the adjacent land. Caddisfly larvae (A) are present and some species are decomposers, but they are not an energy source. Decomposition of dead fish (B) will contribute to the detritus but is not a major component of the detritus. The fast-moving water limits the presence of pelagic algae (D). The main type of primary producer present is the attached algae or periphyton (E) but it is not a main energy source.

76. **(C)**

The marsh is recognized as an area with significant amounts of emergent vegetation, algae, and high productivity. Except near hydrothermal vents where organisms use chemicals to obtain energy, there is no primary production in the abyssal (no light) zone of the ocean (A). There is little or no mixing of the bottom sediments and the water in a deep tropical lake (B), and thus, the material that dies and goes to the bottom is not returned to the water column. The lake is a net sink of nutrients and has low productivity. The whole of the ocean is the most productive aquatic ecosystem due to its size, but the pelagic zone of the ocean (D), on the basis of kcal $m^{-2} yr^{-1}$, is less productive than a marsh. The mouth of a river may be very productive, but the productivity of parts of the river, particularly the headwaters, is low; therefore, the productivity of rivers (E) is low.

77. **(A)**

Decomposers obtain energy from all the producers and consumers and are the major secondary producers (consumers) and thus, have the greatest respiratory heat loss. They have greater efficiency because they use partially decomposed material (B), but this acts to decrease E_R. They are small (C), can live in many areas, and are not selective about their food (E) which contributes to their abundance—not to the amount of E_R. Metabolic rate (D) affects efficiency, not total production E_R.

78. **(A)**

January has a low mean temperature and high precipitation, making snow highly likely.

79. **(B)**

The temperatures show warm and cold seasons which are indicative of temperate climates. The mean temperatures are above freezing for all months and thus it is not arctic tundra (A). A tropical alpine biome (C) has cyclic daily temperatures; the yearly variation is low. Tropical areas cycle primarily with respect to wet and dry conditions. The given area does have a wet and dry season but the temperature change is also significant. Therefore, it is not a tropical grassland (D) or forest (E).

80. **(D)**

A community is composed of *all* of the populations present. The algae (A) are the primary producers but they are only one part of the community. The invertebrates and the fish (B) are the consumers but as with the algae, they are only one part of the community. Many of the invertebrates live in the sediment (C) but the sediment is not part of the community. The fish (E) are what is probably of most interest to people, but the fish alone are not a community.

SAT Biology E/M Practice Test 4

(Answer sheets appear in the back of this book.)

TIME: 1 Hour
80 Questions

BIOLOGY CORE SECTION

DIRECTIONS: The lettered or numbered choices below refer to the questions or statements that immediately follow them. Pick the best answer choice and fill in the correct oval on your answer sheet. An answer choice may be used more than once or not at all.

Questions 1–3 refer to the following dichotomous key and drawings. Take each organism through the key for correct genus identification.

I. a. long, slender body form - go to step II

    b. short, thick body form - go to step III

II. a. body has stripes - *Albus*

    b. body lacks stripes - *Taxus*

III. a. body has stripes - *Leus*

    b. body lacks stripes - *Unus*

(A) *Albus.*

(B) *Leus.*

(C) *Taxus.*

(D) *Xenus.*

(E) *Unus.*

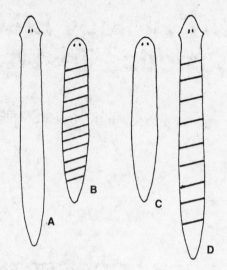

1. Organism A belongs to genus

   C

2. Organism B belongs to genus

   B

3. Organism C belongs to genus

   E

Questions 4–5 refer to the following diagram.

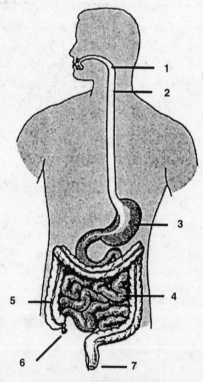

HUMAN DIGESTIVE TRACT

(A) 1   (D) 4

(B) 2   (E) 5

(C) 3

4. A region of this tract shared with the respiratory tract is found in _B_.

5. Absorption of digested nutrients takes place in _D_.

DIRECTIONS: The questions or incomplete statements below are followed by five possible answers or completions. Pick the answer choice that best answers or completes the question or incomplete statement and then fill in the correct oval on your answer sheet.

---

6. Which of the following is a pioneer organism?

(A) Man   (D) Lichen

(B) Tree   (E) Fungus

(C) Insect

7. Angiosperms are unique in that they

(A) are seed-producing plants.

(B) have vascular tissue.

(C) have a gametophyte that is retained in the sporophyte.

(D) have true roots and leaves.

(E) produce flowers and fruit.

8. The Hardy-Weinberg equilibrium would not prevail under which one of the following conditions?

(A) Absence of selection

(B) Large population

(C) Presence of random mating

(D) Presence of mutation

(E) Absence of immigration or emigration

9. Reproduction in which an unfertilized egg develops into an adult animal is termed

   (A) conjugation.
   (D) parthenogenesis.

   (B) hermaphroditism.
   (E) regeneration.

   (C) metamorphosis.

10. Select the monosaccharide from the following list of carbohydrates.

    (A) Glucose
    (D) Starch

    (B) Lactose
    (E) Sucrose

    (C) Maltose

11. The pH of a trout pond contaminated with acid rain is 5. Its hydrogen ion concentration (moles per liter) is

    (A) 0.01.
    (D) 0.0000001.

    (B) 0.0001.
    (E) 1.

    (C) 0.00001.

12. Two nutrient subunits are bonded together and release a water molecule in which process?

    (A) Decondensation buildup
    (D) Hydration

    (B) Dehydration synthesis
    (E) Hydrolysis

    (C) Dehydrolysis

Question 13 refers to the following.

Under certain conditions of stability, allelic frequencies and genotypic frequencies remain constant for generations in a sexually-reproducing population.

13. The founders of this principle for genetic equilibrium were

    (A) Boyle and Dalton.
    (D) Lamarck and Darwin.

    (B) Darwin and Wallace.
    (E) Watson and Crick.

    (C) Hardy and Weinberg.

14. Release of simple substances into the ecosystem for use by producers depends on activity of the

    (A) carnivores.

    (B) decomposers.

    (C) herbivores.

    (D) primary consumers.

    (E) secondary consumers.

15. The particle likely to move most rapidly by diffusion is

    (A) hemoglobin.

    (B) insulin.

    (C) oxygen.

    (D) sucrose.

    (E) starch.

16. Cloning is a reproductive process which involves

    (A) a sexual reproductive process.

    (B) the formation of genetic duplicates.

    (C) a combination of meiosis and mitosis.

    (D) the production of genetic variability.

    (E) the yielding of sex cells.

17. As energy is passed through a food web

    (A) decomposers cannot break down organisms' wastes.

    (B) herbivores dominate the last links of the web by numbers of organisms.

    (C) less useful energy remains available at each successive feeding level.

    (D) producers feed on remaining nutrients unused by other trophic levels.

    (E) species numbers increase from link to link in the web.

18. An animal's sex cells have a chromosome number of 28. Its diploid chromosome number is

    (A) 7.

    (B) 14.

    (C) 28.

    (D) 56.

    (E) 84.

19. In an alga-minnow-bass-bear food chain, organisms are listed in successive trophic levels. The alga is a producer followed by successive consumer levels. The bass can behave as a

(A) decomposer.

(D) secondary consumer.

(B) fourth level consumer.

(E) tertiary consumer.

(C) producer.

20. The complementary half of a DNA double helix strand with base sequence TCGATC is

(A) ACGATC.

(D) GGCUTA.

(B) AGCTAG.

(E) UGCUAG.

(C) GATCGA.

21. A protein currently synthesized from bacteria through the research of genetic engineering and gene splicing is

(A) ATP.

(D) hemoglobin.

(B) glucose.

(E) thyroid hormone.

(C) growth hormone.

Questions 22–23 refer to the following drawing.

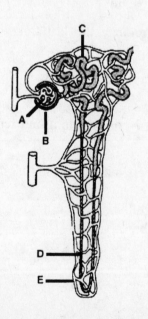

22. Circulatory components of the nephron occur at

    (A) A to B.   (D) B to D.

    (B) A to E.   (E) D to E.

    (C) B to C.

23. Components A and B conduct the renal process of

    (A) absorption.   (D) reabsorption.

    (B) filtration.   (E) secretion.

    (C) osmosis.

24. In human cancer, affected cells tend to

    (A) divide too rapidly.   (D) remain in a given area.

    (B) divide too slowly.   (E) use much more oxygen.

    (C) produce sex cells.

25. One thousand offspring are counted from a genetic cross. All have the recessive phenotype. The most likely genotypes of the parents are

    (A) AA, AA.   (D) Aa, aa.

    (B) AA, Aa.   (E) aa, aa.

    (C) Aa, Aa.

26. Sex-linked traits are

    (A) controlled by genes on the X chromosome.

    (B) inherited by sons from their fathers.

    (C) more common in females.

    (D) produced by gene pairs in males.

    (E) usually caused by dominant genes.

27. Which is the homozygous recessive condition in humans?

    (A) Blood type A

    (B) Brown hair

(C) Dark eyes

(D) Pituitary Dwarfism

(E) High cholesterol in the blood

28. Which one of the following is an angiosperm?

(A) Fern

(B) Mushroom

(C) Oak tree

(D) Pine tree

(E) Spruce

29. Mollusks

(A) all have a mantle.

(B) all have shells.

(C) are spiny-skinned animals.

(D) have some evolutionary links to animals.

(E) have a closed circulatory system.

30. A leg bone is the

(A) femur.

(B) humerus.

(C) radius.

(D) scapula.

(E) ulna.

31. Light passes through structures of the eye in the order:

(A) aqueous humor-cornea-lens-vitreous body-retina.

(B) aqueous humor-lens-cornea-vitreous body-retina.

(C) cornea-aqueous humor-lens-vitreous body-retina.

(D) lens-retina-cornea-aqueous humor-vitreous body.

(E) retina-aqueous humor-cornea-lens-vitreous body.

32. Exhaled air flows through the respiratory passages by the sequence:

(A) alveolus-bronchus-trachea-bronchiole-larynx.

(B) alveolus-bronchiole-bronchus-trachea-larynx.

(C) bronchiole-alveolus-trachea-larynx-bronchus.

(D) bronchiole-trachea-larynx-bronchus-alveolus.

(E) larynx-trachea-bronchus-bronchiole-alveolus.

33. Over 24 hours the kidneys eliminate 900 ml. of urine. Five hundred ml. of liquid are removed by solid wastes and 300 ml. by perspiration and exhalation. Food consumption adds 400 ml, and 800 ml. of liquids are consumed. For water balance, body metabolism contributes

(A) 100 ml.

(B) 300 ml.

(C) 500 ml.

(D) 700 ml.

(E) 900 ml.

34. Sperm cells are stored and mature in the

(A) Cowper's gland.

(B) epididymis.

(C) prostate gland.

(D) testis.

(E) vas deferens.

35. Ovulation in the menstrual cycle corresponds with a peak in the hormone

(A) estrogen.

(B) FSH.

(C) ICSH.

(D) LH.

(E) progesterone.

36. Each of the following is a key component of Darwin's principles of natural selection EXCEPT

(A) competition for limiting resources develops.

(B) less population members are produced than can survive.

(C) populations' reproduction potential is large.

(D) reproductive fitness is the key to a species' future.

(E) variation is a fact of population makeup.

37. Members of the phylum Arthropoda

(A) contain a backbone.

(B) have jointed appendages.

(C) include a mantle.

(D) lack an exoskeleton.

(E) lack appendages.

38. The gene for a given trait may survive and increase in time if it is

(A) adaptive.

(B) inferior.

(C) heterozygous.

(D) homozygous.

(E) multiple.

39. The most common of the four ABO blood types in the United States is

(A) A.

(B) AB.

(C) AO.

(D) B.

(E) O.

40. An autosomal recessive genotype is correctly written as

(A) A.

(B) AA.

(C) Aa.

(D) a.

(E) aa.

41. Groups of different population kinds (species) interact to form a

(A) chemical cycle.

(B) community.

(C) habitat.

(D) niche.

(E) organ system.

42. The soil particle with greatest diameter is

(A) calcium.

(B) clay.

(C) humus.

(D) sand.

(E) silt.

Questions **43–44** refer to the graphs below of the menstrual cycle of a guinea pig.

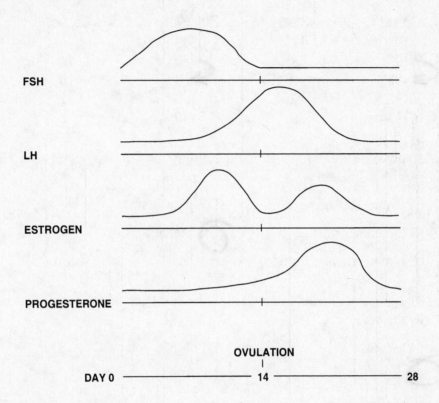

43. The hormone stimulating ovulation is

    (A) estrogen.   (D) LH.

    (B) FSH.   (E) progesterone.

    (C) ICSH.

44. Progesterone's possible effect is to

    (A) dominate the first half of the menstrual cycle.

    (B) keep this particular cycle running indefinitely.

    (C) prepare the uterus for possible embryo acceptance.

    (D) stimulate increased production of FSH.

    (E) work against the effect of estrogen.

Questions 45–47 refer to the following data computed from a field study.

Year	Acres	(No. of) Pheasants	(No. of) Foxes
1980	12	200	6
1981	18	180	14
1982	10	80	18
1983	16	100	12
1984	20	140	8

45. A possible symbiotic process relating population change in the species displayed is

(A) amensalism.

(B) commensalism.

(C) mutualism.

(D) parasitism.

(E) predation.

46. The greatest change in population density from either species occurs by the year

(A) 1980.

(B) 1981.

(C) 1982.

(D) 1983.

(E) 1984.

47. The population density of pheasants decreases from

(A) 1980–1984.

(B) 1981–1984.

(C) 1982–1983 only.

(D) 1980–1983 only.

(E) The density never decreases.

Questions 48–49 refer to the following crosses. You own a pet store and order a group of short hair, black rabbits and a group of long hair, white rabbits. From past experience you know that long hair and black are dominant traits. And since the rabbits are pure bred, short hair and white are each homozygous for the rabbits you just bought. You cross these two groups of rabbits (parent generation) and 64 offspring are born in the next generation (first generation).

48. How many first-generation rabbits were expected to be long hair and black?

(A) 64   (D) 4

(B) 36   (E) 0

(C) 12

49. Three hundred twenty second-generation rabbits are born by crossing first-generation rabbits. If the two genes were on two different tet-rads, how many second-generation rabbits were expected to be short hair and black?   320

(A) 320   (D) 20

(B) 180   (E) 0

(C) 60   9:3:3:1

Questions 50–54 refer to the following experiment that is designed to establish if yeast belongs to the fungus kingdom. A fungus will secrete enzymes that digest food particles outside the organism, then the fungus will absorb the nutrients.

Procedure:

- A packet of yeast is placed in a beaker of water, stirred, and then filtered. The filter paper will allow sucrose enzymes through but not the yeast cells. The solution collected is called the filtrate. The sucrase enzyme will break down sucrose into glucose and fructose.

- Two test tubes are filled ¼ full of 5% sucrose (table sugar) solution.

- In one tube, put 6 ml of the yeast filtrate. In the other tube put 6 ml of distilled water.

- Let the tubes sit for 30 minutes for the breakdown of sucrose into glucose and fructose.

- Add 1 ml of Benedict's solution to both tubes. The Benedict's solution will turn the solution blue.

- Place the tubes into a hot water bath. If the blue solution turns orange or red, this indicates the presence of glucose.

50. The independent variable of the yeast experiment is the

   (A) Benedict's solution.

   (B) color change from blue to orange or red.

   (C) filtrate solution.

   (D) yeast cells.

   (E) 5% sucrose solution.

51. The dependent variable of the yeast experiment is the

   (A) Benedict's solution.

   (B) color change from blue to orange or red.

   (C) filtrate solution.

   (D) yeast cells.

   (E) 5% sucrose solution.

52. If yeast is a fungus,

   (A) both tubes will stay blue.

   (B) both tubes will turn orange or red.

   (C) the tube with distilled water will turn orange or red.

   (D) the tube with the filtrate solution will turn orange or red.

   (E) the tube with the filtrate solution will stay blue.

53. The data collected in the yeast experiment is

   I.   quantitative.

   II.   qualitative.

   III. categorical.

   (A) I only.   (D) I and III.

   (B) II only.   (E) II and III.

   (C) III only.

54. The experimental control in the yeast experiment is having

   I.   equal quantities of yeast solution.

II.   equal quantities of 5% sucrose solution.

III. one tube with yeast filtrate and one tube with an equal amount of distilled water.

(A) I only.   (D) I and II.

(B) II only.   (E) I, II, and III.

(C) III only.

Questions 55–57 refer to the following genetic mutations in vertebrates.

I.   Mammary glands

II. Teeth of various shapes

III. Viviparous

IV. Hair

V.   Endothermy

55. Which evolutionary change(s) allowed vertebrates to exploit a wide variety of food sources?

(A) I only.   (D) II and III.

(B) II only.   (E) IV and V.

(C) III only.

56. Which evolutionary change(s) allowed vertebrates to live in varied climates?

(A) II only.   (D) III and IV.

(B) III only.   (E) IV and V.

(C) IV only.

57. Which evolutionary change(s) allowed vertebrates to carry and nourish unborn young inside their bodies so they could move without leaving the unborn unprotected?

(A) I only.   (D) I and III.

(B) III only.   (E) III and V.

(C) V only.

Questions 58–60 refer to the following.

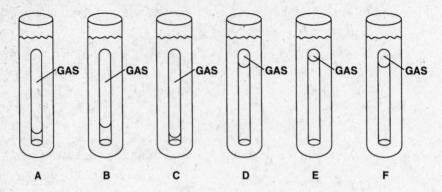

Each of the above tubes was filled with a solution that contained an equivalent number of yeast cells. A small tube was put in each tube to collect any gas produced by the yeast cells. In tubes A, B, and C, 1 ml of grape juice was added. In tubes D, E, and F, 1 ml of sucrose solution was added. The amount of gas collected in one day is shown for each tube.

58. In this particular experiment, the independent variable is the

    (A) growth of yeast.

    (B) source of energy for yeast (grape juice, sucrose).

    (C) amount of gas produced.

    (D) equal amount of yeast put into each tube.

    (E) number of tubes in the experiment.

59. The dependent variable of this experiment is the

    (A) growth of yeast.

    (B) source of energy for yeast (grape juice, sucrose).

    (C) amount of gas produced.

    (D) equal amount of yeast put into each tube.

    (E) number of tubes in the experiment.

60. It can be concluded from this experiment that

    (A) grape juice was a more effective medium for producing yeast cells.

(B) sucrose was a more effective medium for producing carbon dioxide.

(C) grape juice was a more effective medium for producing carbon dioxide.

(D) sucrose was a more effective medium for producing yeast cells.

(E) grape juice was a more effective medium for producing oxygen.

If you are taking the Biology–M Test, continue with questions 81–100. Be sure to start this section of the test by filling in oval 81 on your answer sheet.

BIOLOGY-M SECTION

DIRECTIONS: The questions or incomplete statements below are followed by five possible answers or completions. Pick the answer choice that best answers or completes the question or incomplete statement and then fill in the correct oval on your answer sheet.

---

81. Mitosis is a form of cell division in which

    (A) the daughter cells contain half the number of chromosomes as the parent cell.

    (B) a cell experiences an invagination of the cell membrane.

    (C) the daughter cells have the same number of chromosomes as the parent cell.

    (D) the daughter cells undergo three successive cell divisions.

    (E) the daughter cells undergo five successive cell divisions.

82. In prophase

    (A) the chromosomes arrange themselves around the equator of the spindle fiber.

    (B) the sister chromatids separate and move to opposite poles.

    (C) the chromatids first appear and are short and thick.

    (D) the nuclear membrane reappears.

    (E) None of the above.

83. Anaphase is the process by which

    (A) the nucleoli reappear.

    (B) the nuclear membrane reforms.

    (C) the sister chromatids separate.

    (D) the paired chromosomes attach to the spindle.

    (E) the spindle apparatus forms.

Questions 84–85 refer to the effects of pH on enzyme activity as illustrated in the following graph.

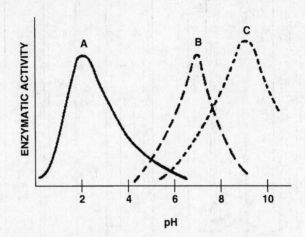

84. At which one of the following pHs are enzymes A, B, and C functioning simultaneously?

    (A) 4

    (B) 4.5

    (C) 5.8

    (D) 7

    (E) 7.5

85. Which one of the following is true at pH 8?

    (A) Activity of enzyme A is decreasing.

    (B) Activity of enzyme B is increasing.

    (C) Activity of enzyme A is increasing.

    (D) Activity of enzyme C is increasing.

    (E) Activities of enzymes B and C are increasing.

Questions 86–88

The following four graphs illustrate the influence of various environmental factors on the rate of photosynthesis.

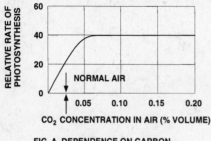

FIG. A. DEPENDENCE ON CARBON
DIOXIDE CONCENTRATION

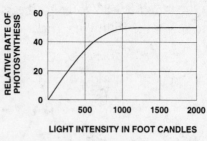

FIG. B. DEPENDENCE ON LIGHT INTENSITY

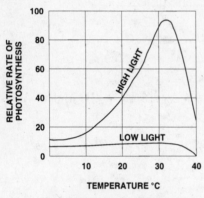

FIG. C. INFLUENCE OF TEMPERATURE

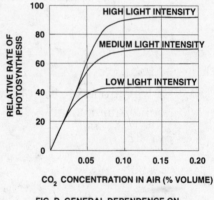

FIG. D. GENERAL DEPENDENCE ON
LIMITING FACTORS

86. At 30°C, the rate of photosynthesis at high light intensity compared to the rate at low light intensity is

(A) equal to the rate at low light intensity.

(B) less than the rate at low light intensity.

(C) two times greater than the rate at low light intensity.

(D) four times greater than the rate at low light intensity.

(E) nine times greater than the rate at low light intensity.

87. Which one of the following statements is not supported by data in figures A through D?

(A) Photosynthetic rate increases as the concentration of chlorophyll increases.

(B) As the concentration of CO_2 increases, photosynthetic rate increases up to a limit.

(C) Photosynthetic activity decreases at temperatures above 35°C.

(D) When enough CO_2 is available, light is a limiting factor in photosynthesis.

(E) As the light intensity increases, photosynthetic activity increases up to a limit.

88. The rate of photosynthesis increases in a linear fashion between light intensities of

(A) 0 and 500.

(B) 500 and 1,000.

(C) 1,000 and 1,500.

(D) 1,500 and 2,000.

(E) 2,000 and 2,500.

89. A cell with 42 chromosomes divides mitotically. After conclusion of the process, each daughter cell produced has a chromosome number equaling

(A) 21.

(B) 42.

(C) 44.

(D) 84.

(E) 168.

90. Mitosis produces cells that are

(A) diploid.

(B) haploid.

(C) homologous.

(D) tetraploid.

(E) zygotes.

91. Turgor is exhibited by a cell from a(n)

(A) alga.

(B) *Amoeba.*

(C) human.

(D) *Paramecium.*

(E) virus.

Questions 92–93

Samples of blood were taken from three different individuals and chemically analyzed for different forms of hemoglobin. Individuals A and C are phenotypically normal, and individual B suffers from sickle cell anemia. The following chart shows the types of hemoglobin for the three different individuals.

Forms of Hemoglobin

Individual	Type 1	Type 2
A	+	−
B	−	+
C	+	+

(+ present, − absent)

92. Which one of the following statements about this experiment is correct?

(A) A is heterozygous.

(B) B is heterozygous.

(C) C is heterozygous.

(D) A person with sickle cell anemia carries a normal gene for hemoglobin.

(E) The gene for sickle cell anemia behaves as a dominant gene when we look at the expression of disease.

93. The allele for sickle cell anemia is different from the normal hemoglobin allele, because

(A) it contains ribose.

(B) it is missing.

(C) it has a base substitution.

(D) it is made of RNA instead of DNA.

(E) it contains uracil.

Questions 94–95 refer to the following drawing.

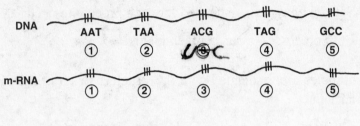

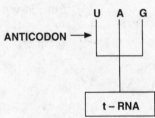

94. The third codon of the mRNA molecule is

    (A) ACG.   (D) TGC.

    (B) AGC.   (E) UGC.

    (C) TAG.

95. The tRNA with its anticodon will couple with mRNA base triplet number

    (A) 1.   (D) 4.

    (B) 2.   (E) 5.

    (C) 3.

96. A cell's enzyme system is subjected to a temperature of 70°C for 30 minutes. Its enzymes will experience

    (A) active site loss.   (D) denaturation.

    (B) allosterism.   (E) modulation.

    (C) competitive inhibition.

97. In comparing photosynthesis and cellular respiration, which one of the following statements would not be true?

    (A) ATP is formed during both processes.

    (B) CO_2 is produced during both processes.

(C) O_2 is released during photosynthesis only.

(D) Several enzymes are needed for each process to occur.

(E) Both processes occur in green plants.

98. Microtubules are associated with the structure of all of the following EXCEPT the

(A) centriole.

(D) mitochondrion.

(B) cilium.

(E) spindle fiber.

(C) eukaryotic flagellum.

99. The correct sequence of the following events in skeletal muscle contractions at the sarcomere is:

1. Myosin filaments slide actin filaments.

2. Acetylcholine is released from axon terminals.

3. Calcium ions are released from sacs of the sarcoplasmic reticulum.

4. Depolarization of the muscle cell membrane occurs.

5. Acetylcholine diffuses across the synaptic cleft.

(A) 3-2-5-4-1

(D) 2-4-5-3-1

(B) 2-3-5-4-1

(E) 1-2-4-3-5

(C) 2-5-4-3-1

100. If all 300 bases of an mRNA molecule are translated, it will code for _____ amino acids.

(A) 3

(D) 600

(B) 100

(E) 900

(C) 300

STOP

If you finish before time is called, you may check your work on the entire
Biology-M test only. Do not turn to any other test in this book.

SAT Biology E/M
Practice Test 4

ANSWER KEY

BIOLOGY CORE SECTION

1.	(C)	16.	(B)	31.	(C)	46.	(B)
2.	(B)	17.	(C)	32.	(B)	47.	(D)
3.	(E)	18.	(D)	33.	(C)	48.	(A)
4.	(A)	19.	(D)	34.	(B)	49.	(C)
5.	(D)	20.	(B)	35.	(D)	50.	(C)
6.	(D)	21.	(C)	36.	(B)	51.	(B)
7.	(E)	22.	(B)	37.	(B)	52.	(D)
8.	(D)	23.	(B)	38.	(A)	53.	(E)
9.	(D)	24.	(A)	39.	(E)	54.	(D)
10.	(A)	25.	(E)	40.	(E)	55.	(B)
11.	(C)	26.	(A)	41.	(B)	56.	(E)
12.	(B)	27.	(D)	42.	(D)	57.	(B)
13.	(C)	28.	(C)	43.	(D)	58.	(B)
14.	(B)	29.	(A)	44.	(C)	59.	(C)
15.	(C)	30.	(A)	45.	(E)	60.	(C)

BIOLOGY-M SECTION

81.	(C)	86.	(E)	91.	(A)	96.	(D)
82.	(C)	87.	(A)	92.	(C)	97.	(B)
83.	(C)	88.	(A)	93.	(C)	98.	(D)
84.	(C)	89.	(B)	94.	(E)	99.	(C)
85.	(D)	90.	(A)	95.	(D)	100.	(B)

DETAILED EXPLANATIONS
OF ANSWERS
PRACTICE TEST 4

BIOLOGY CORE SECTION

1. **(C)**
    This snake is long and slender, lacking stripes.

2. **(B)**
    This snake is short and thick, with stripes.

3. **(E)**
    This snake is short and thick, lacking stripes.

4. **(A)**   5. **(D)**
    This question requires you to identify the correct answer, so you must be familiar with the human digestive system. The pharynx (throat) of the upper digestive tract also accepts air in the upper respiratory tract at 1. The ten-inch esophagus (2), moves swallowed food into the stomach at 3. In the 20-foot small intestine at 4, chemical digestion is completed and the subunits of larger ingested molecules can now enter the blood by absorption for body needs. The next digestive compartment is the large intestine (5) where mostly water is reclaimed into the blood to prevent body dehydration (reabsorption). The appendix (6) is a vestigial organ. The anus (7) is the site of elimination of solid waste at the end of the digestive tract.

6. **(D)**
    A pioneer organism is the first organism to populate a region. It must be autotrophic and able to withstand the harshest conditions. Lichens require little water and can survive a variety of temperatures. Lichens can be found on bare rock and in the Antarctic.

7. **(E)**
    This question requires some knowledge of the characteristics of angiosperms as compared with those of other plants. Tracheophytes have vascular tissue and have true roots and leaves. The seed-producing plants

(gymnosperms and angiosperms) have a gametophyte that is dependent upon the sporophyte. Only angiosperms produce flowers and fruit.

8. **(D)**
The Hardy-Weinberg equilibrium states that in a large population in which there is random mating, the frequency of alleles will remain constant in the absence of mutation, migration, and selection.

9. **(D)**
The development of an egg without fertilization is termed parthenogenesis.

10. **(A)**
Glucose is a simple sugar, or monosaccharide. Lactose, sucrose, and maltose are disaccharides. Two monosaccharides are bonded in their molecular structure. Starch is a polysaccharide.

11. **(C)**
ph= $^-$log [H+] in which [H+] is the concentration of protons (in moles per liter) in the solution. $0.00001 = 10^{-5}$. -5 is the log $-(-5) = 5$.

12. **(B)**
This choice represents a formation of molecule by the bonding of two smaller molecules (synthesis) accompanied by water liberation (dehydration). The H^+ and OH^- that are removed from the molecules leave a vacant bond on each. The two molecules are then combined in order to form a dimer.

13. **(C)**
This is a historical fact. They provided a set of conditions that would maintain constant gene frequencies in a population. If natural selection does not affect a large, isolated population, and if no mutations occur within the population, then no change in gene frequencies will occur; the population will not evolve.

14. **(B)**
Decomposers are the bacteria, fungi, and other microorganisms that digest organisms' carcasses and waste. Their actions return elements from an ecosystem's biotic component back to the abiotic sector of the environment.

15. **(C)**
Light, gaseous particles move most rapidly. Larger, more massive macromolecules are far less likely to do so. Oxygen is the lightest

molecule listed. All other choices represent molecules of much greater molecular weights.

16. **(B)**
This is a simple description of cloning. If body cells are undifferentiated (such as the zygote), they can produce new organisms by cell division, asexually. Cloning has been done commonly with plant structures, and cells from the bellies of salamanders, for example.

17. **(C)**
Producers and the herbivores that feed on them start a food web. Each step of food chain energy conversion leads to dissipation of some energy into useless heat. This limits numbers that can be supported at each successive link, as less energy to support them becomes available. Decomposers act on organisms and their wastes throughout.

18. **(D)**
Sex cells are haploid (half number). The diploid number in somatic cells is double the haploid number in a species. In somatic cells, two copies of each chromosome type are present.

19. **(D)**
The bass is a second-level feeder. It is not at a third step nor fourth step of feeding. It is also not a producer starting the chain, as is the alga. The minnow is an herbivore and a primary consumer. The bear is a third-order consumer.

20. **(B)**
Memorization of the base-pairing rules of A-T and G-C is necessary to answer this. This six-base DNA readout has only one possible complement. Thus, the base T calls A in the other half. C attracts G, etc.

21. **(C)**
Growth hormone, insulin, and interferon are all current producers now synthesized bacterially by gene transplants.

22. **(B)**
The nephron is the microscopic kidney unit. It has two capillary networks: the glomerulus (A) inside the Bowman's capsule and the peritubular capillaries (E) surrounding the nephron's tubular portion.

23. **(B)**

Filtration is the bulk flow, unselective passage of blood plasma substances from the glomerulus into the Bowman's capsule. This is the first step of renal physiology and introduces blood substances into the urinary tract at the microscopic level. Reabsorption involves reclaiming blood substances from the filtrate back into the blood. Secretion is the final renal step eliminating substances from blood into the nephron tract. The other choices are not renal processes.

24. **(A)**

Cancer is mitosis of an organism's body cells at abnormally high rates. The body cells, such as white blood cells in leukemia, divide more rapidly than needed to merely replace worn-out cells. These rapidly dividing cells tend to break away and wander, seeding other body regions. Their continual relocation and rapid division spreads the cancer.

25. **(E)**

Homozygous recessive parents can donate only recessive alleles in sex cells and thus reproduce homozygous recessive offspring. All other choices produce 50%, 75%, or 100% dominant-appearing offspring. The large number of counted offspring statistically affirms the inheritance of only recessive genes.

26. **(A)**

Sex-linked traits, such as hemophilia and color-blindness, are some times called X linked because they are controlled by recessive genes on X chromosomes. Sons inherit this gene from their mother who is usually a carrier for the trait, i.e., heterozygous. The expression of such traits are more common in males. They have only a single gene since they possess only one X chromosome. The Y chromosome does not have a second gene. Therefore, a recessive allele on the X chromosome is not masked by a second gene.

27. **(D)**

aa × aa can yield only aa offspring (dwarfs).

28. **(C)**

Ferns are lower vascular plants. They bear fronds which produce spores. Mushrooms belong to the Kingdom Fungi. The pine tree and spruce are both gymnosperms. They bear cones as reproductive structures. The oak tree is an angiosperm. It bears flowers and "hidden" seeds.

29. **(A)**

The mantle is a membrane for respiration and cell secretion. Advanced members, octopus and squid, have lost their shells but retain the mantle. They have some evolution parallels to annelids but are echinoderms—spiny-skinned animals, such as starfish.

30. **(A)**

The humerus (upper arm) and the radius (lateral forearm) and ulna (medial forearm) are upper appendage bones. The scapula, or shoulder blade, articulates the humerus to the axial skeleton.

31. **(C)**

The outward bulging, clear cornea intercepts light rays which then pass through the water-like aqueous humor in the cavity behind it. The football-shaped lens next refracts light rays, concentrating them on the retina's focal point as they pass through the jellylike vitreous body.

32. **(B)**

Exhaled air leaves microscopic alveoli and enters the tubelike bronchioles and larger bronchi as air leaves the lungs. Remaining respiratory structures liberate air in the order given by the choice. Choice (E) gives the correct sequence for air *inhalation*.

33. **(C)**

Total outputs (urine, solid wastes, perspiration, exhalation) equal 1,700 ml. The two given inputs total 1,200 ml. leaving 500 ml. produced by metabolism for an input-output balance.

34. **(B)**

The epididymis resides somewhat on top of and in back of the testis. It stores maturing sperm cells after their synthesis in the testis.

35. **(D)**

LH, the luteinizing hormone from the pituitary gland, peaks in concentration during ovulation. This occurs 14 days before the beginning of the next female reproductive cycle. It also converts the follicle, having released the migrating ovum, into a corpus luteum. FSH is another pituitary hormone. Its upswing initiates the cycle. Estrogen and progesterone are ovarian hormones maintaining the uterus. ICSH is a male hormone.

36. **(B)**

Darwin stated that populations reproduce many more members than can possibly be supported by environmental resources. Thus, competition occurs for limited resources. Those best equipped to survive have a higher probability to leave offspring and contribute to the gene pool of the next generation.

37. (B)
These invertebrates, with exoskeleton and jointed appendages, include insects as their largest class. A mantle, found in mollusks, is lacking.

38. (A)
Adaptive means promoting survival. Organisms adaptively equipped with their gene have a higher probability to leave offspring and influence the future gene pool.

39. (E)
The approximate frequency is O (45%), A (40%), B (10%), and AB (4-5%).

40. (E)
A recessive allele is always indicated by a lowercase letter (a, for example). A dominant allele is always indicated by a capital letter (A, for example). A genotype indicates the genetic composition. The autosomal traits are in pairs in the normal cell. (One is found on each of the two chromosomes of a given chromosome pair in the diploid individual.) The genotype of the recessive individual is therefore aa. AA is the genotype for the homozygous dominant individual. Recessives always contain two recessive alleles for a given trait.

41. (B)
This is a strict definition of an ecosystem's community. A habitat is the natural environment of an organism. A niche is the sum of all resources used by an organism in the environment.

42. (D)
Silt is smaller and clay is the smallest. Calcium is an element and humus is a collective term for decaying organic matter in soil.

43. (D)
Ovulation is marked on the menstrual cycle graph and corresponds to a peaking of LH (luteinizing hormone) levels. Its peak keys the rupture of an ovarian sex cell and its release into the oviduct. The remaining ovarian

follicle, a jacket of cells that had encased the sex cell, is converted into the corpus luteum by the LH signal. FSH (follicle stimulating hormone) initiates the cycle by its increase. Estrogen and progesterone are ovarian hormones maintaining the uterus. ICSH is a male hormone.

44. (C)

Progesterone's levels dominate in the phase of the cycle beyond ovulation. By then the female sex cell has entered the oviduct for possible fertilization. If this occurs, it arrives in the uterus as an early embryo. Progesterone, the "hormone of pregnancy," prepares the uterine lining for this possible acceptance.

45. (E)   46. (B)   47. (D)

The fox is a possible predator of pheasants in an ecosystem food chain. Notice how a decrease in pheasant prey correlates with annual gains in fox success by numbers. The density of a population is determined by dividing the number of individuals in the population by the number of acres. The largest change in the population density of either organism occurs in the year 1981. The pheasant population density decreases from 16 (in 1980) to 10 (in 1981). The pheasant population density decreases from 16 to 10 to 8 to 6 from 1980 to 1983, respectively. The population density of pheasants increases slightly in 1984.

If the pheasants were eating something toxic to the fox but not to themselves, one might expect the fox population density to increase slightly in response to the large number of pheasants. However, since the pheasants are poisonous, the fox population would suddenly decrease. The decrease would be quite rapid. Under such conditions, the number of pheasant would increase rapidly due to the decreased number of predators.

48. (A)   49. (C)

Alleles: H = long hair
           h = short hair
           C = black hair
           c = white hair

Parent Cross: hhCC × HHcc

For question 48, all of the first-generation (64) rabbits would be long hair, black rabbits. They would be heterozygous for both traits (HhCc).

First-Generation Cross (dihybrid cross): HhCc × HhCc

Question 49 assumes that the two genes are on two different tetrads (chromosome pairs). Therefore, the Law of Independent Assortment will apply for the distribution of the gametes. The possible allele combinations for the first generation are shown in the following Punnett square.

	HC	Hc	hC	hc
HC	HHCC	HHCc	HhCC	HhCc
Hc	HHCc	HHcc	HhCc	Hhcc
hC	HhCC	HhCc	hhCC	hhCc
hc	HhCc	Hhcc	hhCc	hhcc

Results:

9/16 H_C_	$9/16 \times 320 = 180$ long hair, black hair
3/16 H_cc	$3/16 \times 320 = 60$ long hair, white hair
3/16 hhC_	$3/16 \times 320 = 60$ short hair, black hair
1/16 hhcc	$1/16 \times 320 = 20$ short hair, white hair

50. (C)   51. (B)   52. (D)   53. (E)   54. (D)

The independent variable of the yeast experiment is the filtrate solution. If yeast is a fungus, then sucrose enzymes would be secreted and go through the filter paper into the filtrate solution. The independent variable is the one difference between the two tubes. One tube contained the filtrate solution, the other tube had distilled water in place of the filtrate solution.

The dependent variable of the yeast experiment is the color change from blue to orange or red. The dependent variable is the data collected during the experiment. If the filtrate solution contained the sucrase enzyme, then sucrose sugar would be broken down into glucose and fructose. When heated, the Benedict's solution would react with glucose and cause a color change from blue to orange or red. If yeast is a fungus, the tube with the filtrate will turn color.

The data collected is the color of the solution which is qualitative data. Qualitative data is information that can be fitted into a category like color (i.e., categorical data). Quantitative data has a number value.

Experimental control is having the exact same conditions for both treatments except the independent variable. Both tubes had equal quantities of yeast and 5% sucrose solutions.

55. **(B)**

Mammals evolved a variety of teeth shapes to carry out the following functions: incisors in the front to bite and cut; long, sharp canines to grip, puncture, and tear; bicuspids to shear and shred; and molars to grind and crush. With such a variety of teeth, mammals can consume at all levels of the food chain.

56. **(E)**

It is thought that the birds first invented endothermy. Birds, along with mammals, can generate and regulate body heat internally. This allows them to be active during cold seasons and in cold climates. Hair keeps the body warm and thus, allowed vertebrates to go into colder climates in which they otherwise would not have been able to survive.

57. **(B)**

Being viviparous allowed females to carry their unborn in the uterus during development. Females did not have to leave their unborn unprotected like amphibians, reptiles, and birds.

58. **(B)**

When designing an experiment, all treatments (groups) should be the same except for the independent variable. In this experiment, the independent variable was the energy source. Tubes A, B, and C received grape juice and tubes D, E, and F received sucrose as the energy source.

59. **(C)**

The dependent variable is the data collected or the results from manipulating the independent variable. In this experiment, the data is the amount of gas that is collected in the smaller tubes.

60. **(C)**

Grape juice is a complete medium for yeast. It contains fructose, vitamins, and minerals for energy and amino acids for growth. Tubes D, E, and F produced less carbon dioxide because sucrose is not a complete medium for yeast. The gas produced was carbon dioxide from yeast respiration. Oxygen would not be the gas since yeast cells do not have chloroplasts for photosynthesis. The drawings only show the amount of gas produced. The number of cells for each treatment can only be determined by counting them under the microscope or growing yeast colonies on an agar medium.

BIOLOGY-M SECTION

81. **(C)**
    Mitosis is a form of cell division in which the daughter cells contain the same number of chromosomes as the parent cells, because the cell undergoes only one successive division.

82. **(C)**
    Prophase is the stage of mitosis during which the chromatids first appear and are short and thick.

83. **(C)**
    During anaphase the sister chromatids are pulled apart and move to opposite poles.

84. **(C)**
    Every enzyme has a minimum, optimum, and maximum pH. The pH at which the rate of the reaction catalyzed by an enzyme is greatest is called the optimum pH. At pHs below the minimum and above the maximum, enzyme activity is virtually zero. Enzymes B and C are inactive at pH 4. Enzyme C is inactive at pH 4.5. At pHs 7 and 7.5, enzyme A is inactive. Note the overlap of enzyme activity, however, at a pH of 5.8.

85. **(D)**
    At pH 8, the activity of enzyme C is increasing, as indicated by the upward slope of the curve.

86. **(E)**
    At 30°C, Figure C shows that the relative rate of photosynthesis at low light intensity is approximately 10, and the rate at high light intensity is approximately 90 or nine times greater. Compare the values on the vertical axis.

87. **(A)**
    None of the figures takes into account the chlorophyll concentration as a factor in photosynthetic rate. Choice (B) is supported by the data shown in Figure A. The results in Figure C support the statement in choice (C). Choice (D) summarizes the results in Figure D. The results in Figure B support the statement in choice (E).

88. **(A)**

Between light intensities (in foot candles) of 0 and 500, the rate of photosynthesis increases in a linear (straight line) fashion. Note the slope of the line on this graph.

89. **(B)**

Barring a rare mutation, mitosis preserves the constancy of a cell's (and its organism's) genetic structure. This includes the somatic cell chromosome number for that species.

90. **(A)**

Mitosis produces daughter cells whose chromosome numbers and gene content are the same as those of the parent cell. A cell is referred to as being diploid if it contains two of each type of chromosome. For example, the 46 human chromosomes are maintained as 23 homologous pairs.

91. **(A)**

Plant or plant-like cells can take up water osmotically, yet due to their rigid outer cell walls, not burst. The tremendous incompressible fluid buildup causes pressure buildup, or turgor. Choices (B) through (E) are not plants or plant-like.

Questions 92–93

For this set of questions you must be familiar with the inheritance of the gene for sickle cell anemia.

92. **(C)**

This question asks you to interpret the data given in the table concerning the chemical makeup of hemoglobin. Remembering that a particular gene codes for one protein (polypeptide), if only one form exists, the homologous genes must be the same. Likewise, if two forms of hemoglobin are present, then two forms of the gene for hemoglobin must also be present. Therefore, individuals A and B are homozygous for the hemoglobin gene, while individual C is heterozygous. Thus, individual B does not carry any normal hemoglobin gene.

To determine dominance we must look at the heterozygote. However, in this case the question of dominance depends upon whether we are looking at the presence of disease or the chemistry of the individual. The heterozygote is phenotypically normal, and, therefore, the gene for sickle cell anemia would be classified as a recessive gene. However, the heterozygote contains both types of hemoglobin, and, therefore, shows codominance for the hemoglobin gene. Many other genes show typical dominant-recessive behavior when looking at the physical appearance of the offspring, but codominance or intermediate inheritance when we look at the chemistry of the gene.

93. (C)
To answer this question you must know how alleles (forms of the same gene) generally differ. First of all, a gene is made of DNA rather than RNA, and, therefore, would not contain uracil or ribose. A different form of a gene might mean that the gene is missing or that there is a base substitution. Since a different form of hemoglobin is found when the defective gene is present, the gene must be present but in altered form. This change of one base is called a point mutation.

94. (E)
A codon is a base triplet. Its identity is determined by the corresponding DNA codon. The third DNA codon, ACG, transcribes UGC in a manner compliant with the following complementary base-pairing rules:

DNA	RNA
A	U
C	G
G	C
T	A

95. (D)
The tRNA has an anticodon of UAG, which is complementary to the mRNA codon AUC. This must be mRNA codon #4, as the fourth DNA codon, TAG, determines the mRNA codon by transcription. RNA base-pairing rules are:

mRNA	tRNA
A	U
C	G
C	C
U	A

96. (D)
Denaturation is the physical breakdown of a protein under extremes of temperature or pH. Allosterism and modulation are normal changes in the enzyme's shape to accommodate its fitting to a substrate. The active site is the part of an enzyme binding to a substrate. Competitive inhibition refers to inhibition whereby a molecule resembling the substrate enters

and binds with the active site. This decreases the availability of the active site for the normal substrate and it decreases the reaction rate.

97. **(B)**

CO$_2$ is incorporated into carbohydrates during the Calvin cycle of photosynthesis. CO$_2$ is formed during cellular respiration.

98. **(D)**

Both a cilium and a eukaryotic flagellum contain nine double microtubules arranged in a circle near the periphery and two separate microtubules in the center of the circle; a "9 + 2" arrangement. A centriole contains nine triplets of microtubules arranged in a circle near the periphery. Each spindle fiber is one microtubule. The mitochondrion is the powerplant of the cell.

99. **(C)**

The correct sequence of steps is:
2. Acetylcholine is released from axon terminals.
5. Acetylcholine diffuses across the synaptic cleft.
4. Depolarization of the muscle cell membrane occurs.
3. Calcium ions are released from sacs of the sarcoplasmic reticulum.
1. Myosin filaments slide actin filaments.

100. **(B)**

Three mRNA bases (codon) constitute the code for one amino acid attached to its tRNA. Thus, 300 to 100 is the proper ratio.

SAT Biology E/M
Practice Test 5

(Answer sheets appear in the back of this book.)

TIME: 1 Hour
80 Questions

BIOLOGY CORE SECTION

DIRECTIONS: The lettered or numbered choices below refer to the questions or statements that immediately follow them. Pick the best answer choice and fill in the correct oval on your answer sheet. An answer choice may be used more than once or not at all.

Questions 1–2 refer to the following.

(A) Commensal

(D) Saprophyte

(B) Parasite

(E) Scavenger

(C) Predator

1. A fox catches and eats a mouse. C

2. A squirrel lives in a nest it built in a tulip poplar tree. A

Questions 3–5 refer to the following.

(A) Apical meristem

(D) Vascular cambium

(B) Pericycle

(E) Xylem

(C) Phloem

3. Tissue that gives rise to secondary (lateral) roots D

4. The main tissue involved in transporting water from roots to leaves E

5. Growth in height of the stem results from the addition of cells in this area *A*

Questions 6–8 refer to the following.

(A) Biome (D) Ecosystem

(B) Biosphere (E) Population

(C) Community

6. A group of similar individuals living in one particular area at a given time *E*

7. The portion of the earth inhabited by living organisms *B*

8. All of the different kinds of organisms that live and interact in one place at a given time *C*

Questions 9–11 refer to the following.

(A) Small flowers

(B) Small colorful fruits

(C) Winged seeds

(D) Hollow fruits

(E) Woody ovary wall

9. An adaptation that favors wind pollination *C*

10. An adaptation that favors water dispersal *D*

11. An adaptation that favors animal dispersal *B*

Questions 12–16 refer to the five kingdoms of organisms. Match each letter to its correct description.

(A) *Monera* (D) *Fungi*

(B) *Protista* (E) *Animalia*

(C) *Plantae*

12. Upon observation, it has been determined that the unknown organism is multicellular and the cells contain chloroplasts. The organism belongs to the Kingdom _____C_____.

13. Upon observation, it has been determined that the unknown organism is unicellular and has very small ribosomes. The organism belongs to the Kingdom _____.

14. Upon observation, it has been determined that the unknown organism is unicellular and reproduces by mitosis. The organism belongs to the Kingdom _____.

15. Upon observation, it has been determined that the unknown organism is unicellular and has cell walls with chitin. The organism belongs to the Kingdom _____.

16. Upon observation, it has been determined that the unknown organism is a string of unicellular organisms that reproduce by fission. The organism belongs to the Kingdom _____.

> **DIRECTIONS:** The questions or incomplete statements below are followed by five possible answers or completions. Pick the answer choice that best answers or completes the question or incomplete statement and then fill in the correct oval on your answer sheet.

17. Which one of the following taxonomic groups includes all of the others?

    (A) Family   (D) Species

    (B) Genus   (E) Order

    (C) Class

18. The group that includes members that have RNA as their genetic material is the

    (A) bacteria.   (D) viruses.

    (B) fungi.   (E) insects.

    (C) protozoa.

419

19. Two unrelated organisms that become similar in appearance and ways of life as they adapt to similar environmental situations exhibit

    (A) adaptive radiation.   (D) homology.

    (B) convergent evolution.   (E) parallel evolution.

    (C) divergent evolution.

20. In flowering plants, the process that enables the sperm to approach the egg is

    (A) fertilization.

    (B) growth of the pollen tube.

    (C) motility of the sperm.

    (D) pollination.

    (E) (B) and (D).

21. In the karyotype of an organism, an XXX individual

    (A) is a male.

    (B) has Down's syndrome.

    (C) has three Barr bodies.

    (D) has an X-linked trait.

    (E) results following nondisjunction.

22. A cell formed by meiosis contains 12 chromosomes. The cell that divided to form it contained

    (A) 6 chromosomes.   (D) 36 chromosomes.

    (B) 12 chromosomes.   (E) 48 chromosomes.

    (C) 24 chromosomes.

23. Vitamins are required by animals and many microorganisms for use as

    (A) energy sources.

    (B) structural materials.

    (C) parts of enzyme systems.

(D) mineral sources.

(E) parts of hormones.

24. According to the heterotroph hypothesis, which gas was not present in the early atmosphere as the organic molecules that gave rise to the earliest life forms on earth were forming?

(A) Ammonia (NH_3)   (D) Oxygen (O_2)

(B) Hydrogen (H_2)   (E) Water vapor (H_2O)

(C) Methane (CH_4)

25. The form of learning exhibited by fish that swim to the surface in response to the turning-on of a light when they originally responded to the presence of food provided at the same time a light was lit is known as

(A) conditioning.   (D) insight.

(B) habituation.   (E) instinct.

(C) imprinting.

26. An animal hormone that causes the heart to beat more rapidly is

(A) epinephrine.   (D) oxytocin.

(B) estrogen.   (E) parathyroid hormone.

(C) insulin.

27. A tissue/Tissues that lack(s) blood vessels and must receive nutrients by diffusion from a neighboring tissue is/are

I.   cartilage

II. epithelium

III. muscular tissue

(A) I only.   (D) I and II.

(B) II only.   (E) I and III.

(C) III only.

28. Which of the following are characteristic of normal mature human red blood cells?

I.   They have nuclei.

II. They contain hemoglobin.

III. They are capable of amoeboid movement.

(A) I only.

(D) I and II.

(B) II only.

(E) I, II, and III.

(C) III only.

29. All of the following are examples of homeostatic mechanisms EXCEPT:

(A) after exercising vigorously you perspire and the evaporation of water from the skin lowers body temperature.

(B) phagocytic cells in a rabbit detect and eat bacteria.

(C) a frog deposits its eggs in a pond.

(D) shivering occurs outdoors when the air temperature is low.

(E) a small cut in a finger triggers the clotting reaction.

30. Which of the following answer choices lists the organisms in a sequence that corresponds to the following?

intracellular digestion only → digestion in an unbranched cavity that has one opening → digestion partly in a branched cavity that has one opening → digestion in a tube that has two openings

1. *hydra*

2. earthworm

3. sponge

4. planarian

(A) 1-2-3-4

(D) 1-4-3-2

(B) 3-1-4-2

(E) 1-3-4-2

(C) 3-4-1-2

31. Flowering plants and conifers have all of the following in common EXCEPT

(A) vascular tissue for conduction and support.

(B) pollen.

(C) seeds.

(D) conspicuous sporophytes.

(E) fruits.

32. The abnormal hemoglobin of individuals with sickle cell anemia is a result of nucleotide

I. addition.

II. deletion.

III. substitution.

(A) I only.   (D) I and III.

(B) II only.   (E) II and III.

(C) III only.

33. A classification scheme that places pine trees, tomato plants, and pepper plants in one group and ferns and liverworts in another group is based on

I. vascular versus nonvascular.

II. flowering versus nonflowering.

III. seed-forming versus non seed-forming.

(A) I only.   (D) I and II.

(B) II only.   (E) I and III.

(C) III only.

34. How could you account for the presence of coniferous forests in West Virginia or California, since such forests characteristically form a broad band across North America, Europe, and Asia at latitudes to the north of that of the Great Lakes?

(A) They occur only in areas of very low rainfall.

(B) They occur only in areas having similar animals.

(C) They occur only in areas with colder temperatures at higher elevations on mountains.

(D) They occur only in areas of permafrost.

(E) They occur only in areas having well-drained soil.

35. Over time, a single population gives rise to two animal species. The most likely sequence of events would be

1. reproductive isolation.

2. variation.

3. natural selection.

4. geographic isolation.

(A) 1-2-3-4   (D) 4-2-3-1

(B) 3-1-2-4   (E) 4-1-3-2

(C) 4-1-2-3

36. A son with hemophilia could result from which of the following crosses?

I. $X^H X^H$ $\times$ $X^H Y$

II. $X^H X^H$ $\times$ $X^h Y$

III. $X^H X^h$ $\times$ $X^h Y$

(A) I only.   (D) I and II.

(B) II only.   (E) II and III.

(C) III only.

37. All of the following are not true of mutations that occur in humans EXCEPT

(A) only mutations that are dominant are passed to the offspring.

(B) none of the mutations are passed to the offspring.

(C) only mutations occurring in the cells that form gametes are passed to the offspring.

(D) only mutations that are recessive are passed to the offspring.

(E) all mutations occurring in parents are passed to their offspring.

38. What characteristic(s) does an oak tree have in common with a mushroom?

(A) Utilization of chlorophyll

(B) Possession of eukaryotic cells

(C) Heterotrophic capabilities

(D) Utilization of chlorophyll and possession of eukaryotic cells

(E) Possession of eukaryotic cells and heterotrophic capabilities

39. Given the genetic code below and the sequence of bases on a sense strand of DNA is 3' TAC-AAA-GAC-TAT 5', what would the last amino acid be in the translated amino acid chain?

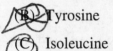

(A) Methionine   (D) Leucine

(B) Tyrosine   (E) Phenylalanine

(C) Isoleucine

The Genetic Code
(Based on Messenger RNA Codons)

First Base	Second Base				Third Base
	U	C	A	G	
U	Phenylalanine	Serine	Tyrosine	Cysteine	U
	Phenylalanine	Serine	Tyrosine	Cysteine	C
	Leucine	Serine	Stop	Stop	A
	Leucine	Serine	Stop	Tryptophan	G
C	Leucine	Proline	Histidine	Arginine	U
	Leucine	Proline	Histidine	Arginine	C
	Leucine	Proline	Glutamine	Arginine	A
	Leucine	Proline	Glutamine	Arginine	G
A	Isoleucine	Threonine	Asparagine	Serine	U
	Isoleucine	Threonine	Asparagine	Serine	C
	Isoleucine	Threonine	Lysine	Arginine	A
	start Methionine	Threonine	Lysine	Arginine	G
G	Valine	Alanine	Aspartic acid	Glycine	U
	Valine	Alanine	Aspartic acid	Glycine	C
	Valine	Alanine	Glutamic acid	Glycine	A
	Valine	Alanine	Glutamic acid	Glycine	G

40. Given the amino acid inserted in a protein is alanine, which one of the following could be the DNA triplet that coded for it?

(A) CGU

(D) CAT

(B) CAA

(E) CGA

(C) CTA

41. In addition to pyruvate and ATP, what is the other end-product of glycolysis?

(A) O_2

(D) $FADH_2$

(B) CO_2

(E) $NADPH_2$ (NADPH + H$^+$)

(C) $NADH_2$ (NADH + H$^+$)

42. If the three-nucleotide sequence on one strand of DNA is 3' TAC 5', what is the three-nucleotide sequence on its DNA complement?

(A) 5' AUG 3'

(D) 3' TAG 5'

(B) 5' ATG 3'

(E) 5' CGA 3'

(C) 3' AUG 5'

43. On a small island off the coast of China, a large number of people are polydactyl (having more than five fingers or toes). Which factor most likely contributed to this phenomenon?

(A) Overcrowding

(D) Natural selection

(B) Overproduction

(E) Isolation

(C) Variation

44. A substance secreted by an individual that affects the behavior of other members of the same species is a

(A) histone.

(D) prostaglandin.

(B) hormone.

(E) steroid.

(C) pheromone.

Base Composition in Mole Percent

Organism	Base			
	Adenine	Thymine	Guanine	Cytosine
Human	30.9	29.4	19.9	19.8
Locust	29.3	29.3	20.5	20.7
Wheat	27.3	27.1	22.7	22.8
Hobbit	30.1	—	—	—

45. Given the information above, what is the approximate percentage of guanine in a hobbit?

(A) 10

(B) 20

(C) 30

(D) 40

(E) 60

Questions 46–48 refer to the breeding of curly-haired and straight-haired hobbits. The results are from five different crosses.

	Parents		Offspring	
Cross	Female	Male	Curly	Straight
1	Curly	Straight	0	58
2	Straight	Curly	48	52
3	Straight	Straight	38	119
4	Curly	Curly	48	0
5	Straight	Curly	0	49

46. If two curly-haired hobbits resulting from cross 3 mate with each other, what is the probability that their offspring will have straight hair?

(A) 3/4

(B) 1/2

(C) 1/4

(D) 1/8

(E) 0

47. If the breeder wanted to obtain homozygous straight-haired hobbits only, he would select which of the following as parents?

(A) a female of   cross 2   and a male of   cross 1

(B) a female of   cross 3   and a male of   cross 1

(C) a female of   cross 2   and a male of   cross 3

(D) a female of   cross 3   and a male of   cross 3

(E) a female of   cross 5   and a male of   cross 1

48. If two curly-haired individuals are mated, what is the probability that a curly-haired female will be produced?

(A) 0%   (D) 75%

(B) 25%   (E) 100%

(C) 50%

Questions 49–51 refer to the following chart.

Biome							Month						
		J	F	M	A	M	J	J	A	S	O	N	D
A	T	1.1	1.7	6.1	12.2	17.8	22.2	25.0	23.3	20.0	13.9	7.8	2.2
	P	8.1	7.6	8.9	8.4	9.2	9.9	11.2	10.2	7.9	7.9	6.4	7.9
B	T	25.6	25.6	24.4	25.0	24.4	23.3	23.3	24.4	24.4	25.0	25.6	25.6
	P	25.8	24.9	31.0	16.5	25.4	18.8	16.8	11.7	22.1	18.3	21.3	29.2
C	T	12.8	15.0	18.3	21.1	25.0	29.4	32.8	32.2	28.9	22.2	16.1	13.3
	P	1.0	1.3	1.0	0.3	0.0	0.0	0.3	1.3	0.5	0.5	0.8	1.0
D	T	−20.0	−18.9	−12.2	−2.2	5.6	12.2	16.1	15.0	10.6	3.9	−5.6	−15.0
	P	3.3	2.3	2.8	2.5	4.6	5.6	6.1	8.4	7.4	4.6	2.8	2.8
E	T	24.6	25.1	26.4	28.5	30.6	31.9	31.1	30.3	31.1	28.8	26.5	25.1
	P	0.8	0.5	1.3	0.5	0.3	0.3	0.0	0.3	0.3	0.3	0.3	0.3

Monthly variations in temperature (T) in degrees celsius and precipitation (P) in centimeters from five major land biomes of the earth are listed above as A, B, C, D, and E.

49. Which data set above (A, B, C, D, or E) is consistent with a tropical desert?

50. The following climatogram represents which data set (A, B, C, D, or E)?

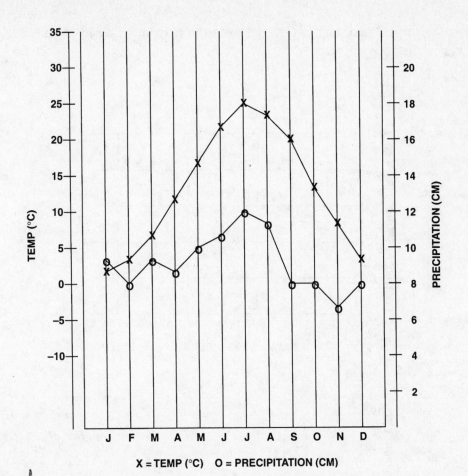

X = TEMP (°C)   O = PRECIPITATION (CM)

51. The temperature and precipitation data graphed in question 50 is most consistent with which one of the following land biomes?

(A) Tropical rain forest

(B) Mid-latitude desert

(C) Tropical desert

(D) Northern coniferous forest

(E) Mid-latitude deciduous forest

Questions 52–53 refer to the following.

In the early 1950s, Eckhard H. Hess and A. O. Ramsey studied the imprinting of mallard ducklings at various ages after hatching and at various distances traveled. Figure A shows the percent of positive responses versus critical age, and Figure B shows the percent of positive responses versus distance traveled.

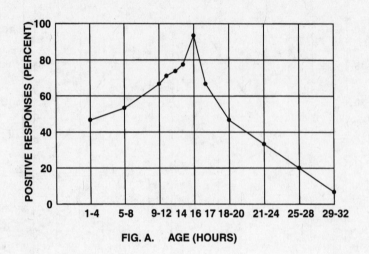

FIG. A.   AGE (HOURS)

FIG. B.   DISTANCE (FEET)

52. The data above indicates that ducklings are most sensitive to imprinting between

(A) 1-4 hours after hatching.

(B) 5-8 hours after hatching.

(C) 13-16 hours after hatching.

(D) 17-20 hours after hatching.

(E) 41-44 hours after hatching.

53. The greatest percentage of increase in imprinting in relation to distance traveled occurred between

(A) 1 and 3 feet.

(D) 25 and 50 feet.

(B) 3 and 12.5 feet.

(E) 50 and 100 feet.

(C) 12.5 and 25 feet.

Questions 54–55 refer to the following.

Two sets of test tubes were set up as shown below. All of the tubes contained water and a few drops of the pH indicator bromthymol blue. The indicator is blue when the pH is above 7.5 and yellow when the pH is less than 6.0. All of the tubes are yellow at the start of the experiment. Tubes II and IV contain snails of similar size. Tubes III and VI contain comparable sprigs of the aquatic plant *Elodea*. Tubes I-III are kept in the light; tubes IV-VI sit in the dark. When the tubes are examined 12 hours later, the indicator in tube III is blue and the indicators in the remaining tubes are still yellow.

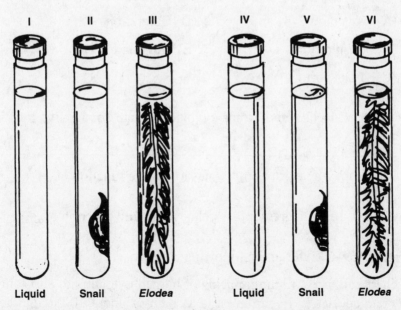

| I | II | III | IV | V | VI |

| Liquid | Snail | *Elodea* | Liquid | Snail | *Elodea* |

Kept in the light at 25°   **Kept in the dark at 25°**

54. After 12 hours the indicator in Tube III is blue because

   (A) *Elodea* respired and gave off CO_2 which formed carbonic acid and lowered the pH.

   (B) indicator decomposed in the light causing the medium to become more basic.

   (C) *Elodea* photosynthesized and gave off O_2 which lowers the pH.

   (D) *Elodea* photosynthesized and used up CO_2 which caused the pH to become more basic.

   (E) the snail formed wastes which raised the pH.

55. Which one of the following statements is not supported by the experiment?

   (A) *Elodea* requires light for photosynthesis.

   (B) Snails do not photosynthesize in the light or dark.

   (C) The pH indicator is not altered by the light.

   (D) The pH indicator is not altered by the temperature.

   (E) Green plants produce O_2 in the dark.

Questions 56–58 refer to the following life functions.

   (A) Nutrition   (D) Excretion

   (B) Respiration   (E) Regulation

   (C) Transport

56. The guard cells and stoma of plants relate to the life function of _____.

57. The crop of an earthworm relates to the life function of _____.

58. The sinuses of a grasshopper relate to the life function of _____.

Questions 59–60 refer to the following chart.

The chart compares 13 amino acids of human cytochrome c to four other vertebrate species. Cytochrome c is a chain of about 100 amino acids in the mitochondria of cells. The numbers in the chart refer to the position of the amino acids and the letters represent specific amino acids.

Amino Acid Position	Human	Vert W	Vert X	Vert Y	Vert Z
58	A	L	E	A	E
60	B	J	B	B	B
61	C	J	C	C	C
62	D	D	C	D	D
63	E	E	E	E	E
64	F	F	F	F	F
65	G	G	G	G	G
66	C	C	C	C	C
100	H	K	D	H	K
101	I	I	I	I	I
102	E	E	E	I	B
103	J	K	K	J	K
104	C	—	H	C	H

59. Which vertebrate species is/are most related to humans?

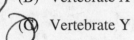

(A) Vertebrate W

(D) Vertebrate Z

(B) Vertebrate X

(E) Vertebrate X and Z

(C) Vertebrate Y

60. Which vertebrate species is/are least related to humans?

(A) Vertebrate W

(D) Vertebrate Z

(B) Vertebrate X

(E) Vertebrate Y and Z

(C) Vertebrate Y

If you are taking the Biology-M test, continue with questions 81-100. Be sure to start this section of the test by filling in oval 81 on your answer sheet.

BIOLOGY-M SECTION

DIRECTIONS: The questions or incomplete statements below are followed by five possible answers or completions. Pick the answer choice that best answers or completes the question or incomplete statement and then fill in the correct oval on your answer sheet.

---

81. Which element is found in all proteins but not in all carbohydrates and lipids?

    (A) Carbon   (D) Oxygen

    (B) Hydrogen   (E) Phosphorus

    (C) Nitrogen

82. During contraction, the shortening of a skeletal muscle results from the interaction of what two proteins?

    (A) Actin and melanin   (D) Keratin and myosin

    (B) Actin and keratin   (E) Keratin and melanin

    (C) Actin and myosin

Questions 83–84 refer to the following chart.

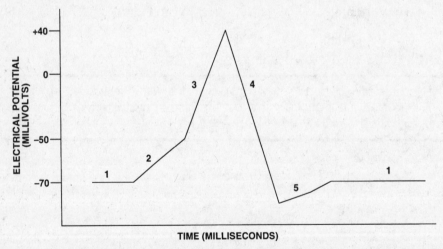

TIME (MILLISECONDS)

83. The polarity change in an axon membrane potential that occurs at #3 during an action potential can best be explained by a

(A) rapid inflow of Cl⁻.   (D) rapid outflow of Ca⁺⁺.

(B) rapid inflow of Na⁺.   (E) rapid outflow of Na⁺.

(C) rapid outflow of K⁺.

84. The axon membrane at #4 is

(A) at resting potential.

(B) depolarized.

(C) hyperpolarized.

(D) repolarizing.

(E) being stimulated at the threshold level.

85. The minimum number of DNA bases needed to code for a single amino acid in a protein is

(A) 1.   (D) 4.

(B) 2.   (E) 5.

(C) 3.

86. An enzyme is all of the following EXCEPT

(A) a catalyst.

(B) made by living organisms.

(C) used up during a chemical reaction.   Recycledbale

(D) specific in its effect.

(E) a protein.

87. A local anesthetic is applied to the skin of an organism. It affects the plasma membrane of sensory neurons communicating pain by

(A) decreasing their permeability to potassium ions only.

(B) increasing their permeability to potassium ions only.

(C) increasing their permeability of sodium ions only.

(D) decreasing their permeability to potassium and sodium ions.

(E) not affecting the permeability of various ions.

88. A bacterial gene 450 bases long will produce a protein containing approximately how many amino acids?

(A) 150

(D) 900

(B) 300

(E) 1,350

(C) 450

89. A tRNA anticodon, UAG, is complementary to an mRNA codon of

(A) AAG.   AUC

(D) UAG.

(B) AUC.

(E) UUC.

(C) AUG.

Questions 90–91 refer to the following diagram of a cell.

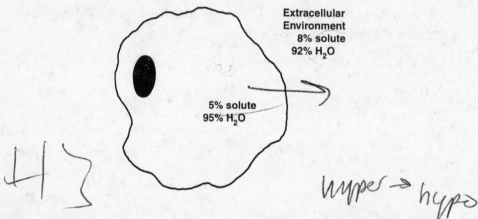

Extracellular
Environment
8% solute
92% H$_2$O

5% solute
95% H$_2$O

90. Select the correct statement about the cell and its setting.

(A) The cell will gain solute.

(B) The cell will lose water.

(C) The extracellular environment is hypotonic.

(D) The intracellular environment is hypertonic.

(E) The two environments are isotonic.

91. Select the concentration hypotonic to both the extracellular and intracellular setting.

(A) 3%

(D) 8%

(B) 5%

(E) 10%

(C) 7%

92. The enzyme used in building a DNA molecule using an RNA template is

   (A) restriction endonuclease.   (D) RNA polymerase.

   (B) DNA ligase   (E) deoxyribonuclease.

   (C) reverse transcriptase.

93. An antibiotic is developed to treat a bacterial disease in humans. It prevents the movement of ribosomes along mRNA in the bacterial cell. Select the event that is inhibited in the bacterial cell.

   (A) Amino acid synthesis   (D) Translation

   (B) DNA replication   (E) tRNA synthesis

   (C) mRNA synthesis

94. This process accounts for the ability of the freshwater alga, *Nitella*, to accumulate a concentration of potassium ions more than a thousand times greater than that of the surrounding water.

   (A) Active transport   (D) Simple diffusion

   (B) Osmosis   (E) Facilitated diffusion

   (C) Phagocytosis

95. The acetyl (two-carbon) group is to oxaloacetic acid in the Krebs cycle as CO_2 is to what compound in the dark reactions (Calvin cycle) of photosynthesis?

   (A) Glucose

   (B) Phosphoglyceric acid (PGA)

   (C) Phosphoglyceraldehyde (PGAL)

   (D) Pyruvic acid

   (E) Ribulose bisphosphate

96. Cellular respiration is a series of chemical reactions that break down organic materials in the body to extract energy. When the body temperature of an organism increases, we would expect

   (A) the rate of cellular respiration to increase.

   (B) less energy production.

(C) the formation of more enzymes.

(D) no change in cellular respiration or energy production.

(E) a decrease in the ability to perform other energy dependent activities.

Question 97 refers to the following drawing showing bacterial conjugation.

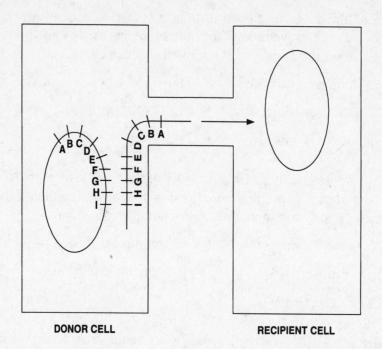

DONOR CELL   RECIPIENT CELL

97. Over the next 24 hours, which donor gene will the recipient cells receive least out of all the transferred genes?

(A) Gene A

(D) Gene G

(B) Gene C

(E) Gene I

(C) Gene D

98. Eukaryotic cells that produce and export large quantities of proteins, such as liver cells, would be well supplied with which organelle?

(A) Centriole

(D) Mitochondrion

(B) Lysosome

(E) Rough endoplasmic reticulum

(C) Microtubule

99. A white blood cell ingests a food particle. The sequence of cell structures that process this particle is

(A) ER – plasma membrane – lysosome – vacuole.

(B) ER – vacuole – lysosome – plasma membrane.

(C) plasma membrane – mitochondrion – vacuole – lysosome.

(D) plasma membrane – vacuole – lysosome – mitochondrion.

(E) vacuole – ER – plasma membrane – lysosome.

100. Rank the following events of a muscle cell contraction in the correct order.

a. calcium ion

b. calcium ions are released from the SR

c. plasma membrane depolarizes

d. myosin slides actin

e. T tubule depolarizes

(A) a – e – b – c – d

(B) b – d – a – c – e

(C) c – e – b – a – d

(D) d – c – b – a – e

(E) e – b – d – a – c

STOP
If you finish before time is called, you may check your work on the entire
Biology-M test only. Do not turn to any other test in this book.

SAT Biology E/M
Practice Test 5

ANSWER KEY

BIOLOGY CORE SECTION

1.	(C)	16.	(A)	31.	(E)	46.	(E)
2.	(A)	17.	(C)	32.	(C)	47.	(E)
3.	(B)	18.	(D)	33.	(C)	48.	(E)
4.	(E)	19.	(B)	34.	(C)	49.	(E)
5.	(A)	20.	(E)	35.	(D)	50.	(A)
6.	(E)	21.	(E)	36.	(C)	51.	(E)
7.	(B)	22.	(C)	37.	(C)	52.	(C)
8.	(C)	23.	(C)	38.	(B)	53.	(B)
9.	(A)	24.	(D)	39.	(C)	54.	(D)
10.	(D)	25.	(A)	40.	(E)	55.	(E)
11.	(B)	26.	(A)	41.	(C)	56.	(B)
12.	(C)	27.	(D)	42.	(B)	57.	(A)
13.	(A)	28.	(B)	43.	(E)	58.	(C)
14.	(B)	29.	(C)	44.	(C)	59.	(C)
15.	(D)	30.	(B)	45.	(B)	60.	(A)

BIOLOGY-M SECTION

81.	(C)	86.	(C)	91.	(A)	96.	(A)
82.	(C)	87.	(B)	92.	(C)	97.	(E)
83.	(B)	88.	(A)	93.	(D)	98.	(E)
84.	(D)	89.	(B)	94.	(A)	99.	(D)
85.	(C)	90.	(B)	95.	(E)	100.	(C)

DETAILED EXPLANATIONS
OF ANSWERS

PRACTICE TEST 5

BIOLOGY CORE SECTION

1. **(C)**   2. **(A)**
   A predator (i.e., a hawk) is an animal that captures, kills, and consumes another animal – its prey (i.e., a mouse).

   A commensal is an organism that benefits from its association with another type of organism, while the other organism neither benefits nor is harmed.

3. **(B)**
   Secondary (lateral, or branch) roots arise by division of cells in the pericycle.

4. **(E)**
   Xylem conducts water while phloem conducts sucrose and other material both up *and* down the plant body.

5. **(A)**
   The increase in height of a tree results from the division and subsequent differentiation and elongation of cells located in apical meristems.

6. **(E)**
   A population is a group of similar organisms living in one particular area at a given time.

7. **(B)**
   The biosphere constitutes the portion of the earth (atmosphere, hydrosphere, lithosphere) inhabited by living organisms. A biome is a complex of ecological communities characterized by distinctive type of vegetation, as determined by climate. Examples of biomes include: tundra, taiga, temperate deciduous forest, tropical rainforest, desert, and grassland.

An ecosystem is the biotic and abiotic factors of an ecological community considered together.

8. **(C)**
The biological community consists of all of the different kinds of organisms that live and interact in one place at a given time.

9. **(A)**
Many small flowers, like grass, with feathery stigma are needed to capture pollen blowing in the wind.

10. **(D)**
Hollow fruits with air chambers will allow the fruit to float. Coconuts may float for hundreds of miles in the ocean before finding land.

11. **(B)**
Small colorful fruits invite mammals and birds to eat the fruit whole. The seed then goes quickly through the digestive system and is dispersed.

12. **(C)**   13. **(A)**   14. **(B)**   15. **(D)**   16. **(A)**
When classifying organisms, the first step is to determine if the cells are prokaryotic or eukaryotic cells. If the cells are prokaryotic, they will not have a nucleus; no multiple copies of chromosomes, and no mitochondria. The cell lacks membrane-bound structures. The ribosomes will be very small. Bacteria and cyanobacteria are prokaryotic cells and belong to the Kingdom Monera. The organisms from all the other kingdoms (Protista, Fungi, Plantae, Animalia) are made of eukaryotic cells. Cells that have a nucleus with multiple chromosomes and many other cell structures like mitochondria. When compared to prokaryotic cells, the ribosomes of eukaryotic cells are large.

Single-celled animals and algae along with the slime molds are in the Kingdom Protista. Protists can be autotropic (obtain nutrition through photosynthesis) or heterotrophic (obtain nutrition through consumption or absorption) and the cell reproduces by the process of mitosis. Yeasts, molds, mildews, and mushrooms are in the Kingdom Fungi. Fungi are heterotrophs that secrete digestive enzymes and then absorb nutrients. They are unicellular or filamentous. Their cell walls may have chitin or cellulose. Mosses, ferns, and seed-producing plants belong to the Kingdom Plantae. Plants are multicellular, autotrophic, and have cell walls made of cellulose. The invertebrate and vertebrate animals belong to the Kingdom Animalia. Animals are multicellular heterotrophs that consume their nutrients.

17. **(C)**

The correct sequence of taxonomic categories from largest to smallest is Kingdom, Phylum, Class, Order, Family, Genus, and Species.

18. **(D)**

Prokaryotes and eukaryotes are built of cells that contain both DNA and RNA. In them, DNA serves as the genetic material. DNA codes for RNAs, a process called transcription. In turn, one type of RNA, messenger RNA, codes for protein; a process called translation. Fungi, insects, and protozoa have eukaryotic cells. Bacteria have prokaryotic cells. On the other hand, viruses are not cellular. They are infectious particles consisting of DNA or RNA (but not both), a protein coat, or capsid, and in some cases an envelope containing lipids and glycoproteins. The nucleic acid of a virus serves as its genetic material.

19. **(B)**

Divergent evolution and adaptive radiation are associated with increasing dissimilarity. The independent occurrence of similarities resulting from common ancestry is termed homology and the process is termed parallel evolution. Similar features (e.g., wings of insects and birds) that occur independently in distantly related organisms in response to adapting to similar environments illustrate convergence. From different evolutionary origins, unrelated organisms become similar. One example is the evolution of wings in insects and birds.

20. **(E)**

Two processes enable the nonmotile sperm to approach the egg for fertilization to be accomplished. First, pollen is transferred from the anther of a male stamen to the stigma of a female pistil, a process called pollination. Second, pollen germinates, forming a pollen tube that grows through the style to the egg inside the ovary.

21. **(E)**

Nondisjunction occurs when one or more chromosome pairs fail to separate normally during meiosis, resulting in the formation of gametes containing one or more extra chromosomes. If an egg containing 22 autosomes and two X chromosomes is fertilized by a sperm that contains an X chromosome, the resulting individual would be an XXX female. The number of Barr bodies in the cells of such an individual would be two (one less than the number of X chromosomes).

22. **(C)**

During meiosis (reduction division), the chromosome number is halved. If a cell formed by meiosis contains 12 chromosomes, then the cell that divided to form it must have contained 24 chromosomes.

23. **(C)**

Vitamins form part of the structures of small organic molecules called coenzymes, which are essential to the functioning of certain enzymes.

24. **(D)**

The composition of the early atmosphere was an important factor in the origin and evolution of life on earth. Presumably, the early atmosphere was a reducing atmosphere, lacking molecular oxygen (O_2). Its simple gases included ammonia (NH_3), hydrogen (H_2), methane (CH_4), and water vapor (H_2O). They contained the basic elements needed for the foundation of life. Over time, in the absence of O_2, organic molecules formed and accumulated in the environment until the first forms of life evolved.

25. **(A)**

Conditioning is a form of learning in which a neutral stimulus, associated with a stimulus that normally elicits a behavioral response, causes the response in the absence of the usual stimulus. The fish involved have associated the neutral stimulus (light) with the concomitant introduction of food to their environment. Thus, they react upon seeing the light, even if they cannot yet detect the food.

26. **(A)**

Epinephrine (also called adrenalin) triggers the "fight-or-flight response." This response includes the breakdown of glycogen into glucose. Glycogen is present in the liver and in muscle. Epinephrine also stimulates an increase in heart rate (the animal will need an increased supply of oxygen if it is to be able to utilize glucose).

27. **(D)**

Both cartilage and epithelium are avascular tissues that receive nutrients from neighboring tissues. Muscular tissue, however, is highly vascularized.

28. **(B)**

Erythrocytes, or red blood cells, which develop from nucleated cells in bone marrow, lose their nuclei as they enter the circulating blood. They contain the oxygen-transporting pigment hemoglobin and are incapable of independent movement such as that exhibited by amoeboid white blood cells.

29. **(C)**

Homeostasis refers to the tendency of an organism to maintain a more or less constant internal environment. The internal environment is the extracellular fluid bathing its cells. The situations represented by all of the choices except (C) are ones in which an external or internal stress changes some normal condition to an abnormal condition. Homeostatic mechanisms serve to counteract the effects of any stresses on an organism. Therefore, when one exercises vigorously and one's internal body temperature increases, one perspires in order to remove excess internal heat, and to have one's internal body temperature return to normal.

30. **(B)**

Sponges depend on intracellular digestion exclusively. Both *hydra* and planaria have digestive cavities with one opening. Such a digestive cavity is called a gastrovascular cavity. In planaria, the gastrovascular cavity is highly branched. Earthworms have a complete digestive tract with two openings, a mouth and an anus.

31. **(E)**

In reality, a fruit is the ripened ovary of a flower and may incorporate other closely associated flower parts. Conifers do not bear flowers, and so they also bear no fruit.

32. **(C)**

Sickle-cell hemoglobin (hemoglobin S) differs from normal adult hemoglobin (hemoglobin A) in that a single amino acid, valine, is substituted for the glutamic acid residue that is normally present as the sixth residue of each of the two beta polypeptides of hemoglobin. This change in amino acid sequence is caused by the substitution of a single nucleotide in the DNA triplet that codes for glutamic acid.

33. **(C)**

Pines, tomato, pepper plants, and ferns are vascular plants. Of the plants that are mentioned, only tomato and pepper plants are flowering plants. However, pine trees, tomato plants, and pepper plants all produce seeds. Ferns and liverworts produce spores.

34. (C)

Extensions or isolated segments of coniferous forest (taiga, boreal forest) occur on the slopes of mountains, where the temperatures at the higher altitudes approximate those at more northern latitudes.

35. (D)

An ancestral population may be split into two or more subgroups by geographic isolation. If, because of isolation, gene flow between the subgroups is prevented, mutations, natural selection, and other factors cause the subgroups to become increasingly different genetically. Over time, they may become so different genetically that interbreeding is not possible.

36. (C)

The gene for hemophilia is recessive and X-linked, thus, a son with hemophilia (X^hY) can only result from a mating in which the mother is either a carrier (X^HX^h) or a hemophiliac (X^hX^h). The father donates the Y chromosome and so it does not matter if the father carries the gene for hemophilia or not. The Punnett squares show this below.

1.

	X^H	X^H
X^H	X^HX^H	X^HX^H
Y	X^HY	X^HY

2.

	X^H	X^H
X^h	X^HX^h	X^HX^h
Y	X^HY	X^HY

3.

	X^H	X^h
X^h	X^HX^h	X^hX^h
Y	X^HY	X^hY*

* hemophilic son

37. (C)

In humans, only mutations occurring in the gametes (sperm and eggs) have the potential of being passed to offspring. These mutations can be either dominant or recessive, since such attributes do not affect whether or not a mutant gene will actually be present in a gamete; dominance and recessiveness only come into play in the determination of phenotype.

38. **(B)**
    The oak tree, a flowering plant, contains chlorophyll and is autotrophic. The mushroom, a fungus, lacks chlorophyll and is heterotrophic. Both have eukaryotic cells.

39. **(C)**
    The DNA triplet TAT codes for the mRNA codon AUA. The AUA codon results in the insertion of the amino acid isoleucine in the amino acid chain. You must remember the proper reading direction, which is from 5' to 3'. Thus, you have the following:

    3' TAC-AAA-GAC-TAT 5' (DNA sense strand)
    5' AUG-UUU-CUG-AUA 3' (mRNA strand)

    Reading the mRNA from 5' to 3', the last codon is AUA.

40. **(E)**
    The DNA triplet CGA codes for the mRNA codon GCU which is translated into the amino acid alanine in a polypeptide. Choice (A) is incorrect because the base, uracil, is found in RNA, not DNA.

41. **(C)**
    As phosphoglyceraldehyde (PGAL) is oxidized during glycolysis, oxidized nicotinamide adenine dinucleotide (NAD$^+$) is reduced, forming NADH + H$^+$. O$_2$ is an electron acceptor in oxidative phosphorylation. CO$_2$ is produced in the conversion of pyruvate to acetyl coenzyme A and in the Krebs cycle. FADH$_2$ is produced in the Krebs cycle. NADPH$_2$ is produced by the pentose phosphate pathway.

42. **(B)**
    The two strands of a DNA double-helix run in opposite directions, 5' to 3' and 3' to 5'. 3' and 5' refer to the third and fifth carbons of deoxyribose. Wherever adenine occurs in one strand, thymine always appears in the complementary strand. Similarly, cytosine is always paired with guanine. Memorize the base pairing rules A–T and G–L.

43. **(E)**
    Isolation most likely contributed to the incidence of polydactyl (more than five fingers or toes). This caused the inhabitants off the shore of China to develop characteristics unlike those of the inhabitants of China. The sea that separates the island from the mainland is the reproductive barrier which prevents interbreeding.

44. **(C)**

Pheromones are compounds released into the environment by an individual to influence the behavior (e.g., attract a mate, mark a trail or territory) of other individuals of the same species. Histones are proteins that are associated with DNA. A hormone is a substance that is secreted by certain somatic cells that affects specific cells at other locations in the body. Prostaglandins are hormones that are fatty-acid derivatives. Steroids, many of which are hormones, all have structures that have three six-membered rings and one five-membered ring.

45. **(B)**

Since thymine is the complement of adenine and since there is just as much thymine in DNA as there is adenine, 30.1% of the bases are thymine. Therefore, 60.2% of the bases are adenine and thymine. The remaining 39.8% of the bases must include equal amounts of guanine and cytosine. Half of 39.8% is 19.9%, which is approximately 20%.

46. **(E)**

Results indicate that the allele for straight hair is dominant to the allele for curly hair. Using "S" to represent the dominant allele for straight hair and "s" to represent the recessive allele for curly hair, the cross can be interpreted as follows:

| | Genotypes of Parents | | Offspring |
Cross	Female	Male	Phenotypic Ratio
1	ss	SS	All straight
2	Ss	ss	1/2 curly, 1/2 straight
3	Ss	Ss	1/4 curly, 3/4 straight
4	ss	ss	All curly
5	SS	ss	All straight

The two curly-haired hobbits referred to in this question would produce the same results as Cross 4 above.

47. **(E)**

In order to produce only progeny that are homozygous for the dominant allele for straight hair, both parents must also be homozygous for this allele. Of the listed parents, only female #5 and male #1 have this genotype.

48. **(E)**

The cross is: ss x ss. All offspring of either sex will also be ss, with curly hair.

49. **(E)**

In a tropical desert, precipitation is uniformly low and temperature uniformly high throughout most of the year. Note the figures in the table citing this.

50. **(A)**

If the data for each of the biomes were plotted, the resulting figure for biome A would resemble the figure provided in the question. Note, for example, that the highest figures for temperature and precipitation are in July.

51. **(E)**

Temperature extremes are too low for the tropics but too high for a Northern coniferous forest. Yearly precipitation is too high for deserts. The data for biome B indicates a tropical rain forest. Biome C is a desert climate with high temperatures and low precipitation. A coniferous forest or taiga is indicated by the data in biome D.

52. **(C)**

The highest percentage of positive responses occurred at 13 to 16 hours after hatching. Note where the peak responses are located.

53. **(B)**

The increase in imprinting in relation to distance traveled was about 30 percent for distances between 3 and 12.5 feet. The next highest percentage of increase was about 20 percent for distances between 12.5 and 25 feet. Read the graph, and compare the changing slopes of the line.

54. **(D)**

In light of sufficient intensity, the rate of photosynthesis by *Elodea* would be expected to exceed the rate of respiration resulting in a net decrease in the CO_2 content of the solution. As CO_2 is used in photosynthesis, carbonic acid in the water is converted to CO_2 (which is subsequently utilized) and H_2O resulting in an elevation of the pH of the solution and the blue color of tube III.

55. **(E)**

Green plants only produce O_2 in the light during photosynthesis. The light-dependent reactions of photosynthesis produce oxygen.

56. **(B)**

Living organisms need to exchange oxygen and carbon dioxide between themselves and their environment. This life function is called respiration. Guard cells of plant leaves open and close stomata, openings in the leaf. This allows excess oxygen to leave the leaf and carbon dioxide to enter the leaf.

57. **(A)**

Organisms need to take in nutrients to live. This life function is called nutrition. The crop of the earthworm stores what comes from the mouth and esophagus until it goes to the grinding organ called the gizzard.

58. **(C)**

The sinuses of grasshoppers are large spaces receiving blood from the dorsal aorta. The grasshopper has an open circulatory system for transporting digested food to the organs. Circulatory systems carry out the transport life function.

59. **(C)**   60. **(A)**

Cytochrome c is needed by all aerobic organisms. Therefore, the amino acid sequence can be studied to infer how closely organisms are related to each other. The longer the time organisms have been diverging from a common ancestor, the greater the difference in the sequence of their amino acids. This is based on the assumption that different species have similar rates in the change of amino acid sequence. Vertebrate Y (monkey) is the most closely related to humans. Compare the Human and Vertebrate Y columns. Note the high percentage of amino acids matching. Monkeys have only one difference in amino acid sequence. Vertebrate W (tuna) is the least related to humans. Tuna has six differences in amino acid sequence. Vertebrate X is turtle and vertebrate Z is frog. Compare Vertebrate W column to the Human column of amino acids. Note the high percentage of dissimilarity.

BIOLOGY-M SECTION

81. **(C)**
    Nitrogen occurs in all amino acids, which are the basic building blocks of proteins, but does not occur in all carbohydrates and lipids. All three biomolecules contain carbon, hydrogen, and oxygen. Phospholipids contain phosphorus.

82. **(C)**
    According to the sliding filament hypothesis of skeletal muscle contraction, thin filaments of actin slide along thick filaments of myosin from both ends of the thick filaments (myosin) toward the middle of each sarcomere.

83. **(B)**
    During an action potential in a nerve fiber, depolarization, which is depicted at #3, occurs as a result of a rapid inflow of sodium ions (Na^+).

84. **(D)**
    At #4 the axon membrane is repolarizing as a result of a rapid outflow of potassium ions (K^+). Resting potential is indicated by 1. Number 2 represents the threshold level and number 5 represents hyperpolarization. Depolarization occurs between 4 and 5.

85. **(C)**
    Coding for amino acids is based on a triplet code. The "alphabet" contains four letters (bases) and the words contain three letters (bases) each. Thus, you can have 64 different codes.

86. **(C)**
    To answer this question you must know the characteristics of an enzyme. Enzymes are specialized proteins made by living organisms. They serve to speed up chemical reactions in the body. Thus, they serve as biological catalysts. They are specific in their actions reacting with particular substrates. Enzymes are not used up during the reaction, but rather can react over and over again with new molecules of substrate.

87. **(B)**
    The concentration of potassium ions is higher intracellularly. Increasing the permeability of the plasma membrane to potassium allows more of

these ions to leave the inside of the neuron and enter the extracellular fluid. This establishes a more positive extracellular environment, hyperpolarizing the outside of the cell. This makes the cell less likely to depolarize and fire an impulse.

More sodium is found extracellularly. Increasing the plasma membrane permeability to sodium causes the neuron to depolarize, making it more likely to fire an impulse.

88. **(A)**

This question asks you to calculate the number of amino acids that would be present in a protein coded for by a bacterial gene containing a certain number of bases. Since the genetic code is a triplet code, a sequence of three bases codes for one amino acid. Therefore, 450 bases should code for 150 amino acids. This is an approximate number, since three different codes (UGA, UAG, and UAA) do not code for any amino acids. These are terminator codes, and one of them would be expected to end the reading of the gene.

89. **(B)**

The base-pairing RNA rules of A-U and C-G must be memorized to answer this question.

90. **(B)**

The extracellular-intracellular settings are not isotonic (equal in solute concentration). The extracellular environment is *hypertonic,* higher in solute concentration. The intracellular environment is *hypertonic,* 5% is less than 8%. Water will flow from the cell, 95%, to the outside, 92%, by osmosis. By osmosis water flows from a higher to lower concentration through a membrane permeable to it. The solute gradient goes into the cell, from 8% to 5%. It will not pass in, however, because the membrane is impermeable to it. Hypertonic and hypotonic are relative terms. For example, a 5% solute solution is *hypotonic* to a 10% solution but *hypertonic* to a 2% solution.

91. **(A)**

Only 3% is less than both 5% and 8%, thus, hypotonic to both solute concentrations. Remember that these figures on tonicity refer to solute concentrations.

92. **(C)**

Restriction endonucleases are bacterial enzymes that split DNA into pieces with specific nucleotides at their ends. In nature, the restriction enzymes are thought to protect bacteria from invading DNA viruses (bacteriophages or phages) by cleaving their DNA into useless fragments. In recombinant DNA technology, humans make use of over 250 restriction endonucleases for introducing DNA of one organism into the cells of another. DNA ligase is used to join short pieces of DNA to form a strand during DNA replication. Prior to that, a DNA polymerase is used to join DNA nucleotides. The enzyme deoxyribonuclease hydrolyzes (digests) DNA into nucleotides. RNA polymerase is used to join RNA nucleotides when RNA is transcribed from DNA. Reverse transcriptase, also called RNA-dependent DNA polymerase, is an enzyme that can build DNA using an RNA template.

93. **(D)**

For translation to occur, the ribosome must move along the mRNA to read the codons on this messenger molecule. Translating the codons correctly places the amino acids in the correct order for protein synthesis.

94. **(A)**

Energy expended during active transport enables cells to accumulate substances despite the fact that these substances are in greater concentration inside the cell and will tend to diffuse out of the cell. The K^+ ions move from lower to higher concentration into the cell.

95. **(E)**

Just as acetyl-coenzyme A is combined with oxaloacetic acid to initiate the Krebs cycle, the first step in the synthesis of carbohydrate by the Calvin cycle involves the combination of CO_2 and a molecule of the five-carbon sugar ribulose bisphosphate.

96. **(A)**

To answer this question, you must know how chemical reactions work in the living organism and apply that knowledge to a specific situation. The rate of chemical reactions increases with an increase in temperature. This typically happens with poikilotherms (cold-blooded animals) as the environmental temperature increases, but also happens during fever. Since cellular respiration is a series of chemical reactions, the rate of cellular respiration will also increase, resulting in greater energy production. Thus, energy-dependent activities will not be limited by an increase in body temperature. Temperature changes should not affect the formation of enzymes.

97. **(E)**

More and more chromosomal material will enter the recipient cell as time accrues. Note that gene A is the first to enter the recipient cell. Gene I is the last to enter.

98. **(E)**

Proteins synthesized on ribosomes associated with endoplasmic reticula can enter the channels of the endoplasmic reticula and become enclosed in sacs; these sacs move to the membrane to export their contents to the outside.

99. **(D)**

The plasma membrane surrounds the particle outside the cell, pinching it off and forming a vacuole inside the cell. Next, lysosomes break down the particle, digesting it for a source of energy. The mitochondrion is the powerplant of the cell. It has enzymes to extract energy from nutrient molecules.

100. **(C)**

A muscle membrane depolarizes when excited by a nerve cell. From the plasma membrane, the T tubule sends electrical energy transversely into the cell. This energy arrives at the SR (sarcoplasmic reticulum), releasing calcium ions from this organelle into the muscle cell cytoplasm (sarcoplasm). Troponin blocks the interaction between actin and myosin. However, the release of calcium ions from the SR inhibits the action of troponin, allowing myosin to slide the actin and shorten the muscle cell.

SAT Biology E/M
Practice Test 6

(Answer sheets appear in the back of this book.)

TIME: 1 Hour
80 Questions

BIOLOGY CORE SECTION

DIRECTIONS: The lettered or numbered choices below refer to the questions or statements that immediately follow them. Pick the best answer choice and fill in the correct oval on your answer sheet. An answer choice may be used more than once or not at all.

Questions 1–3 refer to the following.

(A) Law of Segregation

(B) Law of Dominance

(C) Law of Independent Assortment

(D) Codominance

(E) Multiple alleles

1. The random separation of two different traits (two different genes) during sex cell formation is called _____A_____.

2. One allele masking the expression of another allele of a gene is called _____B_____.

3. More than two alleles expressing a trait is called _____E_____.

Questions 4–6 refer to the following.

Complete the correct sequence of blood flow through the heart.

    (A) Right ventricle   (D) Left atrium

    (B) Left ventricle   (E) Aorta

    (C) Right atrium

4. From lungs to pulmonary veins to the _____

5. From the body to the _____ to the right ventricle

6. From the left atrium to the left ventricle to the _____

Questions 7–9 refer to the following.

    (A) commensal   (D) prey

    (B) parasite   (E) scavenger

    (C) predator

7. A crow feeds on a dead rabbit lying on the road. The crow is a _____.

8. A barnacle is moved from one feeding place to another while attached to the shell of a horseshoe crab. The barnacle is a _____.

9. A leech feeds on blood after attaching to a swimmer in a freshwater pond. The leech is a _____.

Questions 10–11 refer to the following.

    (A) Anaphase   (D) Prophase

    (B) Interphase   (E) Telophase

    (C) Metaphase

10. A characteristic number of double strand chromosomes appears and spindle formation begins.

11. A distinct nucleus is evident throughout this phase although the chromosomes are not visible.

Questions 12–13 refer to the following.

    (A) Grassland

    (B) Taiga

    (C) Temperature deciduous forest

    (D) Tropical rainforest

    (E) Tundra

12. This biome is characterized by permafrost and the absence of trees.

E

13. Temperature changes very little throughout the year in this biome which contains a tremendous number and variety of plants.

D

Questions 14–15 refer to the following.

    (A) Antibiotic   (D) Complement

    (B) Antibody   (E) Interferon

    (C) Antigen

14. A protein produced by virus infected vertebrate cells which spreads to neighboring cells and helps protect them from the virus.

A

15. A protein, produced in the body of a vertebrate, that reacts with the foreign protein, or polysaccharide that stimulated its formation.

B

Questions 16–17 refer to the following.

    (A) Photosynthetic   (D) Prokaryotic

    (B) Autotrophs   (E) Eukaryotic

    (C) Parasitic

16. All bacteria are _____. *D*

17. All animals are _____. *E*

18. As compared to the success of other vascular plants and bryophytes (liverworts and mosses), how could you account for the success and predominance of flowering plants and conifers on land?

(A) They have roots, stem, and leaves.

(B) They use chlorophyll-a as a light-trapping pigment in photosynthesis.

(C) They form large conspicuous gametophytes.

(D) Exposed parts are covered by a waxy cuticle.

(E) The evolution of pollen and seeds eliminated the need for external water for fertilization.

19. The classification of a perch, a frog, and a rabbit in the same group is based on

(A) being warm-blooded.

(B) using lungs for gas exchange.

(C) using gills for gas exchange.

(D) having backbones of vertebrae.

(E) having four-chambered hearts.

20. If a male is colorblind and the female is a carrier, what genotypes would be possible in their daughters?

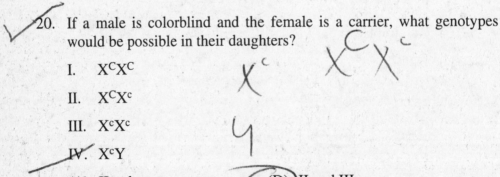

I. $X^C X^C$

II. $X^C X^c$

III. $X^c X^c$

IV. $X^c Y$

(A) II only.

(B) III only.

(C) IV only.

(D) II and III.

(E) I, II, and III.

Question 21 refers to the following graph.

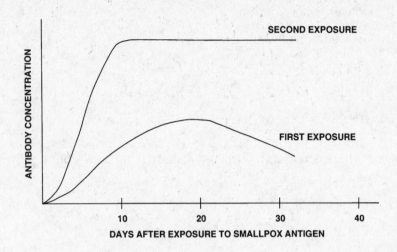

21. Based on the graph, which one of the following is true about exposure to the smallpox antigen?

    (A) The antibody concentration increases faster in a first exposure.

    (B) The concentration of antibody produced is greater in a first exposure.

    (C) The antibody concentration peaks within 10 days after a first exposure.

    (D) The concentration of antibody produced is greater after a second exposure.

    (E) The concentration of antibody produced is the same after a first and a second exposure.

22. All of the following are associated with the light dependent reactions of photosynthesis EXCEPT

    (A) carbon dioxide.   (D) NADPH.

    (B) chlorophyll-a.   (E) plastoquinone.

    (C) ferredoxin.

23. The 14 species of Darwin's finches on the Galapagos Islands are believed to have evolved from competing populations of an ancestral finch that colonized the islands from the South American mainland. If so, this would be an example of

I.   adaptative radiation.

II. convergent evolution.

III. divergent evolution.

(A) I only.   (D) I and II.

(B) II only.   (E) I and III.

(C) III only.

24. What characteristic(s) does a yeast cell have in common with an elephant?

I.   Chlorophyll

II. Eukaryotic

III. Heterotrophic

(A) I only.   (D) I and II.

(B) II only.   (E) II and III.

(C) III only.

25. Ferns and flowering plants have all of the following in common EXCEPT

(A) eukaryotic cells.

(B) dominant sporophyte generation.

(C) free swimming sperm cells.

(D) true roots, stems, and leaves.

(E) vascular tissues.

26. The two-carbon acetyl group enters the Krebs cycle by combining with which four-carbon molecule?

(A) Citrate   (D) Pyruvate

(B) Fumarate   (E) Succinate

(C) Oxaloacetate

27. A representative sample of a large population revealed that 1,600 out of the 10,000 individuals examined displayed a given recessive phe-

notype. Assuming the population is in Hardy-Weinberg equilibrium, how many individuals out of 100 would be expected to be homozygous dominant for the trait?

(A) 16

(D) 48

(B) 24

(E) 84

(C) 36

28. The conversion of atmospheric nitrogen (N_2) by certain eubacteria and blue-green bacteria into a form usable by other living organisms is termed

(A) ammonification.

(D) nitrogen fixation.

(B) denitrification.

(E) transformation.

(C) nitrification.

Questions 29–30 refer to the following.

Crosses among radishes of three phenotypes produced the following results:

Cross	Parents	Offspring (types of radishes)
1	Oval × Round	156 Oval, 154 Round
2	Long × Round	301 Oval
3	Long × Oval	153 Long, 150 Oval

29. In a cross between two plants of the long type, what percentage of plants producing long radishes would be expected?

(A) 0

(D) 75

(B) 25

(E) 100

(C) 50

30. In which cross would 1/2 of the offspring be expected to show the dominant phenotype?

(A) Dd × DD

(D) Dd × Dd

(B) DD × dd

(E) dd × dd

(C) Dd × dd

31. Growth of a dicot stem in length results from cells produced in the

(A) apical meristem.

(D) pericycle.

(B) cork cambium.

(E) vascular cambium.

(C) endodermis.

Question 32 refers to the following.

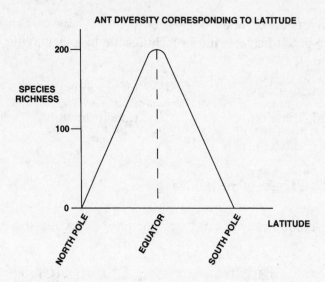

ANT DIVERSITY CORRESPONDING TO LATITUDE

32. Based on the information in the graph, what could you conclude about species diversity on land?

(A) Species diversity is greatest at latitudes north and south of the equator.

(B) Species diversity increases at higher latitudes.

(C) Species diversity decreases as one travels toward the equator.

(D) Species diversity remains constant as one travels north or south of the equator.

(E) Species diversity is greatest at latitudes near the equator.

33. According to the endosymbiont theory

(A) certain prokaryotic cells gradually changed to form eukaryotic cells.

(B) eukaryotic cells arose when certain prokaryotic cells entered and "took up residence" inside other prokaryotic cells.

(C) the earliest cells were eukaryotic.

(D) certain prokaryotic cells gradually degenerated to form viruses.

(E) certain eukaryotic cells gradually degenerated to form prokaryotic cells.

34. The hormone that stimulates release of milk and contraction of smooth muscle during childbirth is

(A) cortisol.

(B) glucagon.

(C) oxytocin.

(D) prolactin.

(E) testosterone.

35. A classification scheme that places crocodiles, robins, and foxes in one group and perch and frogs in another group is based on

I. no backbone versus backbone of vertebrae.

II. gill breathing versus lung breathing.

III. heart with one ventricle versus heart with two ventricles.

(A) I only.

(B) II only.

(C) III only.

(D) I and II.

(E) I and III.

Question 36 refers to the following graph.

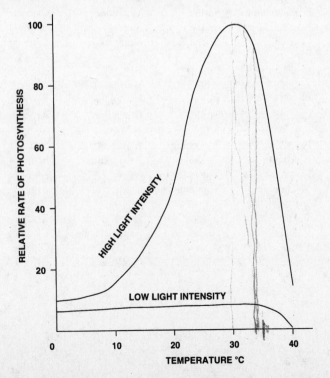

36. Based on data in the graph, at which of the following light and temperature combinations is the rate of photosynthesis greatest?

(A) Low light intensity; 20°C

(B) High light intensity; 20°C

(C) High light intensity; 30°C

(D) High light intensity; 34°C

(E) High light intensity; 38°C

37. If guanine composes 30 percent of the nitrogen bases in a DNA molecule, what percentage of the bases would be adenine in the molecule of mRNA transcribed from the sense strand?

(A) 10 (D) 40

(B) 20 (E) Uncertain

(C) 30

Questions 38–39 refer to the following.

The Genetic Code

(Based on Messenger RNA Codons)

First Base	U	C	A	G	Third Base
U	Phenylalanine	Serine	Tyrosine	Cysteine	U
	Phenylalanine	Serine	Tyrosine	Cysteine	C
	Leucine	Serine	Stop	Stop	A
	Leucine	Serine	Stop	Tryptophan	G
C	Leucine	Proline	Histidine	Arginine	U
	Leucine	Proline	Histidine	Arginine	C
	Leucine	Proline	Glutamine	Arginine	A
	Leucine	Proline	Glutamine	Arginine	G
A	Isoleucine	Threonine	Asparagine	Serine	U
	Isoleucine	Threonine	Asparagine	Serine	C
	Isoleucine	Threonine	Lysine	Arginine	A
Start	Methionine	Threonine	Lysine	Arginine	C
G	Valine	Alanine	Aspartic acid	Glycine	U
	Valine	Alanine	Aspartic acid	Glycine	C
	Valine	Alanine	Glutamic acid	Glycine	A
	Valine	Alanine	Glutamic acid	Glycine	G

38. Given the genetic code and the sequence of bases on a sense strand of DNA is 3' CAT TAG CAT TAG 5', what would the two types of amino acids be in the translated amino acid chain?

   (A) Isoleucine, leucine   (D) Valine, threonine

   (B) Isoleucine, threonine   (E) Valine, methionine

   (C) Valine, isoleucine

39. If a mutation results in the substitution of C for G in the DNA triplet 3' ACG 5', then the amino acid _____ instead of the amino acid _____ would be built into the amino acid chain during translation.

   (A) leucine, arginine   (D) tryptophan, cysteine

   (B) tryptophan, arginine   (E) arginine, leucine

   (C) tryptophan, proline

Questions 40–41 refer to the following.

ABO Blood Group
Agglutination Results

Individual	Antiserum	
	Anti-A	**Anti-B**
1	+	−
2	−	−
3	+	−
4	−	+
5	+	+

40. From the results shown above, which individual has blood group O?

   (A) 1   (D) 4

   (B) 2   (E) 5

   (C) 3

41. Which individual above has genotype $I^A I^B$?

   (A) 1   (D) 4

   (B) 2   (E) 5

   (C) 3

Questions 42–44 refer to the following figure.

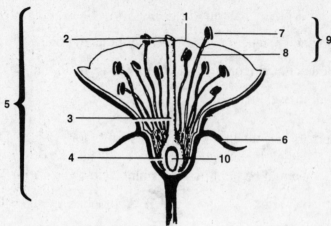

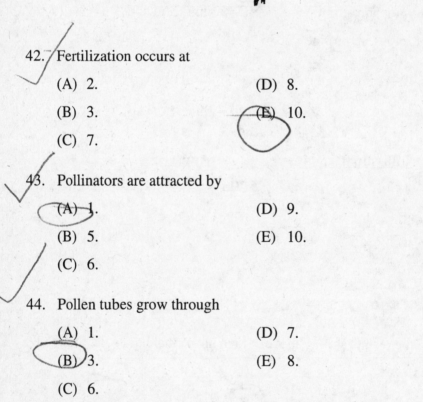

42. Fertilization occurs at

    (A) 2.   (D) 8.

    (B) 3.   (E) 10.

    (C) 7.

43. Pollinators are attracted by

    (A) 1.   (D) 9.

    (B) 5.   (E) 10.

    (C) 6.

44. Pollen tubes grow through

    (A) 1.   (D) 7.

    (B) 3.   (E) 8.

    (C) 6.

Questions 45–48 refer to the following.

The effect of various altitudes on the partial pressure of oxygen (P_{O_2}), the percentage of blood by volume occupied by corpuscles, and the percent of saturation of hemoglobin at various oxygen partial pressures at 38°C are shown in the graph and table.

The effect of altitude on P_{O_2}:

Altitude (ft. above sea level)	P_{O_2} in arterial blood (mm Hg)	% Red blood cells
0	100	46%
2,000	92	48%
4,000	85	51%
6,000	79	53%
8,000	74	56%
10,000	69	58%
20,000	35	61%
30,000	19	

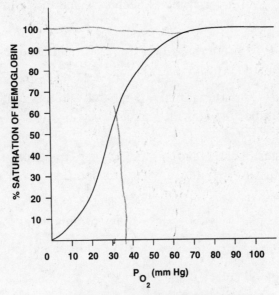

OXYHEMOGLOBIN DISSOCIATION AT 38°C

 45. What would the approximate percent of saturation of hemoglobin with O_2 be when the oxygen partial pressure (P_{O_2}) in arterial blood equals 100 mm Hg?

(A) 40

(B) 50

(C) 75

(D) 90

(E) 100

46. Everything else being equal, what would the approximate percent of saturation of arterial blood hemoglobin with O_2 be at an elevation of 20,000 feet?

(A) 40

(B) 50

(C) 70

(D) 90

(E) 100

47. Which one of the following statements would be true at higher elevations?

(A) The P_{O_2} in arterial blood increases but the number of red blood corpuscles remains the same.

(B) The P_{O_2} in arterial blood decreases and so does the number of red blood corpuscles.

(C) The P_{O_2} in arterial blood decreases and the number of red blood corpuscles increases.

(D) The P_{O_2} in arterial blood increases and so does the number of red blood corpuscles.

(E) The P_{O_2} in arterial blood decreases and the number of red blood corpuscles remains the same.

48. The greatest percentage of the oxygen transport in blood occurs in conjunction with the oxygen transporting pigment, hemoglobin, in the

(A) plasma.

(B) platelets.

(C) red blood cells.

(D) thrombocytes.

(E) white blood cells.

Questions 49–50 refer to the following graph.

Use the data on the average height of males and females from birth to age 18 shown in the following graph to answer the questions.

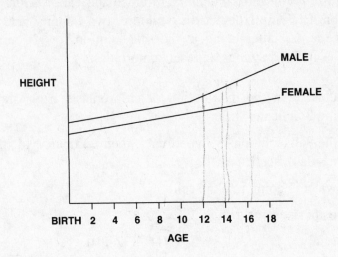

HEIGHT

MALE

FEMALE

BIRTH 2 4 6 8 10 12 14 16 18

AGE

49. The average height data in the graph indicates that

(A) females are shorter than males at all ages.

(B) males increase in height faster than females between ages 10 and 12.

(C) most females are shorter than 160 cm.

(D) males continue to grow in height longer than females.

(E) females increase in height faster than males between ages 14 and 16.

50. Beyond age 6 the greatest increase in average height of males occurs between what age groups?

(A) 6 and 8   (D) 12 and 14

(B) 8 and 10   (E) 14 and 16

(C) 10 and 12

Questions 51–52 refer to the following.

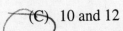
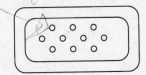
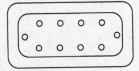
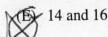
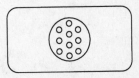

DRAWING 1   DRAWING 2   DRAWING 3

Drawing 1 shows an *Elodea* plant cell immediately after being placed in a salt solution. Drawing 2 depicts the cell after two minutes, and drawing 3 represents the cell after being in the salt solution for six minutes. The small circles in the drawings represent chloroplasts.

51. The change in the distribution of chloroplasts from drawing 1 to drawing 3 indicates that

    I.   the salt solution is hypertonic when compared to the solution inside the cell.

    II. water is going into the cell.

    III. osmosis is occurring.

    (A) I only.   (D) I and III.

    (B) II only.   (E) II and III.

    (C) III only.

52. The change in the distribution of chloroplasts from drawing 1 to drawing 3 indicates all of the following EXCEPT

    (A) the solution inside the cell is hypotonic relative to the salt solution.

    (B) osmosis is occurring.

    (C) the cell membrane is contracting.

    (D) water is leaving the cell.

    (E) drawing 2 shows the *Elodea* cell in an isotonic solution.

Questions 53–54 refer to the following graph.

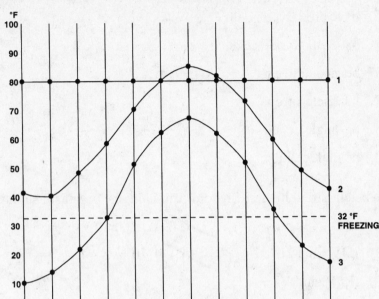

MEAN MONTHLY TEMPERATURE

53. Line 2 on the graph is representative of a city in a

(A) polar evergreen forest.

(B) temperate deciduous forest.

(C) tropical rainforest.

(D) tropical desert.

(E) polar grassland.

54. The number of species of breeding birds in the location represented by line 3 on the graph is 80; the location of line 2 has 200 breeding bird species; and the location of line 1 has 1,110 breeding bird species. Looking at the data, it can be suggested that the most important reason for having a high diversity of organisms is

(A) consistent, high temperatures throughout the year.

(B) frost-free temperatures and abundant precipitation throughout the year.

(C) high competition among species.

(D) climate stability over long periods of time.

(E) the high productivity of the ecosystem.

Questions 55–58 refer to the following classification attributes.

I.   have prokaryotic cells.

II. have eukaryotic cells.

III. be an autotroph.

IV. be a heterotroph.

V.   be single celled.

VI. be multicellular.

55. To be classified in the Kingdom Animalia, the organism should

(A) II, IV, and V.

(B) I, IV, and VI.

(C) II, IV, and VI.

(D) II, III, and VI.

(E) I, III, and VI.

56. To be classified in the Kingdom Monera, the organism should

(A) I, III or IV, and V.

(B) I, IV, and VI.

(C) II, III, and V.

(D) II, III, or IV.

(E) I, IV, and V.

57. To be classified in the Kingdom Plantae, the organism should

(A) II, III, and V.

(B) II, III, or IV.

(C) I, III, and VI.

(D) II, III, and VI.

(E) II, V, or VI.

58. To be classified in the Kingdom Fungi, the organism should

(A) I, V, or VI.

(B) II, III, and VI.

(C) I, IV, and VI.

(D) II, IV, and V.

(E) II, V, or VI.

Questions 59–60 refer to the following evolutionary inventions.

In Antarctica there are 94 species of cold water fish called notothenioids.

I. Antifreeze proteins

II. Lighter skeletons and scales

III. No red blood cells

IV. Added layers of fat

59. Millions of years ago, only thick-bodied, bottom-feeding notothenioids swam the icy waters of Antarctica. Which evolutionary
change(s) allowed these ghostly-white fish to live in icy-cold waters?

(A) I only.   (D) II and IV.

(B) III only.   (E) I, III, and IV.

(C) I and III.

60. The ancient, bottom-dwelling, notothenioids lost their swim bladder.
In order to radiate and exploit more vertical habitats, what did some
notothenioids have to develop?

(A) I only.   (D) II and IV.

(B) III only.   (E) I, III, and IV.

(C) I and III.

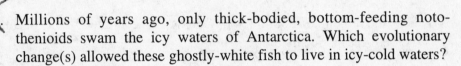

If you are taking the Biology-M test, continue with questions 81–100.
Be sure to start this section of the test by filling in oval 81 on your answer
sheet.

BIOLOGY-M SECTION

81. The movement of sodium ions across the cell membrane during a nerve impulse occurs by

    I.   diffusion.

    II. osmosis.

    III. active transport.

    (A) I only.   (D) I and II.

    (B) II only.   (E) I and III.

    (C) III only.

82. The oxygen that is involved in photosynthesis

    (A) is an end product.

    (B) is used to make ATP. $6CO_2 + 6O_2 +$

    (C) is a raw material for glucose.

    (D) captures the energy from sunlight.

    (E) is needed for NADPH production.

83. Cells usually convert carbohydrate molecules into energy-currency molecules of

    (A) ADP.   (D) oxygen.

    (B) ATP.   (E) starch.

    (C) glucose.

84. During exercise

    (A) ADP yields ATP plus P plus energy release.

    (B) ADP yields ATP plus P plus energy storage.

    (C) ATP yields ADP plus P plus energy release.

    (D) ATP yields ADP plus P plus energy storage.

    (E) P plus ADP yields ATP plus energy release.

85. Which characteristic differentiates RNA from DNA? RNA

    (A) contains the base uracil.

    (B) has a phosphate group.

    (C) has five bases.

    (D) is double-stranded.

    (E) lacks a sugar in its nucleotide.

Questions 86–89 refer to the following diagram.

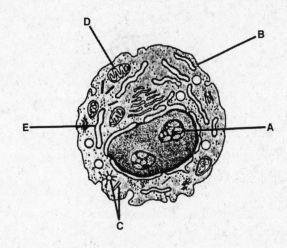

86. Large amounts of RNA are synthesized in the structure that is labeled

    (A) A.   (D) D.

    (B) B.   (E) E.

    (C) C.

87. Internal transport is possible in this cell due to the structure that is labeled

(A) A.   (D) D.

(B) B.   (E) E.

(C) C.

88. Surrounded by astral rays is the structure that is labeled

(A) A.   (D) D.

(B) B.   (E) E.

(C) C.

89. ATP molecules are generated by the structure that is labeled

(A) A.   (D) D.

(B) B.   (E) E.

(C) C.

90. A genotype AaBBccDd produces _____ kinds of gametes genetically by independent assortment.

(A) two   (D) eight

(B) four   (E) twelve

(C) six

91. A person develops mitochondrial myopathy in the cells of the heart. In these cells, this disease specifically affects

(A) atoms and energy use.

(B) atoms and storage capacity.

(C) molecules and transport.

(D) organelles and energy use.

(E) organelles and storage capacity.

92. All of the following statements apply to carbohydrates EXCEPT

(A) they contain C:H:O in a 1:2:1 ratio.

(B) they are the primary energy source for living things.

(C) they are made of glycerol.

(D) they may form polysaccharides.

(E) they are organic compounds.

93. The formation of a peptide bond involves

I. two monosaccharides.

II. two amino acids.

III. a condensation reaction.

(A) I only.   (D) I and III.

(B) II only.   (E) II and III.

(C) III only.

94. The scientific name of a dog is a *Canis dingo*. This name represents its

(A) class and order.   (D) kingdom and phylum.

(B) family and genus.   (E) phylum and species.

(C) genus and species.

95. A person develops a lactose intolerance. This condition specifically involves the ability to digest a

(A) disaccharide in the small intestine.

(B) disaccharide in the stomach.

(C) monosaccharide in the large intestine.

(D) polysaccharide in the oral cavity.

(E) polysaccharide in the large intestine.

96. Saturated fatty acids

(A) are the structural building blocks of carbohydrates.

(B) have many hydrogens on carbon chains.

(C) compose sugars and starches.

(D) generally store less energy than protein.

(E) store small amounts of energy.

Questions 97–98 refer to the following.

This is the arrangement used and the initial contents of five beaker and sac combinations.

Set Up	Beaker Contents	Sac Contents
1	Water	Starch + Amylase + Iodine
2	Starch + Water	Amylase + Iodine
3	Water	Starch + Boiled Amylase + Iodine
4	Amylase + Water	Starch + Iodine
5	Water	Amylase + Iodine

97. After 45 minutes, in which setup would you expect the beaker contents to show a positive test for sugar when heated with Benedict's reagent?

(A) 1

(B) 2

(C) 3

(D) 4

(E) 5

98. In which of the setups would the sac contents be black in color at the start?

(A) 1 only.

(B) 2 only.

(C) 4 only.

(D) 1 and 4.

(E) 1, 3, and 4.

Questions 99–100 refer to the following.

In the lab, an experiment is designed based on the equation $2H_2O_2 \rightarrow 2H_2O + O_2$. This equation represents a chemical change that occurs in liver cells. All of these substances are found in a test tube and studied in the experiment.

99. Select the correct statement about the chemical reaction studied in this experiment.

(A) Catalase is the reactant.

(B) Hydrogen peroxide is a product.

(C) Oxygen is a reactant.

DETAILED EXPLANATIONS OF ANSWERS

PRACTICE TEST 6

BIOLOGY CORE SECTION

1. **(C)**
The Law of Independent Assortment states that each character for a trait operates as a unit and the distribution of one pair of factors is independent of another pair of factors linked on different chromosomes. If you are studying two traits on two different chromosomes, such as texture of hair (curly is dominant; straight is recessive) on chromosome 1 and color of eyes (brown is dominant; blue is recessive) on chromosome 2, it is possible to have 4 different combinations of alleles in the sperm or egg after meiosis. For example, a parent that has a dominant and recessive allele for both traits can have the following allele combinations in the sperm or egg: curly hair, brown eyes; curly hair, blue eyes; straight hair, brown eyes; or straight hair, blue eyes.

2. **(B)**
Gregor Mendel discovered that a dominant allele masked the effect of a recessive allele. Alleles are different forms of a gene. An example would be to cross plants with purple flowers with plants with white flowers. All the plants from the cross were purple. The purple color was produced by a dominant allele.

3. **(E)**
There are three alleles for the gene that expresses human blood type. One allele will produce antigen A; another allele will produce antigen B; and the third allele will produce no antigens (O). There are six combinations of alleles for human blood type: AO or AA (type A); BO or BB (type B); AB (type AB); and OO (type O).

4. **(D)** 5. **(C)** 6. **(E)**
On the right side of the heart, blood from the body flows into the right atrium through the right atrioventricular or tricuspid valve to the right ventricle. The right ventricle then pumps the blood through the pul-

monary artery to the lungs. On the left side of the heart, the blood comes from the lungs through the pulmonary veins into the left atrium through the left atrioventricular bicuspid valve to the left ventricle. The left ventricle then pumps the blood into the aorta which takes blood to the body.

7. **(E)**   8. **(A)**   9. **(B)**
A scavenger is an animal that feeds on dead animals.

A commensal is an organism that benefits by existing in a symbiotic relationship with another type of organism without harming or benefiting it.

A parasite is an organism that gains its existence by feeding on and, to some degree, harming another type of living organism, its host. A predator seeks and kills another animal for food. The animal which is hunted by a predator is called the prey.

10. **(D)**   11. **(B)**
The various phases of mitosis have characteristics which allow us to identify them. During interphase, the nucleus is metabolically very active, chromosomal duplication is occurring, and the chromosomes appear as vague, dispersed thread-like structures, and are referred to as chromatin material. Prophase begins when the chromatin threads begin to condense and appear as a tangled mass of threads within the nucleus. During metaphase the chromosomes are lined-up along the metaphase plate or equator of the cell. In anaphase, the chromosomes are pulled away from the equator of the cell. In telophase, the chromosomes relax, elongate, and return to the resting condition in which only chromatin threads are visible. A nuclear membrane forms around each new daughter nucleus.

12. **(E)**   13. **(D)**
Grasslands are characterized by short, herbaceous (grassy) plants. The taiga has a relatively long harsh winter, cool summer, and an abundance of pine or evergreen trees.

14. **(E)**   15. **(B)**
Interferons are proteins produced by virus infected cells spread to neighboring cells to cause inhibition of virus multiplication.

An antibody (immunoglobulin) is a glycoprotein produced in the body of a vertebrate in response to an antigen (e.g., a component of a microorganism, a pollen grain, a fungal spore, food, etc.). The antibody usually reacts with the antigen. For example, antioxins are antibodies that react with toxins.

Natural, semisynthetic, and synthetic antibiotics are used today as drugs mainly in treating infectious diseases caused by bacteria. Generally, they are effective in killing or inhibiting microorganisms at very low concentrations.

16. **(D)**   17. **(E)**
All bacteria have prokaryotic cells. Some bacteria are autotrophic (photosynthetic, chemosynthetic). Autotrophs can make organic molecules from simple inorganic molecules and an outside energy source. Others are heterotrophic (parasitic, saprophytic, etc.). Heterotrophs require an organic carbon source for energy.

All animals are heterotrophs with eukaryotic cells.

18. **(E)**
Among the vascular plants and bryophytes, only the flowering plants and conifers have pollen and seeds. Two adaptations, pollination and growth of the pollen tube, enable flowering plants to accomplish fertilization in the absence of external water. Their seeds, which can remain dormant for extended periods of time, are adapted to protect and transport the embryonic plants contained in them.

19. **(D)**
They, a perch, a frog, and a rabbit, are all classified as vertebrates because of their backbones of vertebrae. Of the animals that are listed, only rabbits have four-chambered hearts and are warm-blooded. Both rabbits and adult frogs (three-chambered heart) use lungs for gas exchange, while perch (two-chambered heart) and frog tadpoles have gills.

20. **(D)**
A colorblind male (X^cY) and a carrier female (X^CX) can produce daughters of two genotypes: X^CX^c and X^cX^c.

21. **(D)**
In a second exposure to an antigen, the concentration (titer) of antibody produced is greater and production time is shorter than in a first exposure. This is the strategy behind administering a booster injection to a person. It rapidly increases antibody production.

22. **(A)**
Carbon dioxide is incorporated into organic compounds during the Calvin cycle (dark reactions of photosynthesis) when it combines with ribulose diphosphate to form a sugar.

23. **(E)**

   When populations of a single ancestral type change over time to form several distinct species both divergent evolution and adaptive radiation have occurred.

24. **(E)**

   A yeast cell and an elephant cell are both eukaryotic. Neither contains chlorophyll. Thus, they must both be heterotrophic.

25. **(C)**

   While free swimming sperm cells are characteristic of ferns, in flowering plants a generative nucleus inside a pollen grain divides to form two nonmotile sperm which are brought close to the egg by pollination and growth of a pollen tube.

26. **(C)**

   Citric acid is formed when the acetyl group and oxaloacetate combine. Each of the acids listed is a component in the Krebs cycle.

27. **(C)**

   In the inheritance of a two allele system, the frequency of the two alleles (dominant versus recessive) is represented by the equation $p + q = 1$ and the frequencies of the genotypes (homozygous dominant versus heterozygous versus homozygous recessive) is represented by $p^2 + 2pq + q^2 = 1$. Since 1,600 out of 10,000 individuals sampled showed the recessive phenotype and are homozygous recessive, the frequency of the recessive genotype, q^2, is determined as follows: $q^2 = 1,600/10,000 = 0.16$ (or 16%). The frequency of the recessive allele, q, is determined by taking the square root of q^2:

   $$q = \sqrt{q^2} = \sqrt{.16} = .4$$ The frequency of the dominant allele, p, is determined by subtracting q from 1: $p = 1 - q = 1 - 0.4 = 0.6$.

   Finally, the frequency of homozygous dominant individuals, p^2, is determined by squaring p: $p^2 = 0.6^2 = 0.36$ (or 36%).

28. **(D)**

   The conversion of atmospheric nitrogen into substances generally usable by living organisms is termed nitrogen fixation.

29. **(E)**

   The crosses illustrated involve intermediate inheritance or incomplete dominance. Both the long, LL, and round, L^1L^1, phenotypes are homozygous. The heterozygous condition, LL^1, results in the oval phenotype. A cross between two long plants (LL × LL) would be expected to produce only long radishes.

30. **(C)**

Using a Punnett square illustrates this best.

	D	d
d	Dd	dd
d	Dd	dd

31. **(A)**

Cells of the apical meristem divide and subsequently elongate, thus increasing stem length. The cork cambium and vascular cambium result in growth in width or compensate for such growth. The pericycle is that group of cells which forms lateral roots. The endodermis gives the plant selective uptake of minerals from the soil.

32. **(E)**

Species diversity is greatest in tropical rainforests located on or near the equator.

33. **(B)**

Many biologists believe that eukaryotic cells evolved when formerly free-living prokaryotes established a symbiotic relationship. Perhaps one prokaryotic cell ingested another and instead of digesting it began to co-exist with it. Much of the evidence for the symbiont theory involves similarities between bacteria and two of the main organelles of eukaryotic cells: chloroplasts and mitochondria.

34. **(C)**

Oxytocin, which is produced by the hypothalamus and released from the posterior pituitary gland, stimulates milk ejection from the breasts and uterine muscle contraction both during and after childbirth.

35. **(C)**

All of the animals listed are vertebrates with a backbone consisting of vertebrae. Only the perch uses gills to breathe throughout its life. A frog begins life as a gill breathing tadpole which metamorphoses into a lung breathing adult. Finally, the heart of a perch consists of one atrium and one ventricle, the frog heart of two atria and one ventricle, and the four-chambered heart of crocodiles, robins, and foxes consists of two atria and two ventricles.

36. **(D)**
Note the peak of the high light intensity graph past 30°C.

37. **(E)**
Unless the base composition of the sense strand of DNA that codes for the mRNA is known, the answer cannot be determined with certainty. In addition, intron-coded RNA segments are not incorporated into mRNA.

38. **(C)**
The sequences of bases on the segment of mRNA transcribed would be 5' GUA AUC GUA AUC 3'. The codon "GUA" codes for the amino acid valine and the codon "AUC" codes for isoleucine.

39. **(D)**
The DNA triplet "ACG" is transcribed to the mRNA codon "UGC" which is, in turn, translated to the amino acid cysteine. If a mutation results in the substitution of C for G in the DNA triplet, the new DNA triplet "ACC" is transcribed to the mRNA codon "UGG" which is translated to the amino acid tryptophan.

40. **(B)**
Since an individual with type O has neither antigen A nor B in his/her red blood cells, agglutination will not occur in the presence of either anti-A or anti-B.

41. **(E)**
An individual with the genotype I^AI^B forms both A and B antigens. So, agglutination would occur in the presence of both anti-A and anti-B.

42. **(E)**   43. **(A)**   44. **(B)**
Number 10 is an ovule which contains an egg. The pollen tube grows down the style (3) to the ovary (4). The pollen tube penetrates the ovule and releases two sperm nuclei. One fertilizes the egg, the other fertilizes the polar nucleus.

The petal (1) is usually colored if pollinators are used to transfer pollen from the anther to the stigma (2).

Structure (5) is the entire female structure: the pistil or carpel.

45. **(E)**

   At a P_{O_2} of 100 mm Hg, hemoglobin is approximately 100 percent saturated. As the P_{O_2} decreases, the percent of saturation of hemoglobin decreases. Note the plateau of the graph at P_{O_2} of 100mm Hg.

46. **(C)**

   At an elevation of 20,000 feet, the P_{O_2} in arterial blood is 35 mm Hg and hemoglobin is approximately 70 percent saturated.

47. **(C)**

   As altitude increases, the P_{O_2} in arterial blood decreases and the percentage of blood by volume occupied by red blood cells (corpuscles) increases. The increase in red blood cell production and counts is an adaptation for higher altitudes.

48. **(C)**

   The bulk of the oxygen transport (about 97 percent) occurs in conjunction with hemoglobin located inside red blood cells. A small percentage of oxygen is dissolved in the plasma.

49. **(D)**

   Note the growth spurt in males ages 12–16 years.

50. **(D)**

   Based on data in the table, the greatest increase in average height of males of 13 cm occurs between ages 12 and 14. The next greatest increase of 11 cm occurs between ages 8 and 10.

51. **(D)**   52. **(E)**

   Drawings 1, 2, and 3 show an *Elodea* plant cell losing water through the process of osmosis. The salt solution outside the cell is hypertonic, which means that there are more sodium and chlorine ions (solute) outside the cell than inside the cell. Hypotonic would be the opposite—less sodium and chlorine ions outside the cell than inside the cell. The water inside the cell is more concentrated and therefore, will diffuse out of the cell. Drawing 2 shows the chloroplasts being forced against the cell membrane as water leaves the cell. It leaves the cell and enters the hypertonic solution outside the cell. Drawing 3 shows the contracted cell membrane with the chloroplasts bunched together. The cell is now dehydrated. If the salt solution is replaced by distilled water, water will go into the cell, expanding the membrane.

53. **(B)**
    Line 2 is temperature data from Nashville, Tennessee which is in a temperate deciduous forest. Line 1 is characteristic of a tropical rainforest. The temperature changes very little throughout the year. It is interesting to contrast a tropical rainforest with a tropical desert. The temperature of a tropical desert throughout the year has a range of about 20°F. This is because temperatures will fluctuate more in dry air. Line 3 is data from Moscow, Russia which is in a polar evergreen forest. The data from a polar grassland would have 8–9 months below freezing with January and February getting minus 10° to 20°F below zero.

54. **(A)**
    Only temperature data is given; therefore, the only appropriate answer that related to just temperature was a consistent, high temperature throughout the year. Abundant precipitation, a stable climate, high competition, and high productivity are also important for explaining high diversity. But, the most important reason for high diversity is high, frost-free temperatures.

55. **(C)**
    Animals are multicellular organisms with eukaryotic cells. Eukaryotic cells have a nucleus, multiple chromosomes, and many other cell structures like mitochondria. They obtain their nutrition through consumption of other organisms or their by-products (heterotroph).

56. **(A)**
    Monera are single-celled organisms with prokaryotic cells. Prokaryotic cells have no nucleus, no multiple copies of chromosomes, and no mitochondria. They obtain their nutrition through consumption (heterotroph), absorption (heterotroph), or photosynthesis (autotroph).

57. **(D)**
    Plants are multicellular organisms with eukaryotic cells. Eukaryotic cells have a nucleus, multiple chromosomes, and many other cell structures like mitochondria. They obtain their nutrition through photosynthesis (autotroph).

58. **(E)**
    Fungi are single-celled (yeast) or multicellular organisms (molds, mildew, mushrooms) with eukaryotic cells. Eukaryotic cells have a nucleus, multiple chromosomes, and many other cell structures like mitochondria. They obtain their nutrition by secreting digestive enzymes and then absorbing nutrients (heterotroph).

59. **(C)**   60. **(D)**

Scientists are just now discovering the wide variety of notothenioid fish living in the frigid waters of Antarctica. This is an excellent opportunity to study the adaptive radiation of the notothenioids. Today, notothenioids vary from bottom-feeders to small schooling herring-like fish to large hark-like creatures. The notothenioids have two evolutionary inventions for living in the icy waters. First, they no longer have red blood cells. This gives them a ghostly white appearance and keeps the blood from becoming too viscous in the frigid waters. Oxygen is dissolved in their plasma. Second, they have evolved antifreeze proteins to keep their bodies from freezing. Fish living nearest to the icy surface have about twice as much antifreeze in their blood. Since the early bottom-feeding notothenioids lost their swim bladders, later species had to add layers of fat (lighter than water), lighter skeletons, and lighter scales to exploit a variety of environmental niches.

BIOLOGY-M SECTION

81. **(E)**

Sodium is found in higher concentrations on the outside of the cell membrane. When the nerve is stimulated, the membrane becomes more permeable to sodium, and the sodium moves along the concentration gradient into the cell. Thus, the beginning of a nerve impulse is marked by sodium diffusing into the cell.

Na^+ (outside +)   (outside –)

_____   _____

K^+ (inside –) Na^+ and K^+ (inside +)

_____   _____

At the end of a nerve impulse, the positive charge has been restored to the membrane. However, sodium that diffused into the cell must be removed and the potassium which diffused out must be returned to the inside of the cell.

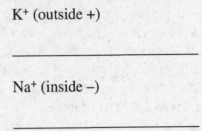

K⁺ (outside +)

_____

Na⁺ (inside −)

_____

The sodium is pumped out and the potassium is pumped in, using energy in the form of ATP. Thus, the end of the action potential is marked by a restoration of the sodium to its proper place by active transport. Therefore, sodium moves across the cell membrane during a nerve impulse by both diffusion and active transport.

82. **(A)**
The reaction for photosynthesis is:

$$6\ CO_2 + 12\ H_2O + light \rightarrow C_6H_{12}O_6 + 6\ H_2O + 6\ O_2$$

(carbon   (glucose)
dioxide)

Note that O_2 is a product on the right of the equation.

83. **(B)**
ATP, adenosine triphosphate, is the universal "energy currency" of cells. Metabolic pathways of glycolysis, the Krebs cycle, and pathways leading to them, convert molecules not immediately usable into a form that is "spendable."

84. **(C)**
ATP, adenosine triphosphate, is the immediate source of energy for the cell. Chemical bonds store energy. The breakdown of ATP, into ADP plus P, releases energy from the terminally-bonded phosphate of ATP. The breakage of this terminal bond releases energy.

85. **(A)**
Both nucleic acids have adenine, cytosine, or guanine as three of their four possible nucleotide bases. However, their fourth bases differ—DNA contains thymine, and RNA contains uracil. Both have nucleotide phosphate groups. The other statements about RNA are untrue.

86. **(A)**

Structure A, the nucleolus, is the site of a great deal of RNA synthesis, especially the synthesis of rRNA (ribosomal RNA).

87. **(E)**

The endoplasmic reticulum (ER) offers a series of channels throughout the cell cytoplasm for transport. It thus serves as a microcirculatory system.

88. **(C)**

The centrioles are two cylinder-shaped organelles in the cytoplasm that are close to the nucleus. They are involved with spindle formation during cell reproduction. The spindle fibers attach to chromosomes, pulling and manipulating them during the division process. At all times, the centrioles are surrounded by short segments of microtubules, also referred to as astral rays.

89. **(D)**

This cell organelle is the mitochondrion. It is the site of cell respiration, where glucose is oxidized. Released energy is coupled to the formation of adenosine triphosphate, ATP. This universal energy currency is then spent by cells to run their metabolic activities: muscle contraction, active transport, etc.

90. **(B)**

The four sex cells produced are ABcD, ABcd, aBcD, and aBcd. The genotype AaBBccDd has two heterozygous gene pairs, accounting for the variability. The formula 2^n is used to predict the number of genetically different sex cells. The exponent n is the number of heterozygous gene pairs. 2^n equals four. The following branching pattern is used to derive the identity of the sex cells.

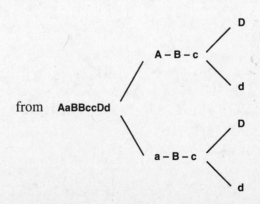

91. **(D)**

Organelles and energy use are specifically affected. The mitochondrion is an organelle in the cell, including heart cells, and is the site of chemical reactions that provide the cell with energy. This organelle has the enzyme system to extract energy from nutrients such as glucose.

92. **(C)**

For this question you must know the structural and functional characteristics of carbohydrates. Carbohydrates are organic compounds, or carbon compounds. They contain carbon, hydrogen, and oxygen in a 1:2:1 ratio. The simple sugars are the basic unit of carbohydrates, usually containing three to six carbon atoms. These simple sugars, or monosaccharides, may be combined to form starches, or polysaccharides. Carbohydrates, once broken down, are energy sources for living things. Glycerol is not a raw material for carbohydrates, but rather is necessary for the formation of fats.

93. **(E)**

Knowing the answer to this question depends upon your ability to recognize the fact that a peptide bond is the bond that forms between two amino acids. This bond forms because an –OH group is removed from the acid portion (–COOH) of one amino acid and a –H is removed from the amino portion (–NH$_2$) of the second amino acid. The –OH and –H combine to form H$_2$O. This linking of amino acids is called a condensation reaction. (Note: R is different for each amino acid).

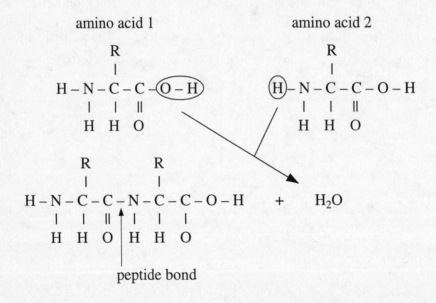

94. **(C)**

The binomial scientific name of an organism is its genus (e.g., *Canus*) and species name (e.g., *dingo*). The genus name is written first and capitalized. The species name is written second and is not capitalized. For example, the scientific name for humans is *Homo sapiens.*

95. **(A)**

Lactose is a disaccharide that can be broken down into two mono-saccharides, glucose and galactose. This normally occurs in the small intestine. It is controlled enzymatically by lactase. During a lactose intolerance, the enzyme is missing and this ability to produce a chemical change on lactose is lost.

96. **(B)**

The term "saturated" refers to saturation of the fatty acid's carbon chain with hydrogen. These hydrogens are a source of energy when removed by oxidation during metabolism. Fatty acids, building blocks of fats, contain more hydrogen per gram than the other listed molecule types, such as carbohydrates and proteins.

97. **(A)**

Neither starch, a polysaccharide, or amylase, a protein, can pass through the sac membrane. However, small sugar molecules can. Digestion of starch to simple sugars that pass through the sac membrane and react with Benedict's reagent occurs in Set Up #1.

98. **(E)**

Starch, in combination with iodine, turns black.

99. **(D)**

In this reaction, the enzyme catalase increases the rate of converting the reactant hydrogen peroxide into the products, water and oxygen gas. The production of bubbles, oxygen gas, is evidence that the enzyme is converting a reactant into products.

100. **(B)**

The rate of most enzymatic reactions is optimal at 37°C. At 50°C, the proteins of an enzyme denature, meaning that they decompose physically. This decreases the concentration of the enzyme and reduces its activity. Removal of the products, water or oxygen gas, pulls the reaction to the right, increasing the reaction rate. Adding hydrogen peroxide increases the reaction rate, as more reactant is available for this chemical change.

SAT Biology E/M
Practice Test 1

ANSWER SHEET

BIOLOGY CORE SECTION

1. Ⓐ Ⓑ Ⓒ Ⓓ Ⓔ
2. Ⓐ Ⓑ Ⓒ Ⓓ Ⓔ
3. Ⓐ Ⓑ Ⓒ Ⓓ Ⓔ
4. Ⓐ Ⓑ Ⓒ Ⓓ Ⓔ
5. Ⓐ Ⓑ Ⓒ Ⓓ Ⓔ
6. Ⓐ Ⓑ Ⓒ Ⓓ Ⓔ
7. Ⓐ Ⓑ Ⓒ Ⓓ Ⓔ
8. Ⓐ Ⓑ Ⓒ Ⓓ Ⓔ
9. Ⓐ Ⓑ Ⓒ Ⓓ Ⓔ
10. Ⓐ Ⓑ Ⓒ Ⓓ Ⓔ
11. Ⓐ Ⓑ Ⓒ Ⓓ Ⓔ
12. Ⓐ Ⓑ Ⓒ Ⓓ Ⓔ
13. Ⓐ Ⓑ Ⓒ Ⓓ Ⓔ
14. Ⓐ Ⓑ Ⓒ Ⓓ Ⓔ
15. Ⓐ Ⓑ Ⓒ Ⓓ Ⓔ
16. Ⓐ Ⓑ Ⓒ Ⓓ Ⓔ
17. Ⓐ Ⓑ Ⓒ Ⓓ Ⓔ
18. Ⓐ Ⓑ Ⓒ Ⓓ Ⓔ
19. Ⓐ Ⓑ Ⓒ Ⓓ Ⓔ
20. Ⓐ Ⓑ Ⓒ Ⓓ Ⓔ

21. Ⓐ Ⓑ Ⓒ Ⓓ Ⓔ
22. Ⓐ Ⓑ Ⓒ Ⓓ Ⓔ
23. Ⓐ Ⓑ Ⓒ Ⓓ Ⓔ
24. Ⓐ Ⓑ Ⓒ Ⓓ Ⓔ
25. Ⓐ Ⓑ Ⓒ Ⓓ Ⓔ
26. Ⓐ Ⓑ Ⓒ Ⓓ Ⓔ
27. Ⓐ Ⓑ Ⓒ Ⓓ Ⓔ
28. Ⓐ Ⓑ Ⓒ Ⓓ Ⓔ
29. Ⓐ Ⓑ Ⓒ Ⓓ Ⓔ
30. Ⓐ Ⓑ Ⓒ Ⓓ Ⓔ
31. Ⓐ Ⓑ Ⓒ Ⓓ Ⓔ
32. Ⓐ Ⓑ Ⓒ Ⓓ Ⓔ
33. Ⓐ Ⓑ Ⓒ Ⓓ Ⓔ
34. Ⓐ Ⓑ Ⓒ Ⓓ Ⓔ
35. Ⓐ Ⓑ Ⓒ Ⓓ Ⓔ
36. Ⓐ Ⓑ Ⓒ Ⓓ Ⓔ
37. Ⓐ Ⓑ Ⓒ Ⓓ Ⓔ
38. Ⓐ Ⓑ Ⓒ Ⓓ Ⓔ
39. Ⓐ Ⓑ Ⓒ Ⓓ Ⓔ
40. Ⓐ Ⓑ Ⓒ Ⓓ Ⓔ

41. Ⓐ Ⓑ Ⓒ Ⓓ Ⓔ
42. Ⓐ Ⓑ Ⓒ Ⓓ Ⓔ
43. Ⓐ Ⓑ Ⓒ Ⓓ Ⓔ
44. Ⓐ Ⓑ Ⓒ Ⓓ Ⓔ
45. Ⓐ Ⓑ Ⓒ Ⓓ Ⓔ
46. Ⓐ Ⓑ Ⓒ Ⓓ Ⓔ
47. Ⓐ Ⓑ Ⓒ Ⓓ Ⓔ
48. Ⓐ Ⓑ Ⓒ Ⓓ Ⓔ
49. Ⓐ Ⓑ Ⓒ Ⓓ Ⓔ
50. Ⓐ Ⓑ Ⓒ Ⓓ Ⓔ
51. Ⓐ Ⓑ Ⓒ Ⓓ Ⓔ
52. Ⓐ Ⓑ Ⓒ Ⓓ Ⓔ
53. Ⓐ Ⓑ Ⓒ Ⓓ Ⓔ
54. Ⓐ Ⓑ Ⓒ Ⓓ Ⓔ
55. Ⓐ Ⓑ Ⓒ Ⓓ Ⓔ
56. Ⓐ Ⓑ Ⓒ Ⓓ Ⓔ
57. Ⓐ Ⓑ Ⓒ Ⓓ Ⓔ
58. Ⓐ Ⓑ Ⓒ Ⓓ Ⓔ
59. Ⓐ Ⓑ Ⓒ Ⓓ Ⓔ
60. Ⓐ Ⓑ Ⓒ Ⓓ Ⓔ

BIOLOGY-E SECTION

61. Ⓐ Ⓑ Ⓒ Ⓓ Ⓔ
62. Ⓐ Ⓑ Ⓒ Ⓓ Ⓔ
63. Ⓐ Ⓑ Ⓒ Ⓓ Ⓔ
64. Ⓐ Ⓑ Ⓒ Ⓓ Ⓔ
65. Ⓐ Ⓑ Ⓒ Ⓓ Ⓔ
66. Ⓐ Ⓑ Ⓒ Ⓓ Ⓔ
67. Ⓐ Ⓑ Ⓒ Ⓓ Ⓔ

68. Ⓐ Ⓑ Ⓒ Ⓓ Ⓔ
69. Ⓐ Ⓑ Ⓒ Ⓓ Ⓔ
70. Ⓐ Ⓑ Ⓒ Ⓓ Ⓔ
71. Ⓐ Ⓑ Ⓒ Ⓓ Ⓔ
72. Ⓐ Ⓑ Ⓒ Ⓓ Ⓔ
73. Ⓐ Ⓑ Ⓒ Ⓓ Ⓔ
74. Ⓐ Ⓑ Ⓒ Ⓓ Ⓔ

75. Ⓐ Ⓑ Ⓒ Ⓓ Ⓔ
76. Ⓐ Ⓑ Ⓒ Ⓓ Ⓔ
77. Ⓐ Ⓑ Ⓒ Ⓓ Ⓔ
78. Ⓐ Ⓑ Ⓒ Ⓓ Ⓔ
79. Ⓐ Ⓑ Ⓒ Ⓓ Ⓔ
80. Ⓐ Ⓑ Ⓒ Ⓓ Ⓔ

SAT Biology E/M
Practice Test 2

ANSWER SHEET

BIOLOGY CORE SECTION

1. Ⓐ Ⓑ Ⓒ Ⓓ Ⓔ   21. Ⓐ Ⓑ Ⓒ Ⓓ Ⓔ   41. Ⓐ Ⓑ Ⓒ Ⓓ Ⓔ
2. Ⓐ Ⓑ Ⓒ Ⓓ Ⓔ   22. Ⓐ Ⓑ Ⓒ Ⓓ Ⓔ   42. Ⓐ Ⓑ Ⓒ Ⓓ Ⓔ
3. Ⓐ Ⓑ Ⓒ Ⓓ Ⓔ   23. Ⓐ Ⓑ Ⓒ Ⓓ Ⓔ   43. Ⓐ Ⓑ Ⓒ Ⓓ Ⓔ
4. Ⓐ Ⓑ Ⓒ Ⓓ Ⓔ   24. Ⓐ Ⓑ Ⓒ Ⓓ Ⓔ   44. Ⓐ Ⓑ Ⓒ Ⓓ Ⓔ
5. Ⓐ Ⓑ Ⓒ Ⓓ Ⓔ   25. Ⓐ Ⓑ Ⓒ Ⓓ Ⓔ   45. Ⓐ Ⓑ Ⓒ Ⓓ Ⓔ
6. Ⓐ Ⓑ Ⓒ Ⓓ Ⓔ   26. Ⓐ Ⓑ Ⓒ Ⓓ Ⓔ   46. Ⓐ Ⓑ Ⓒ Ⓓ Ⓔ
7. Ⓐ Ⓑ Ⓒ Ⓓ Ⓔ   27. Ⓐ Ⓑ Ⓒ Ⓓ Ⓔ   47. Ⓐ Ⓑ Ⓒ Ⓓ Ⓔ
8. Ⓐ Ⓑ Ⓒ Ⓓ Ⓔ   28. Ⓐ Ⓑ Ⓒ Ⓓ Ⓔ   48. Ⓐ Ⓑ Ⓒ Ⓓ Ⓔ
9. Ⓐ Ⓑ Ⓒ Ⓓ Ⓔ   29. Ⓐ Ⓑ Ⓒ Ⓓ Ⓔ   49. Ⓐ Ⓑ Ⓒ Ⓓ Ⓔ
10. Ⓐ Ⓑ Ⓒ Ⓓ Ⓔ   30. Ⓐ Ⓑ Ⓒ Ⓓ Ⓔ   50. Ⓐ Ⓑ Ⓒ Ⓓ Ⓔ
11. Ⓐ Ⓑ Ⓒ Ⓓ Ⓔ   31. Ⓐ Ⓑ Ⓒ Ⓓ Ⓔ   51. Ⓐ Ⓑ Ⓒ Ⓓ Ⓔ
12. Ⓐ Ⓑ Ⓒ Ⓓ Ⓔ   32. Ⓐ Ⓑ Ⓒ Ⓓ Ⓔ   52. Ⓐ Ⓑ Ⓒ Ⓓ Ⓔ
13. Ⓐ Ⓑ Ⓒ Ⓓ Ⓔ   33. Ⓐ Ⓑ Ⓒ Ⓓ Ⓔ   53. Ⓐ Ⓑ Ⓒ Ⓓ Ⓔ
14. Ⓐ Ⓑ Ⓒ Ⓓ Ⓔ   34. Ⓐ Ⓑ Ⓒ Ⓓ Ⓔ   54. Ⓐ Ⓑ Ⓒ Ⓓ Ⓔ
15. Ⓐ Ⓑ Ⓒ Ⓓ Ⓔ   35. Ⓐ Ⓑ Ⓒ Ⓓ Ⓔ   55. Ⓐ Ⓑ Ⓒ Ⓓ Ⓔ
16. Ⓐ Ⓑ Ⓒ Ⓓ Ⓔ   36. Ⓐ Ⓑ Ⓒ Ⓓ Ⓔ   56. Ⓐ Ⓑ Ⓒ Ⓓ Ⓔ
17. Ⓐ Ⓑ Ⓒ Ⓓ Ⓔ   37. Ⓐ Ⓑ Ⓒ Ⓓ Ⓔ   57. Ⓐ Ⓑ Ⓒ Ⓓ Ⓔ
18. Ⓐ Ⓑ Ⓒ Ⓓ Ⓔ   38. Ⓐ Ⓑ Ⓒ Ⓓ Ⓔ   58. Ⓐ Ⓑ Ⓒ Ⓓ Ⓔ
19. Ⓐ Ⓑ Ⓒ Ⓓ Ⓔ   39. Ⓐ Ⓑ Ⓒ Ⓓ Ⓔ   59. Ⓐ Ⓑ Ⓒ Ⓓ Ⓔ
20. Ⓐ Ⓑ Ⓒ Ⓓ Ⓔ   40. Ⓐ Ⓑ Ⓒ Ⓓ Ⓔ   60. Ⓐ Ⓑ Ⓒ Ⓓ Ⓔ

BIOLOGY-E SECTION

61. Ⓐ Ⓑ Ⓒ Ⓓ Ⓔ   68. Ⓐ Ⓑ Ⓒ Ⓓ Ⓔ   75. Ⓐ Ⓑ Ⓒ Ⓓ Ⓔ
62. Ⓐ Ⓑ Ⓒ Ⓓ Ⓔ   69. Ⓐ Ⓑ Ⓒ Ⓓ Ⓔ   76. Ⓐ Ⓑ Ⓒ Ⓓ Ⓔ
63. Ⓐ Ⓑ Ⓒ Ⓓ Ⓔ   70. Ⓐ Ⓑ Ⓒ Ⓓ Ⓔ   77. Ⓐ Ⓑ Ⓒ Ⓓ Ⓔ
64. Ⓐ Ⓑ Ⓒ Ⓓ Ⓔ   71. Ⓐ Ⓑ Ⓒ Ⓓ Ⓔ   78. Ⓐ Ⓑ Ⓒ Ⓓ Ⓔ
65. Ⓐ Ⓑ Ⓒ Ⓓ Ⓔ   72. Ⓐ Ⓑ Ⓒ Ⓓ Ⓔ   79. Ⓐ Ⓑ Ⓒ Ⓓ Ⓔ
66. Ⓐ Ⓑ Ⓒ Ⓓ Ⓔ   73. Ⓐ Ⓑ Ⓒ Ⓓ Ⓔ   80. Ⓐ Ⓑ Ⓒ Ⓓ Ⓔ
67. Ⓐ Ⓑ Ⓒ Ⓓ Ⓔ   74. Ⓐ Ⓑ Ⓒ Ⓓ Ⓔ

SAT Biology E/M
Practice Test 3

ANSWER SHEET

BIOLOGY CORE SECTION

1. Ⓐ Ⓑ Ⓒ Ⓓ Ⓔ
2. Ⓐ Ⓑ Ⓒ Ⓓ Ⓔ
3. Ⓐ Ⓑ Ⓒ Ⓓ Ⓔ
4. Ⓐ Ⓑ Ⓒ Ⓓ Ⓔ
5. Ⓐ Ⓑ Ⓒ Ⓓ Ⓔ
6. Ⓐ Ⓑ Ⓒ Ⓓ Ⓔ
7. Ⓐ Ⓑ Ⓒ Ⓓ Ⓔ
8. Ⓐ Ⓑ Ⓒ Ⓓ Ⓔ
9. Ⓐ Ⓑ Ⓒ Ⓓ Ⓔ
10. Ⓐ Ⓑ Ⓒ Ⓓ Ⓔ
11. Ⓐ Ⓑ Ⓒ Ⓓ Ⓔ
12. Ⓐ Ⓑ Ⓒ Ⓓ Ⓔ
13. Ⓐ Ⓑ Ⓒ Ⓓ Ⓔ
14. Ⓐ Ⓑ Ⓒ Ⓓ Ⓔ
15. Ⓐ Ⓑ Ⓒ Ⓓ Ⓔ
16. Ⓐ Ⓑ Ⓒ Ⓓ Ⓔ
17. Ⓐ Ⓑ Ⓒ Ⓓ Ⓔ
18. Ⓐ Ⓑ Ⓒ Ⓓ Ⓔ
19. Ⓐ Ⓑ Ⓒ Ⓓ Ⓔ
20. Ⓐ Ⓑ Ⓒ Ⓓ Ⓔ

21. Ⓐ Ⓑ Ⓒ Ⓓ Ⓔ
22. Ⓐ Ⓑ Ⓒ Ⓓ Ⓔ
23. Ⓐ Ⓑ Ⓒ Ⓓ Ⓔ
24. Ⓐ Ⓑ Ⓒ Ⓓ Ⓔ
25. Ⓐ Ⓑ Ⓒ Ⓓ Ⓔ
26. Ⓐ Ⓑ Ⓒ Ⓓ Ⓔ
27. Ⓐ Ⓑ Ⓒ Ⓓ Ⓔ
28. Ⓐ Ⓑ Ⓒ Ⓓ Ⓔ
29. Ⓐ Ⓑ Ⓒ Ⓓ Ⓔ
30. Ⓐ Ⓑ Ⓒ Ⓓ Ⓔ
31. Ⓐ Ⓑ Ⓒ Ⓓ Ⓔ
32. Ⓐ Ⓑ Ⓒ Ⓓ Ⓔ
33. Ⓐ Ⓑ Ⓒ Ⓓ Ⓔ
34. Ⓐ Ⓑ Ⓒ Ⓓ Ⓔ
35. Ⓐ Ⓑ Ⓒ Ⓓ Ⓔ
36. Ⓐ Ⓑ Ⓒ Ⓓ Ⓔ
37. Ⓐ Ⓑ Ⓒ Ⓓ Ⓔ
38. Ⓐ Ⓑ Ⓒ Ⓓ Ⓔ
39. Ⓐ Ⓑ Ⓒ Ⓓ Ⓔ
40. Ⓐ Ⓑ Ⓒ Ⓓ Ⓔ

41. Ⓐ Ⓑ Ⓒ Ⓓ Ⓔ
42. Ⓐ Ⓑ Ⓒ Ⓓ Ⓔ
43. Ⓐ Ⓑ Ⓒ Ⓓ Ⓔ
44. Ⓐ Ⓑ Ⓒ Ⓓ Ⓔ
45. Ⓐ Ⓑ Ⓒ Ⓓ Ⓔ
46. Ⓐ Ⓑ Ⓒ Ⓓ Ⓔ
47. Ⓐ Ⓑ Ⓒ Ⓓ Ⓔ
48. Ⓐ Ⓑ Ⓒ Ⓓ Ⓔ
49. Ⓐ Ⓑ Ⓒ Ⓓ Ⓔ
50. Ⓐ Ⓑ Ⓒ Ⓓ Ⓔ
51. Ⓐ Ⓑ Ⓒ Ⓓ Ⓔ
52. Ⓐ Ⓑ Ⓒ Ⓓ Ⓔ
53. Ⓐ Ⓑ Ⓒ Ⓓ Ⓔ
54. Ⓐ Ⓑ Ⓒ Ⓓ Ⓔ
55. Ⓐ Ⓑ Ⓒ Ⓓ Ⓔ
56. Ⓐ Ⓑ Ⓒ Ⓓ Ⓔ
57. Ⓐ Ⓑ Ⓒ Ⓓ Ⓔ
58. Ⓐ Ⓑ Ⓒ Ⓓ Ⓔ
59. Ⓐ Ⓑ Ⓒ Ⓓ Ⓔ
60. Ⓐ Ⓑ Ⓒ Ⓓ Ⓔ

BIOLOGY-E SECTION

61. Ⓐ Ⓑ Ⓒ Ⓓ Ⓔ
62. Ⓐ Ⓑ Ⓒ Ⓓ Ⓔ
63. Ⓐ Ⓑ Ⓒ Ⓓ Ⓔ
64. Ⓐ Ⓑ Ⓒ Ⓓ Ⓔ
65. Ⓐ Ⓑ Ⓒ Ⓓ Ⓔ
66. Ⓐ Ⓑ Ⓒ Ⓓ Ⓔ
67. Ⓐ Ⓑ Ⓒ Ⓓ Ⓔ

68. Ⓐ Ⓑ Ⓒ Ⓓ Ⓔ
69. Ⓐ Ⓑ Ⓒ Ⓓ Ⓔ
70. Ⓐ Ⓑ Ⓒ Ⓓ Ⓔ
71. Ⓐ Ⓑ Ⓒ Ⓓ Ⓔ
72. Ⓐ Ⓑ Ⓒ Ⓓ Ⓔ
73. Ⓐ Ⓑ Ⓒ Ⓓ Ⓔ
74. Ⓐ Ⓑ Ⓒ Ⓓ Ⓔ

75. Ⓐ Ⓑ Ⓒ Ⓓ Ⓔ
76. Ⓐ Ⓑ Ⓒ Ⓓ Ⓔ
77. Ⓐ Ⓑ Ⓒ Ⓓ Ⓔ
78. Ⓐ Ⓑ Ⓒ Ⓓ Ⓔ
79. Ⓐ Ⓑ Ⓒ Ⓓ Ⓔ
80. Ⓐ Ⓑ Ⓒ Ⓓ Ⓔ

SAT Biology E/M
Practice Test 4

ANSWER SHEET

BIOLOGY CORE SECTION

1. Ⓐ Ⓑ Ⓒ Ⓓ Ⓔ	21. Ⓐ Ⓑ Ⓒ Ⓓ Ⓔ	41. Ⓐ Ⓑ Ⓒ Ⓓ Ⓔ
2. Ⓐ Ⓑ Ⓒ Ⓓ Ⓔ	22. Ⓐ Ⓑ Ⓒ Ⓓ Ⓔ	42. Ⓐ Ⓑ Ⓒ Ⓓ Ⓔ
3. Ⓐ Ⓑ Ⓒ Ⓓ Ⓔ	23. Ⓐ Ⓑ Ⓒ Ⓓ Ⓔ	43. Ⓐ Ⓑ Ⓒ Ⓓ Ⓔ
4. Ⓐ Ⓑ Ⓒ Ⓓ Ⓔ	24. Ⓐ Ⓑ Ⓒ Ⓓ Ⓔ	44. Ⓐ Ⓑ Ⓒ Ⓓ Ⓔ
5. Ⓐ Ⓑ Ⓒ Ⓓ Ⓔ	25. Ⓐ Ⓑ Ⓒ Ⓓ Ⓔ	45. Ⓐ Ⓑ Ⓒ Ⓓ Ⓔ
6. Ⓐ Ⓑ Ⓒ Ⓓ Ⓔ	26. Ⓐ Ⓑ Ⓒ Ⓓ Ⓔ	46. Ⓐ Ⓑ Ⓒ Ⓓ Ⓔ
7. Ⓐ Ⓑ Ⓒ Ⓓ Ⓔ	27. Ⓐ Ⓑ Ⓒ Ⓓ Ⓔ	47. Ⓐ Ⓑ Ⓒ Ⓓ Ⓔ
8. Ⓐ Ⓑ Ⓒ Ⓓ Ⓔ	28. Ⓐ Ⓑ Ⓒ Ⓓ Ⓔ	48. Ⓐ Ⓑ Ⓒ Ⓓ Ⓔ
9. Ⓐ Ⓑ Ⓒ Ⓓ Ⓔ	29. Ⓐ Ⓑ Ⓒ Ⓓ Ⓔ	49. Ⓐ Ⓑ Ⓒ Ⓓ Ⓔ
10. Ⓐ Ⓑ Ⓒ Ⓓ Ⓔ	30. Ⓐ Ⓑ Ⓒ Ⓓ Ⓔ	50. Ⓐ Ⓑ Ⓒ Ⓓ Ⓔ
11. Ⓐ Ⓑ Ⓒ Ⓓ Ⓔ	31. Ⓐ Ⓑ Ⓒ Ⓓ Ⓔ	51. Ⓐ Ⓑ Ⓒ Ⓓ Ⓔ
12. Ⓐ Ⓑ Ⓒ Ⓓ Ⓔ	32. Ⓐ Ⓑ Ⓒ Ⓓ Ⓔ	52. Ⓐ Ⓑ Ⓒ Ⓓ Ⓔ
13. Ⓐ Ⓑ Ⓒ Ⓓ Ⓔ	33. Ⓐ Ⓑ Ⓒ Ⓓ Ⓔ	53. Ⓐ Ⓑ Ⓒ Ⓓ Ⓔ
14. Ⓐ Ⓑ Ⓒ Ⓓ Ⓔ	34. Ⓐ Ⓑ Ⓒ Ⓓ Ⓔ	54. Ⓐ Ⓑ Ⓒ Ⓓ Ⓔ
15. Ⓐ Ⓑ Ⓒ Ⓓ Ⓔ	35. Ⓐ Ⓑ Ⓒ Ⓓ Ⓔ	55. Ⓐ Ⓑ Ⓒ Ⓓ Ⓔ
16. Ⓐ Ⓑ Ⓒ Ⓓ Ⓔ	36. Ⓐ Ⓑ Ⓒ Ⓓ Ⓔ	56. Ⓐ Ⓑ Ⓒ Ⓓ Ⓔ
17. Ⓐ Ⓑ Ⓒ Ⓓ Ⓔ	37. Ⓐ Ⓑ Ⓒ Ⓓ Ⓔ	57. Ⓐ Ⓑ Ⓒ Ⓓ Ⓔ
18. Ⓐ Ⓑ Ⓒ Ⓓ Ⓔ	38. Ⓐ Ⓑ Ⓒ Ⓓ Ⓔ	58. Ⓐ Ⓑ Ⓒ Ⓓ Ⓔ
19. Ⓐ Ⓑ Ⓒ Ⓓ Ⓔ	39. Ⓐ Ⓑ Ⓒ Ⓓ Ⓔ	59. Ⓐ Ⓑ Ⓒ Ⓓ Ⓔ
20. Ⓐ Ⓑ Ⓒ Ⓓ Ⓔ	40. Ⓐ Ⓑ Ⓒ Ⓓ Ⓔ	60. Ⓐ Ⓑ Ⓒ Ⓓ Ⓔ

BIOLOGY-M SECTION

81. Ⓐ Ⓑ Ⓒ Ⓓ Ⓔ	88. Ⓐ Ⓑ Ⓒ Ⓓ Ⓔ	95. Ⓐ Ⓑ Ⓒ Ⓓ Ⓔ
82. Ⓐ Ⓑ Ⓒ Ⓓ Ⓔ	89. Ⓐ Ⓑ Ⓒ Ⓓ Ⓔ	96. Ⓐ Ⓑ Ⓒ Ⓓ Ⓔ
83. Ⓐ Ⓑ Ⓒ Ⓓ Ⓔ	90. Ⓐ Ⓑ Ⓒ Ⓓ Ⓔ	97. Ⓐ Ⓑ Ⓒ Ⓓ Ⓔ
84. Ⓐ Ⓑ Ⓒ Ⓓ Ⓔ	91. Ⓐ Ⓑ Ⓒ Ⓓ Ⓔ	98. Ⓐ Ⓑ Ⓒ Ⓓ Ⓔ
85. Ⓐ Ⓑ Ⓒ Ⓓ Ⓔ	92. Ⓐ Ⓑ Ⓒ Ⓓ Ⓔ	99. Ⓐ Ⓑ Ⓒ Ⓓ Ⓔ
86. Ⓐ Ⓑ Ⓒ Ⓓ Ⓔ	93. Ⓐ Ⓑ Ⓒ Ⓓ Ⓔ	100. Ⓐ Ⓑ Ⓒ Ⓓ Ⓔ
87. Ⓐ Ⓑ Ⓒ Ⓓ Ⓔ	94. Ⓐ Ⓑ Ⓒ Ⓓ Ⓔ	

SAT Biology E/M
Practice Test 5

ANSWER SHEET

BIOLOGY CORE SECTION

1. Ⓐ Ⓑ Ⓒ Ⓓ Ⓔ
2. Ⓐ Ⓑ Ⓒ Ⓓ Ⓔ
3. Ⓐ Ⓑ Ⓒ Ⓓ Ⓔ
4. Ⓐ Ⓑ Ⓒ Ⓓ Ⓔ
5. Ⓐ Ⓑ Ⓒ Ⓓ Ⓔ
6. Ⓐ Ⓑ Ⓒ Ⓓ Ⓔ
7. Ⓐ Ⓑ Ⓒ Ⓓ Ⓔ
8. Ⓐ Ⓑ Ⓒ Ⓓ Ⓔ
9. Ⓐ Ⓑ Ⓒ Ⓓ Ⓔ
10. Ⓐ Ⓑ Ⓒ Ⓓ Ⓔ
11. Ⓐ Ⓑ Ⓒ Ⓓ Ⓔ
12. Ⓐ Ⓑ Ⓒ Ⓓ Ⓔ
13. Ⓐ Ⓑ Ⓒ Ⓓ Ⓔ
14. Ⓐ Ⓑ Ⓒ Ⓓ Ⓔ
15. Ⓐ Ⓑ Ⓒ Ⓓ Ⓔ
16. Ⓐ Ⓑ Ⓒ Ⓓ Ⓔ
17. Ⓐ Ⓑ Ⓒ Ⓓ Ⓔ
18. Ⓐ Ⓑ Ⓒ Ⓓ Ⓔ
19. Ⓐ Ⓑ Ⓒ Ⓓ Ⓔ
20. Ⓐ Ⓑ Ⓒ Ⓓ Ⓔ

21. Ⓐ Ⓑ Ⓒ Ⓓ Ⓔ
22. Ⓐ Ⓑ Ⓒ Ⓓ Ⓔ
23. Ⓐ Ⓑ Ⓒ Ⓓ Ⓔ
24. Ⓐ Ⓑ Ⓒ Ⓓ Ⓔ
25. Ⓐ Ⓑ Ⓒ Ⓓ Ⓔ
26. Ⓐ Ⓑ Ⓒ Ⓓ Ⓔ
27. Ⓐ Ⓑ Ⓒ Ⓓ Ⓔ
28. Ⓐ Ⓑ Ⓒ Ⓓ Ⓔ
29. Ⓐ Ⓑ Ⓒ Ⓓ Ⓔ
30. Ⓐ Ⓑ Ⓒ Ⓓ Ⓔ
31. Ⓐ Ⓑ Ⓒ Ⓓ Ⓔ
32. Ⓐ Ⓑ Ⓒ Ⓓ Ⓔ
33. Ⓐ Ⓑ Ⓒ Ⓓ Ⓔ
34. Ⓐ Ⓑ Ⓒ Ⓓ Ⓔ
35. Ⓐ Ⓑ Ⓒ Ⓓ Ⓔ
36. Ⓐ Ⓑ Ⓒ Ⓓ Ⓔ
37. Ⓐ Ⓑ Ⓒ Ⓓ Ⓔ
38. Ⓐ Ⓑ Ⓒ Ⓓ Ⓔ
39. Ⓐ Ⓑ Ⓒ Ⓓ Ⓔ
40. Ⓐ Ⓑ Ⓒ Ⓓ Ⓔ

41. Ⓐ Ⓑ Ⓒ Ⓓ Ⓔ
42. Ⓐ Ⓑ Ⓒ Ⓓ Ⓔ
43. Ⓐ Ⓑ Ⓒ Ⓓ Ⓔ
44. Ⓐ Ⓑ Ⓒ Ⓓ Ⓔ
45. Ⓐ Ⓑ Ⓒ Ⓓ Ⓔ
46. Ⓐ Ⓑ Ⓒ Ⓓ Ⓔ
47. Ⓐ Ⓑ Ⓒ Ⓓ Ⓔ
48. Ⓐ Ⓑ Ⓒ Ⓓ Ⓔ
49. Ⓐ Ⓑ Ⓒ Ⓓ Ⓔ
50. Ⓐ Ⓑ Ⓒ Ⓓ Ⓔ
51. Ⓐ Ⓑ Ⓒ Ⓓ Ⓔ
52. Ⓐ Ⓑ Ⓒ Ⓓ Ⓔ
53. Ⓐ Ⓑ Ⓒ Ⓓ Ⓔ
54. Ⓐ Ⓑ Ⓒ Ⓓ Ⓔ
55. Ⓐ Ⓑ Ⓒ Ⓓ Ⓔ
56. Ⓐ Ⓑ Ⓒ Ⓓ Ⓔ
57. Ⓐ Ⓑ Ⓒ Ⓓ Ⓔ
58. Ⓐ Ⓑ Ⓒ Ⓓ Ⓔ
59. Ⓐ Ⓑ Ⓒ Ⓓ Ⓔ
60. Ⓐ Ⓑ Ⓒ Ⓓ Ⓔ

BIOLOGY-M SECTION

81. Ⓐ Ⓑ Ⓒ Ⓓ Ⓔ
82. Ⓐ Ⓑ Ⓒ Ⓓ Ⓔ
83. Ⓐ Ⓑ Ⓒ Ⓓ Ⓔ
84. Ⓐ Ⓑ Ⓒ Ⓓ Ⓔ
85. Ⓐ Ⓑ Ⓒ Ⓓ Ⓔ
86. Ⓐ Ⓑ Ⓒ Ⓓ Ⓔ
87. Ⓐ Ⓑ Ⓒ Ⓓ Ⓔ

88. Ⓐ Ⓑ Ⓒ Ⓓ Ⓔ
89. Ⓐ Ⓑ Ⓒ Ⓓ Ⓔ
90. Ⓐ Ⓑ Ⓒ Ⓓ Ⓔ
91. Ⓐ Ⓑ Ⓒ Ⓓ Ⓔ
92. Ⓐ Ⓑ Ⓒ Ⓓ Ⓔ
93. Ⓐ Ⓑ Ⓒ Ⓓ Ⓔ
94. Ⓐ Ⓑ Ⓒ Ⓓ Ⓔ

95. Ⓐ Ⓑ Ⓒ Ⓓ Ⓔ
96. Ⓐ Ⓑ Ⓒ Ⓓ Ⓔ
97. Ⓐ Ⓑ Ⓒ Ⓓ Ⓔ
98. Ⓐ Ⓑ Ⓒ Ⓓ Ⓔ
99. Ⓐ Ⓑ Ⓒ Ⓓ Ⓔ
100. Ⓐ Ⓑ Ⓒ Ⓓ Ⓔ

SAT Biology E/M
Practice Test 6

ANSWER SHEET

BIOLOGY CORE SECTION

1. Ⓐ Ⓑ Ⓒ Ⓓ Ⓔ
2. Ⓐ Ⓑ Ⓒ Ⓓ Ⓔ
3. Ⓐ Ⓑ Ⓒ Ⓓ Ⓔ
4. Ⓐ Ⓑ Ⓒ Ⓓ Ⓔ
5. Ⓐ Ⓑ Ⓒ Ⓓ Ⓔ
6. Ⓐ Ⓑ Ⓒ Ⓓ Ⓔ
7. Ⓐ Ⓑ Ⓒ Ⓓ Ⓔ
8. Ⓐ Ⓑ Ⓒ Ⓓ Ⓔ
9. Ⓐ Ⓑ Ⓒ Ⓓ Ⓔ
10. Ⓐ Ⓑ Ⓒ Ⓓ Ⓔ
11. Ⓐ Ⓑ Ⓒ Ⓓ Ⓔ
12. Ⓐ Ⓑ Ⓒ Ⓓ Ⓔ
13. Ⓐ Ⓑ Ⓒ Ⓓ Ⓔ
14. Ⓐ Ⓑ Ⓒ Ⓓ Ⓔ
15. Ⓐ Ⓑ Ⓒ Ⓓ Ⓔ
16. Ⓐ Ⓑ Ⓒ Ⓓ Ⓔ
17. Ⓐ Ⓑ Ⓒ Ⓓ Ⓔ
18. Ⓐ Ⓑ Ⓒ Ⓓ Ⓔ
19. Ⓐ Ⓑ Ⓒ Ⓓ Ⓔ
20. Ⓐ Ⓑ Ⓒ Ⓓ Ⓔ

21. Ⓐ Ⓑ Ⓒ Ⓓ Ⓔ
22. Ⓐ Ⓑ Ⓒ Ⓓ Ⓔ
23. Ⓐ Ⓑ Ⓒ Ⓓ Ⓔ
24. Ⓐ Ⓑ Ⓒ Ⓓ Ⓔ
25. Ⓐ Ⓑ Ⓒ Ⓓ Ⓔ
26. Ⓐ Ⓑ Ⓒ Ⓓ Ⓔ
27. Ⓐ Ⓑ Ⓒ Ⓓ Ⓔ
28. Ⓐ Ⓑ Ⓒ Ⓓ Ⓔ
29. Ⓐ Ⓑ Ⓒ Ⓓ Ⓔ
30. Ⓐ Ⓑ Ⓒ Ⓓ Ⓔ
31. Ⓐ Ⓑ Ⓒ Ⓓ Ⓔ
32. Ⓐ Ⓑ Ⓒ Ⓓ Ⓔ
33. Ⓐ Ⓑ Ⓒ Ⓓ Ⓔ
34. Ⓐ Ⓑ Ⓒ Ⓓ Ⓔ
35. Ⓐ Ⓑ Ⓒ Ⓓ Ⓔ
36. Ⓐ Ⓑ Ⓒ Ⓓ Ⓔ
37. Ⓐ Ⓑ Ⓒ Ⓓ Ⓔ
38. Ⓐ Ⓑ Ⓒ Ⓓ Ⓔ
39. Ⓐ Ⓑ Ⓒ Ⓓ Ⓔ
40. Ⓐ Ⓑ Ⓒ Ⓓ Ⓔ

41. Ⓐ Ⓑ Ⓒ Ⓓ Ⓔ
42. Ⓐ Ⓑ Ⓒ Ⓓ Ⓔ
43. Ⓐ Ⓑ Ⓒ Ⓓ Ⓔ
44. Ⓐ Ⓑ Ⓒ Ⓓ Ⓔ
45. Ⓐ Ⓑ Ⓒ Ⓓ Ⓔ
46. Ⓐ Ⓑ Ⓒ Ⓓ Ⓔ
47. Ⓐ Ⓑ Ⓒ Ⓓ Ⓔ
48. Ⓐ Ⓑ Ⓒ Ⓓ Ⓔ
49. Ⓐ Ⓑ Ⓒ Ⓓ Ⓔ
50. Ⓐ Ⓑ Ⓒ Ⓓ Ⓔ
51. Ⓐ Ⓑ Ⓒ Ⓓ Ⓔ
52. Ⓐ Ⓑ Ⓒ Ⓓ Ⓔ
53. Ⓐ Ⓑ Ⓒ Ⓓ Ⓔ
54. Ⓐ Ⓑ Ⓒ Ⓓ Ⓔ
55. Ⓐ Ⓑ Ⓒ Ⓓ Ⓔ
56. Ⓐ Ⓑ Ⓒ Ⓓ Ⓔ
57. Ⓐ Ⓑ Ⓒ Ⓓ Ⓔ
58. Ⓐ Ⓑ Ⓒ Ⓓ Ⓔ
59. Ⓐ Ⓑ Ⓒ Ⓓ Ⓔ
60. Ⓐ Ⓑ Ⓒ Ⓓ Ⓔ

BIOLOGY-M SECTION

81. Ⓐ Ⓑ Ⓒ Ⓓ Ⓔ
82. Ⓐ Ⓑ Ⓒ Ⓓ Ⓔ
83. Ⓐ Ⓑ Ⓒ Ⓓ Ⓔ
84. Ⓐ Ⓑ Ⓒ Ⓓ Ⓔ
85. Ⓐ Ⓑ Ⓒ Ⓓ Ⓔ
86. Ⓐ Ⓑ Ⓒ Ⓓ Ⓔ
87. Ⓐ Ⓑ Ⓒ Ⓓ Ⓔ

88. Ⓐ Ⓑ Ⓒ Ⓓ Ⓔ
89. Ⓐ Ⓑ Ⓒ Ⓓ Ⓔ
90. Ⓐ Ⓑ Ⓒ Ⓓ Ⓔ
91. Ⓐ Ⓑ Ⓒ Ⓓ Ⓔ
92. Ⓐ Ⓑ Ⓒ Ⓓ Ⓔ
93. Ⓐ Ⓑ Ⓒ Ⓓ Ⓔ
94. Ⓐ Ⓑ Ⓒ Ⓓ Ⓔ

95. Ⓐ Ⓑ Ⓒ Ⓓ Ⓔ
96. Ⓐ Ⓑ Ⓒ Ⓓ Ⓔ
97. Ⓐ Ⓑ Ⓒ Ⓓ Ⓔ
98. Ⓐ Ⓑ Ⓒ Ⓓ Ⓔ
99. Ⓐ Ⓑ Ⓒ Ⓓ Ⓔ
100. Ⓐ Ⓑ Ⓒ Ⓓ Ⓔ

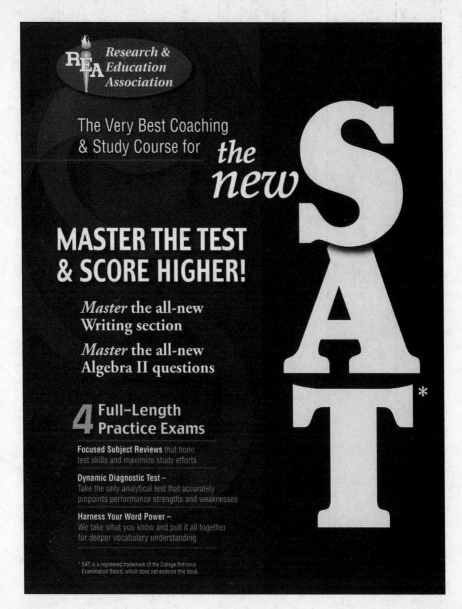

The Best Test Preparation for the

AP*

ADVANCED

PLACEMENT

EXAMINATION

BIOLOGY

7th Edition

6 Full-Length Practice Exams with detailed explanations

Based on official exams released by the College Board

Completely New & Expanded Review of Exam Topics

All 12 AP Biology Labs are covered

AP Biology review topics include...

• Chemistry of Life
• Molecules & Cells
• Botany
• Zoology
• Genetics
• Evolution
• Ecology

REA *Research & Education Association*
* AP is a registered trademark of the College Entrance Examination Board, which does not endorse this book.

Available at your local bookstore or order directly from us by sending in coupon below.

"The ESSENTIALS" of Math & Science

Each book in the ESSENTIALS series offers all essential information of the field it covers. It summarizes what every textbook in the particular field must include, and is designed to help students in preparing for exams and doing homework. The ESSENTIALS are excellent supplements to any class text.

The ESSENTIALS are complete and concise with quick access to needed information. They serve as a handy reference source at all times. The ESSENTIALS are prepared with REA's customary concern for high professional quality and student needs.

Available in the following titles:

Advanced Calculus I & II
Algebra & Trigonometry I & II
Anatomy & Physiology
Anthropology
Astronomy
Automatic Control Systems /
   Robotics I & II
Biology I & II
Boolean Algebra
Calculus I, II, & III
Chemistry
Complex Variables I & II
Computer Science I & II
Data Structures I & II
Differential Equations I & II
Electric Circuits I & II
Electromagnetics I & II

Electronics I & II
Electronic Communications I & II
Fluid Mechanics /
   Dynamics I & II
Fourier Analysis
Geometry I & II
Group Theory I & II
Heat Transfer I & II
LaPlace Transforms
Linear Algebra
Math for Computer Applications
Math for Engineers I & II
Math Made Nice-n-Easy Series
Mechanics I, II, & III
Microbiology
Modern Algebra
Molecular Structures of Life

Numerical Analysis I & II
Organic Chemistry I & II
Physical Chemistry I & II
Physics I & II
Pre-Calculus
Probability
Psychology I & II
Real Variables
Set Theory
Sociology
Statistics I & II
Strength of Materials &
   Mechanics of Solids I & II
Thermodynamics I & II
Topology
Transport Phenomena I & II
Vector Analysis

If you would like more information about any of these books,
complete the coupon below and return it to us or visit your local bookstore.

RESEARCH & EDUCATION ASSOCIATION
61 Ethel Road W. • Piscataway, New Jersey 08854
Phone: (732) 819-8880   **website: www.rea.com**

Please send me more information about your Math & Science Essentials books

Name _____

Address _____

City _____ State _____ Zip _____

REA's Test Preps
The Best in Test Preparation

REA's Test Prep Books Are The Best!

(a sample of the <u>hundreds of letters</u> REA receives each year)

(more on front page)